Private Enforcement of EU Competition Law and Class Actions

International Competition Law Series

VOLUME 93

Editor

In its series editor, Alastair Sutton, Kluwer is fortunate to engage and benefit from the experience and expertise of one of the world's outstanding authorities on European Union and international economic law.

Introduction

In their efforts to regulate competition in an increasingly complex business environment, competition authorities face a daunting task. The European Commission and Courts, as well as national courts and legislatures, policymakers, and regulators, are constantly proposing, enacting, reviewing, and enforcing new legal measures, often addressing novel situations. Every industry and service is affected.

Contents/Subjects

With many titles currently available and new ones appearing regularly, the series' coverage includes detailed analyses of relevant legislation and case law in major global trading jurisdictions, defences used in cases involving the digital network economy, state aid cases, enforcement methodologies and a great deal more.

Objective & Readership

The purpose of Kluwer's International Competition Law Series is to follow the ever-changing contours of this dynamic area of the law, keeping the practice in sharp focus so that practising lawyers (including in-house counsel) and academics can be assured of the most up-to-date guidance and sources, in the widest possible range of applications.

The titles published in this series are listed at the end of this volume.

Private Enforcement of EU Competition Law and Class Actions

Has the Force Awakened?

Sílvia Bessa Venda

Wolters Kluwer

Published by:
Kluwer Law International B.V.
PO Box 316
2400 AH Alphen aan den Rijn
The Netherlands
E-mail: lrs-sales@wolterskluwer.com
Website: www.wolterskluwer.com/en/solutions/kluwerlawinternational

Sold and distributed by:
Wolters Kluwer Legal & Regulatory U.S.
920 Links Avenue
Landisville, PA 17538
United States of America
E-mail: customer.service@wolterskluwer.com

ISBN 978-94-035-2139-8

e-Book: ISBN 978-94-035-2149-7
web-PDF: ISBN 978-94-035-2159-6

To my Mother,
The most beautiful flower in the gardens of life.
I am writing this dedication while doing one of the things my mother,
Cândida Bessa, loved most: 'flying'.
And almost at midnight on her birthday, 17th September.
Even before it happened, I often feared I wouldn't be able to finish this book, and I told her so.
She replied with serene certainty: 'Of course you will,
there is nothing you set out to do that you cannot accomplish.'
Psychology, her domain of mastery, explains that the image we have of ourselves is defined by how those we love most see us.
How could I not fulfil this dream, if she knew I would?

'The value of things is not in how long they last,
but in the intensity with which they happen.
That's why there are unforgettable moments,
inexplicable things and incomparable people.'

Table of Contents

Note to Readers

This book is a translated, adapted, and updated version of the author's doctoral thesis of the same title, originally supervised by Professor Sofia Oliveira Pais and defended at the Portuguese Catholic University on 11 March 2024.

It reflects a long, inquisitive, and at times stubborn journey into one of the most overlooked corners of EU law: how we (fail to) compensate small victims - SMEs and consumers - of competition law infringements.

Whether you are a student, a practitioner, a policymaker, or simply someone who enjoys a good legal puzzle, I hope this book offers not only insights to reflect on but also ideas that inspire action and change.

'A Europe that protects,
a Europe that empowers,
a Europe that defends (...) its citizens
when and where it matters.'
Jean-Claude Juncker

'Try not. Do or do not. There is no try.'
Yoda, Star Wars Episode V: The Empire Strikes Back

List of Abbreviations

ADR	Alternative Dispute Resolution
CAT	UK's Competition Appeal Tribunal
CCBE	Council of Bars and Law Societies of Europe
CFREU	Charter of Fundamental Rights of the European Union
CJEU	Court of Justice of the European Union (EGC + ECJ)
CMA	Competition and Markets Authority
Directive 2020/1828	Directive 2020/1828 of the European Parliament and of the Council of 25 November 2020 on representative actions for the protection of the collective interests of consumers and repealing Directive 2009/22/EC
ECHR	European Convention on Human Rights
ECJ	European Court of Justice
ECON	Committee on Economic and Monetary Affairs
ECSC	European Coal and Steel Community
ECtHR	European Court of Human Rights
EGC	European General Court
EESC	European Economic and Social Committee
EPRS	European Parliamentary Research Service
EU	European Union
EU Damages Directive	Directive 2014/104/EU of the European Parliament and of the Council of 26 November 2014 on certain rules governing actions for damages under national law for infringements of the competition law provisions of the Member States and of the European Union Text with EEA relevance
Green Paper	Green Paper on damages actions for breach of the EC antitrust rules (SEC(2005) 1732)

IMCO	Committee on the Internal Market and Consumer Protection
JURI	Committee on Legal Affairs
MEP	Members of the European Parliament
NCAs	National Competition Authority(ies)
PCA	Portuguese Competition Authority
PCL	Portuguese Competition Law
Portuguese Law 23/2018	Law No. 23/2018, of 5 June, transposing Directive 2014/104/EU of the European Parliament and of the Council of 26 November 2014 on certain rules governing actions for damages under national law for infringements of the provisions of the competition law of the Member States and of the European Union, and making the first amendment to the RJC, as well as the fourth amendment to the Law on the Organisation of the Judicial System, approved by Law No. 62/2013, of 26 August
Regulation 1/2003	Council Regulation (EC) No. 1/2003 of 16 December 2002 on the implementation of the rules on competition laid down in Articles 81 and 82 of the Treaty
SMEs	Small- and Medium-Sized Enterprises
TCRS	Portuguese Competition, Regulation and Supervision Court (*Tribunal da Concorrência, Regulação e Supervisão*)
TEU	Treaty on European Union
TFEU	Treaty on the Functioning of the European Union
TPLF	Third-Party Litigation Funding
UK	United Kingdom
US	United States of America
White Paper	White Paper on damages actions for breach of the EC antitrust rules (2008/2154(INI))

Foreword

The doctoral thesis entitled 'Private Enforcement of EU Competition Law and Class Actions: Has the Force Awakened?', authored by Sílvia Bessa Venda and developed under my supervision at the Faculty of Law of the Portuguese Catholic University, evidences rigorous analytical insight and a comprehensive expertise on the subject. It tackles one of the most dynamic and evolving areas of EU law, offering an original contribution to the understanding of private enforcement mechanisms and collective redress in competition law.

The book originates from the recognition of a persistent paradox within EU competition law: despite the widespread recognition of the right to compensation for infringements of Articles 101 and 102 of the TFEU, effective access to that right continues to pose significant challenges, particularly for small- and medium-sized enterprises and individual consumers. It is from this tension that the book takes shape. Drawing on a comparative study of four European legal systems – each of which offers a distinct approach and valuable lessons – alongside a detailed analysis of policy and legislative initiatives at EU institutional level, Sílvia makes a compelling case for specific EU legislation in the field of collective redress for competition law infringements. She argues that only a competition law class action mechanism at the EU level, complemented by initiatives to regulate private litigation funding, can ensure meaningful access to justice for all victims of anticompetitive practices.

The author's interest in the field of private enforcement of competition law is not recent. It was already clearly demonstrated in her Master's thesis, where she focused on the complex issue of leniency statements – a topic she approached with the same critical precision that underpins her doctoral research. This continuity reflects a coherent academic trajectory, and reveals a sustained and deepening engagement with one of the most challenging areas of EU law.

Furthermore Sílvia's interest and experience in these matters extends beyond academia, to her work as a lawyer in leading law firms and companies, where she continuously monitored compensation actions for violations of competition rules, both individual and collective. She began this journey in Portugal and now operates at a global level for a multinational company, which allows her to have in-depth experience in this type of action, namely at the EU and US levels. This wealth of hands-on, real-world experience directly informs the analysis and insights presented in this book, making it a valuable resource for both academics and practitioners. It will undoubtedly stand as a landmark work on the subject of class actions in the area of competition law.

Sofia Oliveira Pais

Associate Professor at the Portuguese Catholic University's Faculty of Law, Director of the PhD Program (Porto) and of the Católica Research Centre for the Future of Law. PhD in EU Competition Law (2009), Jean Monnet Chair, Co-founder of the Market and Competition Law Review, and Coordinator of EU-funded projects (namely 'Training Judges on EU Competition Law' and 'Observatory of Competition Law Enforcement').

Preface

The private enforcement of EU competition law has long stood at the intersection of legal principle and practical inaccessibility. While the right of individuals to seek compensation for infringements of Articles 101 and 102 of the Treaty on the Functioning of the European Union (TFEU) is firmly established – first by the Court of Justice of the European Union (CJEU) and later codified in the EU Damages Directive – its exercise remains elusive for many, particularly small- and medium-sized enterprises (SMEs) and consumers.

This book was born from the recognition of that gap. It begins by tracing the evolution of private enforcement in the EU, highlighting the persistent challenges that have hindered its effectiveness. Despite legislative progress, the lack of robust collective redress mechanisms and limited access to funding continue to render the right to redress 'impossible or excessively difficult' for those most in need of protection.

Divided into two parts, the book first lays the groundwork by exploring the historical and legal context of private enforcement. It then turns to the EU Damages Directive, analysing its scope through the lens of CJEU case law and its uneven implementation across Member States. This analysis reveals the Directive's limited impact in overcoming structural barriers to justice.

The heart of the book lies in its second part, which makes the case for EU-level legislation on collective redress in competition law. It examines institutional initiatives such as the Representative Actions Directive and the European Parliament's recommendations on responsible private funding. It also presents a comparative study of four jurisdictions – Portugal, the United Kingdom, Belgium, and France – whose diverse approaches to collective redress offer valuable insights and cautionary lessons.

Drawing on this comparative analysis, the book identifies ten key factors that influence the success or stagnation of antitrust class actions across the EU. It concludes with a six-point legislative proposal designed to harmonise collective enforcement with the legal traditions of Member States, while upholding the EU principles of effectiveness and equivalence.

This book is intended for legal scholars, practitioners, policymakers, and anyone interested in the future of competition law enforcement. It is both a diagnosis of the current shortcomings and a call to action for a more accessible and equitable system of redress.

Introductory Notes on Citations

Bibliographical citations are generally, and where appropriate, presented in the following order: author, title of article, title of publication, volume/number, publisher, edition and/or date, link and page/paragraph.

When citing multiple articles from the same publication, only the publication is included in the bibliography.

Works are listed alphabetically by the author's surname. If there are several works by the same author, they are listed in ascending order according to the year of publication.

Case law citations are generally formatted as follows: case name or parties, date, case number and page/paragraph.

Citations from other documents (other than those mentioned above) are generally, and where appropriate, presented in the following order: document name, reference, link and page/paragraph.

At the end of the book, citations from case law and other documents are generally listed in the order in which they appear throughout the text.

Unless otherwise stated, all translations in this book are the responsibility of the author.

Acknowledgements

To my loved ones,
who walked beside me through this 'marathon'.
And especially, to two extraordinary Women:
To my mother,
Professor Cândida Bessa,
who taught me how to live
and whose ultimate vote of confidence I intend to honour.
To my supervisor,
Professor Sofia Oliveira Pais,
who held my hand every step of the way.

Aos meus amores,
que percorreram comigo esta 'maratona'.
E, particularmente, a duas grandes Mulheres:
À minha mãe,
Professora Cândida Bessa,
que me ensinou a viver
e cujo derradeiro voto de confiança pretendo honrar.
À minha orientadora,
Professora Sofia Oliveira Pais,
que me deu a mão em todos os momentos.

CHAPTER 1
Contextualisation

1.1 PRIVATE ENFORCEMENT OF COMPETITION LAW: WHERE DO WE COME FROM, WHERE ARE WE, AND WHERE DO WE WANT TO GO?

Private enforcement - referring to the private application of competition law - is currently one of the EU's top priorities. Under Regulation 1/2003,[1] the authority to apply Articles 101 and 102 of the TFEU (which set out the EU's competition or antitrust rules)[2] is granted not only to the European Commission and National Competition Authorities (NCAs), but also to National Courts. This framework enables a dual enforcement system: public enforcement, led by the European Commission and NCAs[3] (with National Courts acting as Courts of Appeal for public decisions issued by regulatory authorities), and private enforcement, where National Courts safeguard consumers' and companies' rights. The interplay between these two forms of enforcement is essential to ensure full compliance with EU competition law.

According to Articles 101 and 102 of the TFEU, agreements that restrict competition and abuses of a dominant position are incompatible with the internal market and are therefore prohibited. These treaty provisions create rights and obligations for both

1. Its purpose is to ensure an 'effective and uniform' application of Articles 101 and 102 of the TFEU, avoiding distortions of competition in the common market (*see* Recital 1).
2. This book uses both terms. They have their origins in the US, with the adoption of *the Sherman Act*, in 1890, as a reaction to the high number of trusts and the creation of monopolistic markets (although Canada passed similar provisions in 1889). The EU's competition policy can be traced back to the Treaty of Paris, which created the ECSC in 1951. In this regard, *see* Massimo Motta, *Competition Policy: Theory and Practice*, Cambridge University Press, 2004, pp. 1 et seq.
3. *See* Articles 4 to 6. When applying the antitrust rules of domestic law (which, in Portugal, correspond to Articles 9 to 11 of the PCL, respectively), the NCAs and National Courts must simultaneously apply the EU law, as long as both have essentially the same object (with the exception of matters relating to the control of company mergers), under the terms of Article 3(1) and (3) of Regulation 1/2003. In this regard, *see* Miguel Moura and Silva, *Direito da Concorrência: Uma introdução Jurisprudencial*, Almedina, 2008, p. 66.

Member States and private individuals. As such, they have direct effect, meaning they can be invoked directly by individuals in national contexts, either against the State (vertical direct effect) or against other individuals (horizontal direct effect).[4]

The effective application of antitrust rules requires not only the prevention and punishment of infringements, but also the protection of companies and consumers from such illegal practices and the resulting damages. This protection is achieved mainly through damages actions. As reaffirmed by the European General Court (EGC) in the *CDC Hydrogen Peroxide* judgment:[5] 'Actions for damages before the national courts can make a significant contribution to the maintenance of effective competition in the EU.'

The right of consumers, companies, and public authorities to seek compensation for damages caused by breaches of competition rules (known as effective judicial protection) was first affirmed by the European Court of Justice (ECJ) in the *Courage* judgment.[6] However, the Court did not specify the conditions for exercising this right. Instead, it emphasised that it is the duty of Member States to regulate actions for damages in such a way that they 'are not less favourable than those governing similar domestic actions (principle of equivalence) and that they do not render practically impossible or excessively difficult the exercise of rights conferred by Community law (principle of effectiveness)'.[7]

The right to compensation was reaffirmed by the ECJ in the *Manfredi* judgment,[8] which clarified that it applies to any person and requires a causal link between the damage and the anticompetitive practice. The judgment also established that Member States must ensure a level playing field and enable the effective exercise of this right. Additionally, the ECJ recognised that loss of profit can be considered when calculating compensation.[9]

Ten years after the *Courage* judgment, the ECJ issued a landmark decision aimed at reconciling the tension between the public and private enforcement of competition law. This decision, known as the *Pfleiderer* judgment,[10] addresses the inherent conflict between the interests of injured parties seeking access to leniency statements and the need to preserve the incentives that underpin the effectiveness of the leniency regime. As noted by Fernando Xarepe Silveiro,[11] this judgment underscores the delicate balance between the interests of the injured parties in obtaining access to leniency

4. *See* rulings in *BRT v. SABAM* of 27 March 1974, Case C-127/73, pt. 16, *Courage* of 20 September 2001, Case C-453/99, pt. 23, *Manfredi* of 13 September 2006, Case C-295/04 et seq. C-295/04 et seq., pt. 39 and *Kone,* 5 June 2014, Case C-557/12, pt. 20. *See also* Recital 3 of the EU Damages Directive.
5. Of 15 December 2011, Case T-437/08, p. 77.
6. Of 20 September 2001, Case C-453/99, pt. 26.
7. *See* pt. 29.
8. Of 13 September 2006, Cases C-295/04 et seq.
9. Without prejudice to measures against unjust enrichment, *see* pts 61 and 92-96.
10. Of 14 June 2011, Case C-360/09.
11. In *Commentary on European Union Case Law, Judgment of the Court of Justice of the European Union of 6 June 2013, in Case C-536/11, Donau Chemie,* Revista de Concorrência e Regulação, Year IV, Nos 14 and 15, April/September 2013, pp. 453 and 454.

statements and the incentives that are indispensable for the leniency regime to remain appealing.

The leniency regime is a programme designed to incentivise companies involved in illegal cartels to cooperate in their dismantling. By voluntarily providing information and evidence - typically through leniency statements - these companies facilitate inspections and help establish violations of Article 101 TFEU. The first whistleblower is granted immunity from fines, while subsequent applicants may receive reduced fines, depending on the value and timing of their cooperation.[12]

As Maurice Guerrin and Georgios Kyriazis have observed, among all forms of competition distortion, the creation of a cartel most radically contradicts the principles of a free market economy.[13] Cartels are notoriously difficult to detect due to their inherently secretive nature and increasingly sophisticated methods of communication. In this context, leniency statements function as true confessions and have proven indispensable in uncovering and sanctioning cartels.[14]

For public enforcers,[15] proving the existence of a cartel is challenging without the support of the leniency regime. This is why the European Commission is particularly interested in protecting the confidentiality of leniency statements and related documents to maintain the regime's effectiveness and encourage continued cooperation from cartel participants.[16] For private individuals, who lack investigative powers, proving the existence of a cartel is extremely difficult - if not impossible - unless they bring a follow-on action based on a public decision issued in the context of a sanctioning procedure that has already declared the existence of the infringement.[17]

12. *See* Commission Notice on immunity from fines and reduction of fines in cartel cases (2006/C 298/11), pts 8, 10 to 13 and 23 et seq. This regime was also inspired by the US *Corporate Leniency Policy, Department of Justice,* 10 August 1993. In this regard, Wouter PJ Wils, *Efficiency and Justice in European Antitrust Enforcement,* Hard Publishing, 2008, p. 70.
13. In *Cartels: Proof and Procedural Issues,* Fordham International Law Journal, vol. 16, 2nd ed., 1992, p. 274.
14. In this sense, Richard Whish and David Bailay, *Competition Law,* Oxford University Press, 2012, pp. 517 et seq. Also Wouter PJ Wils, *Efficiency and Justice in European Antitrust Enforcement,* Hard Publishing, 2008, pp. 127 and 128, considers that infringing companies are the EC's best source of information. *See also* Christopher R Leslie, *Editorial: Antitrust Leniency Programmes,* The Competition Law Review, vol. 7, No. 2, July 2011, p. 175, and Yves Botteman and Paul Hughes, *Access to File: Striking the Balance Between Leniency and Private Enforcement Tools, The European Antitrust Review 2013,* Global Competition Review, 2013, p. 3, who refer to leniency as the European Commission's investigative tool of choice.
15. The Member States adopted their own leniency regimes. For example, in Hungary, the immune member could no longer be equally liable for the damages caused by the cartel if they were satisfied by the other members. *See* Paolo Buccirossi, Catarina Marvão and Giancarlo Spagnolo, *Leniency and Damages,* Working Paper No. 32, Stockholm Institute of Transition Economics, February 2015, p. 3. One of the aims of the *European Competition Network* is to harmonise national leniency regimes. *See* Tine Carmeliet, *How Lenient Is the European Leniency System? An Overview of Current (Dis)Incentives to Blow the Whistle,* Jura Falconis Jg. 48, No. 3, 2011-2012, pp. 473 et seq.
16. In this sense, David Ashon and David Henry, *Competition Damages Action in the EU: Law and Practice,* economics contribution from Frank Maier-Rigaud and Ulrich Schawalbe, Elgar, Competition Law and Practice, 2013, p. 71.
17. *See* Gianni de Stefano, *Access of Damage Claimants to Evidence Arising out of EU Cartel Investigations: A Fast-Evolving Scenario,* Global Competition Litigation Review, vol. 3, 2012, p. 108.

Having briefly outlined the conflict of interests underlying the Pfleiderer judgment, let us now return to its core holding. The Court declared that EU law does not preclude 'a person who has been adversely affected by an infringement of European Union competition law and is seeking to obtain damages from being granted access to documents relating to a leniency procedure involving the perpetrator of that infringement. It is, however, for the courts and tribunals of the Member States, on the basis of their national law, to determine the conditions under which such access must be permitted or refused by weighing the interests protected by European Union law'.[18] That is, the ECJ reaffirmed that EU law does not regulate this matter,[19] leaving it to the Member States to establish conditions that are no less favourable than those applicable to similar domestic claims. In their case-by-case assessments, Member States must balance the interests that may justify access to leniency documents against the need to protect the confidentiality of information provided by cartel members under the leniency regime.

Subsequent EU case law[20] has upheld this approach, emphasising that to ensure the effectiveness of the EU law, particularly Article 101 of the TFEU, National Courts must weigh the competing interests of public enforcement (preserving the effectiveness of the leniency regime) and private enforcement (ensuring the right to effective redress), on a case-by-case basis.[21]

1.2 PROBLEM, TOPICALITY AND RELEVANCE OF THE SOLUTION

Private enforcement is a less common form of antitrust enforcement in the EU. In contrast, as Sofia Oliveira Pais points out, private enforcement in the US 'constitutes more than 90 percent of all antitrust cases'[22] and is predominantly based on class actions.

The European Commission has taken steps to encourage private enforcement of competition law within the EU, aiming to do so without jeopardising the confidentiality of leniency statements submitted by companies.[23] These efforts culminated in the adoption of the EU Damages Directive. However, the question remains: are the legislative measures outlined in this instrument sufficient to tackle the persistently low

18. *See* pt. 32.
19. It should be remembered that both the above-mentioned Commission notice on the leniency regime and the Commission notice on cooperation between the Commission and the courts of the Member States of the European Union in the application of Articles 81 and 82 of the EC Treaty [now 101 and 102 of the TFEU] (OJ 2004/C of 27 April 2004) are not binding on the Member States.
20. *See*, for example, *Donau Chemie*, 6 June 2013, Case C-536/11 (before the EU Damages Directive) *and Axa Versicherung*, 7 July 2015, Case T-677/13 (after the EU Damages Directive).
21. *See* Sofia Oliveira Pais, *Between Clemency and Responsibility: A Success Story?, Judgement of the Court (Grand Chamber) of 14.6.2011, Case C-360/09*, Cadernos de Direito Privado, ISSN 1645-7242, No. 37, 2012, p. 8.
22. In *Package on Actions for Damages Based on Breaches of EU Competition Rules: Can One Size Fit All?*, Yearbook of Antitrust and Regulatory Studies, vol. 7, No. 10, 2014, p. 210.
23. *See* Sofia Oliveira Pais, *A União faz a força? Breves reflexões sobre os mecanismos coletivos de reparação no contexto da aplicação privada do direito da concorrência da união, Liber Amicorum* em Homenagem ao Prof. Doutor João Mota de Campos, Coimbra Editora, 2013, p. 880.

levels of private enforcement of competition rules? As Leonor Rossi and Miguel Sousa Ferro highlight,[24] while in the US 'the vast majority of cases result from private enforcement, (...) in the EU this figure is marginal'.[25] In fact, the Impact Assessment of Damages actions for breach of the EU antitrust rules, which accompanied the proposal for the EU Damages Directive, estimated the annual cost of ineffective private enforcement, measured in unclaimed damages by victims, to be around EUR 23 billion.[26]

One of the main reasons for the limited success of private enforcement in the EU, as identified by potential claimants, is the difficulty in accessing the necessary evidence.[27] Indeed, an injured party seeking compensation before a National Court must, in principle, allege and prove all the essential elements of their claim, including the infringement, the damage suffered, and the causal link between the two.[28] The phrase in principle applies because, even prior to the adoption of the EU Damages Directive, Article 16 of Regulation 1/2003 prohibited National Court and NCAs from issuing decisions that contradicted European Commission decisions regarding antitrust infringements. Consequently, in a follow-on action, the injured party is relieved of the burden of proving the infringement if it has already been established by the EC.

Without prejudice to the above, the burden of proving both the existence of damages and the causal link remains, as confirmed by the *Otis I* judgment.[29] In this judgment, as David Ashon points out,[30] the ECJ reaffirmed the principle that any person has the right to claim compensation for damage suffered, provided there is a causal link between that damage and an agreement or practice prohibited by Article 101 TFEU:[31] 'EU law must be interpreted as meaning that, in circumstances such as those at issue in the main proceedings, the Commission is not precluded from representing the EU before a national court hearing a civil action for damages in respect of loss caused to the EU by an agreement or practice prohibited by Articles 81 EC and 101 TFEU which may have affected certain public contracts awarded by various institutions and bodies of the EU,

24. In *Private Enforcement of Competition Law in Portugal (I): An Overview of Case-Law*, Revista de Concorrência e Regulação, Year III, No. 10, April/June 2012, Almedina, pp. 91 and 92.
25. *See also* Richard Whish and David Bailey, *Competition Law*, Oxford University Press, 2012, p. 295.
26. *See Commission Staff Working Paper Document Executive Summary of the Impact Assessment Damages actions for breach of the EU antitrust rules Accompanying the proposal for a Directive of the European Parliament and of the Council on certain rules governing actions for damages under national law for infringements of the competition law provisions of the Member States and of the European Union* (SWD/2013/0204 final), available at EUR-Lex - 52013SC0204 - EN - EUR-Lex (europa.eu), pt. 8.
27. *See* pt. 6.
28. Regarding the essentiality of access to proof of illegality in this matter, *see* David Ashton and David Henry, *Competition Damages Action in the EU: Law and Practice*, economics contribution from Frank Maier-Rigaud and Ulrich Schawalbe, Elgar, *Competition Law and Practice*, 2nd ed., 2018, p. 69. Regarding the requirement of a causal link between the damage and the anticompetitive practice, *see* the analysis above in the context of the *Manfredi* case.
29. Of 6 November 2012, Case C-199/11, pts 65 and 66.
30. In *Competition Damages Action in the EU: Law and Practice*, economics contribution from Frank Maier-Rigaud and Ulrich Schawalbe, *Competition Law and Practice*, Elgar, 2nd ed., 2018, p. 284.
31. *See* pt. 61 of the *Manfredi* judgment.

there being no need for the Commission to have authorisation for that purpose from those institutions and bodies.'[32]

With the adoption of the EU Damages Directive, aimed at ensuring the full application of antitrust rules, the decisions of NCAs and Courts of Appeal declaring infringements of competition rules were expressly given effect in terms of actions for damages. The specific measures introduced and their implementation by Member States will be examined in greater detail in Chapter 2 of this book. Article 9(1) of the Directive provides that an infringement of this nature, declared by a final national decision, is considered 'irrefutably established for the purposes of an action for damages brought before their national courts under Article 101 or 102 TFEU or under national competition law'. Even in relation to Member States other than the NCA or the Court of Appeal issuing the decision, according to paragraph 2 of the same article, it can be presented 'at least prima facie evidence that an infringement of competition law has occurred and, as appropriate, may be assessed along with any other evidence adduced by the parties'. This provision was one of the most controversial when it was transposed and applied in Member States. As Miguel Sousa Ferro points out,[33] decisions by the European Commission, NCAs and Courts of Appeal are often vague and do not provide a clear description of the infringement for the purposes of bringing a follow-on action. This issue has been exacerbated by the practice of 'negotiating' the content of public decisions in exchange for settlements with the companies under investigation, in order to save public resources.

In addition to the legislative option mentioned above, which facilitates the exercise of the right to redress, the EU legislator has chosen to restrict access to evidence included in the file of a competition authority. These rules are also subject to the principle of effectiveness.[34] Specifically, it has been established that National Courts must consider: (1) the specific nature of the request for access; (2) whether it relates to the need to substantiate a claim for damages; and (3) whether it is necessary to safeguard the effectiveness of the application of competition law by public authorities.[35] Furthermore, the so-called black and grey lists have been established. The black list, which includes leniency statements, refers to elements that are absolutely forbidden to access for this purpose.[36] The grey list includes documents that can only be disclosed after the competition authority has finalised its procedure, either by adopting a decision or through other means.[37]

32. *See Otis I* judgment, pt. 36.
33. In *Antitrust Private Enforcement and the Binding Effect of Public Enforcement Decisions*, Market and Competition Law Review, vol. 3, No. 2, pp. 51-80 https://doi.org/10.7559/mclawreview.2019.1830, available at Antitrust Private Enforcement and the Binding Effect of Public Enforcement Decisions | Market and Competition Law Review (ucp.pt), p. 51.
34. *See* Miguel Sousa Ferro, *The Reality of Access in Antitrust Private Enforcement: Overview of 3 Years' Experience in Portugal*, Revista de Concorrência e Regulação, Ano XIII, Nos 46-47, Almedina, 2021, pp. 37-71, available at CR 46-47_Miguel Sousa Ferro.pdf (concorrencia.pt), p. 45.
35. *See* Article 6(4).
36. *See* Article 6(6). In fact, the plaintiffs may only have access to such elements to the extent necessary to ensure that their content corresponds to their category, pursuant to Article 6(7).
37. *See* Article 6(5).

Among the various provisions set out in the EU Damages Directive, it is worth highlighting, by way of introduction, the rebuttable presumption that 'cartel infringements cause harm'.[38] The Directive also establishes provisions concerning the principle of joint and several liability applicable to companies that benefit from immunity from fines. These companies remain liable to their direct and indirect purchasers or suppliers (including those purchasing through intermediaries) and are only liable to other injured parties if the remaining cartel members are unable to fully compensate them.[39]

It is therefore clear that, in addition to promoting the exercise of the right to redress, the EU Damages Directive pursues a secondary objective: to rebalance the relationship between public and private enforcement of antitrust rules. The intersection of the leniency regime in the non-contractual civil liability of offenders has already been implemented in the US (United States of America, where whistleblowers are only liable for damages directly resulting from their conduct) and even in the EU by Hungary, where the liability of the company benefiting from immunity was, until now, merely subsidiary.[40] With the Directive, this principle has been incorporated into EU law, although it remains a contentious issue. Christian Kersting[41] argues that those negatively affected, such as co-offenders and injured parties, should be given an opportunity to be heard.

While acknowledging the cultural and sociological differences that set the US apart from many other jurisdictions, it appears that certain provisions of the EU Damages Directive, such as the prohibition on disclosing leniency statements, may jeopardise the intended balance between public and private enforcement. As the former European Commissioner for Competition Joaquín Almunia[42] has acknowledged, injured parties, ranging from large corporations to individual consumers, will likely have to wait for a final public decision before they can seek compensation for the harm suffered. The JURI (Committee on Legal Affairs) has also criticised the European Commission's proposed black list, arguing that it affords excessive protection to companies involved in illegal cartels and 'that no categories of documents should be excluded, as such, from an evaluation of whether or not they should be disclosed'.[43] At a preliminary

38. *See* Article 17(2).
39. *See* Article 11(4).
40. *See* Caroline Cauffman, *The Interaction of Leniency Programmes and Actions for Damages*, The Competition Law Review, vol. 7, No. 2, July 2011, p. 203 and Catarina Marvão and Giancarlo Spagnolo, *Leniency and Damages*, Working Paper No. 32, Stockholm Institute of Transition Economics, February 2015, pp. 4 and 5.
41. In *Practical Difficulties with Privileging the Successful Leniency Applicant in Relation to the Injured Parties, Proposal for a* EU Damages Directive, COM(2013) 404 final, Heinrich Heine University, 28 September 2013, pp. 1 and 2.
42. In *Speech at College of Europe's Global Competition Law Centre Annual Conference*, 7 November 2013, Antitrust damages in EU Law and Policy, available at http://europa.eu/rapid/press-release_SPEECH-13-887_en.htm.
43. *See* Report on the proposal for a directive of the European Parliament and of the Council on certain rules governing actions for damages under national law for infringements of the provisions of competition law of the Member States and of the European Union (COM(2013)0404 – C7-0170/2013 – 2013/0185(COD)), European Parliament, Session Document, 4 February 2014, pp. 34 and 35.

level, it may be said that the Directive renders private enforcement overly dependent on public enforcement, while also contradicting established case law of the CJEU.

Nevertheless, the EU Damages Directive entered into force on 25 December 2014, with Member States required to transpose it by 27 December 2016. By 2018, all twenty-eight Member States had communicated their full transposition.

In Portugal, for example, the government tasked the Portuguese Competition Authority (PCA) with preparing a transposition proposal. As part of this process, the PCA engaged stakeholders, first through a workshop and later via a public consultation on the preliminary draft. The final proposal was submitted on 22 June 2016. However, the Directive was only transposed into Portuguese law two years later, through Portuguese Law 23/2018.[44]

Subsequently, the European Commission assessed whether the Directive had been fully and correctly implemented by the Member States[45] – an issue that will be further examined in Chapter 2 of this book.

Failure to comply with the transposition deadline may not only be subject to judicial proceedings under Articles 258 et seq. of the TFEU but also give rise to general civil liability for breach of EU law.[46] As Sofia Oliveira Pais notes,[47] the principle of direct effect in the context of directives 'is less obvious'. According to the ECJ's case law, individuals may invoke the provisions of a directive before the State (under vertical direct effect) when those provisions are unconditional and sufficiently precise, and either have not been transposed within the prescribed timeframe or have been transposed incorrectly.[48] However, with regard to horizontal direct effect, i.e., invoking a directive against another private party, the ECJ has consistently held, as in the *Busseni* and *Daihatsu* judgments,[49] that directives do not produce such effect. This limits the ability of individuals to rely on directives in disputes against other private parties or even certain public authorities. Nonetheless, the principle of conforming interpretation,[50] as established in the *Marleasing* judgment,[51] requires national courts

44. Portuguese Law 23/2018 – Law No. 23/2018, of June 5, transposing Directive 2014/104/EU of the European Parliament and of the Council of 26 November 2014 on certain rules governing actions for damages under national law for infringements of the provisions of the competition law of the Member States and of the European Union, and making the first amendment to the PCL, as well as the fourth amendment to the Law on the Organisation of the Judicial System, approved by Law No. 62/2013, of August 26.
45. *See* http://ec.europa.eu/competition/antitrust/actionsdamages/directive_en.html.
46. *See Francovish* judgment of 19 November 1991, Case C-6/90 and C-9/90, pts 39 and 40.
47. In *Judgment of the Court of Justice of 5 February 1963: Case 26/62 Van Gend en Loos v. Dutch Tax Administration, Fundamental Principles of European Union Law, A Jurisprudential Approach*, Almedina, 3rd ed., 2017, p. 26.
48. *See* the *Beentjes* ruling of 20 September 1988, Case C-31/87, pt. 40.
49. Of 22 February 1990, Case C-221/88, pt. 23 and of 4 December 1997, Case C-97/96, pt. 24, respectively.
50. Both of the above principles are ramifications of the principle of the effectiveness of the EU law – which is fundamental to the pursuit of its objectives – and under which the Member States must guarantee its full application. *See EC v. Italy* of 18 January 2001, Case C-162/99, pt. 22. *See also* Miguel Gorjão-Henriques, *Direito da União, História, Direito, Cidadania, Mercado Interno e Concorrência*, Almedina, 7th ed., 2014, p. 345.
51. 13 November 1990, Case C-106/89, pt. 7.

to interpret national law, as far as possible,[52] in a manner consistent with the objectives, structure, and wording of a directive (regardless of whether the national provisions predate or postdate the Directive). This obligation is subject to limits, including general principles of law[53] such as non-retroactivity, legal certainty, and the prohibition of contra legem interpretation.[54]

Notwithstanding the above, the primary focus of this book is precisely the issue on which the EU Damages Directive remains silent: collective actions.[55] Can the problem of the non-exercise of the right to redress be effectively addressed without the adoption of EU legislation on collective actions in the field of competition law? The absence of robust collective mechanisms in this area is likely to hinder access to redress, particularly for SMEs (Small- and Medium-Sized Enterprises) and consumers, due to the high costs associated with such procedures and the relatively low value of individual harm, which may not justify pursuing isolated claims. This concern will be further examined in the chapters that follow.[56]

David Ashon and David Henry,[57] who share the concern regarding the lack of effective collective redress mechanisms, distinguish several types of collective actions based primarily on who initiates the proceedings:

(1) *Collective action in the strict sense* – the aggregation of individual claims into a single action brought on behalf of all affected parties.
(2) *Class action* – an action initiated by a group of claimants, whether individually identified or not.
(3) *Representative action* – an action brought by a representative body, such as a consumer association, on behalf of its members.
(4) *Group action* – a coordinated set of claims brought by a large number of individuals, either within a single proceeding or across multiple proceedings managed collectively.

In addition to these, they identify variants that resemble representative actions but have distinct features:

(5) *Public interest action* – initiated by a representative body for the benefit of the general public.

52. *See* pt. 8.
53. *See* Sofia Oliveira Pais, *Judgment of the Court of Justice of 13 November 1990: Case C-106/89 Marleasing SA v. La Comercial Internacional de Alimentación SA, Fundamental Principles of European Union Law, A Jurisprudential Approach*, Almedina, 3rd ed., 2017, pp. 101 et seq.
54. *See* the *Adeneler* ruling of 4 July 2006, Case C-212/04, pt. 110 – which also confirmed that the obligation to interpret in conformity only exists after the transposition deadline has expired (*See* pt. 115).
55. Recital 13 states that '[t]his Directive should not require Member States to introduce collective redress mechanisms for the enforcement of Articles 101 and 102 TFEU'.
56. *See* Sofia Oliveira Pais and Anna Piszcz, *Package on Actions for Damages Based on Breaches of EU Competition Rules: Can One Size Fit All?*, Yearbook of Antitrust and Regulatory Studies, vol. 7(10), 2014, p. 213.
57. In *Competition Damages Action in the EU: Law and Practice*, economics contribution from Frank Maier-Rigaud and Ulrich Schawalbe, Elgar, Competition Law and Practice, 2013, p. 128.

(6) *Assigned action* - brought by a third party not entitled to compensation, who litigates in its own name in exchange for a share of the awarded damages.
(7) *Parens patriae action* - brought by a public authority on behalf of specific individuals, typically to protect broader societal interests.[58]

For the purposes of this book, we will use the term 'collective' or 'class action' in a broad sense, particularly because, as will be shown, national legal frameworks often exhibit characteristics of more than one of these types.

Class actions can also be distinguished based on whether they require active participation from injured parties in order for a judgment to apply to them. This distinction gives rise to two primary models: opt-in and opt-out actions. In opt-in actions, individuals must provide explicit consent to be included in the proceedings and benefit from any resulting judgment. In contrast, opt-out actions are initiated on behalf of an undefined group of individuals, who are automatically included unless they take specific steps to exclude themselves from the action's effects.[59]

Portugal, for example, adopts an opt-out model for collective actions through a general mechanism known as *actio popularis* or ação popular (popular action,)[60] which is designed to protect diffuse interests. As Leonor Rossi and Miguel Sousa Ferro observe,[61] this instrument could, in theory, serve as an effective means of securing compensation for harm caused by breaches of competition law, were it not for the monetary, legal, and cultural barriers that hinder its practical use. By contrast, the UK (United Kingdom) was the first Member State to introduce a collective action mechanism specifically aimed at enforcing the right to redress for antitrust infringements: the representative action before the CAT (UK's Competition Appeal Tribunal).[62] This topic will be explored in greater detail in Chapter 3 of this book.

1.3 IDENTIFICATION OF KEY PRELIMINARY QUESTIONS

In this opening chapter, the book aims to clearly frame the central questions that have inspired and guided this research. The first and foremost question is whether there is a need to establish horizontal collective action mechanisms, particularly in light of the principle of effectiveness underpinning EU law on compensation for harm caused by

58. *See* Horacio Vedia Jerez, *Competition Law Enforcement and Compliance Across the World: A Comparative Review*, Wolters Kluwer, 2015, pp. 257 et seq.
59. *See* Charlotte Leskinen, *Collective Antitrust Damages Actions in the EU: the Opt-in v. Opt-out Model*, Working Paper IE Law School, 2010, available at http://ssrn.com/abstract=1612731, p. 5.
60. *See* Article 31 of the Code of Civil Procedure, approved by Law No. 41/2013, of 26 June.
61. In *Private Enforcement of Competition Law in Portugal (II): Actio Popularis – Facts, Fictions and Dreams*, Revista de Concorrência e Regulação, Year IV, No. 13, January/March, 2013, Almedina, pp. 74 et seq.
62. *See Commission Staff Working Paper, Annex to the Green Paper on Damages actions for breach of the EC antitrust rules*, COM(2005) 672 final, 2005, available at https://eur-lex.europa.eu/legal-content/EN/TXT/PDF/?uri=CELEX:52005SC1732, p. 55.

infringements of competition law. In other words: are the instruments provided by the EU Damages Directive sufficient to incentivise the exercise of the right to redress?

As previously noted, in the US, the vast majority of competition law actions are pursued through collective claims. This raises a critical question: Do collective mechanisms hold the key to generating procedural momentum in the enforcement of competition law? The issue is particularly complex, given the sophistication of antitrust infringements and the inherent challenges in identifying affected parties and quantifying the harm suffered. This, in turn, prompts a further question: should the appropriate response be the establishment of a dedicated class action mechanism specifically for competition law, such as the model adopted in the United Kingdom, or can existing procedural frameworks adequately serve this purpose?

This brings us to another fundamental question: what legal guidelines should shape the design of a horizontal collective redress mechanism? The first consideration concerns the model and type of action to be adopted[63] - an issue that has sparked considerable debate.[64] Early on, the European Commission expressed a preference for opt-in actions[65] and recommended the creation of a hybrid mechanism combining representative and collective actions. This approach aimed to address the procedural and financial barriers that often prevent small businesses and consumers from pursuing damages claims.[66]

Subsequently, the European Parliament adopted a resolution broadly supporting the Commission's proposal to establish horizontal collective action mechanisms. However, it emphasised that such initiatives should not necessarily take the form of a single instrument. In addition, any legislative proposal should involve the European Parliament and avoid triggering excessive or abusive litigation.[67] This resolution also stressed that any proposal in this area should be preceded by an independent cost-benefit analysis[68] to prevent arbitrary or unnecessary fragmentation of Member States' procedural systems.[69] Following this, the European Commission launched a public consultation in early 2011 to gather input on the general principles of class actions common to the Member States and to explore how a coherent EU-level solution could be constructed.[70] A subsequent resolution by the European Parliament reiterated

63. *See* s. 3.6.1 below.
64. *See* Sofia Oliveira Pais, *Between Clemency and Responsibility: A Success Story?, Judgement of the Court (Grand Chamber) of 14.6.2011, Case C-360/09*, Cadernos de Direito Privado, ISSN 1645-7242, No. 37, 2012, p. 8.
65. *See Commission Staff Working Paper, Annex to the* Green *Paper on Damages actions for breach of the EC antitrust rules*, COM(2005) 672 final, 2005, available at https://eur-lex.europa.eu/legal-content/EN/ALL/?uri=CELEX%3A52005DC0672, p. 56.
66. *See* White Paper, pp. 4 and 5.
67. As is the case in the US. *See* Sofia Oliveira Pais and Anna Piszcz, *Package on Actions for Damages Based on Breaches of EU Competition Rules: Can One Size Fit All?*, Yearbook of Antitrust and Regulatory Studies, vol. 7, No. 10, 2014, p. 213.
68. At the end of 2008, two studies had already been published by the Commission's Directorate-General for Health and Consumer Protection on Member States' collective action mechanisms and possible obstacles to the internal market resulting from the disparity in their legislation. *See also* Green Paper, p. 9 and Green Paper on consumer collective redress (COM(2008)0794).
69. *See* European Parliament resolution on the White Paper on damages actions for breach of the EC antitrust rules (2008/2154(INI)), pts 4, 5, 23 and 24.
70. *See* http://ec.europa.eu/competition/consultations/2011_collective_redress/index_en.html.

these concerns and urged the European Commission to conduct a thorough assessment of the appropriate legal basis for adopting collective redress measures at the EU level. The goal was to ensure alignment with national legal traditions and to avoid a proliferation of manifestly unfounded claims.

In that context, the European Parliament also laid out guidelines on key elements such as legal standing, compensable harm, access to evidence, cost allocation, and third-party litigation funding.[71] These elements will be examined in greater detail in the following chapters, as they are essential to evaluating whether, and under what conditions, collective redress mechanisms can provide an effective solution to the challenges outlined above.

In 2013, the European Commission finally issued a recommendation outlining common principles to guide Member States in establishing collective redress mechanisms for both injunctions and compensations in cases involving violations of rights guaranteed by EU law.[72] However, as previously noted, the core ideas underpinning this recommendation, such as the preference for opt-in models and the combination of representative and collective actions, were ultimately not incorporated into either the proposal or the final text of the EU Damages Directive. This omission was criticised by the European Parliament's Committees. For example, the ECON (Committee on Economic and Monetary Affairs) stated that the 'rapporteur would like to see representative and collective redress mechanisms being introduced. (...) the Commission agreed that there should be an integrated approach to collective redress to ensure consistent treatment of claims for damages in the area of Union competition law. Binding horizontal measures for collective redress are still not a reality. Collective actions would allow for genuine and qualified entities, such as consumer associations or trade organisations, to bring actions forward on behalf of the individual claimant. However, the rapporteur calls for only a clearly identified group of people to be able to act as representative and to take part in the claim. This identification must be completed when the claim is brought, and the rapporteur suggests an opt-in model. Given that only 25 % of cartel cases lead to actions for damages within the Union more has to be done to encourage consumers to exercise their rights'.[73]

The EESC (European Economic and Social Committee) has also advocated that the proposal for a directive and the recommendation on collective actions should be brought closer together since both texts stipulate that Member States must have national collective action mechanisms, particularly with regard to redress actions. It regretted that the initiation of collective action in competition matters, which should be the effective mechanism for consumers, has been dissociated and referred to a

71. *See* European Parliament resolution Towards a coherent European approach to collective redress (2011/2089(INI)), pts 6, 8, 15 et seq.
72. Of 11 June 2013 (2013/396/EU).
73. *See* Report on the proposal for a directive of the European Parliament and of the Council on certain rules governing actions for damages under national law for infringements of the provisions of competition law of the Member States and of the European Union (COM(2013)0404 – C7-0170/2013 – 2013/0185(COD)), European Parliament, Session Document, 4 February 2014, p. 58.

recommendation encouraging Member States to equip themselves with non-binding collective action mechanisms.[74]

In 2018, the European Commission published a report on the application of its 2013 Recommendation and introduced the so-called New Deal for Consumers.[75] This initiative included a proposal for a directive on representative actions aimed at protecting the collective interests of consumers. However, unlike the EU Damages Directive, this new legislative effort focused on consumer protection more broadly, rather than on safeguarding competition per se – a distinction that will be explored in greater detail below.[76]

One of the common criticisms[77] of the European Commission's seemingly preferred model – opt-in collective actions – relates to the limited initiative shown by injured parties. This reluctance is often attributed to the high costs associated with such proceedings, the relatively low value of individual claims, and a broader European cultural tendency to avoid litigation. These factors collectively undermine the effectiveness of opt-in mechanisms as a tool for ensuring access to redress.

As previously noted, the question of who is qualified to bring an action[78] depends on the type of collective mechanism adopted and warrants particular attention. It is closely linked to the concerns raised by European institutions regarding the potential for abusive litigation, especially in the context of representative actions.

The European Commission's Recommendation specifically emphasised that representative bodies should be non-profit entities, and that their purpose must be directly related to the rights granted under EU law that are alleged to have been infringed.[79] This raises an important consideration: should the role of representative bodies be reserved exclusively for legal persons governed by public law?

Given the importance of access to evidence in the context of particularly complex infringements (and the restrictions imposed by the so-called black list under the EU Damages Directive, as previously discussed), this issue will also be examined in the framework of a potential horizontal solution at the EU level.[80]

With regard to compensable damages, it is true that the EU Damages Directive explicitly excludes the possibility of awarding punitive damages, i.e., damages exceeding the actual harm suffered.[81] Nevertheless, exceptions to the traditionally European

74. *See* Opinion of the European Economic and Social Committee on the Proposal for a Directive of the European Parliament and of the Council on certain rules governing actions for damages under national law for infringements of the provisions of competition law of the Member States and of the European Union and the Communication from the Commission on the quantification of damages in actions for damages based on infringements of Articles 101 and 102 of the Treaty on the Functioning of the European Union, para. 1.2.9.
75. *See* Review of EU consumer protection legislation - New Deal for Consumers | European Commission (europa.eu).
76. *See* s. 3.3.6 below.
77. *See* Sofia Oliveira Pais and Anna Piszcz, *Package on Actions for Damages Based on Breaches of EU Competition Rules: Can One Size Fit All?*, Yearbook of Antitrust and Regulatory Studies, vol. 7, No. 10, 2014, p. 214.
78. *See* s. 3.6.2 below.
79. *See* pt. 4.
80. *See* s. 3.6.3 below.
81. *See* Article 3(3).

principle of full compensation for harm caused by anticompetitive practices have previously existed,[82] notably in the UK.[83]

Although the EU legislator has now settled this issue, it is important to acknowledge that the method of calculating compensation, particularly the inclusion of consequential damages and loss of profits, can serve as a powerful incentive for private enforcement. Moreover, it carries a preventive function by deterring future infringements. For these reasons, this topic will also be addressed in the course of this book.[84]

Finally, the feasibility of implementing collective redress mechanisms at the EU level is inextricably linked to the issue of costs, in the broad sense.[85] Third-party funding of compensation claims could increase litigation, particularly in competition law, by alleviating financial barriers for claimants. However, this approach is not without risks, especially in cases involving potential conflicts of interest or abusive practices.

Related concerns include whether representative bodies or third-party funders should be entitled to a share of the awarded compensation in the event of a favourable outcome (in the case of funders, in addition to reimbursement and interest), and whether contingency fee arrangements – such as *quota litis* pacts, common in the US – should be permitted.[86] These agreements link a lawyer's remuneration to the success of the case.

As Charlotte Leskinen points out,[87] '*[t]*he lack of incentive, combined with the fact that, in general, the "loser pays" principle is applied in most Member States, thus increases the risks of bringing a competition law damages action as the claimant may have to pay the defendant's litigation costs in addition to his own costs. Furthermore, the lack of opt-out collective actions makes virtually all low-value cases difficult to enforce'. While the loser pays principle is broadly accepted across the EU, a 2017 study revealed that in practice, some National Courts apply it only partially, particularly when the defendant is a legal person.[88] In the following chapters, we will also examine recent developments in this area, including the EPRS (European Parliamentary Research Service) Study and the European Parliament's Resolution on responsible private funding of litigation.[89]

---

82. Contrary to the line taken by the US. *See* Alan Riley and John Peysner, *Damages in EC Antitrust Actions: Who Pays the Piper?*, European Law Review, ISSN 0307-5400, vol. 31, No. 5, 2006, pp. 748-761, p. 750.
83. *See* Sofia Oliveira Pais and Anna Piszcz, *Package on Actions for Damages Based on Breaches of EU Competition Rules: Can One Size Fit All?*, Yearbook of Antitrust and Regulatory Studies, vol. 7, No. 10, 2014, p. 224.
84. *See* s. 3.6.4 below.
85. *See* s. 3.6.5 below.
86. In Portugal, for example, the prohibition of the *quota litis* pact is laid down in Article 106 of the Statute of the Bar Association, approved by Law No. 145 of 9 September 2015. On the *ratio of* this rule, *see* Susana Neto, *Quota Litis: da Evidência da sua Proibição*, Revista da Ordem dos Advogados, Lisbon, A.61, No. 2, April, 2001, pp. 1121-1140, available at https://portal.oa.pt/publicacoes/revista-da-ordem-dos-advogados/ano-2001/ano-61-vol-ii-abr-2001/temas/susana-neto-quota-litis-da-evidencia-da-sua-proibicao/, p. 1125.
87. In *Collective Actions: Rethinking Funding and National Cost Rules*, The Competition Law Review, vol. 8(1), December 2011, p. 119.
88. *See The Growth of Collective Redress in the EU: A Survey of Developments in 10 Member States*, Institute for Legal Reform, March 2017.
89. *See* s. 3.3.8 below.

CHAPTER 2

Part I: After the EU Damages Directive

2.1 AN ONGOING OBJECTIVE OF EU LAW

The harmonisation introduced by the EU Damages Directive (whose key provisions have already been outlined) has been the subject of criticism, particularly from legal scholars, on the grounds that it may infringe upon the principle of procedural autonomy of the Member States.[90] This principle, however, only applies in the absence of relevant EU legislation.[91]

It is worth noting that EU legislation typically focuses on substantive rather than procedural matters. Nevertheless, the CJEU has been called upon to address procedural issues where they intersect with the principles of effectiveness of EU law and the right to judicial protection for private parties. A notable example is the *Courage* judgment,[92] previously discussed, in which the Court affirmed the importance of ensuring that national procedural rules do not undermine the effective enforcement of EU competition law.

According to Patrícia Fragoso Martins,[93] the principle of procedural autonomy of the Member States is limited by the principles of effectiveness and equivalence, as consistently affirmed in the CJEU's case law cited above.[94] Moreover, EU competition

90. *See*, for example, Alvaro Águila-Real, *Contra la armonización positiva; la Propuesta de la Comisión para reforzar el private enforcemente del Derecho de la Competencia*, *in Indret 3/2009*, pp. 11 and following.
91. *See* Eda Şahin, *Collective Redress and EU Competition Law*, Routledge, 2019, p. 1.
92. *See* Folkert Wilman, *The End of the Absence? The Growing Body of EU Legislation on Private Enforcement and the Main Remedies It Provides for*, Common Market Law Review, vol. 53, No. 4, 2016, p. 889 https://doi.org/10.54648/cola2016088, available at https://kluwerlawonline.com/journalarticle/Common+Market+Law+Review/53.4/COLA2016088.
93. In *Rethinking Access by Private Parties to the Court of Justice of the European Union: Judicial Review of Union Acts Before and After the Lisbon Treaty*, Universidade Católica Editora, 2016, p. 241.
94. Courage judgment of 20 September 2001, Case C-453/99, pt. 29.

rules exert significant influence over national legal frameworks, underscoring the importance of harmonisation not only in substantive law but also in the realm of private enforcement. This is particularly relevant given the still limited application of private enforcement mechanisms across the EU – and, more specifically, the absence of collective redress mechanisms in the EU Damages Directive, a gap often attributed to economic considerations rather than legal or institutional constraints.[95]

Before turning to the collective mechanisms discussed above and considering the potential for a sector-specific EU legislative initiative, it is essential to first examine the scope of the EU Damages Directive. This will allow us to assess, in light of the principles of subsidiarity and proportionality, whether the Directive's provisions are sufficient to effectively leverage the compensation of damages resulting from infringements of EU competition law.

2.2 LESSONS LEARNED FROM KEY CJEU CASES

Since the CJEU is competent, on the one hand, to review the legality of acts adopted by EU institutions, particularly those of the European Commission (EC) – excluding recommendations and opinions – through actions for annulment (Article 263 TFEU) and, on the other hand, to interpret such acts, including the EU Damages Directive adopted by the European Parliament and the Council, through preliminary rulings (Article 267(b) TFEU), in order to ensure the effective and uniform application of EU law, it is essential to begin by examining the CJEU's post-Directive case law to assess its potential effects.

Following the adoption of the EU Damages Directive at the end of 2014, several cases have been brought[96] before the CJEU,[97] resulting in judgments that can be broadly grouped into three thematic categories: (i) the determination of the competent jurisdiction to adjudicate actions for damages under the Brussels I Regulation;[98] (ii) the relationship between public and private enforcement mechanisms; and (iii) the

95. *See* Andreas Stephan, *Does the EU's Drive for Private Enforcement of Competition Law Have a Coherent Purpose?*, 2018, pp. 11 and 16, available at Accepted_manuscript.pdf (uea.acórdãouk).
96. *See EC Staff Working Document on the implementation of Directive 2014/104/EU of the European Parliament and of the Council of 26 November 2014 on certain rules governing actions for damages under national law for infringements of the competition law provisions of the Member States and of the European Union*, Brussels, 14 December 2020, SWD(2020) 338 final, available at report_on_damages_directive_implementation.pdf (europa.eu), pp. 12 et seq.
97. E.g., 5/7/18 C-27/17 *flyLAL-Lithuanian Airlines C. Toader/Room 2* EU:C:2018:533; 14/3/19 C-724/17 *Skanska A. Arabadjiev/Room 2* EU:C:2019:204; 28/3/19 C-637/17 *Cogeco A. Arabadjiev/Room 2* EU:C:2019:263; 29/7/19 C-451/18 *Tibor-Trans C. Toader/Room 6* EU:C:2019:635; 12/12/19 C-435/18 *Otis II I. Jarukaitis/Room 5* EU:C:2019:1069; 15/7/21 C-30/20 *Volvo M. Safjan/Room 1* EU:C:2021:604; 6/10/21 C-882/19 *Sumal D. Šváby/Gran Room* EU:C:2021:800; 22/6/22 C-267/20 *DAF Trucks & AB Volvo A. Arabadjiev/Sala 1* EU:C:2022:494 and 28/1/2025 C–253/23 *ASG 2* ECLI:EU:C:2025:40.
98. *See* Regulation (EU) No. 1215/2012 of the European Parliament and of the Council of 12 December 2012 on jurisdiction and the recognition and enforcement of judgments in civil and commercial matters.

interpretation, in the strict sense, of the substantive principles enshrined in the EU Damages Directive.[99]

Given the specific focus of this book, it does not seek to examine all three categories outlined above in detail. However, categories (ii) and (iii) are particularly relevant for analysing the solution currently provided by EU law in relation to the subject at hand. They are also essential for an assessment of the adequacy of the existing legal framework. For this reason, we will briefly address these two categories below.

The first judgment of the CJEU – in this case, delivered by the EGC – to reference the EU Damages Directive was the aforementioned[100] *Axa Versicherung* ruling[101] in 2015. The case concerned access to documents contained in the European Commission's file,[102] specifically in the context of access to evidence. At issue was the applicant's request for full versions of the index and a set of documents from the file, based on the intention to seek compensation.

The EGC once again applied the general presumption established in the pre-Directive case law on private enforcement – namely, Pfleiderer and Donau Chemie – that the disclosure of documents contained in the European Commission's file would, in principle, undermine the protection of the objectives of the Commission's inspection and investigation activities. This presumption applies 'irrespective of any specific considerations relating to the nature or content of the documents collected under the leniency programme'.[103] Nevertheless, the Commission is still required to 'establish whether the general considerations normally applicable to a particular type of document are in fact applicable to the document which it has been asked to disclose'.[104] However, the applicant, in turn, failed to demonstrate why access to the documents contained in the file was necessary for the exercise of the right to seek compensation.[105]

Moreover, the EGC confirmed that '[a]lthough this case-law concerns leniency programmes established by national competition authorities, the same reasoning may be applied, by analogy, to the leniency programme of the Commission'.[106] In addition, it reaffirmed that both the European Commission and National Courts 'must refrain from taking an inflexible and absolute stance liable to undermine either the effective application of the competition rules by the public authorities entrusted with ensuring their observance or the effective exercise of individuals' rights flowing from these rules'.[107] Following this reasoning, the Court also held that the European Commission, despite conducting a case-by-case analysis, failed to demonstrate the existence of a

99. *See* Rafael Amaro (ed.), *Private Enforcement of Competition Law in Europe: Directive 2014/104/EU and Beyond*, Bruylant, 2021, pp. 14 and 15.
100. *See* pt. 41.
101. 7 July 2015, Case T-677/13. *See* Sílvia Bessa Venda, *The Disclosure of Documents Collected by Competition Authorities Before and After the EU Damages Directive, in 60 Years of EU Competition Law: Stocktaking and Future Prospects,* Roberto Mastroianni and Amedeo Arena (eds), Editoriale Scientifica, Naples, 2017, pp. 99-112, p. 109.
102. *See* AT.39125 – *Carglass*, available at https://ec.europa.eu/competition/elojade/isef/case_details.cfm?proc_code=1_AT_39125.
103. *See* pts 46, 54 and 95.
104. *See* pts 94 and 97.
105. *See* pt. 73.
106. *See* pt. 118.
107. *See* pt. 123.

reasonably foreseeable risk of specific and actual harm to the interests invoked, one that would justify an absolute refusal to disclose references to the leniency documents listed in the index. This refusal could not be justified solely on the basis of 'any confidential information they may contain or reveal'.[108]

Specifically with regard to the EU Damages Directive, the EGC merely noted that the Directive explicitly states it does not affect the rules established by Regulation 1049/2001 (*see* Recital 20 and Article 6(2) of the Directive). At the same time, the Court reaffirmed that the public interest in safeguarding the effectiveness of leniency programmes 'cannot be considered to take precedence, in a general and absolute way, over the other public and private interests at stake, which are also worthy of protection and must be reconciled with it on a case-by-case basis'.[109]

It should be noted that the case concerned an index containing references to leniency documents, rather than the leniency documents themselves. The ECJ used this distinction to avoid[110] applying Article 6(2) of the EU Damages Directive and instead reaffirmed its earlier case law.

As developed in greater detail elsewhere[111] and briefly referenced in this book,[112] the case law of the CJEU has thus far favoured a case-by-case balancing of interests in this area, rather than the adoption of an absolute rule, such as the categorical prohibition on access to leniency statements introduced by the EU Damages Directive. According to the Court, such an absolute prohibition would be incompatible with the principle of effectiveness of EU law.[113]

In 2019,[114] the Court delivered three key rulings directly relevant to the private enforcement of competition law: *Skanska*,[115] *Cogeco*,[116] and, more recently, *Otis II*.[117] These decisions will be analysed in greater detail below.

108. *See* pt. 126.
109. *See* pt. 135.
110. *See* Claudia Massa, *The Disclosure of Leniency Statements and Other Evidence under Directive 2014/104/EU: An Undue Prominence of Public Enforcement?*, Market and Competition Law Review, vol. 2(1), 2018, pp. 149-169 https://doi.org/10.7559/mclawreview.2018.336, available at The Disclosure of Leniency Statements and Other Evidence under Directive 2014/104/EU: An Undue Prominence of Public Enforcement? | Market and Competition Law Review (ucp.pt), p. 163.
111. *See* Sílvia Bessa Venda, *As regras antitrust e o direito a uma reparação efetiva: O acesso às declarações de clemência*, Colecção Estudos Instituto do Conhecimento AB No. 6, Almedina, 2017, pp. 299-343, available at Estudos do Instituto do Conhecimento AB N.º 6 (abreuadvogados.com), pp. 324 and 336.
112. *See* s. 3.1 above.
113. *See* pt. 49 of the *Donau Chemie* judgment: 'the principle of effectiveness precludes a provision of national law under which access to documents on the file relating to national proceedings concerning the application of Article 101 TFEU, including documents communicated under a leniency programme, by third parties who are not parties to those proceedings and who intend to bring actions for damages against participants in a cartel (...) [does] not allow any possibility of weighing up the interests at stake to be left to national courts'.
114. Between 2016 and 2018, the ECJ issued approximately six judgments touching on this issue, which again will not be examined here in detail given the specific focus of this book.
115. *See* C-724/17, of 14 March 2019.
116. *See* C-637/17, of 28 March 2019.
117. *See* C-435/18, of 12 December 2019.

Indeed, *Skanska* represents a turning point in the attribution of liability for damages arising from infringements of EU competition law. The Referring Court acknowledged that, while it was well established in the case law of the ECJ that any individual may claim compensation for harm caused by a breach of Article 101 TFEU, provided there is a causal link, it remained unclear whether the identification of the liable party should be determined directly under Article 101 TFEU or in accordance with the procedural rules of each Member State.

Under the first approach, the Referring Court noted that it would be necessary to clarify which entities could be held liable, and, in particular, whether the same principles the Court has applied in the context of fines - such as liability based on belonging to the same economic entity or on the principle of economic continuity[118] - would also apply in the context of this damages.

In essence, the ECJ was asked to determine whether EU law or national law governs the identification of the party responsible for compensating harm caused by a competition law infringement. The Court held unequivocally that 'the determination of the entity which is required to provide compensation for damage caused by an infringement of Article 101 TFEU is directly governed by EU law'.[119]

The European Commission argued that Article 11(1) of the EU Damages Directive - which provides that Member States must ensure that undertakings infringing competition law through joint behaviour are jointly and severally liable for the resulting harm - implies that it is for the domestic legal systems of the Member States to determine which entity is liable for compensation, in accordance with the principles of equivalence and effectiveness.[120] However, the ECJ disagreed. It held that this provision not only was inapplicable ratione temporis to the facts of the case but also does not concern the identification of the entities liable for damages. Rather, it addresses the allocation of liability among those entities once identified. It therefore does not confer discretion on Member States to determine who is liable.[121]

On this basis, the Court ruled that successor companies[122] may be held liable for the harm caused by the cartel in question since they ensured, as legal persons, the economic continuity of the undertakings originally involved in the infringement and which have since been dissolved.[123]

The ECJ rightly clarified that the concept of a causal link, necessary to establish liability for an infringement of Article 101 TFEU, is determined by EU law. Consequently, national legal provisions that seek to limit or redefine this notion are not applicable in the context of actions for damages. This position is grounded in the

118. *See* pts 16 and 21.
119. *See* pt. 28.
120. *See* pt. 33.
121. *See* pts 34 and 35.
122. *See* Chantal Lavoie, *Court of Justice Ruling in Skanska: EU Competition Law Concept of 'Undertakings' and Principle of Economic Continuity to the Rescue in Civil Damages Claims*, Kluwer Competition Law Blog, 22 March 2019, available at http://competitionlawblog.kluwercompetitionlaw.com/2019/03/22/court-of-justice-ruling-in-skanska-eu-competition-law-concept-of-undertakings-and-principle-of-economic-continuity-to-the-rescue-in-civil-damages-claims/?doing_wp_cron=1591108238.9130420684814453125000.
123. *See* pt. 50.

principle of effectiveness, which requires the uniform application of Article 101 across all Member States to ensure that the rights conferred by EU competition law are fully realised.

Notwithstanding the above, it is worth noting that in its preliminary ruling, the ECJ did not rely on the EU Damages Directive. Instead, it grounded its reasoning in the general principle of effectiveness and the uniform concept of 'undertaking' under EU law – even though the case concerned a follow-on action for damages arising from a breach of competition rules. For this reason, some legal scholars, such as Marco Botta,[124] have argued that the decision is 'nothing extraordinary', as it simply reaffirms established principles of EU competition law.

However, this book takes a different view from the author mentioned above. Regardless of the reasoning path followed by the ECJ, the *Skanska* judgment constitutes a landmark in the evolution of private enforcement within the EU. While the application of the concept of 'undertaking' and the principle of economic continuity is well established in public enforcement (albeit still frequently challenged by infringing companies), this case law is groundbreaking in the context of private enforcement because it affirms, for the first time, that the determination of the entity liable for damages in follow-on actions is governed directly by EU law. In doing so, it introduces into civil liability proceedings a concept previously confined to public enforcement,[125] thereby reinforcing the uniform and effective application of Article 101 TFEU across Member States.

This book is not alone in recognising the significance of the *Skanska* judgment. Benedikt Freund,[126] for example, acknowledges that the ECJ has further 'Europeanised' the rules governing the right to compensation for damages resulting from infringements of competition law. He does, however, caution that the Court did not explore the full implications of its conclusion, given the specific circumstances of the case.

Csongor István Nagy[127] goes even further, arguing that the *Skanska* judgment forms part of a broader trend towards the 'federalisation' of EU competition law, particularly in the area of private enforcement. According to him, the ECJ did more than merely frame national private law rules; it laid the foundation for an autonomous body of EU

124. In *The Economic Succession Doctrine in Private Enforcement of EU Competition Law: 'Nothing Extraordinary' after Skanska Industrial?*, Market and Competition Law Review, vol. 3(2), 2020, pp. 171-186 https://doi.org/10.7559/mclawreview.2019.1828, available at https://revistas.ucp.pt/index.php/mclawreview/article/view/1828, p. 185.

125. *See* Martina Anzini et al., *Making European Policies Work, Evolving Challenges and New Approaches in EU Law Enforcement*, October 2021, available at https://www.eipa.eu/wp-content/uploads/2025/03/Edward-Best_Making_European_Policies_Work_Evolving_Challenges.pdf, pp. 12 and 13.

126. In *Heralds of Change: In the Aftermath of Skanska (C-724/17) and Sumal (C-882/19)*, International Review of Intellectual Property and Competition Law, vol. 53, Springer, 15 February 2022, pp. 246-263 https://doi.org/10.1007/s40319-022-01150-5, available at https://link.springer.com/content/pdf/10.1007/s40319-022-01150-5.pdf, p. 255.

127. *Has the Time Come to Federalise Private Competition Law? The Autonomous Concept of Undertaking in the CJEU's Ruling in Case C-724/17 Vantaa v. Skanska*, Maastricht Journal of European and Comparative Law, vol. 26, No. 5, 2019, pp. 720-728, p. 6 https://doi.org/10.1177/1023263x19875354.

private competition law. He finds it 'curious' that, in the earlier *Kone* case,[128] the ECJ treated the question of causation as a matter of national law, subject to the principle of effectiveness, whereas in *Skanska*, the same Court signalled 'the twilight of national procedural autonomy and the advent of European "private competition law"'.[129]

Once again, this book respectfully disagrees with the position advanced by Csongor István Nagy. First, it is important to recall that the *Kone* judgment predates the adoption of the EU Damages Directive (handed down in June 2014, whereas the Directive was adopted in November of that year). At that time, in line with the *Courage* judgment,[130] it was for the Member States to regulate actions for damages resulting from competition law infringements, provided they respected the principles of equivalence and effectiveness.

Second, as previously noted,[131] the principle of national procedural autonomy only applies in the absence of relevant EU legislation. Since November 2014, the right to compensation for harm caused by infringements of Articles 101 and 102 TFEU - stemming from their direct effect - has been governed by EU law through the EU Damages Directive. In this light, the ECJ cannot be said to have created a body of European private competition law in *Skanska*, as such a framework already derives from the Treaties and has been further harmonised by secondary legislation.

The second 2019 case mentioned above, *Cogeco*, concerns preliminary questions referred to the ECJ regarding the temporal scope of the EU Damages Directive - making it, in fact, the first judgment to directly address this issue.[132] The case also examined whether the limitation period for bringing actions for damages, as provided under the Portuguese Civil Code,[133] was compatible with EU competition law and the principles of equivalence and effectiveness.

To briefly understand the context, *Cogeco* concerned an action for damages brought by Cogeco Communications, which had been a shareholder of Cabovisão - Televisão por Cabo S.A. between 3 August 2006 and 29 February 2012. On 27 February 2015, Cogeco filed a claim before the Lisbon District Court against Sport TV Portugal and its parent companies. The claim was based on a decision by the PCA dated 14 June 2013, which found that Sport TV Portugal had abused its dominant position. This decision was later upheld by the Portuguese Competition, Regulation and Supervision Court (TCRS, Tribunal da Concorrência, Regulação e Supervisão), although the fine was reduced to EUR 2.7 million on the grounds that the conduct in question was not likely to affect trade between Member States within the meaning of Article 102 TFEU.[134]

First, the ECJ held that the EU Damages Directive was not applicable ratione temporis to the dispute in the main proceedings. This was because Article 22(1) of the

128. ECJ, of 5 June 2014, Case C-557/12.
129. *See* p. 8.
130. *See* pt. 29.
131. *See* s. 2.1 above.
132. *See* Catarina Vieira Peres, *The Cogeco Case: The First Preliminary Ruling on the* EU Damages Directive, Market and Competition Law Review, vol. 3, No. 2, pp. 81-106 https://doi.org/10.7559/mclawreview.2019.1827, available at The Cogeco Case: The First Preliminary Ruling on the EU Damages Directive | Market and Competition Law Review (ucp.pt), p. 81.
133. *See* Article 498(1).
134. *See* s. 3.4.3.6 below.

Directive prohibits the retroactive application of the substantive provisions of Portuguese law adopted to transpose the Directive.[135]

The ECJ reached the same conclusion regarding the procedural provisions. Specifically:

(1) Article 22(2) of the Directive grants Member States discretion to decide whether the procedural rules should apply retroactively to actions for damages brought after 26 December 2014 but before the Directive's transposition or, at the latest, before the transposition deadline of 27 December 2016;[136]
(2) in this case, Cogeco's action for damages was filed on 27 February 2015, prior to both the transposition deadline and the actual transposition of the Directive into Portuguese law via Law No. 23/2018;[137]
(3) the Portuguese legislator explicitly decided, in Article 24 of Law No. 23/2018, that the national rules transposing the procedural provisions of the Directive would not apply to actions brought before the law's entry into force.[138]

Second, the ECJ found national legislation to be incompatible with EU law if it: (i) establishes a three-year limitation period for damage claims, starting from when the injured party becomes aware of their right to compensation, regardless of their knowledge of the infringer's identity, or/and (ii) fails to allow any suspension or interruption of the limitation period during proceedings before the NCA.[139]

According to the Court, such rules are liable to render the exercise of the right to claim compensation for infringements of EU competition law impossible or excessively difficult in practice. In particular, short limitation periods that begin before the injured party can identify the perpetrator of the infringement undermine the effectiveness of the right to full compensation.[140]

Once again, the ECJ reached the correct conclusion. This case clearly illustrates the inadequacy of the national legal framework for handling actions for damages arising from breaches of competition law. It also underscores the necessity of harmonising the applicable rules at the EU level to ensure the effective enforcement of competition law.[141]

---

135. Point 33.
136. Point 28.
137. *See* pt. 31.
138. *See* pt. 32.
139. *See* pt. 55.
140. *See also* the aforementioned *Kone* judgment of the ECJ of 5 June 2014, Case C-557/12 (prior to the EU Damages Directive), which reaffirmed in pt. 25 that 'the rules applicable to actions intended to safeguard rights deriving for individuals from the direct effect of EU law must not be less favourable than those applicable to similar actions of a domestic nature (principle of equivalence) and must not make it impossible in practice or excessively difficult to exercise the rights conferred by the EU legal order (principle of effectiveness)'.
141. *See*, in this regard, Guilherme Oliveira and Costa, in *The First Preliminary Ruling on Directive 2014/104/EU: Case 637/17 Cogeco*, 3 July 2019, available at The first preliminary ruling on Directive 2014/104/EU: Case 637/17 Cogeco - European Law Blog.

Despite the ECJ's judgment, it appears that the Portuguese Competition Court may not have ruled in full alignment with it (or at least, the reasoning is not entirely clear).[142] While this issue falls outside the scope of this analysis, it nonetheless reinforces the importance of the principle of effectiveness of EU Law. This principle serves as a safeguard for the uniform application of EU law across Member States, particularly in relation to Article 102 TFEU, irrespective of the applicability of the EU Damages Directive.[143]

The ECJ has once again demonstrated its capacity[144] to fill legislative gaps in the private enforcement of competition law, particularly in cases where the provisions of the EU Damages Directive are not yet applicable. This proactive role reinforces the Court's commitment to ensuring the effective application of EU competition law.

Finally, the 2019 judgment in *Otis II,*[145] referenced above, addressed a request for a preliminary ruling from the Austrian Supreme Court (Oberster Gerichtshof). The case arose from a damages action brought, among others, by Land Oberösterreich against five companies previously convicted of participating in a cartel in the market for the installation and maintenance of lifts and escalators. The cartel's objective was to ensure that the favoured company could secure contracts at inflated prices.

The plaintiff did not initiate the action as a direct or indirect customer of the products affected by the cartel. Instead, it acted in its capacity as a public body responsible for granting subsidies. According to the plaintiff, the cartel-induced increase in lift installation costs (reflected in the overall construction expenses) led to the allocation of higher subsidies, specifically in the form of promotional loans for construction projects. This, in turn, deprived the plaintiff of the opportunity to allocate those funds differently.

The defendant companies argued, and the National Court agreed, that under Austrian law, the damage claimed by the plaintiff did not have a sufficiently close connection to the objective of the prohibition on anticompetitive agreements, namely the protection of competition within the market affected by the cartel. In light of this, the Austrian Supreme Court referred a question to the ECJ, asking whether parties who are neither suppliers nor customers in the market impacted by the anticompetitive agreement may nonetheless seek compensation for damages they have suffered, even if only indirectly.

142. For further developments, *see* Charley Connor, *Portuguese Court Rejects ECJ's Cogeco Preliminary Ruling*, 13 November 2020, available at Portuguese court rejects ECJ's Cogeco preliminary ruling - Global Competition Review.
143. *See* Michiel Verhulst, *CJEU Finds National Limitation Periods in Conflict with the EU Law Principle of Effectiveness*, 2 July 2020, available at CJEU finds national limitation periods in conflict with the EU law principle of effectiveness - CDC (carteldamageclaims.com).
144. *See* Magnus Strand, *Competition Damages Betwixt and Between Past and Future: Cogeco*, Common Market Law Review, vol. 57, 2020, pp. 569-590, p. 589 https://doi.org/10.54648/cola2020038.
145. *See* Sílvia Bessa Venda, *Otis II: Light at the End of the Tunnel for Damages Indirectly Caused by Competition Law Infringements*, ULP Law Review/Revista de Direito da ULP, vol. 13, No. 1, 2020, available at Otis II: light at the end of the tunnel for damages indirectly caused by competition law infringements | ULP Law Review - Revista de Direito da ULP (ulusofona.pt).

In that context, the Opinion of Advocate General Juliane Kokott is particularly significant. The central issue, as she framed it, was whether there exists a sufficiently direct causal link between the cartel and the damage claimed, or whether the harm is too remote to justify imposing liability on the cartel participants.[146] Importantly, the Advocate General emphasised that this question does not concern the procedural modalities of enforcing the right to compensation but rather the substantive precondition for the existence of such a right under EU law.

Accordingly, the real issue becomes whether Article 101 TFEU also confers a right to compensation on an entity, such as a public creditor, that did not act as a supplier or customer in the market affected by the cartel, but nonetheless suffered harm as a result of it. For the Advocate General (and rightly so, as will be argued further below), this is a matter of EU law, specifically the interpretation of the Treaties, as it concerns the scope of persons entitled to claim compensation for infringements of EU competition law.[147]

As to the existence of a sufficiently direct causal link between the lift cartel and the damages claimed, Advocate General Juliane Kokott concluded that the relationship between the inflated prices of the installed lifts and the corresponding percentage of each promotional loan granted to finance them could, in principle, be demonstrated on a case-by-case basis.

As the Advocate General emphasised,[148] this case exemplifies the wide range of harm that anticompetitive conduct can cause. Such harm is not limited to losses suffered directly or indirectly by suppliers or customers in the affected or adjacent markets, nor is it confined to damage incurred in the course of a profit-oriented activity.

Philipp Kirst highlights[149] an apparent tension between the Opinion of Advocate General Juliane Kokott and the *Manfredi* judgment, both cited earlier. While the Advocate General suggested that the conditions for awarding compensation should be assessed by National Courts in light of EU law,[150] the ECJ in *Manfredi* had stated that the concept of a causal link falls within the scope of national law, provided the principles of equivalence and effectiveness are respected.

According to Kirst, the Advocate General sought to reconcile her position with *Manfredi* by distinguishing between the definition and the application of the causal link. In her view, the legal concept of causation comprises multiple layers,[151] and *Manfredi* addressed only the application of that concept – not its substantive definition under EU law.[152]

This book respectfully disagrees with the author's criticism, as it appears to overlook the temporal and legal evolution of EU competition law. Again, the *Manfredi* judgment

146. *See* pt. 47.
147. *See* pt. 52.
148. *See* pt. 79.
149. In *The Impact of the Damages Directive on the Enforcement of EU Competition Law: A Law and Economics Analysis*, Edward Elgar, 2021, p. 39.
150. *See* pt. 41.
151. *See* pts 46 and 50.
152. *See* Philipp Kirst, *The Impact of the Damages Directive on the Enforcement of EU Competition Law: A Law and Economics Analysis*, Edward Elgar, 2021, p. 40.

dates back to 2006, whereas the EU Damages Directive was only adopted in late 2014, and the *Otis II* case – where the Advocate General's opinion in question was delivered – was decided in 2019. At the time of *Manfredi*, the EU Treaties did not yet regulate the rules governing actions for damages under national law for infringements of EU or Member State competition provisions. It is therefore entirely natural that both the Advocate General's reasoning and the subsequent case law reflect a development from the legal framework that existed prior to the adoption of the Directive.

In its judgment, the ECJ began by recalling its established case law, particularly concerning the direct effect of Article 101 TFEU on the legal sphere of individuals. It reaffirmed that the full effectiveness of this provision requires that any person who has suffered harm as a result of an infringement of competition rules must be able to claim compensation.[153]

Substantively, the ECJ agreed with the Advocate General that limiting the right to claim damages solely to suppliers and customers within the market affected by the cartel would jeopardise[154] the effectiveness of that right. Accordingly, the Court held that 'any loss which has a causal connection with an infringement of Article 101 TFEU must be capable of giving rise to compensation in order to ensure the effective application of Article 101 TFEU and to guarantee the effectiveness of that provision'.[155]

Furthermore, the ECJ held, in abstract terms, that even entities which do not operate as suppliers or customers in the market affected by a cartel must be entitled to claim compensation for the harm they have suffered. This includes situations where such entities, like public bodies, were compelled to grant higher subsidies than they would have in the absence of the cartel, thereby losing the opportunity to allocate those funds more profitably.

In concrete terms, however, it is for the national courts to assess whether such damage occurred and whether a causal link exists between the harm and the cartel in question.[156]

As demonstrated above, the *Otis II* judgment is particularly significant in that it clarified that neither the identity ('who') nor the market position ('where') of the claimant is determinative, provided there is a causal link between the harm suffered and the infringement of competition law. The Court confirmed that cartel members are liable for all damage caused by their unlawful conduct,[157] regardless of the person or market in which that damage materialises. In short, the right to compensation under Article 101 TFEU extends to *anyone* who has suffered harm as a result of a competition law infringement.

153. *See* pts 21 and 22.
154. *See* pt. 27.
155. *See* pt. 30.
156. *See* pts 32 and 33.
157. *See* Albert Knigge and Rick Cornelissen, *The Judgment of the CJEU in Otis and Others (C-435/18): Indirect Losses May Need to Be Compensated*, Lexology, 16 January 2020, available at https://www.lexology.com/library/detail.aspx?g=bb549a7b-d0da-4bb6-9a91-37a5ca375637.

Additionally, the *Otis II* judgment clarified that the conditions for liability arising from infringements of EU competition law are governed by EU law.[158] As such, it falls within the jurisdiction of the ECJ to determine, in abstract terms, whether those conditions apply. Conversely, it is for the National Courts to assess, in each specific case, whether the facts satisfy those conditions.[159]

Despite the undeniable importance of this judgment for the private enforcement of competition law, it is worth noting that the ECJ did not specify which concrete elements must be established in an individual case to demonstrate the existence of a 'causal relationship'.[160] While the Court reaffirmed the principle that any harm causally linked to an infringement of Article 101 TFEU must be compensable, it left the task of determining the specific criteria and evidentiary thresholds to the National Courts.

The ECJ's reluctance to articulate the specific requirements for establishing a right to compensation even in abstract terms creates a risk of divergent interpretations across Member States. This variability may undermine the principle of equivalence, as it allows National Courts to apply EU competition law inconsistently, potentially weakening the uniform enforcement of rights derived from Article 101 TFEU.

In any case, the three 2019 decisions above – including *Otis II* – have significantly contributed to clarifying the division of competences between EU and national law in the context of the private enforcement of competition rules. This division mirrors the distinction between substantive rights and the procedural mechanisms for enforcing them. In other words, the conditions under which a right to compensation arises are a matter of EU law. However, it is up to National Courts to determine whether those conditions are met in each specific case.

Between late 2021 and early 2025,[161] the ECJ issued seven decisions which, in the view of this book, are of particular relevance[162] to the present research and will therefore be addressed herein, albeit in a concise manner.

The first is the *Sumal* judgment,[163] which – like *Skanska* – addresses the application of the concept of 'undertaking' in the context of private enforcement. The fact that a concept so extensively applied in public enforcement for many years is only now being scrutinised in private enforcement (prompting two rulings by the ECJ) is indicative of

158. *See* Miguel Sousa Ferro and Guilherme Oliveira and Costa, *Otis: Another Great Judgment on Private Enforcement from the CJEU ... But It Could be Better*, Competition Policy International, 22 January 2020, available at https://www.competitionpolicyinternational.com/otis-another-great-judgment-on-private-enforcement-from-the-cjeu-but-it-could-be-better/.

159. *See* pt. 143 of the GA Opinion.

160. *See* David van Wamel, *Otis II: A Lost Opportunity to Clear the Mist*, Lexxion Competition Blogs, 25 March 2020, available at https://www.lexxion.eu/en/coreblogpost/otis-ii-a-lost-opágs. ortunity-to-clear-the-mist/.

161. Years have not consistently produced significant decisions, with 2020 being particularly unproductive due to the disruptions caused by the pandemic.

162. Without prejudice, once again, to other judgments, namely those concerning the determination of the competent jurisdiction to adjudicate actions for damages under the Brussels I Regulation, which fall outside the scope of this book.

163. Of 6 October 2021, Case C-882/19.

the relative underdevelopment of private enforcement compared to its public counterpart.[164]

The case concerns a follow-on action for damages brought in Spain by Sumal against Mercedes Benz Trucks España ('Mercedes'), following a European Commission[165] decision that sanctioned fifteen[166] European truck manufacturers for cartel practices. Sumal had purchased two trucks from Mercedes via Stern Motor SL, a dealer within the Daimler group - one of the companies penalised in the Commission's decision.

Sumal sought EUR 22,204.35 in compensation from the Commercial Court of Barcelona. However, in its judgment of 23 January 2019, the National Court dismissed the claim, holding that Mercedes lacked standing because it was not an addressee of the Commission's decision.

Sumal appealed, raising the question of whether a damages action based on a competition authority's decision can be brought against a subsidiary that was not directly addressed in the decision but is wholly owned by a sanctioned parent company. The referring court noted divergent interpretations in Spanish case law: some National Courts have applied the concept of economic continuity, allowing liability to extend to subsidiaries; others have held that while a parent company may be liable for a subsidiary's conduct, the reverse does not apply.

Advocate General Giovanni Pitruzzella, drawing on the *Skanska* judgment, proposed that the ECJ should affirm that, in the context of a follow-on action for damages arising from a competition law infringement, liability may extend to a company even if only its parent company was formally sanctioned. He argued that, where the parent and subsidiary formed a single economic unit at the time of the infringement, and the subsidiary's market conduct substantially contributed to the realisation of the anticompetitive objective and its effects, the subsidiary may also be held liable.[167]

In other words, does the obligation to respect the European Commission's decision, enshrined in Article 16(1) of Regulation 1/2003,[168] preclude National Courts from holding an entity liable for damages in a follow-on action if that entity was not formally addressed in the Commission's decision?

According to Advocate General Pitruzzella, the answer is negative. The European Commission has broad discretion in determining which entities to address in a statement of objections or a final decision. However, this does not imply - either

164. *See* Benedikt Freund, *Heralds of Change: In the Aftermath of Skanska (C-724/17) and Sumal (C-882/19)*, International Review of Intellectual Property and Competition Law, vol. 53, Springer, 15 February 2022, pp. 246-263 https://doi.org/10.1007/s40319-022-01150-5, available at https://link.springer.com/content/pdf/10.1007/s40319-022-01150-5.pdf, p. 247.

165. EC decision in case AT.39824 - *Trucks*, of 19 July 2016, available at https://ec.europa.eu/competition/antitrust/cases/dec_docs/39824/39824_8750_4.pdf.

166. These are *MAN SE, MAN Truck & Bus AG, MAN Truck & Bus Deutschland GmbH (together 'MAN'); Daimler AG (hereinafter 'Daimler'); Fiat Chrysler Automobiles N.V., CNH Industrial N.V., Iveco S.p.A., Iveco Magirus AG (together 'Iveco'); AB Volvo (publ), Volvo Lastvagnar AB, Renault Trucks SAS, Volvo Group Trucks Central Europe GmbH, (together 'Volvo/Renault'); PACCAR Inc., DAF Trucks Deutschland GmbH, DAF Trucks N.V., DAF (together 'DAF').*

167. *See* pt. 77.

168. As a result, it should be recalled that the National Courts must avoid taking decisions that conflict with a decision adopted by the EC in proceedings that the EC has initiated on agreements, decisions or practices under Articles 101 and 102 of the TFEU.

expressly or implicitly – that entities not formally sanctioned are exempt from liability. If such entities formed part of the same economic unit that committed the infringement, they may still be held liable in follow-on damages actions.[169]

The ECJ endorsed Advocate General Pitruzzella's opinion and grounded its reasoning in the principles established in the *Manfredi* and *Skanska* judgments. It emphasised that the right to compensation in competition law infringements extends beyond direct harm to include indirect damage – particularly the structural and functional harm to the market, which undermines its economic effectiveness and ultimately harms consumers.[170]

The ECJ reaffirmed that the concept of an 'undertaking' is an autonomous notion under EU competition law and must be interpreted consistently across both public and private enforcement.[171] Consequently, in cases where an infringement has been established solely against a parent company, injured parties may still bring a damages action against a subsidiary, provided they can demonstrate that the subsidiary formed part of the same economic unit at the time of the infringement. To establish such liability, the claimant must prove – either through the Commission's decision under Article 101 TFEU or by other means – that the subsidiary was economically, organisationally, and legally linked to the parent company, and that its activities were concretely related to the subject matter of the infringement. This is particularly relevant where the Commission's decision is silent on the subsidiary's role or has not yet addressed it.[172]

Indeed, although National Courts have exclusive jurisdiction over private enforcement of competition law, the concept of 'undertaking' must be interpreted uniformly in accordance with EU law. Applying the theory of economic unity, it follows that the specific legal entity named in a public enforcement decision is not decisive. Rather, what matters is whether the parent company and its subsidiaries collectively form a single economic unit that is responsible for the infringement and resulting harm.

So, from the *Sumal* judgment it can be inferred that when a claimant seeks damages from an entity that was not formally addressed in a European Commission decision but is part of the same economic unit as the sanctioned undertaking, it must demonstrate two key elements before the National Court:

(1) the existence of economic, organisational, and legal links between the parent company and the subsidiary, establishing that they formed a single economic unit at the time of the infringement; and
(2) a specific connection between the subsidiary's economic activity and the subject matter of the infringement committed by the parent company, showing that the subsidiary contributed to the implementation or effects of the anticompetitive conduct.

169. *See* pts 69, 73 and 74.
170. *See* pt. 36.
171. *See* pt. 38.
172. *See* pt. 51.

It is true that companies within the same economic group may engage in very different activities. Therefore, in follow-on or stand-alone actions for damages, injured parties must always establish a causal link between the specific conduct of the defendant entity and the harm suffered, regardless of whether a prior public enforcement decision exists.[173]

However, as Benedikt Freund rightly observes,[174] this evidentiary burden can be particularly onerous. Proving both the economic unity and the concrete connection between the subsidiary's market activity and the infringement committed by the parent company often requires detailed documentation and economic analysis, which may not be readily accessible to claimants.

In this regard, Miguel Sousa Ferro[175] highlights that allowing actions to be brought against subsidiaries or affiliates - rather than solely against parent companies - can offer practical advantages for consumers. It enables them to litigate in their own language and avoid the significant time and financial costs associated with translating documents. Moreover, subsidiaries may have fewer resources and less sophisticated means to mount a legal defence, potentially levelling the playing field. However, Sousa Ferro also cautions that in the context of class actions, plaintiffs are unlikely to target subsidiaries due to the persistent legal uncertainty surrounding the binding effects of public enforcement decisions in follow-on actions.

We agree with the arguments advanced by Miguel Sousa Ferro and would add that the *Sumal* judgment imposes a heightened burden of proof on claimants seeking to hold a subsidiary liable. Specifically, it requires demonstrating both the economic unity between the parent and subsidiary and a concrete link between the subsidiary's activities and the infringement committed by the parent company. This evidentiary threshold may, in practice, discourage injured parties from pursuing compensation claims against subsidiaries, particularly in complex or resource-intensive proceedings.

In June 2022 and March 2023, the ECJ delivered two key rulings addressing the temporal applicability of the EU Damages Directive, with particular focus on Article 10 concerning limitation periods.

The 2022 judgment referred to is the *Volvo* and DAF *Trucks* case,[176] which - like the earlier *Sumal* case - involved a follow-on action for damages brought in Spain, this time before the Commercial Court of León. The plaintiff had purchased three trucks manufactured by Volvo and DAF Trucks and filed the initial claim on 1 April 2018, relying on the European Commission's decision concerning the so-called trucks cartel.

In its judgment of 15 October 2019, the National Court partially upheld the claim, awarding compensation equal to 15% of the purchase price of the trucks, plus statutory interest, but declined to award costs. The defendants raised a limitation defence,

173. *See* pt. 34.
174. In *Heralds of Change: In the Aftermath of Skanska (C-724/17) and Sumal (C-882/19)*, International Review of Intellectual Property and Competition Law, vol. 53, Springer, 15 February 2022, pp. 246-263 https://doi.org/10.1007/s40319-022-01150-5, available at https://link.springer.com/content/pdf/10.1007/s40319-022-01150-5.pdf, p. 255.
175. In *Consumer antitrust private enforcement in Europe: as complete a survey as possible (extended version)*, 23 October 2022, available at https://ssrn.com/abstract=4223770, p. 37.
176. Of 22 June 2022, Case C-267/20.

arguing that the EU Damages Directive was inapplicable because the infringement had ceased on 18 January 2011, so prior to the Directive's transposition. This argument led to an appeal, and the National Court referred preliminary questions to the ECJ, focusing in particular on the temporal scope[177] of Article 10 (limitation periods) and Article 17 (quantification of harm) of the Directive.

It is important to recall that Article 22 of the EU Damages Directive distinguishes between substantive and procedural provisions based on temporal application. Specifically, national provisions transposing the substantive rules of the Directive – such as those concerning liability or the quantification of harm – do not apply retroactively. In contrast, procedural provisions, including those governing disclosure or limitation periods, may apply retroactively, but only to actions for damages brought before National Courts on or after 26 December 2014, the Directive's transposition deadline.

Advocate General Athanasios Rantos observed[178] that although Article 22 of the EU Damages Directive does not explicitly define which provisions are substantive and which are procedural, its reference to 'substantive provisions of this Directive' suggests that the classification is a matter of EU law,[179] not national discretion. He warned that leaving this distinction to the Member States would risk inconsistent and non-uniform application of the Directive's provisions across different legal systems – an outcome that would undermine the Directive's objectives of ensuring effective and harmonised private enforcement of EU competition rules.[180]

To that extent, Advocate General Athanasios Rantos concluded that Articles 10 and 17(2) of the EU Damages Directive – concerning limitation periods and the rebuttable presumption that cartels cause harm – are substantive in nature and therefore not retroactively applicable. This contrasts with Article 17(1), which imposes an obligation on Member States to ensure that National Courts can estimate the amount of harm when precise quantification is impractical or excessively difficult. The Advocate General considered Article 17(1) to be procedural, and thus capable of applying to actions brought after the Directive's transposition date even if the infringement occurred earlier.[181]

In reaching this conclusion, Advocate General Athanasios Rantos relied primarily on the case law of the ECJ. First, in *Evropaïki Dynamiki,*[182] the Court held that limitation periods are part of substantive law, distinguishing them from procedural time limits. The rationale lies in their dual function: to protect the injured party – by ensuring sufficient time to gather relevant information and identify the liable party – and to prevent indefinite delays in exercising the right to compensation.[183]

177. *See* Charlotte de Meeûs, *The EU Court of Justice Clarifies the Temporal Scope of the Damages Directive (Volvo/DAF Trucks)*, e-Competitions, 22 June 2022, Article No. 107667.
178. *See* pt. 60.
179. *See Truck cartel in Spain: Opinion of the EU Advocate General in the case C-267/20,* 28 October 2021, available at Truck cartel in Spain: Opinion of the EU Advocate General in the case C-267/20 - INSIGHT EU MONITORING (ieu-monitoring.com).
180. *See* pt. 61.
181. *See* pts 69, 77 and 86.
182. Of 8 November 2012, Case C-469/11.
183. *See* pt. 66.

Second, in *Tsapalos and Diamantakis,*[184] the Court clarified that rules concerning the attribution and scope of non-contractual liability of companies that have infringed Article 101 TFEU through their participation in a cartel - such as those that place the burden of proof on the infringer and exempt the injured party from having to prove the existence of harm caused by the cartel or a causal link between that harm and the cartel - may be classified as 'substantive rules', as they do not serve a merely evidentiary purpose.[185]

According to the Advocate General, Article 17(1) of the EU Damages Directive does not introduce a new substantive obligation for the parties involved in the proceedings. Rather, it imposes a duty on Member States to ensure compliance[186] with the principle of effectiveness in EU competition law, as established by the ECJ. This means that neither the burden nor the standard of proof required to quantify damages should render the right to compensation[187] practically impossible or excessively difficult to exercise. For this reason, under Article 22 of the Directive, Article 17(1) is considered procedural in nature and may therefore apply retroactively to the case at hand.

The Advocate General also considered that, in the context of a follow-on action such as the one at issue, the publication of a European Commission decision declaring an infringement of competition rules in the Official Journal of the European Union provides a clear, precise, and transparent reference point for determining the *dies a quo* - the starting date for calculating the limitation period. This moment is equally identifiable for both the infringing undertakings and the injured parties, thereby ensuring legal certainty and procedural fairness.[188]

This book aligns with the view expressed by Ignacio García-Perrote Martínez,[189] who notes that the Advocate General closely followed the case law of the ECJ while also seeking to ensure compatibility with the legal practices of the Member States, thereby promoting legal certainty. For instance, regarding the *dies a quo* for calculating the limitation period, the Advocate General's position does not alter the existing approach in Spain. Under current Spanish interpretation, the limitation period is generally understood to begin on the date of publication of either the summary or the full text of the Commission's decision - unless specific circumstances justify a different starting point.[190]

The ECJ partly followed the opinion of Advocate General Athanasios Rantos. Specifically, it held that:

184. Of 1 July 2004, Cases C-361/02 and C-362/02.
185. *See* pt. 81.
186. *See* Cogeco, 28 March 2019, Case C-637/17 and *Otis II,* 12 December 2019, Case C-435/18.
187. *See* pts 71 and 73.
188. *See* pt. 123.
189. In *AG Rantos: Temporal Scope of the Damages Directive, Substantive and Procedural Provisions and Limitation Periods,* Kluwer Competition Law Blog, 19 February 2022, available at AG Rantos: Temporal scope of the Damages Directive, substantive and procedural provisions and limitation periods - Kluwer Competition Law Blog.
190. *See* Judgment of the Supreme Court of Madrid of 4 September 2013, Case STS 4739/2013, pt. 7, available at Consejo General del Poder Judicial: Buscador de contenidos.

(1) the classification of provisions in the EU Damages Directive as either substantive or procedural must be determined under EU law, not national law. This interpretation stems from Article 22 of the Directive, which makes no reference to national legal systems;[191]

(2) Article 10, which governs limitation periods, is a substantive provision. However, it may still apply to an action for damages concerning an infringement that ended before the Directive's entry into force, 'in so far as the limitation period for bringing that action under the old rules had not elapsed before the date of expiry of the time limit for the transposition of the directive';[192]

(3) Article 17(2), which establishes a rebuttable presumption that cartels cause harm, is also substantive. As such, it cannot be applied ratione temporis to actions concerning infringements that ended before the Directive's transposition deadline, even if the action was filed after that date;[193]

(4) in contrast, Article 17(1) – which requires Member States to ensure that National Courts can estimate the amount of harm when precise quantification is impractical – is procedural. Therefore, it applies to actions brought after 26 December 2014 and after the entry into force of the national transposing provisions, even if the infringement occurred earlier;[194]

(5) finally, the Court clarified that the *dies a quo* (the starting point for calculating the limitation period) should be the date of publication of the summary of the Commission's decision in the Official Journal of the European Union (6 April 2017 in this case), rather than the date of the press release (19 July 2016).[195] This is because press releases are not legally binding, often lack detail, and are not necessarily published in all official EU languages.[196]

Juraj Siska and Martin Seegers[197] have noted that the *Volvo* and *DAF Trucks* judgment provided important and long-awaited clarification on the private enforcement of EU competition law, particularly for Member States like Spain, where pre-Directive limitation periods were relatively short. The ECJ's interpretation of the temporal scope of the EU Damages Directive, especially regarding Article 10 on limitation periods, offers greater legal certainty and harmonisation across jurisdictions, helping to ensure that claimants are not unfairly barred from seeking redress due to restrictive national rules.

191. *See* pt. 39.
192. *See* pts 47 and 79.
193. *See* pts 92 and 104.
194. *See* pts 85 and 89.
195. *See* pt. 71.
196. *See* pts 67 and 69.
197. In *CJEU Clarifies the Temporal Application of the New EU Damages Directive's Five-Year Limitation in Cartel Cases*, Cartel Damage Claims, 24 June 2022, available at CJEU clarifies the temporal application of the new EU Damages Directive's five-year limitation in cartel cases - CDC (carteldamageclaims.com).

Strictly speaking, the Court had already addressed the issue of temporal applicability in the *Cogeco* ruling. However, in the 2022 *Volvo* and *DAF Trucks* judgment, the ECJ provided further clarification by holding that the five-year limitation period set out in Article 10 of the EU Damages Directive applies to actions for damages even where the underlying infringement occurred before the Directive entered into force. In the absence of an explicit transitional provision in the Directive, the Court effectively formulated a transitional rule: the new five-year limitation period applies as long as the claim had not already become time-barred under the previously applicable national rules before the Directive's transposition deadline (27 December 2016).

The ECJ's final formulation in the *Volvo* and *DAF Trucks* judgment marks a partial departure from the opinion of Athanasios Rantos. While the Advocate General proposed a more straightforward interpretation of the Directive's transitional regime, the Court introduced a nuanced approach that hinges on whether the limitation period under national law had already expired before the Directive's transposition deadline. This layered reasoning adds a degree of complexity to determining the temporal applicability of the Directive's provisions – particularly Article 10 – and may pose interpretative challenges for National Courts and claimants.

According to Ann-Christin Richter,[198] the ECJ's reasoning in *Volvo* and *DAF Trucks* reveals a notable inconsistency with the underlying logic of the EU Damages Directive. The Directive appears to accept the compatibility of longstop limitation periods – i.e., absolute deadlines for bringing claims that begin to run independently of the claimant's knowledge – with the principle of effectiveness. However, the ECJ's approach, which ties the start of the limitation period to the claimant's awareness (e.g., the publication of the Commission's decision), may undermine this assumption. As Richter points out, this inconsistency raises doubts as to whether the judgment effectively signals the end of longstop limitation periods in EU competition law.

This book partially agrees with the contradiction identified by Ann-Christin Richter, particularly in light of the final clause of Recital 36 of the EU Damages Directive.[199] However, it is important to note – as will be further developed below – that recitals do not carry binding legislative force. In contrast, Article 10(2) of the Directive explicitly states that the limitation period does not begin to run until two conditions are met: (i) the infringement has ceased, and (ii) the claimant has complete knowledge, or can reasonably be expected to have knowledge, of the infringement.

Still on the subject of the *dies a quo*, it is worth noting that the ECJ did not exclude the possibility that the injured party may have had knowledge of the essential elements required to bring an action for damages well before the publication of the summary of a Commission decision in the Official Journal of the European Union, or even prior to

198. In *ECJ Rules on Temporal Applicability of the Cartel Damages Directive and Clarifies the Statute of Limitation in Cartel Damage Cases*, Competition Bulletin, 24 August 2022, available at Hausfeld | ECJ rules on temporal applicability of the cartel Damages Directive and clarifies the statute of limitation in cartel damage cases.

199. According to this, 'Member States should be able to maintain or introduce absolute limitation periods that are of general application, provided that the duration of such absolute limitation periods does not render practically impossible or excessively difficult the exercise of the right to full compensation.'

the release of the corresponding press statement. This applies even in cartel cases, although the Court did not find that such circumstances were present in the case at hand.[200]

The 2023 judgment concerning the temporal application of the EU Damages Directive is the *Deutsche Bank* case,[201] which essentially mirrors the reasoning adopted by the ECJ in the *Volvo* and *DAF Trucks* judgment. Accordingly, no further elaboration is necessary here, other than to underscore the Court's consistent and well-established interpretation on this matter.

The *Trucks* case also led to the *Paccar* and *DAF Trucks* judgment,[202] delivered at the end of 2022, which – together with the *RegioJet v. České* judgment[203] of January 2023 – addresses the issue of access to evidence.

The first case also involved truck purchasers who, on 25 March 2019, petitioned Barcelona Commercial Court No. 7 for access to evidence allegedly held by the defendants. Their aim was to quantify the artificial price increase – specifically, to compare the recommended prices before, during, and after the period of collusion in question.[204]

Since the documents requested likely did not previously exist, compliance with the National Court's access order would have required the defendants to undertake work to aggregate and classify data according to the parameters defined by the claimants (effectively creating new documents). In light of this, the National Court referred a question to the ECJ regarding the applicability of Article 5(1), first subparagraph, of the EU Damages Directive. This provision allows a National Court to order a defendant or a third party to disclose relevant evidence that lies within their control.[205]

Advocate General Maciej Szpunar argued in favour of the provision's applicability, primarily because it aligns more closely with the spirit of the EU Damages Directive, namely to address the information asymmetry between infringers and injured parties. He emphasised that, under Article 5(3)(b) of the Directive, it is for National Courts to assess the proportionality of disclosure costs, including the need to avoid 'non-specific searches for information which is unlikely to be of relevance for the parties in the procedure'.[206]

The ECJ was receptive to these arguments, stating, first, that providing injured parties with pre-existing raw documents, potentially voluminous, only imperfectly satisfies their request and only partially addresses the asymmetry of information between the parties to the dispute. Second, the Court noted that excluding the disclosure of newly created documents in such contexts could create barriers that hinder the effective private enforcement of EU competition rules. In doing so, the Court implicitly invoked the principle of effectiveness, even if not expressly mentioned.[207]

200. *See* pt. 64.
201. Of 6 March 2023, Cases C-198/22 and C-199/22.
202. Of 10 November 2022, Case C-163/21.
203. Of 12 January 2023, Case C-57/21.
204. *See* pt. 20.
205. *See* pts 23 and 26.
206. *See* pts 69, 83 and 90.
207. *See* pts 61 and 62.

Thus, the ECJ confirmed the applicability to this case of the rule of access to documents based on the principle of proportionality, with the National Court having to assess the adequacy of the workload, as well as the cost associated with the ex novo production of the requested evidence.[208]

Nevertheless, it is noteworthy that the ECJ does not fail to point out that the above-mentioned access to evidence 'cannot result in defendants to main proceedings taking the place of claimants to main proceedings in their task of demonstrating the existence and scope of damage suffered' and that the provisions of the EU Damages Directive 'must be implemented in compliance with the fundamental rights and principles recognised by the Charter of Fundamental Rights of the European Union'.[209]

Indeed, although Recital 15 of the EU Damages Directive (which carries interpretative value) states that 'claimants are afforded the right to obtain the disclosure of evidence relevant to their claim, without it being necessary for them to specify individual items of evidence', in the view of this book, the ECJ may have gone too far in requiring defendants, even under the principle of proportionality, to produce documents 'on request', the content of which may ultimately be used against them in court. Such an obligation risks conflicting with the right against self-incrimination and, by extension, with the protection of the rights of the defence enshrined in Article 48(2) of the CFREU (Charter of Fundamental Rights of the European Union).

A different and particularly contentious issue – already discussed above – is the possibility of accessing leniency statements and settlement submissions. These are documents previously prepared by the claimants and held by a competition authority. While the Directive explicitly prohibits such access, this position appears to stand in tension with the case law of the CJEU, which has not always drawn a clear line excluding such materials from disclosure.

Moreover, Article 17(1) of the EU Damages Directive provides that where, on the basis of the available evidence, it is practically impossible or excessively difficult for the injured party to quantify the harm suffered with precision, National Courts are required to estimate the amount of damages.

The second judgment on access to evidence, *RegioJet v. České,*[210] addressed several preliminary questions once again concerning documents forming part of a public enforcement procedure in competition law. Access to these documents was denied on the grounds that the administrative procedure had not yet been concluded. The documents had been requested in the context of a damages action – suspended in the meantime – based on the alleged infringement at issue in the earlier procedure. The concern was that granting access at this stage could undermine the effectiveness of public enforcement of competition law, thereby highlighting the ongoing tension between private and public enforcement mechanisms.[211] The case involved an alleged abuse of dominance by České dráhy, the Czech state-owned national railway operator.

208. *See* pt. 68.
209. *See* pts 66 and 67.
210. Of 12 January 2023, Case C-57/21.
211. *See* pt. 29.

Although the administrative procedure was initiated in the Czech Republic in 2012,[212] it remained unresolved due to the European Commission launching its own investigation into the same facts, which was ultimately closed on 29 September 2022.[213]

Advocate General Maciej Szpunar and the ECJ were notably aligned in their reasoning, clarifying several key points:

(1) National Courts may order the disclosure of evidence even if the action for damages is suspended due to an ongoing administrative procedure, provided the principle of proportionality under Articles 5 and 6 of the EU Damages Directive is respected.
(2) The suspension of a public enforcement procedure by an NCA because the European Commission has initiated an investigation into the same facts does not constitute a conclusion of that procedure 'by adopting a decision or otherwise' within the meaning of Article 6(5) of the Directive (the so-called grey list).[214]
(3) The Directive precludes national legislation that temporarily restricts not only the disclosure of information 'prepared' specifically for public enforcement proceedings but also any information 'submitted' for that purpose.[215]
(4) Subject to the principle of proportionality, National Courts may defer the assessment of whether the requested evidence includes information prepared specifically for competition authority proceedings until such documents are in their possession.
(5) In the event of such a deferral, the National Court must ensure that neither the applicant nor any other party to the proceedings (including their representatives) gains access to the evidence before the Court has completed its review, or, in the case of grey list materials, before the competition authority has concluded its proceedings.

In our view, by invoking the principle of proportionality embedded in the EU Damages Directive's provisions on access to evidence, the ECJ is essentially seeking to preserve continuity with its pre-Directive case law.[216] That earlier jurisprudence favoured a case-by-case balancing of competing interests, particularly when public and private enforcement of competition law coexist. Rather than introducing a rigid framework, the Court appears to be reaffirming a flexible, context-sensitive approach that allows National Courts to weigh the need for effective private enforcement against the integrity of ongoing public investigations.

212. *See* pt. 24.
213. *See* AT.40156 *Czech Rail,* available at https://ec.europa.eu/competition/elojade/isef/case_details.cfm?proc_code=1_AT_40156.
214. *See* s. 1.2 above.
215. *See* Articles 5(8) and 6(5)(a) and 9.
216. *See* s. 3.1 below.

According to Nils Imgarten,[217] the ruling once again favours disclosure, but highlights the principle of proportionality as the greatest potential obstacle for claimants. This principle, he argues, can be strategically invoked by defendants and National Courts to deny access to evidence. In his view, the application of proportionality is inherently subjective, relying heavily on the individual judgment of national judges. Such interpretative ambiguity – what he refers to as a 'grey area' – is only compatible with the EU Law and the EU Damages Directive insofar as it does not render the right to disclosure impossible or excessively difficult to exercise.

This book takes a different stance from the view expressed above. The case-by-case balancing of interests for and against the disclosure of specific evidence has long been upheld in the CJEU's case law, precisely to ensure that the right to compensation for harm caused by infringements of competition law is not rendered impossible or excessively difficult. This approach was later codified in Article 5 of the EU Damages Directive. On this basis, the book contends that rigid rules, such as the absolute prohibition on disclosure of documents listed in the so-called black list under Article 6(6) of the Directive, contradict both the earlier jurisprudence and the principle of effectiveness.[218]

The sixth judgment issued by the ECJ relevant to this study is Tráficos Manuel Ferrer.[219] This case, also related to the 'trucks cartel', is particularly significant because it addresses several key themes as highlighted by AG Juliane Kokott: the structural imbalance between the injured claimant and the infringing defendant (primarily due to information asymmetry disadvantaging the claimant) and the challenges in presenting evidence and quantifying damages, as outlined in Articles 5, 6, and 17 of the EU Damages Directive.[220]

The plaintiffs sought damages from only one member of the cartel, submitting an expert report estimating an average overcharge of 16.35% in the affected market. The defendant countered with its own expert report, which was made available to the plaintiffs in a data room at the defendant's offices. This access aimed to facilitate a more thorough critique and potentially lead to a revised version of the plaintiffs' report. The plaintiffs subsequently submitted a technical opinion based on this consultation.[221]

Following the hearing, the National Court referred two key questions to the ECJ: whether a national rule stipulating that, if a claim is partially upheld, each party bears its own costs and shares common costs (except in cases of abusive conduct) is compatible with the right to full compensation for damages caused by competition law

217. In *Disclosure of Documents in Parallel Public and Private Enforcement of Competition Law: The ECJ's Judgment in C-57/21 – RegioJet*, 1 February 2023, available at Disclosure of Documents in Parallel Public and Private Enforcement of Competition Law – The ECJ's Judgment in C-57/21 – RegioJet – Kluwer Competition Law Blog.
218. For further details, *see* s. 2.3.1 below.
219. Of 16 February 2023, Case C-312/21.
220. *See* pt. 54.
221. *See* pt. 27.

infringements; and whether National Courts may estimate damages in a scenario where the claimant accessed the defendant's expert report and pursued damages against only one infringer, who had only partially commercialised the overpriced products.

The national rule in question has already been found incompatible with Directive 93/13/EEC[222] on unfair terms in consumer contracts. However, the ECJ declined to draw a parallel between the present case and the one in *Caixabank v. Banco Bilbao Vizcaya*,[223] emphasising that Directive 93/13/EEC typically applies to situations involving an imbalance of power – namely, a consumer (the weaker party) contracting with a professional (the stronger party) who sells goods or provides services. According to the ECJ, this structural imbalance, which characterises consumer contracts, is not comparable to the context of the EU Damages Directive.

In particular, the ECJ noted that the EU Damages Directive includes provisions, such as access to evidence, presumptions of harm, and judicial discretion in estimating damages, that are specifically designed to rebalance the relationship between the parties.[224] As such, the Court[225] agreed with the Advocate General[226] that it is both reasonable and consistent with procedural fairness to require a claimant whose claims are only partially upheld to bear their own costs, or at least a proportion of them, as well as a share of the common costs attributable to their actions.

With regard to damages, the ECJ clarified that the mere presence of uncertainties, arising 'from the confrontation of arguments and expert reports in the exchange of arguments, does not correspond to the degree of complexity in the assessment of damages required to allow the application of the judicial estimation provided for in Article 17(1) of that directive'.[227] However, the Court also emphasised that factors such as information asymmetry or whether the claim is brought against all infringers or only one under the principle of joint and several liability are irrelevant to the applicability of that provision.[228]

On the one hand, the ECJ reiterates that National Courts may estimate damages where the precise quantification would render the exercise of the right to compensation practically impossible or excessively difficult. This may occur, for example, in cases involving 'particularly significant difficulties in interpreting the documents disclosed',[229] such as complex expert reports. On the other hand, the ECJ emphasises that the need for a judicial estimate may depend on whether the claimant has exercised the right to request access to evidence under Article 5(1) of the EU Damages Directive. It is therefore incumbent upon the National Court to verify whether the claimant has made

222. Of the Council of 5 April 1993.
223. Of 16 July 2020, Cases C-224/19 and C-259/19.
224. *See* pt. 45.
225. *See* pt. 48.
226. *See* pts 58 and 62.
227. *See* pt. 52.
228. *See* pts 54, 55, 59, 60 and 64.
229. *See* pt. 53.

use of this procedural tool before proceeding with a judicial estimate. The Court further clarifies that '[i]f the practical impossibility of assessing the harm is the result of inaction on the part of the claimant, it is not for the national court to take the place of the latter or to remedy its shortcomings'.[230]

While it is true that the EU Damages Directive explicitly addresses the allocation of costs only in the context of sanctions – such as non-compliance with a National Court's disclosure order under Article 8(1)(a) and (2) – this book concurs with Lena Hornkohl in observing[231] that the Court failed to adequately consider the evidentiary burdens and financial costs inherent in this type of litigation. These actions often necessitate the use of expert analysis, which significantly contributes to the risk of a claimant losing the case, even partially.

Contrary to the ECJ's assertion, the relationship governed by the EU Damages Directive is far from balanced. Litigation costs remain one of the most significant deterrents to the effective exercise of the right to compensation. On this point, Advocate General Juliane Kokott also diverges from the ECJ, arguing that there are clear structural parallels between the imbalance addressed in unfair terms cases and the situation at hand. The injured party is frequently a consumer or an SME and faces multinational corporations with vastly superior resources. This structural disparity underpins the emergence of third-party litigation funding in competition law enforcement and underscores the need to ensure that all injured parties, regardless of the scale of harm, can effectively exercise their right to redress.[232]

This judgment is nonetheless of considerable importance, as it marks the first time the ECJ has interpreted the conditions under which National Courts may substitute themselves for injured parties in the quantification of damages. Crucially, the Court highlights that the failure of measures such as the request for the production of evidence under Article 5 of the EU Damages Directive is a key factor in justifying such judicial intervention. In other words, the National Court's ability to estimate damages hinges on whether the claimant has made reasonable use of the procedural tools available to them and whether those efforts have proven unsuccessful.

Finally, at the beginning of 2025, the ECJ issued a decision addressing a specific type of class action, the assigned action (which, remember,[233] is an action brought by a third party not entitled to compensation, who litigates in their own name in exchange for a share of the awarded damages).[234]

Indeed, the key issue of the *ASG 2*[235] was to determine whether EU law permits national legislation that prevents a legal services provider from bringing a collective action for damages based on claims assigned by multiple injured parties, specifically in

---

230. *See* pt. 57.
231. In *Of Adequate Cost Rules, Judicial Damages Estimation, and Fundamental Principles of Antitrust Damages Actions: Tráficos Manuel Ferrer, C-312/21*, 17 February 2023, available at Of Adequate Cost Rules, Judicial Damages Estimation, and Fundamental Principles of Antitrust Damages Actions – Tráficos Manuel Ferrer, C-312/21 – Kluwer Competition Law Blog.
232. *See* pts 52 a 56.
233. *See* s. 3.2 below.
234. *See* s. 3.6.1.6 below.
235. Of 28 January 2025, Case C–253/23.

the context of a stand-alone competition law infringement (i.e., without a prior infringement decision by a competition authority).

Indeed, the service provider ASG 2 brought a collective action for damages before the Regional Court of Dortmund against the Land Nordrhein-Westfalen, in its own name and at its own expense but on behalf of assignors (in return for fees in the event of success) – thirty-two sawmills located in Germany, Belgium, and Luxembourg, which claimed to have suffered harm due to a cartel that allegedly fixed prices for unwrought coniferous timber ('roundwood') between 2005 and 2019. The Land contested both the substance of the claim and ASG 2's legal standing, arguing that the assignments violated the German law and were therefore invalid.

While this type of collective action has been accepted in Germany in other areas, such as rental disputes and air passenger claims, National Courts have rejected its use in competition law cases, particularly in stand-alone actions that do not follow a final infringement decision by an NCA.

Given this context, the Regional Court of Dortmund questioned whether such a restrictive interpretation of the German law is compatible with EU law, particularly with the EU Damages Directive and Article 47 of the CFREU ('Right to an effective remedy and to a fair trial'), referring three questions to the ECJ: whether EU law precludes national rules that block fiduciary assignments for collective redress; whether this holds true even in stand-alone actions; and whether, if such national rules are incompatible with EU law and cannot be interpreted in conformity, they must be disapplied.[236]

According to Advocate General Szpunar, the central issue in the case was whether German law offers alternative mechanisms that are functionally equivalent for ensuring the effective enforcement of the right to compensation in cases of collective harm arising from cartels. While acknowledging that, in the absence of specific EU rules, Member States retain procedural autonomy to define the detailed rules governing the exercise of rights derived from EU law, the Advocate General emphasised that this autonomy is not unlimited and recalled that the principle of effectiveness requires that national procedural rules must not make the exercise of EU-derived rights practically impossible or excessively difficult.[237]

The ECJ once again aligned with the view of Advocate General Szpunar, concluding that if, upon review, the referring court finds – first – that none of the collective mechanisms available under national law effectively enables injured parties, such as the sawmills in this case, to assert their right to compensation for harm caused by a competition law infringement, and – second – that the conditions for bringing an individual action render the exercise of that right practically impossible or excessively difficult, thereby undermining effective judicial protection, then the national law must be deemed incompatible with EU law.[238]

236. *See* pt. 35.
237. *See* pts 30, 118, 134 and 135.
238. *See* pt. 84.

This decision was warmly welcomed[239] by both potential claimants and litigation funders in Germany, as it effectively clears the path for collective redress mechanisms in competition law cases. Indeed, by affirming that national rules cannot make it excessively difficult to exercise the right to compensation, the ECJ has reinforced the practical enforceability of EU competition law. The judgment is expected to encourage more assigned actions, particularly in cases involving dispersed or low-value harm.

In general terms, Francisco Marcos[240] identifies one of the main challenges in the field of competition law damages as the coexistence of EU and national legal regimes. According to the author, the expansive nature of EU legislation – particularly through the principle of effectiveness – creates persistent uncertainty about the boundaries between EU and national competences. While the scope of the EU Damages Directive is, in principle, clearly defined by its own provisions, interpretative doubts remain, especially due to its transitional regime. These uncertainties often require clarification by the CJEU.

As Philipp Kirst points out[241] (and as will be further illustrated below), significant differences remain among Member States in the rules governing actions for damages for breaches of competition law. Although all Member States have transposed the EU Damages Directive, it only establishes minimum harmonisation, leaving considerable discretion to national legislators in several key areas. Moreover, some Member States have gone further than others, adopting more expansive or claimant-friendly mechanisms that exceed the Directive's baseline requirements.

In fact, contrary to what Francisco Marcos appears to suggest, the presence of EU law in this area is far from excessive. On the contrary, as this book will explore in more detail below, there are still important gaps to be filled. The EU principle of effectiveness actually requires the uniform application of Articles 101 and 102 TFEU across all Member States. Without effective private enforcement, particularly through the exercise of the right to compensation, these provisions risk losing much of their practical effect. This concern was precisely what led to the adoption of the EU Damages Directive, which nonetheless continues to require interpretation and clarification by the EUCJ.

The case law discussed above is likely to significantly ease the path for injured parties seeking[242] damages for breaches of competition law. First and foremost, it has

---

239. *See* www.burfordcapital.com/insights-news-events/insights-research/european-court-of-justice-clears-the-path-for-collective-redress-in-antitrust-damages/.
240. In *Prescripción y daño en las reclamaciones de daños por conductas anticompetitivas: luces y sembras de la sentencia del Tribunal de Justicia UE de 22/6/22 (C-267/20 DAF TRUCKS NV and AB VOLVO/RM) (Statute of Limitations and Harm in Antitrust Damages Claims: Light and Shadows on the CJEU Judgment of 22/6/22 (C-267/20 DAF Trucks NV & AB Volvo))*, 9 September 2022, available at https://ssrn.com/abstract=4244690, pp. 3 and 4.
241. *See* Philipp Kirst, *The Impact of the Damages Directive on the Enforcement of EU Competition Law: A Law and Economics Analysis*, Edward Elgar, 2021, pp. 106 and 107.
242. *See* Ken Edelson, Liam Boylan and Petros Vinis, *in Antitrust and Private Enforcement: A Recent Judgment by EU's Top Court Requires Defendants to Produce New Documents That Can Be Used Against Them*, 21 November 2022, available at Antitrust and Private Enforcement: A Recent Judgment by EU's Top Court Requires Defendants to Produce New Documents That Can Be Used Against Them | Wilson Sonsini (wsgr.com).

clarified that the preconditions for non-contractual liability in this area are governed by EU law. It is for National Courts to assess, in each specific case, whether those conditions are met.[243] In doing so, the CJEU has interpreted these requirements in light of EU competition law, adopting a broad understanding of who may qualify as a claimant or defendant. This approach not only strengthens the remedial function of private enforcement but also enhances its deterrent effect – an essential element for ensuring that Articles 101 and 102 TFEU achieve their full practical impact.[244]

Nevertheless, uncertainties remain regarding how National Courts will apply the liability criteria and the CJEU's case law in practice. In Member States where pre-existing national rules already offered solutions similar to those introduced by the EU Damages Directive, courts may be inclined to rely on earlier national jurisprudence. However, this approach risks diverging from the standards established under EU competition law, potentially undermining the uniformity and effectiveness the Directive seeks to ensure.

As previously noted, despite the valuable clarifications provided by the CJEU in support of harmonising the exercise of the right to redress for competition law infringements across Member States, a wide margin of discretion still remains for National Courts. As will be explored below, there are still significant gaps in the enforcement of the right to compensation that the EU Damages Directive was designed to address. However, these gaps extend beyond the scope of what the ECJ can resolve through interpretation alone, as they stem from legislative choices and structural limitations that require further legislative action at the EU level.

2.3 OVERVIEW OF THE IMPLEMENTATION OF THE DIRECTIVE

In recent years, the implementation of the EU Damages Directive has significantly influenced the development of damages actions for breaches of competition law across the EU. While one of the Directive's core objectives was to establish a baseline of minimum harmonisation, Member States have retained substantial discretion in its transposition. As a result, notable divergences persist among national legal frameworks, reflecting varying interpretations and levels of commitment to the Directive's goals.

First, under Article 288 of the TFEU, a directive is binding upon Member States as to the result to be achieved, while leaving them free to determine the form and methods of implementation within their national legal systems. This flexibility allows Member States to either introduce new legislation or amend existing laws to give effect to the Directive's objectives.[245]

243. *See,* for example, pt. 143 of Juliane Kokott's Opinion in the *Otis II* case.
244. *See,* for example, pt. 67 of Giovanni Pitruzzella's Opinion in the *Sumal* case.
245. *See* Gentjan Skara, *Europeanisation of Private Enforcement of Competition Law: The Case of Albania*, Springer, 2022, pp. 136 and 137.

The pace and complexity of implementing the EU Damages Directive have varied significantly across Member States, largely depending on the legal frameworks already in place prior to the transposition deadline. In cases where national regimes were already aligned with the Directive's objectives, the process was relatively swift. However, where the Directive's content clashed with existing legislative structures or policy approaches, particularly those no longer compatible with the EU law, transposition proved more complex and time-consuming. The diversity of legislative instruments adopted by Member States, along with the failure of some to meet the transposition deadline of 27 December 2016 (as detailed in Appendix I – EU Damages Directive Implementation Table), underscores the challenges involved in achieving consistent and timely implementation.

Some Member States created an autonomous law, like Ireland; others inserted new provisions into pre-existing sectoral legislation, like Belgium; others did both, like Luxembourg, which created new legislation and amended the competition law; others amended civil procedure legislation, like Latvia; others went further than the Directive and amended pre-existing legislation on class actions, such as Portugal; and other Member States made all the above and more, such as Sweden, which created a specific law on compensation for damages caused by infringements of competition rules and, in addition, amended competition, class action and even intellectual property laws.

As for the transposition deadline, only five Member States (Denmark, Slovakia, Finland, Luxembourg and Sweden) have complied with it. Portugal was the last to transpose the Directive, doing so on 5 June 2018, nearly eighteen months after the deadline.

The disparities noted above – particularly regarding the timely and correct transposition of EU law – have long been the subject of academic and institutional analysis. Researchers have identified a range of justifying factors for these divergences. At the EU level, issues such as delays in notification and administrative coordination play a role. At the national level, several variables influence the transposition process, including the financial and administrative costs involved, differing regulatory philosophies, the date of accession to the EU, the economic sectors most affected by the Directive, internal legislative procedures, and the institutional configuration of each Member State. These factors help explain both the variation in transposition strategies and the frequent delays in meeting EU-imposed deadlines.[246]

It is not uncommon for transposed legislation to rely on EU legal concepts that do not fully align with those of national law. A clear example is found in Portugal, where the national leniency programme applies broadly to all anticompetitive agreements,[247] not just cartels, as is the case under EU law.[248] The EU Damages Directive, however,

246. *See* Thomas König and Brooke Luetgert, *Troubles with Transposition? Explaining Trends in Member-State Notification and the Delayed Transposition of EU Directives*, Cambridge University Press, 10 November 2008, available at ConantBackgroundReading4 (eui.eu), p. 190.
247. *See* Article 75 of the PCL.
248. *See* Commission Notice on immunity from fines and reduction of fines in cartel cases (2006/C 298/11), pt. 8.

defines both the leniency programme and leniency statements in accordance with the EU concept. In this context, Article 6(6) of the Directive prohibits access to leniency statements, and the Portuguese legislator transposed this provision by restricting access to statements submitted for the purposes of exemption or reduction of fines, i.e., according to its national concept.

As a result, Portuguese law appears to offer broader protection than the Directive itself. But is this permissible? The Directive's general rule, as outlined in Article 5(8), allows Member States to adopt more permissive rules on access to evidence, provided they do not infringe the Directive's mandatory prohibitions - such as the protection of leniency statements. Moreover, Article 6(3) clarifies that the article is without prejudice to national or EU rules on the protection of internal documents of NCAs and their correspondence.

Therefore, while Portugal's approach may seem more restrictive, it arguably remains within the bounds of EU law. Nonetheless, this example illustrates the interpretative challenges and legal uncertainties that often arise during the transposition of EU directives, particularly when national legal concepts diverge from those embedded in EU law.

The EU legislator appears to be fully aware of the complexities involved in transposing the EU Damages Directive. It is no coincidence that the Directive contains fifty-six recitals - twelve more than the original European Commission proposal - and twenty-four articles. While recitals do not carry binding legislative force, several of them, such as Recital 37, seem to introduce substantive obligations not explicitly reflected in the articles themselves. Recital 37, for example, states that a co-infringer who pays compensation exceeding their share should have a right of recourse against the other co-infringers. It further notes that national law, subject to the principles of effectiveness and equivalence, should determine the allocation of liability based on factors such as turnover, market share, or the role played in the infringement.

However, the articles of the Directive mention the right of recourse only once, in Article 19, and only in the context of the effects of amicable settlements. Specifically, it provides that co-infringers who did not participate in a settlement cannot seek recourse from those who did, with respect to the settled portion of the claim. While this article presupposes the existence of a right of recourse, it does not establish it. Ideally, the substance of Recital 37 should have been codified in an article to ensure legal clarity and enforceability. This discrepancy illustrates the interpretative challenges that arise when recitals appear to extend beyond the scope of the binding provisions, complicating both transposition and judicial application.

Notwithstanding the foregoing, recitals possess interpretative value. Indeed, the CJEU has relied on them in this capacity.[249] The European Commission's Legal Service, in its 2014 document titled 'Complexity of EU law in the domestic implementing

249. *See* Tadas Klimas and Jflrate Vaitiukait, *The Law of Recitals in European Community Legislation*, ILSA Journal of International & Comparative Law, vol. 15(1), 2008, pt. 76.

process', referred to recitals as interpretative instruments in the EU legal order.[250] For instance, Recital 27 of the EU Damages Directive states that 'National courts should themselves be able, upon request by a claimant, to access documents in respect of which the exemption is invoked in order to verify whether the contents thereof fall outside the definitions of leniency statements and settlement submissions laid down in this Directive.' The very assumption that multiple definitions of leniency statements may exist reinforces the earlier observations – both regarding the proper transposition of this provision into Portuguese law and the interpretative diligence required for its implementation.[251]

In addition to the significant discretion afforded to Member States and the interpretative ambiguities surrounding the implementation of the EU Damages Directive, its provisions tend to favour certain types of claims, particularly follow-on actions related to cartel infringements. This inherent bias not only shapes the way the Directive is transposed and applied but may also undermine its broader objectives.[252]

The EU Damages Directive also leaves several important areas unregulated. Chief among these is the issue of collective actions – the central focus of this book – but it also omits other forms of private enforcement beyond compensation.[253] Notably, it does not address injunctions (requests for court orders to cease infringements and/or eliminate their effects) or declaratory actions aimed at establishing the invalidity of agreements.[254] As Anna Piszcz aptly observes, '[t]he Directive is selective – hence the harmonisation of private enforcement of EU competition law is selective'.[255]

Now, the book explores the selective nature of the harmonisation introduced by the EU Damages Directive, setting the stage for 'Part II: Class Actions'. In addition to examining post-Directive case law, it is essential to analyse how the Directive has been implemented within individual Member States. This analysis serves as a foundation for assessing whether there is a need to establish horizontal collective action mechanisms or whether the system created by the Directive is itself adequate, a possibility that must

250. *See EU Legislative Drafting: Views from those applying EU law in the Member States': Complexity of EU law in the domestic implementing process,* available at Complexity of EU law in the domestic implementing process (europa.eu), p. 9.
251. On a similar Polish case, *see* Gentjan Skara, *Europeanisation of Private Enforcement of Competition Law: The Case of Albania*, Springer, 2022, p. 138.
252. *See* Francisco Marcos, Barry Rodger and Miguel Sousa Ferro, *Promotion and Harmonisation of Antitrust Damage Claims by Directive EU/2014/104*, Working Paper IE Law School AJ8-242-I, 13 June 2018, p. 27.
253. *See* Sara Landini, *Private Enforcement and Market Regulation*, Market and Competition Law Review, vol. 2, No. 2, pp. 47-70 https://doi.org/10.7559/mclawreview.2018.324, available at Private Enforcement and Market Regulation | Market and Competition Law Review (ucp.pt), p. 51.
254. *See* Anna Piszcz, *Piecemeal Harmonisation Through the Damages Directive? Remarks on What Received Too Little Attention in Relation to Private Enforcement of EU Competition Law*, Yearbook of Antitrust and Regulatory Studies, vol. 8, No. 12, CARS, 2015, p. 88 https://doi.org/10.7172/1689-9024.yars.2015.8.12.4.
255. In *Piecemeal Harmonisation Through the Damages Directive? Remarks on What Received Too Little Attention in Relation to Private Enforcement of EU Competition Law*, Yearbook of Antitrust and Regulatory Studies, vol. 8, No. (12), CARS, 2015, p. 96 https://doi.org/10.7172/1689-9024.yars.2015.8.12.4.

be critically considered. Such an enquiry is also vital for evaluating the design and coherence of any future reforms.

2.3.1 Harmonisation Versus Discretion

The very title of the EU Damages Directive reveals its core focus: it lays down '<u>certain</u> rules governing actions for damages under national law for infringements of the competition law provisions' (emphasis added).

The principal aim of the Directive is articulated in Recital 6: '[t]o ensure effective private enforcement actions under civil law and effective public enforcement by competition authorities, both tools are required to interact to ensure maximum effectiveness of the competition rules'. This objective is divided into the two contained in Article 1(1) and (2), i.e., if on the one hand the Directive aims to realise the right to redress, on the other, it seeks to balance this exercise with public enforcement. In the words of the European Commission, in its Report on the implementation of Directive 2014/104/EU:[256] 'the Directive includes rules that remove practical obstacles in exercising this right. Article 1(2) highlights that the Damages Directive also aims at fine-tuning the interplay between private damages actions and public enforcement of the EU antitrust rules by the Commission and national competition authorities'.

As a result of the above, the EU Damages Directive effectively seeks to establish a framework of minimum harmonisation. This approach addresses not only the disparities among Member States regarding the conditions under which victims may exercise their right to compensation for damages resulting from competition law infringements but also the broader issue of insufficient private enforcement in certain jurisdictions. Notably, in 2013 – the year preceding the Directive's adoption – the European Commission estimated that the annual harm caused by hardcore cartels alone could amount to as much as EUR 69 billion across the EU.[257] This figure excludes losses stemming from other anticompetitive practices, underscoring the scale of the enforcement gap the Directive aims to close.

However, as previously discussed,[258] the EU legislator introduced measures within the EU Damages Directive that appear to contradict the objective of promoting private enforcement – and even diverge from the case law of the CJEU. A notable example is the so-called black list, which grants special protection to leniency statements. This provision was subject to criticism during the legislative process, particularly by the CCBE (Council of Bars and Law Societies of Europe), for exceeding what was necessary to maintain a fair balance between public and private enforcement. As advanced, it

256. *See EC Staff Working Document on the implementation of Directive 2014/104/EU of the European Parliament and of the Council of 26 November 2014 on certain rules governing actions for damages under national law for infringements of the competition law provisions of the Member States and of the European Union*, Brussels, 14 December 2020, SWD(2020) 338 final, available at report_on_damages_directive_implementation.pdf (europa.eu), p. 5.

257. *See EC Staff Working Document 'Damages actions for breach of the EU antitrust rules'*, which accompanied the proposal for a Directive, available at impact_assessment_en.pdf (europa.eu), pt. 65.

258. *See* s. 3.2 below.

was also seen as inconsistent with CJEU jurisprudence, which has held that no category of documents should be categorically excluded from judicial scrutiny regarding disclosure. This is why, as noted earlier, the Directive may be said to render private enforcement dependent on public enforcement, thereby undermining the established case law.[259]

In addition to potentially falling short in addressing the lack of private enforcement, the EU legislator's intention to preserve a degree of national discretion is also evident in the choice of legislative instrument - rather than opting for a regulation, the legislator adopted a directive. As set out in Article 288 of the TFEU, both directives and regulations can establish binding rules for Member States at the EU level. However, while a regulation is directly applicable in all Member States and has full direct effect - both vertically (against the state) and horizontally (between individuals) - a directive requires transposition into national law. This allows Member States to determine the most appropriate means of implementation within their own legal systems. The choice of a directive, therefore, reflects a deliberate decision to leave room for national variation in the enforcement of competition law.[260]

The choice of a directive itself adds value by obligating Member States to pursue the EU's objectives and facilitating application to national realities. In any case, it marks a departure from the EU institutions' tendency to choose regulation as the preferred form of legislation, as was the case with data protection and financial services.[261]

The truth is that the legislator was aware that this matter could clash with the traditions and civil procedural legal systems of the various Member States, as evidenced by the transposition difficulties mentioned in the previous point. The legislator wanted to find a middle ground between the principle of the effectiveness of EU law[262] and the principle of procedural autonomy of the Member States.[263] Whether the legislator succeeded is a question this book will attempt to answer below.

As mentioned above,[264] the EU Damages Directive places important limitations on the procedural autonomy of Member States in certain areas, which constitutes significant progress towards the effective application of Articles 101 and 102 of the TFEU.[265] At the same time, the Directive leaves room for national legal systems to exercise

259. For further developments on the violation of ECJ case law with the protection of leniency statements operated by the EU Damages Directive, *see* Sílvia Bessa Venda, *As regras antitrust e o direito a uma reparação efetiva: O acesso às declarações de clemência*, Colecção Estudos Instituto do Conhecimento AB No. 6, Almedina, 2017, 299-343, available at Estudos do Instituto do Conhecimento AB N.° 6 (abreuadvogados.com).
260. *See* EUR-Lex - l14547 - EN - EUR-Lex (europa.eu).
261. *See* Elisabetta Rotondo, *Is the EU's Use of Regulations Becoming a Trend?*, Thomson Reuters Practical Law Public Sector Blog, 24 July 2013 available at Is the EU's use of regulations becoming a trend? | Public Sector Blog (practicallaw.com).
262. *See* ss 2.1 and 2.2 above.
263. *See* Chapter 5 below.
264. *See* s. 1.2 above.
265. For further developments on the content of the EU Damages Directive, *see* Sílvia Bessa Venda, *As regras antitrust e o direito a uma reparação efetiva: O acesso às declarações de clemência*, Colecção Estudos Instituto do Conhecimento AB No. 6, Almedina, 2017, 299-343, available at Estudos do Instituto do Conhecimento AB N.° 6 (abreuadvogados.com).

discretion in other areas, provided that the EU principles of effectiveness and equivalence[266] are respected. This analysis will focus on these points next, in a general and exemplary way, to see what is missing in promoting the private application of competition law by SMEs and consumers.

2.3.1.1 Competition Law Infringement

The EU Damages Directive applies to infringements of competition law. It defines these infringements as violations of either Article 101 or Article 102 of the TFEU or of national competition law. National competition law is defined as 'provisions of national law that predominantly pursue the same objective as Articles 101 and 102 TFEU and that are applied to the same case and in parallel to Union competition law'.[267]

In other words, the Directive leaves it to the discretion of Member States to apply the adopted rules to purely national competition offences. However, all Member States have endeavoured to extend the scope of these rules to cases involving EU and/or national competition law.[268] For example, this implies covering abuses of economic dependence in cases such as those in Portugal[269] and France,[270] which have no parallel in the TFEU.[271]

2.3.1.2 Right to Full Reparation and Its Requirements

Article 3 of the EU Damages Directive establishes the right of natural or legal persons who suffer damage caused by infringements of competition law to claim and obtain full compensation for such damage. This includes consequential damages, loss of profits, and interest. This compensation is granted in compliance with some of the principles resulting from the ECJ's Courage, Manfredi, Donau Chemie, Kone, and CDC Hydrogen Peroxide judgments, referred to above.[272] However, it excludes excessive compensation, i.e., punitive damages, which this book will explore later.[273]

---

266. *See* Ana Vlahek and Klemen Podobnik, *in Implementation of the EU Damages Directive in Central and Eastern European Countries*, Anna Piszcz (ed.), Centre for Antitrust and Regulatory Studies, University of Warsaw Faculty of Management Press, 2017, available at CARS 24 Implementation of the EU.indd (uw.edu.pl), p. 269.
267. *See* Articles 1(1) and 2(1) and (3).
268. *See* Barry Rodger, Miguel Sousa Ferro and Francisco Marcos, *The EU Antitrust Damages Directive: Transposition in the Member States*, Oxford University Press, 2018, p. 429.
269. *See* Article 12 of the PCL.
270. Article L. 420-2 of the Code de commerce, available at Code de commerce - Légifrance (legifrance.gouv.fr).
271. *See* Vassili Moussis and Atsushi Yamada, *Abuse of Economic Dependence, Global Dictionary of Competition Law, Concurrences*, Article No. 86372. For more recent developments, *see* Marion Baumann et al., *The Enforcement of Abuse of Economic Dependence in the EU*, 28 January 2021, available at The Enforcement of Abuse of Economic Dependence in the EU | HUB | K&L Gates (klgates.com).
272. *See* ss 1.1 and 2.2 above.
273. *See* s. 3.6.4 below.

According to the European Commission,[274] all Member States have incorporated this right into their national laws. As stated in the aforementioned ECJ judgments, the right to reparation was already enshrined in Articles 101 and 102 of the TFEU (which take direct effect in all Member States); however, the EU legislator felt the need to clarify this right. Some Member States, such as Denmark,[275] transposed it literally. Others, e.g., Portugal, transposed this directive provision into two articles: one addressing the civil liability of offending companies and the other addressing the calculation of compensation and defining the damages to be included.[276]

The EU Damages Directive does not define the requirements for this compensation, such as the level of proof, fault, or the causal link.[277] These issues are left to the Member States, subject to compliance with the EU principles and CJEU case law. However, as seen above, the CJEU in particular has been reluctant to delve into these requirements, even though it has already stated that the assumptions of liability for infringements of EU competition rules are a matter of EU law and has addressed them, notably in the *Otis II* judgment.[278]

In Recital 11 of the EU Damages Directive, the EU legislator states that: '[i]n the absence of Union law, actions for damages are governed by the national rules and procedures of the Member States. (...) All national rules governing the exercise of the right to compensation for harm resulting from an infringement of Article 101 or 102 TFEU, including those concerning aspects not dealt with in this Directive such as the notion of causal relationship between the infringement and the harm, must observe the principles of effectiveness and equivalence'.

Which means that, where Member States lay down other conditions for reparation under national law, such as imputability, adequacy or culpability, they should be able to maintain them provided that they are not formulated or applied in a way that makes it excessively difficult or practically impossible to exercise the right to redress guaranteed by the TFEU (or applied in a less favourable way than the rules applicable to similar national actions).

This is why the principles of effectiveness and equivalence are reiterated in Article 4 of the EU Damages Directive. The EU legislator's decision to leave these issues open will likely lead to significant differences in the private enforcement of competition rules.[279]

274. *See EC Staff Working Document on the implementation of Directive 2014/104/EU of the European Parliament and of the Council of 26 November 2014 on certain rules governing actions for damages under national law for infringements of the competition law provisions of the Member States and of the European Union*, Brussels, 14 December 2020, SWD(2020) 338 final, available at report_on_damages_directive_implementation.pdf (europa.eu), p. 5.
275. *See* Appendix I – EU Damages Directive Implementation Table, Chapter 2 of the Danish legislation.
276. *See* Articles 3 and 4 of Law 23/2018.
277. *See* Barry Rodger, Miguel Sousa Ferro and Francisco Marcos, *The EU Antitrust Damages Directive: Transposition in the Member States*, Oxford University Press, 2018, p. 33.
278. *See* s. 2.2 above.
279. *See* Philipp Kirst, *The Impact of the Damages Directive on the Enforcement of EU Competition Law: A Law and Economics Analysis*, Edward Elgar, 2021, p. 55.

2.3.1.3 *Disclosure of Evidence*

As access to evidence is crucial to exercising the right to compensation,[280] and potential claimants have pointed out for several years that the difficulty of accessing it is one of the main causes of the failure of private enforcement of competition law, the EU Damages Directive devotes a substantial part to the disclosure of evidence (Articles 5 to 7).

In general, procedural rules on access to evidence vary considerably across Member States. Although the Directive's regime was praised during the transmission process, giving the impression that some Member States wanted to extend it to other matters, the truth is that none did.[281]

Regarding actions for damages for infringements of competition law, the rule is as follows: National Courts may order the defendant, claimant, or third party to disclose relevant evidence under their control, subject to the principle of proportionality. This takes into account: (i) the extent to which the facts and evidence supporting the request justify disclosure; (ii) the scope and cost of disclosure compared to its relevance to the proceedings; and (iii) whether the evidence contains confidential information and the procedures adopted to protect it.[282] In other words, the Directive leaves it up to the Member States to ensure that National Courts have the power to order the disclosure of confidential information and have effective measures in place to protect its confidentiality when ordering its disclosure,[283] as well as to analyse on a case-by-case basis whether or not to order such disclosure. Although this will result in disparate applications in the Member States, it is in line with the ECJ's case law already mentioned.[284]

Although the EU legislator emphasised that '[t]he interest of undertakings to avoid actions for damages following an infringement of competition law shall not constitute an interest that warrants protection',[285] it adopted rules aimed at protecting public enforcement rather than facilitating redress.[286] Indeed, the EU legislator has chosen to restrict access to evidence included in a competition authority's file by adding criteria

280. *See EC Staff Working Document on the implementation of Directive 2014/104/EU of the European Parliament and of the Council of 26 November 2014 on certain rules governing actions for damages under national law for infringements of the competition law provisions of the Member States and of the European Union*, Brussels, 14 December 2020, SWD(2020) 338 final, available at report_on_damages_directive_implementation.pdf (europa.eu), p. 5.
281. For further developments, *see* Barry Rodger, Miguel Sousa Ferro and Francisco Marcos, *A Panacea for Competition Law Damages Actions in the EU? A Comparative View of the Implementation of the EU Antitrust Damages Directive in Sixteen Member States*, Maastricht Journal of European and Comparative Law, vol. 26, No. 4, 2019, pp. 480-504, p. 487 https://doi.org/10.1177/1023263x19861032.
282. *See* Article 5(1) to (3).
283. *See* Article 5(4).
284. *See* s. 2.2 above.
285. *See* Article 5(5).
286. *See* s. 1.2 above.

for National Courts to consider when deciding on disclosure requests: (i) the specificity of the request, (ii) whether it relates to substantiating a claim for damages, and (iii) whether disclosure would jeopardise safeguarding the effectiveness of public enforcement.[287] The legislator has also prohibited disclosing certain evidence contained in the above-mentioned black and grey lists.

The black list refers to evidence whose access for this purpose is absolutely prohibited: leniency statements and settlement proposals.[288] The grey list includes evidence that can be disclosed but only after the competition authority has concluded its proceedings (by adopting a decision or otherwise). This includes: (i) information prepared by a natural or legal person specifically for the proceedings of a competition authority; (ii) information prepared by a competition authority and sent to the parties in the course of its proceedings; and (iii) settlement submissions that have been withdrawn.[289] It should be noted that this (iii) type of document was not included in the European Commission's proposal.[290] The year after the EU Damages Directive was adopted, the Commission tried to circumvent it by preventing the parties from unilaterally withdrawing transaction proposals.[291]

Evidence obtained in breach of Article 6(5) and (6) of the EU Damages Directive is inadmissible; the same goes for any evidence obtained by a person exclusively through access to the file of a competition authority if its use in a damages action is not carried out by that person or by a successor person (including a person that acquired that person's claim).[292]

These restrictions mean that injured parties must wait for the public competition law enforcement decision to access the aforementioned documents. Access to these documents is crucial because the non-confidential version of the competition authority's decision is published several months or more than a year later and is not widely publicised. Usually, only competition law specialists are aware of this, and it is insufficient for preparing a claim for damages, even considering the rule of binding effect discussed in the next section. Indeed, based on this decision alone, it is difficult for an injured party, especially a consumer or an SME, to understand the scope of the infringement and, consequently, the extent of the damage they may have suffered. This is particularly true of decisions based on leniency statements or settlements because victims cannot access these documents.[293]

287. *See* Article 6(4).
288. As already mentioned, the plaintiffs may only have access to such elements to the extent necessary to ensure that their content corresponds to the respective category, pursuant to Article 6(7).
289. *See* Article 6(5).
290. *See* EUR-Lex - 52013PC0404R(01) - EN (europa.eu).
291. By amending the wording of pt. 22 of the Commission Notice on the conduct of settlement procedures for the purpose of adopting decisions pursuant to Article 7 and Article 23 of Council Regulation (EC) No. 1/2003 in cartel cases.
292. *See* Article 7.
293. *See* Miguel Sousa Ferro, *Consumer Antitrust Private Enforcement in Europe: As Complete a Survey as Possible (Extended Version)*, 23 October 2022, available at https://ssrn.com/abstract=4223770, p. 45.

Finally, the EU Damages Directive leaves it up to Member States to impose sanctions for non-compliance with the above rules, such as refusal to comply with a disclosure order, destruction of relevant evidence, non-compliance with obligations imposed by the National Court to protect confidential information, or refusal to comply. This may include drawing conclusions unfavourable to the noncomplying party, such as establishing the facts in question as proven, denying requests for means of defence, and ordering the payment of costs (in which the loser pays principle is derogated from).[294]

According to data collected by the European Commission,[295] while all Member States have implemented the rules on access to evidence established by the EU Damages Directive in a relatively uniform way (albeit using different methods to incorporate them into their legal frameworks), the range of sanctions for violating the disclosure rules, the respective penalties, and who and what behaviour can be sanctioned vary. Some Member States have even established fines and prison sentences.

For example, Portugal has specified the measures that can be used to protect confidential information in disclosed documents. These measures include: (i) concealing sensitive excerpts from documents, (ii) conducting hearings behind closed doors, (iii) restricting access to evidence to authorised parties and their lawyers or experts subject to confidentiality obligations, and (iv) requesting that experts prepare non-confidential summaries of the information.[296] It also provides for a fine for non-compliance with the rules on access to evidence set by the National Court, ranging from 50 to 5,000 UC (between EUR 5,100 and 510,000),[297] with the possibility of adding a penalty payment in the event of non-compliance or refusal to comply with an order to produce evidence and removing the evidential effects of such non-compliance, such as reversing the burden of proof.

The above depends on the seriousness of the conduct and the extent to which it makes it difficult for the plaintiff or defendant to prove their case[298] – and not on the financial capacity of the violating party or the compensation potentially at stake (in other words, depending on the evidence in question, non-compliance can pay off).

Ultimately, the Portuguese legislator surpassed the Directive by regulating pre-action disclosure, as well as measures to preserve evidence, in its Civil and Procedure Codes.[299]

Several Member States have implemented similar measures regarding access to evidence prior to filing a claim for compensation. They have also gone beyond the

294. *See* Article 8.
295. *See EC Staff Working Document on the implementation of Directive 2014/104/EU of the European Parliament and of the Council of 26 November 2014 on certain rules governing actions for damages under national law for infringements of the competition law provisions of the Member States and of the European Union,* Brussels, 14 December 2020, SWD(2020) 338 final, available at report_on_damages_directive_implementation.pdf (europa.eu), pp. 6 and 7.
296. *See* Article 12(7) of Law 23/2018.
297. *See* 103045671390.pdf (sfj.pt).
298. *See* Article 18, paras 1 to 4 of Law 23/2018.
299. *See* Articles 13 and 17 of Law 23/2018.

Directive: Spain, Germany, the Czech Republic, and Estonia, for example.[300] Other Member States did not feel the need to change their legislation to this extent since it already provided for this possibility before the Directive, such as the UK or Ireland. The same applies to the protection of confidentiality: Sweden, the Netherlands and the UK did not introduce new protection measures.[301] The latter, for example, already provided for the possibility of the CAT creating confidentiality rings,[302] which can consist, in particular, of data rooms with restricted access.

Indeed, commercially sensitive information is frequently used in competition law disputes. Often, if this commercial information has been exported from a document, the argument based on this element becomes meaningless. That is why the above-referred rings have been used frequently by the CAT for several years now.[303]

As for the sanctions, they vary greatly. For example, in France, the civil fine (amende civile) can only go up to EUR 10,000,[304] without prejudice to the possibility of claiming damages and the National Court drawing factual consequences from destroying documents, failing to comply with the order to produce them, or failing to protect confidential information. This is a somewhat outrageous figure, considering the amount of damage usually involved.

Finally, Germany has not provided any sanctions other than the right to compensation for damage caused by a party obstructing access to a document.[305] Thus, the injured party ends up doubly injured in this solution. They must prove and quantify two types of damages: the infringement of competition rules and the deprivation of access to the document needed to support the action for damages related to that infringement. They must also establish at least two causal links. They have the same problems with asymmetry of information as before the transposition of the right of access to evidence, provided for by the EU Damages Directive.

2.3.1.4 Binding Effect of National Decisions

One of the most significant (and often debated) provisions of the EU Damages Directive is the binding effect[306] of a final national decision declaring an infringement of

300. *See* Appendix I – EU Damages Directive Implementation Table: Article 283bis(e)1 of Spanish legislation; s. 33(g) of German legislation; Pt. 98 (No. 147) of Czech Republic legislation and s. 244 of Estonian legislation.
301. *See* Philipp Kirst, *The Impact of the Damages Directive on the Enforcement of EU Competition Law: A Law and Economics Analysis*, Edward Elgar, 2021, p. 61.
302. *See* 53(2)(h) of the Competition Appeal Tribunal Rules 2015, available at The Competition Appeal Tribunal Rules 2015 (catribunal.org.uk).
303. *See* Tom Richards, *Cats, Bags, Rings and Rooms: The Problem of Confidentiality*, Competition Bulletin, 11 October 2013, available at Cats, bags, rings and rooms: the problem of confidentiality | Competition Bulletin.
304. *See* Article R.483-14 du Code de commerce.
305. *See* s. 33g(8) GWB (German Competition Act), available at Act against Restraints of Competition (GWB) (gesetze-im-internet.de).
306. *See* s. 3.2 below.

competition law. According to the Directive, such a decision creates an irrebuttable presumption for the National Court hearing the damages action.[307]

If the decision is issued in another Member State, the Directive grants greater discretion to national legal systems, requiring only that such a decision may be treated, at a minimum, as prima facie evidence of a competition law infringement.[308] It is important to distinguish prima facie evidence from a rebuttable presumption: while the latter shifts the burden of proof and allows for counter-evidence, prima facie evidence merely lowers the threshold for the party bearing the burden of proof. It does not reverse that burden;[309] the party must still present sufficient evidence to establish a rebuttable presumption.

As has also been noted, this provision has sparked controversy and even raised constitutional concerns in some Member States. This is largely because, in many of them, a National Court is not bound by the decision of another National Court (even one from the same Member State). The situation becomes even more complex when the binding effect is attributed to an administrative decision that may not have been subject to judicial review.[310] The Bulgarian Constitutional Court, for instance, even has ruled that granting binding effect to decisions by NCAs declaring infringements of competition law would violate constitutional principles such as the rule of law, the separation of powers, and judicial independence.[311] In other words, there is a risk that decisions adopted by National Courts may conflict with the principle of the primacy of the EU law.

Due to the concerns outlined above, Member States have adopted divergent approaches when transposing the EU Damages Directive, particularly regarding the evidentiary effect of decisions from other Member States declaring infringements of competition law:

(1) *Literal transposition of prima facie effect:* Thirteen Member States have either transposed the Directive's wording directly or consider that their existing legal framework already aligns with it (though this assumption may be questionable in some cases, such as Estonia).[312] The countries in

307. *See* Article 9(1).
308. *See* Article 9(2).
309. *See* Rita Lynce de Faria, *A Inversão do ónus da Prova no Direito Civil Português*, Editora Lex, 2001, p. 34.
310. *See* Miguel Sousa Ferro, *Antitrust Private Enforcement and the Binding Effect of Public Enforcement Decisions*, Market and Competition Law Review, vol. 3, No. 2, pp. 51-80 https://doi.org/10.7559/mclawreview.2019.1830, available at Antitrust Private Enforcement and the Binding Effect of Public Enforcement Decisions | Market and Competition Law Review (ucp.pt), p. 76.
311. *See* Evelin Pärn-Lee, *Effect of National Decisions on Actions for Competition Damages in the CEE Countries*, Yearbook of Antitrust and Regulatory Studies, vol. 10, No. 15, 2017, pp. 177-196, available at Effect of National Decisions on Actions for Competition Damages in the CEE Countries by Evelin Pärn-Lee:: SSRN, pp. 186 and 187.
312. *See* fn. 325 below.

this group include: UK,[313] Luxembourg,[314] the Netherlands,[315] Ireland,[316] Sweden,[317] Poland,[318] Italy,[319] Malta,[320] Lithuania,[321] Finland,[322] Belgium,[323] Estonia[324] and Cyprus.[325]

(2) *Rebuttable presumption:* Eleven Member States went further by establishing a rebuttable presumption, thereby shifting the burden of proof unless counter-evidence is presented. This group includes: Portugal,[326] Spain,[327]

313. *See* 58A of the Competition Act 1998 in its current version, available at Competition Act 1998 (legislation.gov.uk).
314. *See* Appendix I – EU Damages Directive Implementation Table, Article 6(2) of Luxembourg law.
315. *Ibid.*, Article 161(a) of Dutch law.
316. *Ibid.*, Article 8(2) of Irish law.
317. National legislation already provided for this prima facie rule. *See* Lars Henriksson, *in The EU Antitrust Damages Directive: Transposition in the Member States,* Barry Rodger, Miguel Sousa Ferro and Francisco Marcos (eds), Oxford University Press, 2018, p. 274.
318. *See* Article 231 of the Polish Civil Code, available at Akt prawny (sejm.gov.pl) – which also provided that the Court may consider facts significant for the outcome of the case to be established facts, if such a conclusion can be inferred from other established facts (presumption of fact). The Polish legislator felt that this provision already encompassed the solution provided for in Article 9(2) of the EU Damages Directive. For further developments, *see* Anna Piszcz and Dominik Wolsk, in *Poland, Implementation of the EU Damages Directive in Central and Eastern European Countries*, Anna Piszcz (ed.), Centre for Antitrust and Regulatory Studies, University of Warsaw Faculty of Management Press, 2017, available at CARS 24 Implementation of the EU.indd (uw.edu.pl), pp. 227 and 228.
319. *See* Appendix I – EU Damages Directive Implementation Table, Article 7(2) of Italian legislation.
320. *Ibid.*, Article 9(2) of Maltese legislation.
321. *Ibid.*, Article 51(4) of Lithuanian legislation.
322. *Ibid.*, Article 3 (second part) of the Finnish legislation.
323. *Ibid.*, Article XVII.82. para. 2 of Belgian law.
324. Nor did it transpose Article 9(2) of the EU Damages Directive, since this was supposedly already covered by Article 272 of the Estonian Code of Civil Procedure, available at Tsiviilkohtumenetluse seadustik-Riigi Teataja. *See* Evelin Pärn-Lee, *in Estonia, Implementation of the EU Damages Directive in Central and Eastern European Countries*, Anna Piszcz (ed.), Centre for Antitrust and Regulatory Studies, University of Warsaw Faculty of Management Press, 2017, available at CARS 24 Implementation of the EU.indd (uw.edu.pl), p. 122. Article 272 only defines documentary evidence: '(1) Documentary evidence is any document or other similar medium, recorded in writing, by means of photography or video, audio or electronic recording or any other form of data recording, which contains information on facts relevant to the resolution of the case and which can be presented in tangible form at the hearing. (2) Documents shall also include official and personal letters, judgements in other cases and opinions of persons with special knowledge submitted to the court by a party to the proceedings.' (emphasis added). This book does not support the view that such a situation establishes prima facie evidence (which, while not amounting to a legal presumption, serves to enhance the probative value of the document in the absence of evidence to the contrary).
325. *See* Appendix I – EU Damages Directive Implementation Table, Article 9(2) of the Cyprus legislation.
326. *See* Article 7(2) and (3) of Law 23/2018.
327. *See* Appendix I – EU Damages Directive Implementation Table, Article 75(2) of Spanish legislation.

France,[328] Denmark,[329] Slovenia,[330] Slovakia,[331] Hungary,[332] Romania,[333] the Czech Republic,[334] Latvia[335] and Croatia.[336]

(3) *Germany:* grants the same evidentiary effect to both national decisions and those from other Member State, provided they are based on German law or on Articles 101 and 102 of the TFEU.[337]

(4) *Austria:* also treats national and foreign decisions equally, including those based on the legislation of other Member State, as long as that legislation pursues the same objectives as Articles 101 and 102 TFEU.[338]

(5) *Bulgaria:* has refused to introduce into its national law a provision on the probative value of a decision produced in another Member State.[339]

Indeed, as Anton Petrov highlights, the Bulgarian legislation transposing the EU Damages Directive (BAPCA) deliberately omits the provision set out in Article 9(2) of the Directive.[340]

Consequently, decisions issued by NCAs from other Member States carry neither binding authority nor enhanced probative value before Bulgarian courts. What is particularly striking is that the European Commission, in its working document on the implementation of the Directive, fails to acknowledge this omission. Instead, it asserts

328. *See* Article L.481-2 of the Code de commerce.
329. *See* Appendix I – EU Damages Directive Implementation Table, Chapter 4, Article 7(2) of Danish legislation.
330. *Ibid.*, Article 62.g(2) of the legislation of Slovenia.
331. *Ibid.*, Article 4(2) of Slovak legislation. In this regard, *see* Ondrej Blažo, *In Slovakia, Implementation of the EU Damages Directive in Central and Eastern European Countries*, Anna Piszcz (ed.), Centre for Antitrust and Regulatory Studies, University of Warsaw Faculty of Management Press, 2017, available at CARS 24 Implementation of the EU.indd (uw.edu.pl), p. 259. *See also* Philipp Kirst, *The Impact of the Damages Directive on the Enforcement of EU Competition Law: A Law and Economics Analysis*, Edward Elgar, 2021. However, the wording of the article is not entirely clear: '[a] final decision on a competition offence issued in another Member State of the European Union shall be considered as evidence of a violation of competition law, unless the contrary is proven in legal proceedings for damages' (emphasis added).
332. *See* Appendix I – EU Damages Directive Implementation Table, Article 88/R(2) of Hungarian legislation.
333. *Ibid.*, Article 9(2) of the Romanian legislation. In this sense, *see* Philipp Kirst, *The Impact of the Damages Directive on the Enforcement of EU Competition Law: A Law and Economics Analysis*, Edward Elgar, 2021. However, this provision is not entirely clear either: '[a] final decision or judgement (...) rendered in another Member State of the European Union proves, until the contrary is proven, that a violation of competition law has occurred and, where appropriate, may be assessed together with other evidence submitted by the parties.' (emphasis added).
334. *See* Appendix I – EU Damages Directive Implementation Table, Article 27(2) of the legislation of the Czech Republic.
335. *Ibid.*, Article 250.69(2) of Latvian legislation.
336. *Ibid.*, Article 11(2) of Croatian legislation.
337. *Ibid.*, Article 33b of German law.
338. *Ibid.*, Article 37i.(2) of Austrian law.
339. *See* Philipp Kirst, *The Impact of the Damages Directive on the Enforcement of EU Competition Law: A Law and Economics Analysis*, Edward Elgar, 2021, p. 73.
340. In *Bulgaria, Implementation of the EU Damages Directive in Central and Eastern European Countries*, Anna Piszcz (ed.), Centre for Antitrust and Regulatory Studies, University of Warsaw Faculty of Management Press, 2017, available at CARS 24 Implementation of the EU.indd (uw.edu.pl), p. 49.

that the transposition of this provision has been 'more or less uniform' – a characterisation that is difficult to reconcile with Bulgaria's clear legislative divergence.[341]

Regarding the scope of the binding effect of national decisions, the EU legislator did not define it in the EU Damages Directive's articles, but rather in Recital 34. According to this recital, a finding of an infringement of competition law encompasses the nature of the infringement, as well as its material, personal, temporal, and territorial scope. Given the significance of this issue, it is questionable that the legislator chose to address it only in a recital rather than in the binding rules of the Directive. Some Member States shared this concern and explicitly incorporated this clarification into their transposition measures – as Portugal[342] and Italy[343] being notable examples.

This issue has led to considerable disagreement among enforcers and National Courts, who often struggle to determine the precise scope of the presumption established by a final infringement decision. As previously noted, the reasoning in public enforcement decisions is not always fully transparent (particularly from the perspective of a potential claimant) and even less so when only a non-confidential version is available. Merely stating that an anticompetitive agreement exists is insufficient; the decision must also specify the products or services involved, the precise conduct agreed upon, and other relevant details. Without such specificity, a claimant cannot adequately assess whether they were affected by the infringement or estimate the extent of the resulting harm.[344]

2.3.1.5 Passing-On Defence and Damage Quantification

The passing-on of overcharges resulting from a competition law infringement and the corresponding quantification of damages are governed by Articles 12 to 17 of the EU Damages Directive. This legal framework addresses situations where a direct purchaser (such as a company affected by a price-fixing cartel) passes on the overcharge, in whole or in part, to its own customers (indirect purchasers or end consumers). In such cases, the harm is transmitted down the supply chain, and damages may arise at multiple levels.

341. *See EC Staff Working Document on the implementation of Directive 2014/104/EU of the European Parliament and of the Council of 26 November 2014 on certain rules governing actions for damages under national law for infringements of the competition law provisions of the Member States and of the European Union*, Brussels, 14 December 2020, SWD(2020) 338 final, available at report_on_damages_directive_implementation.pdf (europa.eu), p. 7.
342. Which provided for an 'inescapable presumption of the existence, nature and material, subjective, temporal and territorial scope of that offence, for the purposes of an action for compensation for the damage resulting from it'. *See* Article 7(1) of Law 23/2018.
343. Which provided that the irrefutable establishment of the offence on the basis of a final decision of the NCA 'concerns the nature of the offence and its material, personal, temporal and territorial scope, but not the causal link and the existence of damage'. *See* Appendix I – EU Damages Directive Implementation Table, Article 7(1) *in fine* of the Italian legislation.
344. *See* Miguel Sousa Ferro, *Antitrust Private Enforcement and the Binding Effect of Public Enforcement Decisions*, Market and Competition Law Review, vol. 3, No. 2, pp. 51-80 https://doi.org/10.7559/mclawreview.2019.1830, available at Antitrust Private Enforcement and the Binding Effect of Public Enforcement Decisions | Market and Competition Law Review (ucp.pt), p. 60.

Proving this harm becomes significantly more complex for indirect purchasers and consumers. Since they did not transact directly with the infringing undertakings, they bear the burden of demonstrating that the cartel's effects were passed on to them. This evidentiary challenge is compounded by the need to establish the causal link between the infringement and the specific harm suffered.

The EU legislator not only acknowledged this difficulty but also sought to prevent overcompensation - such as punitive or multiple damages, which are explicitly prohibited under Article 3(3) of the Directive. The result is a delicate balance: enabling effective redress for victims while safeguarding against unjust enrichment.[345]

To prevent excessive compensation, the EU Damages Directive introduces several key safeguards:

(1) Procedural rules by Member States: the Directive requires Member States to establish procedural mechanisms ensuring that compensation at any level of the supply chain does not exceed the actual harm suffered at that level. However, it does not specify what these mechanisms should be, leaving their design to national discretion.[346]
(2) Passing-On defence: defendants in damages actions may invoke the passing-on defence, arguing that the claimant transferred all or part of the overcharge to subsequent purchasers. While the burden of proof lies with the defendant, they are entitled to request disclosure of relevant information from the claimant or third parties through the National Court.[347]
(3) Consideration of parallel cases: National Courts may take into account parallel proceedings, whether under EU law or national law, when assessing the extent of harm and the applicability of the passing-on defence, using the tools available under the EU or national legal frameworks.[348]

Conversely, to ensure that those who have actually suffered harm, whether direct or indirect purchasers, can effectively claim compensation, the EU Damages Directive establishes several key mechanisms:

(1) *Judicial estimation of pass-on:* National Courts are empowered to estimate the portion of the overcharge that was passed on down the supply chain, based on the European Commission's guidelines[349] developed for this purpose.

345. *See* s. 2.3.1.2 above.
346. *See* Article 12(2).
347. *See* Article 13.
348. *See* Article 15(1) ('(a) actions for damages that are related to the same infringement of competition law, but that are brought by claimants from other levels in the supply chain; (b) judgments resulting from actions for damages as referred to in point (a); (c) relevant information in the public domain resulting from the public enforcement of competition law').
349. *See* Articles 12(5) and 16.

(2) *Access to evidence:* claimants may request disclosure of relevant information from the defendant or third parties, enabling them to substantiate their claim and overcome information asymmetries.
(3) *Rebuttable presumption for indirect purchasers:* recognising that price pass-on is a common commercial practice, the Directive introduces a rebuttable presumption in favour of indirect purchasers. This presumption applies where the claimant can demonstrate that: (i) the defendant committed an infringement of competition law; (ii) the infringement resulted in an overcharge for the direct purchaser; and (iii) the indirect purchaser acquired goods or services that were the subject of the infringement (or were derived from or contained such goods or services).[350]

More broadly (beyond the specific context of indirect purchasers and consumers), the EU Damages Directive also addresses the general challenge of calculating damages. It introduces two key rules:

(1) *Presumption of harm in cartel cases:* the Directive presumes that cartels cause harm, a presumption that has been criticised for lacking a clear evidentiary basis. This presumption simplifies the claimant's task but raises concerns about fairness and proportionality. A more detailed analysis of this issue will follow.
(2) *Judicial estimation of damages:* as advanced, where the claimant has demonstrated that harm was suffered, or where harm is presumed, and it is practically impossible or excessively difficult to quantify the precise amount of damage based on the available evidence, National Courts are empowered to estimate the harm.[351] This provision is grounded in the principle of effectiveness,[352] as articulated in the *Courage* judgment,[353] which requires that the exercise of the right to compensation must not be rendered practically impossible or excessively difficult. Courts may also seek voluntary assistance from NCAs to support this estimation.[354]

Indeed, requiring injured parties to assess how the relevant market would have evolved in the absence of the infringement is an almost insurmountable task. Nevertheless, while the EU Damages Directive's concern with avoiding overcompensation is understandable, it arguably misjudges the actual risk landscape. In practice, the greater concern within the EU is not excessive compensation, but rather the under-enforcement of private damages claims.

350. *See* Article 14.
351. On the circumstances in which the National Court can carry out this calculation, *see* the judgment of the ECJ *Tráficos Manuel Ferrer*, explored in s. 2.2 above.
352. *See* Article 4 (first part).
353. *See* pt. 29.
354. *See* Article 17.

This is evidenced by the fact that most Member States did not need to transpose the Directive's prohibition on punitive or multiple damages, as such forms of compensation are already excluded under their national legal systems. In jurisdictions where the legal framework is silent on the matter, National Courts have occasionally issued decisions that come close to awarding such forms of compensation (though these remain exceptions).[355] For the majority of Member States,[356] the literal transposition of the Directive's provisions on this point serves primarily as a reaffirmation of existing legal principles.[357]

However, the UK and Ireland - historically the only Member States to recognise the application of punitive damages - must be excluded from the general observation above. Their legal systems allow for the awarding of damages beyond mere compensation, including in competition law cases.

This raises an important question under the principle of equivalence: even though neither the EU law nor the CJEU supports awarding damages that exceed what is necessary to restore the injured party's position, should such damages nonetheless be permitted in actions based on EU law if they are available in comparable actions under national law? Where punitive damages may be awarded in domestic tort claims, this could imply that similar remedies should be accessible in EU-based claims to ensure procedural parity.[358]

It is true that when the legislator refers to the risk of excessive compensation in the context of passing-on, the concern primarily lies with the possibility of multiple claims being brought by plaintiffs at different levels of the supply or distribution chain, against the same defendant and for the same infringement.[359] However, when it comes to ensuring that compensation neither exceeds nor falls short of the actual harm suffered, particularly in the case of indirect victims, the practical implementation has been lacking. Despite the Directive's clear mandate in Article 15 for Member States to introduce mechanisms to address this issue, most have failed to adopt specific procedural tools to that end.

355. *See* Thomas Fausten and Robert Hammesfahr, *Punitive Damages in Europe: Concern, Threat or Non-issue*, Richard Heard (ed.), Swiss Re, 2012, available at punitive_damage_in_europe.pdf (biztositasiszemle.hu).

356. *See EC Staff Working Document on the implementation of Directive 2014/104/EU of the European Parliament and of the Council of 26 November 2014 on certain rules governing actions for damages under national law for infringements of the competition law provisions of the Member States and of the European Union*, Brussels, 14 December 2020, SWD(2020) 338 final, available at report_on_damages_directive_implementation.pdf (europa.eu), p. 9.

357. *See* Barry Rodger, Miguel Sousa Ferro and Francisco Marcos, *The EU Antitrust Damages Directive: Transposition in the Member States*, Oxford University Press, 2018, p. 464.

358. *See* Cedric Vanleenhove, *Punitive Damages and European Law: Quo Vademus?, in The Power of Punitive Damages: Is Europe Missing Out?*, Lotte Meurkens and Emily Nordin (eds), Cambridge-Antwerp-Portland, Intersentia, 2012, pp. 337-353, p. 342.

359. This is particularly the case in Recital 44 of the EU Damages Directive, which states that National Courts 'should have at their disposal appropriate procedural means, such as joinder of claims, to ensure that compensation for actual loss paid at any level of the supply chain does not exceed the overcharge harm caused at that level. Such means should also be available in cross-border cases'.

As Barry Rodger, Miguel Sousa Ferro, and Francisco Marcos have pointed out,[360] the real challenge is not so much identifying the existence of parallel damages actions (whether domestic or cross-border) but rather determining the legal and evidentiary impact such actions should have in a given case. This uncertainty continues to undermine the effectiveness and coherence of private enforcement across the EU.

With regard to easing the burden of proof for indirect purchasers and cartel victims, as well as the quantification of damages and the assessment of pass-on, all Member States have transposed the relevant provisions of the EU Damages Directive – albeit using different formulations. Portugal, for example, explicitly provides that National Courts may rely on a rough estimate when calculating damages and may take into account the European Commission's earlier Communication on the quantification of harm.[361] Furthermore, in compliance with Article 16 of the Directive, the European Commission adopted specific guidelines on 9 August 2019 to assist in calculating the share of overcharges passed on to indirect purchasers.[362]

The Portuguese legislator also introduced a requirement that any refusal by the PCA to assist in the quantification of damages must be duly substantiated. As Miguel Sousa Ferro[363] has noted, this provision was likely introduced to avoid potential constitutional concerns – specifically, to ensure that it is the National Court, not the NCA, that determines whether such assistance is warranted. This approach reinforces judicial oversight while preserving the collaborative role of the PCA in complex damages assessments.

The reality is that the PCA has shown reluctance to assist in the quantification of damages, often arguing that such calculations were not part of its original analysis when issuing infringement decisions. This is particularly true in recent cases, which have largely involved infringements by object, where the PCA did not assess the actual effects of the conduct on the market.

While it is understandable that the PCA may wish to conserve resources and avoid becoming entangled in follow-on compensation claims, this was not the rationale behind this rule of the EU Damages Directive. It does not assume that the issue has already been addressed; rather, it seeks to leverage the technical expertise of NCAs in support of judicial proceedings. Damage quantification in competition cases requires not only general economic knowledge but also a deep understanding of competition law and its specific analytical frameworks.

That expertise is scarce, particularly in Portugal, where the pool of qualified professionals is limited. Those who do specialise in this area often charge high fees and

---

360. In *The EU Antitrust Damages Directive: Transposition in the Member States*, Oxford University Press, 2018, p. 469.
361. That is, the Commission Communication (2013/C 167/07) of 13 June 2013 on the quantification of damages in actions for damages based on infringements of Articles 101 and 102 of the TFEU, available at quantification_guide_en.pdf (europa.eu).
362. *See* Commission Notice with Guidance to national courts on how to calculate the share of additional costs passed on to indirect purchasers (2019/C 267/07), available at Commission Notice - Guidance to national courts on how to calculate the share of additional costs passed on to indirect purchasers (europa.eu).
363. In *Portugal, The EU Antitrust Damages Directive: Transposition in the Member States*, Barry Rodger, Miguel Sousa Ferro and Francisco Marcos (eds), Oxford University Press, 2018, p. 320.

typically work with defendants, who are usually large companies with substantial financial resources. In multi-defendant cases, the domestic supply of experts is frequently insufficient, prompting the need to engage specialists from abroad, especially from the UK.

In this context, the involvement of NCAs can be instrumental. Their support can help ensure a more balanced and informed assessment of damages, particularly in jurisdictions where access to independent expertise is constrained.

Ireland, by contrast, has transposed the provision on assistance from the NCA in the calculation of damages in a literal manner. Under Irish law, it is the NCA that determines whether its support in quantifying damages is appropriate. However, the Irish legislature also clarifies that it is ultimately the National Court that is responsible for determining the extent to which any overcharge has been passed on. This dual structure reflects a balance between administrative discretion and judicial authority, aligning with the broader objectives of the EU Damages Directive, while preserving the independence of the judiciary in damage assessment.[364]

Given the minimalist nature of the EU Damages Directive (and, by extension, the national laws that transpose it), there remains a risk of conflicting judicial decisions, particularly in cases involving parallel actions brought by direct and indirect purchasers, even within the same Member State. In response to this fragmentation, the CJEU has played an increasingly active role in filling interpretative gaps and promoting harmonisation.[365]

To address this challenge more systematically, Philipp Kirst has proposed the creation of a European register of private enforcement actions in competition law. Such a register would allow National Courts and authorities to monitor ongoing proceedings across jurisdictions, potentially reducing the risk of inconsistent outcomes. While this solution may not guarantee uniform application, this book agrees that it represents a constructive step towards greater transparency and coordination in cross-border enforcement.

2.3.1.6 Joint and Several Liability

The EU Damages Directive also establishes that liability for infringements of competition law is, as a general rule, joint and several.[366] This means that injured parties may seek full compensation from any one of the infringing undertakings, without prejudice to that undertaking's right to claim contribution from co-infringers, based on their relative responsibility.[367]

However, the Directive provides for two important exceptions. One is for SME infringers, who are exempt from joint and several liability, being liable only to their own direct or indirect purchasers, if all of the following conditions are met: (i) the SME's market share in the relevant market was below 5% at all times during the

364. *See* Appendix I – EU Damages Directive Implementation Table, Article 11(7) of Irish law.
365. *See* s. 2.2 above.
366. *See* s. 1.2 above.
367. *See* Article 11(1) and (5).

infringement period; (ii) applying joint and several liability would irreparably harm the SME's economic viability and completely devalue its assets; (iii) the SME did not lead the infringement or coerce others into participating; and (iv) the SME has not previously been found guilty of a competition law infringement.[368]

The second exception applies to undertakings that have received a full waiver of fines under a leniency programme (as opposed to a mere reduction). These beneficiaries are only jointly and severally liable to injured parties who are not their direct or indirect purchasers or suppliers if full compensation cannot be obtained from the other undertakings involved in the same infringement.[369]

The rule of joint and several liability established by the EU Damages Directive has been correctly implemented in several Member States, including the UK, Ireland, Italy, Germany, Lithuania, and Hungary. However, discrepancies have emerged in countries such as France, Belgium, and Luxembourg.[370] These Member States have historically applied the concept of *in solidum* liability under their general civil law frameworks, rather than adopting the Directive's standard of joint and several liability.

While both forms of liability allow the injured party to claim full compensation from any one of the infringers, *in solidum* liability is less protective of victims. It originated in legal systems that lacked a formal doctrine of joint and several liability and is more limited in its effects. For example, under *in solidum* liability, initiating proceedings against one infringer does not interrupt the limitation period for others, and a judgment against one party does not bind subsequent actions against co-infringers.[371]

France[372] and Belgium[373] have since amended their legislation to explicitly provide for joint and several liability among infringing undertakings, aligning more closely with the Directive's requirements. Luxembourg, however, presents a more ambiguous case: while the title of the relevant legislative provision refers to 'joint and several liability', the body of the article addresses only exceptions. This inconsistency may be viewed as a failure to fully and clearly transpose the Directive's provisions, potentially undermining the effectiveness of private enforcement in that jurisdiction.

This provision has raised several questions among Member States. One key issue concerns the allocation of liability for the purposes of the 'right of recourse'. During the transposition process, both Belgium and Hungary considered including legal guidance for National Courts on this matter; however, such guidance was ultimately omitted from their final legislative texts.[374] Portugal, by contrast, was the only Member State to introduce a (rebuttable) presumption: liability is presumed to correspond to the

368. *See* Article 11(2) and (3).
369. *See* Article 11(4).
370. *See* Barry Rodger, Miguel Sousa Ferro and Francisco Marcos, *The EU Antitrust Damages Directive: Transposition in the Member States*, Oxford University Press, 2018, p. 464.
371. *See* Philipp Kirst, *The Impact of the Damages Directive on the Enforcement of EU Competition Law: A Law and Economics Analysis*, Edward Elgar, 2021, p. 81.
372. *See* Article L.481-9 of the Code de commerce.
373. *See* Appendix I – EU Damages Directive Implementation Table, Article XVII.86 of Belgian law.
374. *See* Barry Rodger, Miguel Sousa Ferro and Francisco Marcos, *The EU Antitrust Damages Directive: Transposition in the Member States*, Oxford University Press, 2018, p. 445.

average market share held by each infringing company in the affected markets during the period of their participation in the infringement.[375]

Another area of persistent uncertainty concerns the liability of parent companies and the application of the concepts of 'undertaking' and 'economic continuity' in the private enforcement of competition law by National Courts. These issues have already given rise to preliminary references and have been the subject of clarifications by CJEU, as outlined above.[376]

Further uncertainty remains regarding the application of the concept of a single and continuous infringement in this context, particularly whether a company that participated only during part of the infringement period can nonetheless be held civilly liable for the full amount of damages.[377]

Finally, regarding the exceptions, it is worth noting that some Member States, such as Belgium, have extended the application of the above-mentioned provision[378] originally intended for immunity recipients under the leniency programme to SMEs.[379] This approach appears to contradict the wording of the Directive and, in our view, constitutes an incorrect transposition by the Belgian legislator.

2.3.1.7 Limitation Periods

The EU legislator has once again granted Member States a degree of discretion in this area, by establishing a minimum limitation period of at least five years for bringing actions for damages. This period must not begin to run until the infringement of competition law has ceased and the claimant knew or could reasonably be expected to have known: (i) the conduct in question and that it constituted an infringement of competition law; (ii) that the infringement caused them harm; and (iii) the identity of the infringer.[380] In addition, Member States are required to either suspend or interrupt this limitation period if an NCA takes action in connection with an investigation or proceedings related to the infringement underpinning the damages claim. Where suspension is chosen, it must last at least one year after the infringement decision becomes final or the proceedings are otherwise concluded.[381]

375. In fact, according to Portuguese legislation, '[t]he right of recourse between co-infringers exists to the extent of their relative liability for the damage caused by the offence, such liability being presumed to be equivalent to the average of their shares in the markets affected by the offence, during their participation in it, unless there is evidence to the contrary, namely as to the role played by each co-infringer in the offence'. *See* Article 5.5 of Law 23/2018.
376. *See* s. 2.2 above.
377. *See* Barry Rodger, Miguel Sousa Ferro and Francisco Marcos, *The EU Antitrust Damages Directive: Transposition in the Member States*, Oxford University Press, 2018, p. 445.
378. In the sense that they will be liable to other injured parties (in addition to their direct or indirect buyers or suppliers) only when it is not possible to obtain full compensation from the other companies involved in the same infringement of competition law.
379. *See* Appendix I - EU Damages Directive Implementation Table, Article XVII.86, para. 2 of Belgian legislation.
380. *See* Article 10(2) and (3).
381. *See* Article 10(4).

On this point, we concur with the European Commission[382] that most Member States have transposed Article 10(2) and (3) of the EU Damages Directive[383] in a manner closely aligned with the Directive's wording. Some Member States, such as Ireland[384] and Cyprus,[385] have opted to retain their pre-directive limitation periods, which are longer (six years in both cases).

In practice, however, there are significant differences in how this limitation period is applied across Member States. Notably, allowing Member States to choose between suspension and interruption introduces meaningful discrepancies, as these legal mechanisms have distinct consequences.[386] In particular, while suspension merely pauses the limitation period, interruption resets it entirely (effectively extending the time available to bring an action for damages).

2.3.1.8 Alternative Dispute Resolution

With regard to ADR (alternative dispute resolution), the EU Damages Directive provides more detailed guidance. It stipulates that the limitation period for bringing an action for damages is suspended during ADR proceedings, for a maximum of two years.[387] Furthermore, in the event of an amicable settlement, any compensation claim by an injured party who participated in the settlement must be offset against the damages caused by the co-infringer who also took part in the settlement.[388] Any remaining claim may only be pursued against non-settling co-infringers, unless those co-infringers are unable to pay and this possibility is not expressly excluded in the settlement agreement.[389] Additionally, non-settling co-infringers are barred from exercising a right of recourse against co-infringers who participated in the amicable settlement in relation to the remaining claim.[390]

The implementation of this provision by Member States has not been without uncertainty, particularly regarding which mechanisms fall within the Directive's definition of ADR – namely those that enable parties to 'reach the out-of-court resolution of a dispute concerning a claim for damages'.[391] Portugal, for instance, opted

382. *See EC Staff Working Document on the implementation of Directive 2014/104/EU of the European Parliament and of the Council of 26 November 2014 on certain rules governing actions for damages under national law for infringements of the competition law provisions of the Member States and of the European Union*, Brussels, 14 December 2020, SWD(2020) 338 final, available at report_on_damages_directive_implementation.pdf (europa.eu), p. 8.
383. *See* Barry Rodger, Miguel Sousa Ferro and Francisco Marcos, *The EU Antitrust Damages Directive: Transposition in the Member States*, Oxford University Press, 2018, p. 457.
384. *See* Appendix I – EU Damages Directive Implementation Table, Article 11A. (1) of Irish law.
385. *Ibid.*, Article 10(1) of Cyprus legislation.
386. *See* Barry Rodger, Miguel Sousa Ferro and Francisco Marcos, *The EU Antitrust Damages Directive: Transposition in the Member States*, Oxford University Press, 2018, p. 458.
387. *See* Article 18(1) and (2).
388. *See* Article 19(1).
389. *See* Article 19(2) first part and Article 19(3) second part.
390. *See* Article 19(2), second part.
391. *See* Article 2(21).

to provide illustrative examples, including mediation, conciliation, arbitration, and the settlement mechanism outlined in Article 1248 of its Civil Code.[392]

While there is no comprehensive data on the number of ADR mechanisms employed across the EU – making it difficult to assess the overall effectiveness of this provision – there is evidence of its practical application in jurisdictions such as the UK, the Netherlands, and Ireland.[393]

2.3.1.9 Temporal Scope of Application

Article 22 of the EU Damages Directive defines its temporal scope of application by distinguishing between substantive and procedural provisions. Advanced, substantive provisions do not apply retroactively, while procedural provisions do not apply to actions for damages brought before National Courts prior to 26 December 2014. However, the Directive does not specify which provisions fall into each category. This omission has left a critical gap, as the absence of clear national transposition measures in some Member States has resulted in a lack of protection for injured parties.

By leaving this determination to the discretion of each Member State, the EU legislator has allowed divergent interpretations of the Directive's applicability to specific cases, thereby perpetuating inequality in the exercise of the right to compensation. Once again, it has fallen to the CJEU to provide the legal certainty that the Directive itself failed to deliver, as seen in the judgments in *Cogeco*, *Volvo* and *DAF Trucks*, and *Deutsche Bank*.[394]

2.3.2 The Directive's Partial Nature and Its Implications

The EU Damages Directive, in carrying out its minimal harmonisation, prioritises and deepens certain themes. For instance, Chapter IV places greater emphasis on harm suffered by actors downstream of the infringer – namely, buyers – while offering comparatively less attention to harm experienced by upstream market participants, such as suppliers.[395] However, the 'preferences' explored in the following sections are even more consequential due to their broader impact on the effectiveness and uniformity of private enforcement across Member States.

392. *See* Article 2(s) of Law 23/2018.
393. *See* Barry Rodger, Miguel Sousa Ferro and Francisco Marcos, *The EU Antitrust Damages Directive: Transposition in the Member States*, Oxford University Press, 2018, p. 470.
394. *See* s. 2.2 above.
395. Furthermore, according to Article 12(4) of the Directive, the rules of this chapter, on the passing-on of additional costs, should be applied by the National Courts when the infringement of competition law is related to a supply to the infringer, with the necessary adaptations. The EU legislator further clarified in Recital 43 that, in such cases, consequential damages may result from the lower price paid by the infringers' suppliers.

2.3.2.1 *Prioritising Public Enforcement and Follow-On Actions*

One of the EU legislator's central concerns, as outlined above, was ensuring effective coordination between private enforcement of competition rules through civil actions and public enforcement by competition authorities. To this end,[396] the Directive restricts access to certain documents held by competition authorities[397] – most notably, leniency statements.[398] These documents are often essential for public enforcers to establish the existence of an infringement and would be even more critical for injured parties seeking compensation. By limiting access, the legislator sought to preserve the effectiveness of public enforcement mechanisms, even if it meant constraining the evidentiary tools available to private claimants.

This approach effectively means that, in practice (as previously noted),[399] injured parties will often need to await the outcome of public enforcement proceedings before initiating a damages action, thereby favouring follow-on actions. The provisions of the EU Damages Directive are generally designed with this type of action in mind. For instance, Article 6(5) (the so-called grey list) restricts the use of certain documents in damages actions until the NCA has concluded its proceedings through a decision or other formal means.[400]

Moreover, the binding effect of final infringement decisions by NCA further incentivises claimants to wait before bringing an action. This is particularly true given that such decisions are frequently appealed, often by economically powerful infringers facing substantial fines and potential damages, which can delay finality for several years. As a result, while the Directive aims to facilitate private enforcement, its structure and evidentiary rules may inadvertently discourage timely stand-alone actions.

2.3.2.2 *Cartel-Centric Enforcement*

While any claimant seeking compensation must meet the burden of proof, doing so in competition law cases is particularly challenging due to the technical complexity of both identifying infringements and demonstrating their effects. This difficulty is even more pronounced in cartel cases, as previously discussed.[401] The inherent opacity of cartel conduct and the challenges faced by competition authorities in detecting and prosecuting such practices led to the creation of leniency programmes. Under these schemes, cartel participants may receive full immunity or a reduction in fines in

396. *See* s. 2.3.1.3 above.
397. For the EU legislator, '[i]t is necessary to regulate the coordination of those two forms of enforcement in a coherent manner, for instance in relation to the arrangements for access to documents held by competition authorities. Such coordination at Union level will also avoid the divergence of applicable rules, which could jeopardise the proper functioning of the internal market'. *See* Recital 6 of the EU Damages Directive.
398. *See* Article 6(6)(a).
399. *See* s. 3.2 below.
400. *See* Article 7(2).
401. *See* s. 3.1 below.

exchange for a leniency statement (essentially, a confession).[402] Without such declarations, neither the European Commission[403] nor NCAs[404] would likely be able to establish the infringement, let alone enable injured parties to do so.

The EU Damages Directive was clearly designed with these challenges in mind. It addresses them through two key topics: (i) the protection of leniency statements,[405] preserving the attractiveness and effectiveness of leniency programmes[406] (which, within the EU, apply exclusively to cartel infringements);[407] and (ii) the establishment of a rebuttable presumption that cartels cause harm.[408]

According to the European Commission,[409] this legislative choice was based on a study[410] prior to the Directive's proposal. The study concluded that over 90% of cartels result in price increases, thereby justifying the presumption of harm and easing the evidentiary burden on claimants in cartel-related damages actions.

Some Member States have gone beyond the minimum harmonisation required by the EU Damages Directive. Although the Directive does not mandate a quantified presumption of harm, certain Member States, such as Hungary[411] and Latvia,[412] have introduced a presumed overcharge rate of approximately 10%. In these jurisdictions,

402. *See* Caroline Cauffman, *The Interaction of Leniency Programmes and Actions for Damages,* The Competition Law Review, vol. 7, No. 2, July 2011, p. 183.
403. In this sense, Richard Whish and David Bailay, *Competition Law,* Oxford University Press, 2012, pp. 517 et seq. Also Wouter PJ Wils, *Efficiency and Justice in European Antitrust Enforcement,* Hard Publishing, 2008, pp. 127 and 128, considers that infringing companies are the European Commission's best source of information. *See also* Christopher R Leslie, *Editorial: Antitrust Leniency Programmes,* The Competition Law Review, vol. 7, No. 2, July 2011, p. 175, and Yves Botteman and Paul Hughes, *Access to File: Striking the Balance Between Leniency and Private Enforcement Tools, The European Antitrust Review 2013,* Global Competition Review, 2013, p. 3, who refer to leniency as the European Commission's investigative tool of choice.
404. *See* Paolo Buccirossi, Catarina Marvão and Giancarlo Spagnolo, *Leniency and Damages,* Working Paper No. 32, Stockholm Institute of Transition Economics, February 2015, pp. 473 et seq.
405. *See* Article 6(6a).
406. In this sense, David Ashon and David Henry, *Competition Damages Action in the EU: Law and Practice,* economics contribution from Frank Maier-Rigaud and Ulrich Schawalbe, Elgar, *Competition Law and Practice,* 2nd ed., 2018, p. 71.
407. On the particularities of transposing this EU concept present in the EU Damages Directive into Member States legislation, *see* s. 2.3 above.
408. *See* Article 17(2).
409. *See EC Staff Working Document on the implementation of Directive 2014/104/EU of the European Parliament and of the Council of 26 November 2014 on certain rules governing actions for damages under national law for infringements of the competition law provisions of the Member States and of the European Union,* Brussels, 14 December 2020, SWD(2020) 338 final, available at report_on_damages_directive_implementation.pdf (europa.eu), p. 9.
410. *See Quantifying Antitrust Damages: Towards Non-binding Guidance for Courts, Study Prepared for the European Commission by Oxera,* December 2009, available at Microsoft Word - Quantifying antitrust damages (europa.eu).
411. *See* Peter Miskolczi Bodnár, *Hungary, Implementation of the EU Damages Directive in Central and Eastern European Countries,* Anna Piszcz (ed.), Centre for Antitrust and Regulatory Studies, University of Warsaw Faculty of Management Press, 2017, available at CARS 24 Implementation of the EU.indd (uw.edu.pl), p. 144.
412. *See* Julija Jerneva and Inese Druviete, *Latvia, Implementation of the EU Damages Directive in Central and Eastern European Countries,* Anna Piszcz (ed.), Centre for Antitrust and Regulatory Studies, University of Warsaw Faculty of Management Press, 2017, available at CARS 24 Implementation of the EU.indd (uw.edu.pl), p. 165.

defendants must rebut the presumption by demonstrating either that the cartel did not cause any harm or that the price increase was lower than the presumed percentage.

Conversely, claimants still bear the burden of proving the existence of the cartel (in stand-alone actions), the causal link between the infringement and the harm, and the specific amount of damages suffered. It is important to note that a presumed 10% price increase does not equate to 10% in damages. The actual harm may vary depending on how the overcharge affected the claimant, particularly if the increased cost was passed on to the next level in the supply chain or if other market dynamics mitigated or amplified the impact.

In short, it is unlikely that a claimant harmed by a cartel will be able to prove[413] the existence of the infringement in a stand-alone action. Despite the rebuttable presumption of harm introduced by the Directive, without access to a leniency statement (protected under the Directive), the claimant will typically have to wait not only for the public enforcement decision but also for that decision to become final. This delay can span several years, particularly in cases involving appeals, thereby significantly postponing access to compensation.

2.3.3 Gaps in the Directive

There are additional areas where the EU legislator has deliberately chosen not to establish even minimal harmonisation, opting instead to leave them outside the scope of the EU Damages Directive. Yet, these omissions may significantly affect the effectiveness of private enforcement, one of the Directive's core objectives. As previously discussed, the absence of guidance on issues such as collective redress mechanisms, litigation funding, cost allocation, and jurisdictional rules creates uncertainty and inconsistency across Member States. This fragmented approach risks undermining the Directive's goal of ensuring effective and uniform access to compensation for victims of competition law infringements.

2.3.3.1 Other Forms of Private Enforcement

Requests for injunctive relief (such as orders to cease anticompetitive conduct) or for the nullity of contractual clauses that infringe competition law are examples of private enforcement mechanisms that National Courts have encountered in practice. However, the EU Damages Directive does not seek to harmonise these forms of relief.[414]

Indeed, these alternative avenues of private enforcement – beyond actions for damages – have consistently been excluded from EU-level policy discussions. This omission is particularly significant given the wide disparities among Member States in

413. *See* Gianni de Stefano, *Access of Damage Claimants to Evidence Arising out of EU Cartel Investigations: A Fast-evolving Scenario,* Global Competition Litigation Review, vol. 3, 2012, p. 108.

414. *See* Giorgio Monti, *Liability Issues Not Codified by the Damages Directive: How to Fill Such Gaps?, in Private Enforcement of EU Competition Law: The Impact of the Damages Directive,* Pier Luigi Parcu, Giorgio Monti and Marco Botta (eds), Elgar, 2018, p. 43.

how such remedies are addressed, both procedurally and substantively.[415] As a result, the Directive's limited scope may hinder the full realisation of effective private enforcement across the internal market.

2.3.3.2 The Competent Court

The EU Damages Directive does not provide any guidance on which National Court should be competent to hear actions for damages for breaches of competition rules, namely whether it should be specialised or not. This has been one of the issues that has most concerned Member States, and the solutions adopted could not be more disparate. Some Member States made no changes following the transposition of the Directive and kept this type of action in the general courts, namely civil and commercial courts, or higher courts; others already had specialised courts or, at least, specialised sections within a general court for this type of matter; and there are Member States that, with the transposition of the Directive, assigned this competence to specialised courts/sections.

Spain, for instance, assigned first-instance jurisdiction for this type of action to the General Commercial Courts.[416] In contrast, the UK and Ireland retained their own specialised court and section, respectively. Nevertheless, until 2015, the UK's CAT only had jurisdiction over stand-alone actions and, even today, does not hold exclusive jurisdiction – it shares competence with the High Court. Portugal, however, designated the TCES – a theoretically specialised court that already handled appeals and similar matters in administrative offence proceedings issued by various regulatory authorities, including the PCA – as the competent forum for damages actions based solely on infringements of competition law.[417]

According to Maria João Melícias,[418] '[t]his solution seeks to take advantage of the usual benefits of specialisation, including to prevent contradictory judicial decisions and to avoid that antitrust damages actions be decided by civil judges spread throughout the country, most of which would have dealt with competition law, at best, once or twice beforehand in their entire legal careers'. Carla Câmara[419] further observes a natural reluctance within the judiciary towards competition law cases, attributing this aversion largely to the lack of specialised training and sustained exposure in the field.

As noted in the previous paragraph, it is difficult to characterise a court – or more precisely, a chamber – as truly specialised when its judges: (i) handle a wide array of

415. For further developments, *see* Sebastian Peyer, *Injunctive Relief and Private Antitrust Enforcement*, CCP Working Paper 11-7, 2011, p. 52.
416. *See* Francisco Marcos, *Spain, The EU Antitrust Damages Directive: Transposition in the Member States*, Barry Rodger, Miguel Sousa Ferro and Francisco Marcos (eds), Oxford University Press, 2018, p. 332.
417. *See* Article 22 of Law 23/2018.
418. In *The Art of Consistency Between Public and Private Antitrust Enforcement: Practical Challenges in Implementing the Damages Directive in Portugal*, Revista de Concorrência e Regulação, Year VII, No. 26, Almedina, April/June, 2016, p. 47.
419. In *Tribunal da Concorrência, Regulação e Supervisão: quo vadis?*, Revista de Concorrência e Regulação, Year VII, No. 30, Almedina, April/June 2017, p. 29.

highly specific matters, ranging from competition law to sectoral regulation, each with its own complexities; (ii) receive limited specialised training; (iii) have minimal practical experience in the field; and (iv) serve for relatively short terms, typically no longer than two or three years.

As Sofia Oliveira Pais rightly observes, the main shortcoming of Article 22 of Law 23/2018 lies in its narrow attribution of jurisdiction to the specialised court, limiting it to damages actions based exclusively on infringements of competition law. We concur with this assessment. Such a single legal basis is typical in follow-on actions, which are expected to become increasingly common due to the binding effect of public enforcement decisions. However, in the context of stand-alone actions, Portuguese judicial practice reveals a different reality: most claims are not grounded solely in competition law but rather combine it with other legal frameworks, such as consumer protection or unfair competition. As Miguel Sousa Ferro has noted,[420] they invoke competition law in defence or as one of several legal grounds for unlawfulness. There are very few cases in which the plaintiff invoked only one breach of competition law. Thus, of the eighty-eight cases of restrictive practices analysed by the author, only seven could fall within the scope of the TCRS' competence thus defined (less than 8 %). This conclusion is echoed by Maria José Costeira,[421] who emphasises that 'it is should be considered that, notwithstanding the fact that there will be a single specialised court to a part of actions and litigation related to competition law, there is still a large amount of cases, perhaps the majority, which stays away from the specialisation'.

Regarding the appellate review of first-instance decisions in damages actions for breaches of competition law, the prevailing rule is the absence of judicial specialisation at the Court of Appeal level. This also raises legitimate concerns about the capacity of appellate judges to adequately assess rulings issued (at least in theory) by judges with greater expertise and familiarity with competition law. Such a disparity in specialisation, particularly in a domain as complex and consequential as competition law, risks undermining both the uniform application of Articles 101 and 102 TFEU and the overall effectiveness of judicial review.[422]

2.3.3.3 Costs and Litigation Funding

The issue of costs and funding is inextricably linked to the practical viability of bringing damages actions for infringements of competition law. As Jason Levine has noted,[423] both individual and collective antitrust damages actions are particularly well suited to

420. In *Jurisprudência de 'Private Enforcement' (Private Enforcement Case-Law), Jurisprudência Portuguesa de Direito da Concorrência Chapter 7: Jurisprudência de private enforcement,* 2016, available at https://papers.ssrn.com/sol3/papers.cfm?abstract_id = 3077488, p. 15.
421. In *The Transposition of the EU Damages Directive: A Critical Perspective,* UNIO – EU Law Journal, vol. 3, No. 2, July 2017, pp. 175-184, p. 182 https://doi.org/10.21814/unio.3.2.12.
422. *See* Barry Rodger, Miguel Sousa Ferro and Francisco Marcos, *The EU Antitrust Damages Directive: Transposition in the Member States,* Oxford University Press, 2018, p. 456.
423. In *The Role of Litigation Finance in Antitrust Lawsuits,* 30 March 2022, available at The role of litigation finance in antitrust lawsuits (omnibridgeway.com).

litigation funding mechanisms, without which such actions may be rendered unfeasible. These cases are distinguished by their complexity, duration, and high financial stakes, often involving substantial damages claims.

Moreover, they typically require specialised legal and economic expertise, which entails significant costs. These include not only legal fees but also the expenses associated with expert reports, hearings, and the production of complex economic evidence. Depending on the jurisdiction and the nature of the action (whether stand-alone or follow-on), litigation costs can reach millions of euros. This financial burden is further exacerbated by the evidentiary challenges faced by claimants, who must establish illegality, harm, and causation, often without access to the infringer's internal documentation.

In this context, litigation funding and collective redress mechanisms emerge as essential tools to ensure access to justice and the effective enforcement of competition law rights.

Indeed, it is difficult to understand why the EU Damages Directive fails to address the issue of litigation funding – whether by regulating private financing agreements or by delegating such regulation to the Member States. As previously noted,[424] the Directive only refers to the payment of costs in the context of sanctions imposed on parties, third parties, and their legal representatives. In such cases, National Courts may order the payment of costs, provided the amount is proportionate to the breach in question.[425] However, it is important to highlight that the term 'costs' in this context is narrower than the broader concept of 'litigation expenses'.

2.3.3.4 Collective Redress and Preliminary Conclusion

Although compensation actions brought by SMEs and consumers were, until the adoption of the EU Damages Directive, largely illusory, the Directive notably excluded collective actions from its scope. This omission has further exacerbated the fragmentation of national systems for enforcing the right to redress in competition law, a disparity that is likely to persist given the Directive's shortcomings and its apparent prioritisation of public enforcement mechanisms.

In a context marked by persistent asymmetries, particularly in terms of access to information and resources, between claimants and defendants, the absence of a robust collective redress mechanism proves especially detrimental to small-scale plaintiffs. Ironically, these are the very actors most frequently harmed by anticompetitive conduct.

Even with the interpretative support of the CJEU, which has sought to align national transpositions of the Directive with the principles of the EU Treaties, the right to redress remains excessively difficult to exercise in practice. In this regard, the Directive falls short of fulfilling the principle of effectiveness, as articulated in the case law and enshrined in Article 4 of the Directive itself.

424. *See* s. 2.2 above.
425. *See* Article 8(2) of the EU Damages Directive.

In our view, the EU legislator's decision to exclude class actions (virtually non-existent in the EU at the time) constitutes the Directive's most significant gap. This exclusion undermines the effective exercise of the right to compensation for the majority of those affected by competition law infringements, namely SMEs and consumers. For this reason, Chapter 3 of this book will be dedicated to a detailed examination of this issue.

CHAPTER 3
Part II: Class Actions

3.1 THE DIRECTIVE'S BLIND SPOT: A GAP UNDERMINING ENFORCEMENT

Has the EU Damages Directive created an imbalance between public and private enforcement of competition law? Could the provisions examined above ultimately undermine its intended objectives? This book believes the answer to both questions is yes. Rather than establishing a fair and functional equilibrium between public and private enforcement, the Directive appears to render private enforcement heavily dependent on a prior, definitive public decision confirming an infringement. Even then, injured parties must still prove both the causal link and the actual harm suffered - an onerous burden, particularly for consumers and small businesses.

In light of this, one must ask: are consumers and SMEs the Directive's most significant blind spot? Despite being the very groups the Directive aims to empower, they remain the least equipped to navigate its procedural hurdles and evidentiary demands.[426]

As Pieter Van Cleynenbreugel rightly observes,[427] while the EU Damages Directive may be seen as a step forward in advancing restorative justice within EU competition law, its current structure and configuration fall short of what is necessary to achieve that goal effectively.

Violations of competition law often produce a wide array of effects across the entire supply chain - from producers to end consumers.[428] This dispersion of harm results in

426. It should be recalled that, according to para. 13 of the Directive, Member States should not be oblige to introduce collective redress mechanisms for the purposes of applying Articles 101 and 102 TFEU.
427. In *Private Damages Actions in EU Competition Law and Restorative Justice: Towards a More Streamlined Institutional Framework?*, Market and Competition Law Review, vol. 3, No. 2, pp. 15-49 https://doi.org/10.7559/mclawreview.2019.1826, p. 28.
428. *See* Nina Bucan Gutta, *The Enforcement of EU Competition Rules by Civil Law*, Maklu Competition Series, 2014, p. 54.

significant aggregate damage, even though the individual harm suffered by each party may be relatively minor. Crucially, such small-scale individual damages very rarely justify the costs of initiating stand-alone legal proceedings. In the absence of accessible and efficient collective redress mechanisms, the Directive risks failing the very actors it aims to protect.

At the end of the day, if competition law enforcement is confined solely to public mechanisms, the deterrent effect is significantly weakened. The benefit an offender derives from anticompetitive conduct may well exceed the fine imposed, and the prohibition alone fails to fulfil its fundamental role of preventing unlawful behaviour. More critically, such an approach does little to advance consumer welfare - often cited as a core objective of competition law.[429]

Consumers, in particular, are left in a vulnerable position. Faced with the high costs of initiating and sustaining legal proceedings, they frequently opt not to pursue claims for damages that, while collectively significant, are individually negligible - amounting to as little as EUR 10 or EUR 20. In the absence of accessible and effective collective redress mechanisms, this economic disincentive perpetuates under-compensation and undermines the Directive's restorative ambitions.

As a result, the vast majority of private enforcement actions are initiated by large companies - typically direct purchasers - who possess the resources and incentives to litigate. In contrast, indirect buyers, SMEs, and consumers rarely bring claims. These groups often lack the time or capacity to wait for a prior and definitive public decision confirming the infringement, and in some cases, they may have already been forced out of the market by the time such a decision is issued.

Even when they remain active, the high costs of litigation and the relatively small value of individual damages act as powerful deterrents. This economic imbalance makes it exceedingly difficult for these parties to pursue stand-alone actions and, consequently, to obtain compensation for harm caused by competition law violations.[430]

To this extent, can the persistent problem of under-enforcement of the right to redress truly be resolved without EU legislation specifically addressing class actions in competition law? This question has long been debated - well before the EU Damages Directive was even proposed - and was reportedly one of the reasons behind the delay in its adoption.[431] Yet, the European Commission appears to have answered in the affirmative. It chose not to include class actions in either the EU Damages Directive or the 2018 proposal on representative actions for the protection of collective consumer interests.

429. *See* Peter C. Carstensen, *The Goals of Competition Law: Ends v. Means, in Albert A. Foer, A Consumer Voice in the Antitrust Arena, Liber Amicorum,* Nicolas Charbit and Sonia Ahmad (eds), Concurrences, 2020, pp. 52 and 53.

430. *See* Sofia Oliveira Pais and Anna Piszcz, *Package on Actions for Damages Based on Breaches of EU Competition Rules: Can One Size Fit All?*, Yearbook of Antitrust and Regulatory Studies, vol. 7, No. 10, 2014, p. 213.

431. *See* Philipp Kirst, *The Impact of the Damages Directive on the Enforcement of EU Competition Law: A Law and Economics Analysis*, Edward Elgar, 2021, p. 44.

And still, the question remains: without a harmonised and accessible collective redress mechanism tailored to competition law, can the Directive's objectives - particularly effective compensation and deterrence - ever be fully realised?

3.2 GLOBAL AND EUROPEAN ORIGINS OF COLLECTIVE REDRESS: LEGAL AND POLICY RATIONALES

The US is widely recognised as the cradle of modern class actions, with its model[432] often serving as the global reference point. However, the roots of collective redress mechanisms trace back to medieval English legal traditions.

Indeed, the formal codification of class actions in the US dates to 1849[433] marking a pivotal moment in the institutionalisation of group litigation.[434] Yet, it is important to recall that the Common Law itself originated in England, and the substitution of individual claims with collective actions can be traced as far back as 17th-century English case law.[435,436]

In 1986, the ECtHR (European Court of Human Rights) addressed the issue of opt-out collective actions for the first time in the case of *Lithgow v. United Kingdom.*[437,438] The Court held that such mechanisms did not violate Article 6 of the ECHR (European Convention on Human Rights), which guarantees the right to a fair trial. This early recognition of collective procedures as compatible with fundamental rights laid an important foundation for future developments.

Later, in 2004, the ECtHR reaffirmed this perspective in *Gorraiz Lizarraga and Others v. Spain*, stating that 'in modern-day societies, (...) recourse to collective bodies such as associations is one of the accessible means, sometimes the only means, available to

---

432. *See* Jasminka Kalajdzie, *The State of Reform in First and Second Generation Class Action Jurisdictions, in Class Actions in Europe: Holy Grail or a Wrong Trail?,* Alan Uzelac and Stefaan Voet (eds), Springer, 2021, p. 304.
433. *See* Hon. Guido Clabresi, *in The Law and Economics of Class Actions in Europe: Lessons from America*, Jürgen G. Backhaus, Alberto Cassone and Giovanni B. Ramello (eds), Edward Elgar Publishing, 2012, p. 12.
434. *See* Christopher Hodges, *The Reform of Class and Representative Actions in European Legal Systems: A New Framework for Collective Redress in Europe*, Oxford, Hart, 2008, p. 1.
435. The *Common Law* system, which emerged in England in the eleventh century and has been adopted by countries such as the US, Canada, New Zealand and Australia, is based mainly on case law, while the Civil Law system, which originated in Roman times and developed in continental Europe, is codified par excellence, with judges being called upon to interpret the rules on the basis of general principals. *See* Caslav Pejovic, *Civil Law and Common Law: Two Different Paths Leading to the Same Goal*, July 2001, available at https://www.researchgate.net/publication/265244573_Civil_Law_and_Common_Law_Two_Different_Paths_Leading_to_the_Same_Goal, p. 9.
436. *See* Eda Şahin, *Collective Redress and EU Competition Law*, Routledge, 2019, p. 17. *See also* Michael A. Eizenga and Emrys Davis, *A History of Class Actions: Modern Lessons from Deep Roots*, Canadian Class Action Review, vol. 7, No. 1, October 2011, p. 11.
437. *See* Cases 9006/80, 9262/81, 9263/81, 9265/81, 9266/81, 9313/81 and 9405/81 *Lithgow v. United Kingdom*, 8 July 1986, available at https://hudoc.echr.coe.int/.
438. *See* s. 3.6.1 below.

them whereby they can defend their particular interests effectively'.[439] This acknowledgement underscores the essential role of collective mechanisms in ensuring access to justice - particularly for individuals or groups whose claims may otherwise be too fragmented or economically unviable to pursue individually.

As far as the CJEU is concerned, the development of jurisprudence on collective redress has been more gradual and sector-specific.[440] Nevertheless, there are notable examples that reflect a growing recognition of the importance of collective mechanisms in safeguarding fundamental rights.

In 2017, in the context of collective consumer protection (*Maximilian Schrems v. Facebook*), Advocate General Michal Bobek emphasised 'that this Court has consistently placed a paramount importance on the objective to protect consumers as weaker parties'.[441] This statement underscores the ECJ's acknowledgement of the structural imbalance between consumers and powerful market actors.

Further, in 2021, Advocate General Jean Richard de la Tour, in *Facebook Ireland Limited v. Bundesverband*, addressed the right to effective judicial protection and the legitimacy of non-profit associations representing data subjects. He affirmed that '[a]n injunctive action brought by a consumer protection association, such as the Federation (...) contributes to ensuring the effective application of the rights protected by Regulation 2016/679 [General Data Protection Regulation]'.[442] This reinforces the view that collective representation is not only compatible with EU law but also essential to its effective enforcement.

In terms of EU policy, collective redress has recently emerged as a prominent topic - both within the broader framework of EU law and, more specifically, in the field of competition law.[443] This is hardly surprising, given that consumer protection is widely regarded as one of the central objectives of competition policy.[444]

Class action mechanisms are increasingly seen as part of the EU's legal and cultural tradition. Although their application in competition law is relatively recent, they have been the subject of sustained academic interest and institutional analysis for over a decade. Both the European Commission and the European Parliament have explored their potential extensively, recognising their role in enhancing access to justice and ensuring effective enforcement of consumer rights.

---

439. Case 62543/00, 27 April 2004, available at Gorraiz Lizarraga and Others v. Spain (coe.int), pt. 38.
440. *See* David Ashton, *Competition Damages Action in the EU: Law and Practice*, economics contribution from Frank Maier-Rigaud and Ulrich Schawalbe, Elgar, *Competition Law and Practice*, 2nd ed., 2018, p. 290.
441. *See* Opinion delivered on 14 November 2017 in Case C-498/16, *Maximilian Schrems v. Facebook Ireland Limited*, pt. 95.
442. *See* Conclusions of 2 December 2021, in Case C-319/20, *Facebook Ireland Limited v. Bundesverband der Verbraucherzentralen und Verbraucherverbände*, p. 77.
443. *See* Christopher Hodges, *The Reform of Class and Representative Actions in European Legal Systems: A New Framework for Collective Redress in Europe*, Oxford, Hart, 2008, p. 9.
444. *See* Barry Rodger (ed.), *Competition Law, Comparative Private Enforcement and Collective Redress Across the EU*, Kluwer Law International, 2014, p. 157. *See also* Silvia Pietrini, *L'action en droit des pratiques anticoncurrentielles – Perspectives nationale, européenne et internationale, Concurrences*, Bruylant, 2012, p. 226.

As early as 1972, a US jurist famously referred to class actions as 'blackmail settlements',[445] highlighting concerns about their potential misuse. Yet, the core purpose of class actions remains clear: to provide injured parties with a viable path to compensation - one that would often be inaccessible through individual litigation.

At their heart, class actions serve as a mechanism for ensuring access to justice in its fullest sense: the right of all individuals and legal entities to access the courts on equal terms.[446] By aggregating claims, they help overcome the economic and procedural barriers that typically deter victims - especially consumers and small businesses - from pursuing redress for harm suffered.

The argument above is also firmly supported in legal scholarship. As Steven Van Uytsel explains,[447] '[c]ollective actions contribute to access to justice. This has been explained by referring to their capacity to "provide a real remedy" to those in the community who individually had uneconomically viable claims, but where overall, the total amount at issue was significant'. This observation is particularly relevant in the field of competition law, where the harm caused by infringements often spans the entire distribution chain - impacting a wide range of actors, from multinational corporations to individual consumers. In such contexts, collective redress mechanisms are not merely procedural tools; they are essential to ensuring that justice is both accessible and meaningful.

The right to an effective remedy - understood here as encompassing collective redress - is intrinsically linked to the substantive rights enshrined in the EU Treaties, particularly Articles 101 and 102 of the TFEU. This connection was firmly established in the landmark *Courage* judgment,[448] where the ECJ affirmed, for the first time, that not only undertakings and public authorities but also consumers have the right to seek compensation for harm caused by infringements of competition law.[449] This recognition marked a pivotal moment in the development of effective judicial protection within the EU legal order.

The Court further emphasised that the exercise of this right must comply with the principles of equivalence and effectiveness: national procedures must not be less favourable than those governing similar domestic actions, and they must not render the exercise of EU rights practically impossible or excessively difficult.[450] This interpretation was later reinforced in the *Manfredi* judgment,[451] which reiterated[452] that Member

445. *See* Charles Silver, *We're Scared to Death: Class Certification and Blackmail*, New York University Law Review, Vol 78, No. 4, October 2003, We're Scared to Death: Class Certification and Blackmail (nyulawreview.org), p. 1.
446. *See* Tom Cornford, *Access to Justice: Beyond the Policies and Politics of Austerity*, Ellie Palmer, Tom Cornford, Yseult Marique and Audrey Guinchard (eds), Bloomsbury Publishing, 26 April 2018, p. 39.
447. In *Collective Actions in a Competition Law Context: Reconciling Multiplayer Interests to Enhance Access to Justice, Collective Actions - Enhancing Access to Justice and Reconciling Multilayer Interests?*, Stefan Wrbka, Steven Van Uytsel and Mathias Siems (eds), Cambridge University Press, 2012, p. 57.
448. Of 20 September 2001, Case C-453/99, pt. 26.
449. *See* s. 1.1 above.
450. *See* pt. 29.
451. Of 13 September 2006, Case App. C-295/04 et seq.
452. *See* s. 1.1 above.

States are obliged to ensure both equal treatment and the effective exercise of the right to reparation for competition law violations.[453]

The EU Damages Directive,[454] as outlined[455] in Article 1(1), states: '[this] This Directive sets out certain rules necessary to ensure that anyone who has suffered harm caused by an infringement of competition law by an undertaking or by an association of undertakings can effectively exercise the right to claim full compensation for that harm from that undertaking or association. It sets out rules fostering undistorted competition in the internal market and removing obstacles to its proper functioning, by ensuring equivalent protection throughout the Union for anyone who has suffered such harm'.[456]

However, as demonstrated above, the Directive falls short of this ambition. In practice, it leaves key stakeholders (particularly consumers and SMEs) insufficiently protected. Even medium-sized companies often refrain from initiating such actions individually, given the disproportionate balance between the high procedural and financial costs involved and the relatively limited damages suffered.

Ultimately, the key question raised by this discussion is: what type of action – individual or collective – can truly guarantee that anyone harmed by a breach of competition law will have access to compensation under equal conditions across the EU? This question goes to the heart of effective judicial protection, as enshrined in EU law.

As the following chapters will demonstrate, the answer lies in class actions. These mechanisms offer a pathway to justice for those whose individual claims may be too small to pursue alone but are collectively significant. However, the legal frameworks governing class actions across Europe remain highly fragmented (and in some Member States, entirely absent).

In addition to its compensatory function, the use of collective mechanisms in the private enforcement of competition law also contributes significantly to deterrence and the promotion of a competition-conscious culture.[457] This reflects the so-called dual function[458] of private litigation: not only does it serve to restore the harm suffered by victims but it also acts as a preventive tool by increasing the likelihood and cost of enforcement for infringing undertakings.

Class actions are generally understood to serve four interrelated objectives: (i) ensuring access to justice; (ii) promoting procedural efficiency; (iii) safeguarding substantive rights; and (iv) preventing future violations.[459]

---

453. Without prejudice to measures against unjust enrichment, *see* pts 61 and 92 to 96.
454. *See* s. 1.2 above.
455. *See* s. 2.3.1 above.
456. Underlining by this book.
457. *See* David Ashton, *Competition Damages Action in the EU: Law and Practice*, economics contribution from Frank Maier-Rigaud and Ulrich Schawalbe, Elgar, *Competition Law and Practice*, 2nd ed., 2018, p. 282.
458. *See* Steven Van Uytsel, *Collective Actions in a Competition Law Context: Reconciling Multiplayer Interests to Enhance Access to justice, Collective Actions – Enhancing Access to Justice and Reconciling Multilayer Interests?*, Stefan Wrbka, Steven Van Uytsel and Mathias Siems (eds), Cambridge University Press, 2012, p. 64.
459. *See* Christopher Hodges, *Evaluating Collective Redress: Models, Evidence, Outcomes and Policy in Class Actions in Europe: Holy Grail or a Wrong Trail?*, Alan Uzelac and Stefaan Voet (eds), Springer, 2021, pp. 19 to 25.

With regard to the first two objectives (access to justice and procedural economy), it is important to recognise that class actions are designed to make justice accessible at a proportionate cost in both time and resources, particularly in cases where individual litigation would be economically unviable. While it is true that class actions can also entail significant costs - such as those related to registration, validation, case management, publicity, and payments to intermediaries like funders and legal counsels - these costs must be weighed against the broader efficiencies they generate.

Moreover, the financial and procedural burden of class actions varies considerably depending on the legal model adopted. Despite their complexity, these mechanisms often result in a net gain for the judicial system by reducing the number of duplicative claims and promoting a more intelligent allocation of judicial resources.[460]

As for the final two objectives (defending the law and preventing its violation), it is essential to recognise that the legitimacy of any legal system depends on public trust in its impartial and consistent application. Individuals, whether victims or infringers, must believe that the law will be enforced fairly, without distortion or favouritism. In the context of competition law, this means that the consequences of infringements must be proportionate and predictable, thereby shaping future behaviour through credible deterrence.

While it is true that human behaviour is often influenced by social, cultural, and emotional factors, competition law primarily targets companies - entities that operate on a cost-benefit rationale. For such actors, the likelihood and magnitude of legal consequences are key variables in strategic decision-making. Collective redress mechanisms, by increasing the risk and cost of non-compliance, play a crucial role in reinforcing the preventive function of private enforcement.

In short, class actions not only enhance access to justice but also generate procedural and economic efficiencies - benefits that may not be achievable even for large companies acting alone. Specifically:

(1) they reduce asymmetries between victims and offenders (in terms of both economic power and access to information), thereby levelling the playing field and enabling a more comprehensive assessment of the effects of anticompetitive conduct;
(2) they create procedural synergies, lowering litigation costs and resource burdens for both the parties involved and the judicial system, contributing to a more efficient use of institutional capacity;
(3) they help prevent inconsistent rulings and reduce legal uncertainty by consolidating similar claims into a single, coherent proceeding.

460. *See* Horacio Vedia Jerez, *Competition Law Enforcement and Compliance Across the World: A Comparative Review*, Wolters Kluwer, 2015, p. 256.

3.3 POLICY AND LEGISLATIVE INITIATIVES AT EU INSTITUTIONAL LEVEL

The debate surrounding the establishment of collective redress mechanisms at the EU level dates back (at least) to the preparatory work for the EU Damages Directive, as previously discussed. In recent years, however, this debate has gained renewed momentum, with significant policy and legislative developments emerging.

At this stage of the analysis, it is essential to examine these developments critically: to assess the strengths and limitations of the solutions adopted, to reflect on what could have been done differently, and to identify the key issues that remain unresolved. This evaluation will serve as the foundation for presenting this book's proposal for a more coherent and effective resolution.

3.3.1 The Green Paper

The discussion on the creation of collective redress mechanisms at the EU level dates back (at least) to the 2005 Green Paper.[461] In that document, the European Commission acknowledged the need to consolidate a large number of small claims into a single action, primarily to save time and reduce costs. It recognised that, in practice, it would be highly unlikely, if not impossible, for consumers or small-scale purchasers to bring individual actions for damages arising from competition law infringements.

In response to questions about the necessity of establishing special procedures for class actions and protecting consumer interests, the Commission proposed two preliminary options:

(1) Allowing consumer associations to bring actions on behalf of affected individuals, without precluding individual claims. However, key issues such as legal standing (e.g., registration or authorisation systems), the distribution of compensation (whether to the association or its members), and the method of calculating damages (based on unlawful gain or individual harm) were left open for further analysis.
(2) Introducing a specific provision for class actions brought by groups of purchasers other than final consumers.[462]

In this document, the European Commission also endorsed the use of representative and class actions initiated by final consumers under an opt-in model,[463] signalling a deliberate move away from the US-style class action regime.

Unlike in the US, participation rates in opt-in class actions within the EU remain notably low. Moreover, actions initiated by consumer associations are particularly

461. *Commission Staff Working Paper, Annex to the Green Paper on Damages actions for breach of the EC antitrust rules*, COM(2005) 672 final, 2005, available at https://eur-lex.europa.eu/legal-content/EN/ALL/?uri=CELEX%3A52005DC0672 and Recital 3 of the EU Damages Directive.
462. *See* p. 9.
463. *See* s. 1.2 above and 3.6.1 below.

susceptible to the principal-agent problem – that is, the potential conflict of interest between the represented individuals (principals) and the associations acting on their behalf (agents).

The principal-agent problem also arises in the US, where, as previously noted and further developed,[464] lawyers (acting as agents) represent victims (principals) in a manner akin to corporate actors. They typically bear the full cost of initiating class actions, anticipating a share of the awarded compensation (through either a court ruling or settlement) as remuneration. This is made possible through *quota litis* agreements, known in the American context as contingency fees. Consequently, if the expected compensation does not significantly exceed the litigation costs, these agents may be incentivised to settle early, potentially at the expense of the victims' best interests.

In addition to the concerns outlined above, the private enforcement of competition law by consumer associations will remain underutilised unless the issue of funding is adequately addressed.[465]

On this matter, Philipp Kirst argues[466] against the opt-out model, suggesting that it exacerbates the principal-agent problem: with a larger class, lawyers may be incentivised to file frivolous claims and invest minimal effort in ensuring that victims' rights are effectively exercised – especially since many affected individuals may be unaware that a claim has even been filed on their behalf.

However, this book respectfully disagrees with this position. A larger class can also justify greater investment and enhance the enforcement of victims' rights. Moreover, the choice between opt-in and opt-out models should not be based on the presumption that legal representatives will breach their ethical obligations. These issues warrant further discussion, which we will return to below.[467]

3.3.2 The White Paper

In the 2008 White Paper, the European Commission went further and declared that there was a 'clear need' to create mechanisms to allow the aggregation of individual claims for compensation from victims of infringements of competition rules. This is because it recognises that consumers and SMEs, especially those who have suffered sporadic or low-value damage, often shy away from bringing these types of actions because of the costs, delays, uncertainties, risks and administrative burdens they entail.

464. *See* s. 3.4.1 below.
465. *See* Roger Van den Bergh, *Private Enforcement of European Competition Law and the Persisting Collective Action Problem*, Maastricht Journal of European and Comparative Law, SAGE Publications, vol. 20, No. 1, 3 January 2013.
466. In *The Impact of the Damages Directive on the Enforcement of EU Competition Law: A Law and Economics Analysis*, Edward Elgar, 2021, p. 45.
467. *See* s. 3.6 below.

Moreover, as acknowledged by the European Commission, on the rare occasions when multiple individual actions have been brought concerning the same infringement, they have led to procedural complexities, not only for plaintiffs and defendants but also for the judicial system as a whole.

To address the persistent barriers to effective private enforcement in competition law, the European Commission has proposed a dual mechanism of complementary collective redress tools. First, it recommends representative actions brought by qualified entities – such as consumer associations, public bodies, or professional organisations – either pre-designated or empowered on an ad hoc basis by a Member State, to act on behalf of identified or, in a limited number of cases, identifiable victims. Second, it supports opt-in collective actions, whereby victims explicitly choose to aggregate their claims into a single proceeding. Recognising that qualified entities may not be able or willing to represent all affected individuals, the Commission considers it essential that both mechanisms operate in tandem to ensure the effectiveness of collective redress for victims of antitrust infringements.

In other words, the European Commission has firmly distanced itself from the US model, which it views as susceptible to litigation abuses.[468] However, the opt-in system it advocates does not appear to resolve the underlying challenges. Given the typically low-value nature of individual harm, it is unrealistic to expect that a mechanism reliant on the initiative of SMEs and consumers will function effectively – particularly in the EU, where litigation culture is less entrenched than in the US, and where lawyers are prohibited from covering litigation costs due to the ban on *quota litis* agreements. Moreover, the Commission's proposed 'dual-track' solution – combining opt-in actions with representative actions brought by qualified entities – presupposes initiative not only from victims but also from entities that often lack the financial and institutional capacity to pursue such claims.

Even at this stage, the European Commission was already signalling the shift in perspective it would formalise in 2010, as discussed in the following section. Notably, the Commission emphasised that its proposals on damages actions in competition law were part of a broader initiative to enhance collective redress mechanisms in the EU – an initiative it acknowledged 'may develop further within this context'.[469]

While the Commission rightly observed that asymmetries between parties are not unique to competition law and also arise in areas such as consumer protection, it failed to account for the fact that these asymmetries are significantly more pronounced in the competition domain. This is due not only to the technical complexity of antitrust violations – many of which go unnoticed by victims – but also to the considerable resources and legal sophistication typically available to infringing companies.[470]

468. *See also Joint information note by Vice-President Viviane Reding, Vice-President Joaquín Almunia and Commissioner John Dalli, Towards a Coherent European Approach to Collective Redress: Next Steps*, 5 October 2010, which preceded the 2011 public consultation mentioned above.
469. *See* pp. 4 and 5.
470. In fact, the European Commission has noted in the White Paper that various obstacles to effective compensation for victims of infringements of EC competition rules, such as mass damages and sporadic low-value damages, information asymmetries and other problems

3.3.3 The European Commission's Strategic Shift in 2010

Until 2010, the European Commission's strategy focused primarily on sector-specific collective redress mechanisms, particularly in the field of competition law. However, that year marked a strategic shift in its work programme.[471] The Commission began to approach collective action as a cross-cutting issue, emphasising the need for coherence across EU policies. It announced its intention to develop a set of common legal principles applicable to all areas of law through EU-level legislative proposals. As a result, in 2011, the Commission launched a public consultation, inviting contributions on the general principles of collective actions shared among Member States and exploring how a harmonised solution could be constructed at the EU level.[472]

The challenge with legislating in such general terms, in our view, lies in the necessary detachment from the specificities of each legal domain. This not only complicates the identification of genuinely common issues across different areas of law but also undermines the effectiveness of transposing such legislation into the legal systems of Member States. By nature, broad-based initiatives tend to be superficial, limiting their practical impact across diverse legal traditions.

Indeed, as we will see, the European Commission ultimately excluded the very area of law that initially prompted its concern over the lack of effective collective redress mechanisms - competition law.

3.3.4 The 2012 European Parliament Resolution

The European Parliament has also addressed this issue on several occasions, as mentioned above, in particular the 2012 Resolution Towards a coherent European approach to collective redress, which followed the recent European Commission trend and was not limited, unlike the Green and White Papers,[473] to collective actions under competition rules.

This book suggests that the European Commission's strategic shift, discussed in the previous section, may have been influenced by the European Parliament. This inference is supported by the Parliament's debate on the White Paper and, in particular, by the remarks of Rapporteur Klaus-Heiner Lehne, who criticised the 'fragmentation of the law' observed in the context of competition law. He advocated instead for the adoption

encountered in damages actions, are not unique to EU competition law cases, but also occur, for example, in areas such as product quality liability and other consumer-related problems.

471. *See Communication from the Commission to the European Parliament, the Council, the European Economic and Social Committee and the Committee of the Regions Commission Work Programme 2010 Time to act*, COM/2010/0135 final, p. 9.

472. *See* http://ec.europa.eu/competition/consultations/2011_collective_redress/index_en.html.

473. *Commission Staff Working Paper, Annex to the Green Paper on Damages actions for breach of the EC antitrust rules*, COM(2005) 672 final, 2005, available at https://eur-lex.europa.eu/legal-content/EN/ALL/?uri=CELEX%3A52005DC0672.

of horizontal instruments that would apply across legal sectors, signalling a preference for a more unified and coherent approach to collective redress.[474]

As a result, the European Parliament recommended that any legislative proposal in this area should establish a horizontal framework, as previously discussed, grounded in a common set of principles to ensure uniform access to justice through collective redress across the EU. The Parliament also endorsed the Commission's preference for the opt-in model, viewing it as a safeguard against the unmeritorious use of collective mechanisms.[475] Furthermore, it emphasised that Member States should ensure that a judge (or an equivalent authority) retains discretionary powers[476] to conduct a preliminary assessment of the admissibility of any proposed class action. This includes verifying whether the qualifying criteria are met and whether the action is suitable to proceed. The Parliament also called for the designation of qualified organisations to bring representative actions, based on criteria defined at the EU level.

This book applauds the National Courts' discretion, particularly regarding access to evidence, but, as will be widely noted below, in a scenario of scarcity of collective redress, limiting access to it on the grounds of abusive litigation seems unreasonable.

Regarding the principles that should govern collective redress mechanisms, the European Parliament recommended the adoption of the following safeguards: (i) a prohibition on punitive damages; (ii) access to evidence equivalent to that in individual actions, requiring each claimant to present their own supporting evidence; (iii) the application of the 'loser pays' principle, whereby the losing party bears the costs of the proceedings - again, with the aim of discouraging unmeritorious claims at the EU level;[477] and (iv) the decision not to legislate on third-party funding at the EU level, such as arrangements where funders receive a portion of the awarded compensation. This last point reflects the fact that such funding models are largely unfamiliar in most Member States, though the Parliament left open the possibility for national rules or guidelines to be developed in this area.[478]

Once again, we believe that the principles outlined above, when taken collectively, impose significant limitations on the exercise of collective redress. There is no compelling evidence to suggest that class actions are being abused within the EU. In

474. Indeed, as stated by the *Rapporteur* Klaus-Heiner Lehne: 'we do not want fragmentation of the law. Now competition law is going off and creating such an instrument. Consumer protection is coming along on the same issue. We know that at some point something similar will be considered in relation to capital market law, environmental law and social law. We consider it absolutely necessary for a horizontal approach to be considered as well and for us at least to support the procedural instruments which are more or less the same in all areas with a horizontal instrument. That is also of decisive importance', *see* Debates - Wednesday, 25 March 2009 (europa.eu), p. 130.
475. According to the European Parliament, in order to avoid unmeritorious claims and the misuse of collective redress, for a representative action to be admissible, there must be a clearly identified group, and the identification of the members of the group must have taken place before the claim was brought, *see Communication from the Commission to the European Parliament, the Council, the European Economic and Social Committee and the Committee of the Regions Commission Work Programme 2010 Time to act*, COM/2010/0135 final, p. 1.
476. *Ibid.*
477. *Ibid.*
478. *Ibid.*

this context, restricting access to such mechanisms on the basis of hypothetical litigation excesses appears unjustified. Most notably, the European Parliament's recommendation not to regulate third-party funding at the EU level is particularly regrettable, given that funding is widely recognised as a key enabler - and one of the primary reasons for the current scarcity - of collective actions. As this book will demonstrate below, even the Parliament itself would later reconsider this position.[479]

3.3.5 The Independent Study

In parallel with the initiatives outlined above, the ECOM commissioned an 'Independent Study', published in June 2012, to explore potential legislative action at the EU level concerning collective redress in the antitrust field.[480] One of the key questions addressed by the study was whether the legislative instrument should adopt a horizontal approach - applying across all areas of EU law, such as competition, consumer protection, and data protection - or focus specifically on antitrust enforcement. The study ultimately supported the latter, advocating for the reinforcement of private enforcement mechanisms in competition law. This approach aimed to reduce disparities among Member States in the judicial protection of individual rights arising directly from Articles 101 and 102 of the TFEU.

This book agrees, as will be discussed further below,[481] with the sector-specific approach advocated by the Independent Study, as it offers a targeted solution to the underdeveloped private enforcement of Articles 101 and 102 TFEU across the EU. This approach respects the principles of subsidiarity and proportionality by addressing the problem without exceeding what is necessary. Moreover, as the study highlights, a horizontal collective redress framework would be less effective in accommodating the specificities of competition law. Such a framework would likely require additional sector-specific measures to address issues like pass-on, access to evidence, and the interaction with the leniency regime.[482] While it is true that some of these concerns have since been partially addressed by the EU Damages Directive, they have not been fully resolved - particularly in the context of collective redress, where the need for access to evidence prior to initiating proceedings may be even more pressing.

Furthermore, the Independent Study argued that the appropriate legal basis for adopting legislation on the collective protection of competition law infringements would be Article 103(1) of the TFEU. This provision empowers the Council to adopt the necessary regulations or directives for the implementation of Articles 101 and 102, based on a proposal from the European Commission and after consulting the European Parliament. Legislation grounded in this article would: (i) address the specificities of competition law; (ii) apply to both cross-border and domestic disputes - excluding infringements of purely national competition rules, which remain under Member State

479. *See* s. 3.3.8 below.
480. *See Collective Redress in Antitrust*, available at https://ec.europa.eu/competition/antitrust/actionsdamages/study_legislative_action_collective_redress.pdf.
481. *See* s. 5.2 below.
482. *See* p. 88.

jurisdiction; (iii) benefit both SMEs and consumers; and (iv) constitute a targeted procedural instrument of EU competition law. More precisely, a regulation is adopted ad hoc and aimed to create a uniform and efficient procedural framework to complement existing national systems.

To justify ruling out the use of a directive in favour of a regulation, the Independent Study cites potential incompatibilities with existing national legislation and the risk of adopting non-harmonised solutions across Member States - given that most national collective redress systems are general in scope and not limited to competition law.

However, this book respectfully disagrees with that conclusion, primarily on the grounds[483] of the principle of proportionality and the procedural particularities of the various Member States. While this book sees no compelling reason to doubt the Directive's capacity to achieve its intended objectives - as was recognised at the time of the EU Damages Directive's adoption - it also acknowledges that the active involvement of Member States in adapting the Directive's provisions to their respective legal systems enhances both the assimilation of those rules and their effective implementation.

Regarding the choice between opt-in and opt-out models, and in an effort to reconcile the European legal tradition with concerns over excessive litigation while ensuring effective access to redress for SMEs and consumers, the Independent Study proposes a hybrid approach. Drawing inspiration from the models adopted in the UK and Belgium (which will be examined in detail below),[484] this solution would establish the opt-in mechanism as the general rule. However, it would allow courts to authorise the use of an opt-out model in specific circumstances, such as when the harm suffered by individual consumers is minimal. This flexibility aims to ensure that a significant proportion of injured parties receive compensation for the damage incurred.

In contrast, this book will advocate[485] for the opt-out class action model as the option offering the greatest benefits to all potential participants in a competition law class action. Nonetheless, we acknowledge that a hybrid regime is more likely to garner political support from the various Member States and may represent a meaningful improvement in many national legal systems, depending on the assessment conducted by the National Courts.

Finally, the Independent Study addressed several points that remain relevant to the framework of the legislative action under consideration:

(1) *Admissibility:* a collective action should be deemed admissible when it concerns the same facts and the same infringement of competition rules, allowing the National Courts to apply a common line of reasoning for all claimants and rely on a shared body of evidence.
(2) *Types of Action*: both representative actions and collective actions *stricto sensu* should be permitted. There appears to be no justification for restricting the ability of consumers (or SMEs in comparable positions) to

483. *See* s. 5.1 below.
484. *See* ss 3.4.4 and 3.4.5 below, respectively.
485. *See* s. 5.3 below.

initiate collective proceedings to seek compensation for harm caused by anticompetitive conduct.

(3) *Financing:* the study identifies the lack of effective financing mechanisms as a key factor behind the limited development of class actions in Europe. It advocates for the use of contingency or conditional fee arrangements, which allocate risk to the party best positioned to bear it and incentivise legal representatives to assess the merits of a case beforehand. The study also supports the assignment of claims to third parties who may then initiate proceedings. It dismisses concerns, drawn from the US experience, that such financing models distort legal incentives or encourage excessive and unmeritorious litigation, arguing that these outcomes result from a unique combination of procedural features not present in the European context.

(4) *Cost sharing:* the 'loser pays' principle should be preserved, as it is widely accepted across Member States. This rule encourages parties to consider the full cost of litigation, deters frivolous claims, and promotes alternative dispute resolution mechanisms such as out-of-court settlements. The study found no evidence that this principle constitutes a significant barrier to the development of class actions in Europe.[486]

This book examined the Independent Study in detail above, as it considers that, for the first time, a study systematically and thoroughly identified the core issues, highlighting the persistent lack of adequate solutions in this area. This research will return to the Independent Study in Chapter VII, where it outlines this book's proposal for achieving the effective exercise of the right to reparation for damages resulting from infringements of competition law by SMEs and consumers in the EU. In that chapter, the book will contrast the positions developed throughout it with the initial proposals for EU-level solutions (among which the Independent Study stands out).

Ultimately, the resolution of existing inequalities, particularly in the area of collective redress, must be driven by EU law. Such an approach is essential to ensure the effectiveness of enforcement mechanisms and to provide Member States with a coherent and reasonable framework for harmonisation. This would bring the EU closer to the functionality of US mechanisms, while fully respecting the foundational legal principles of European legal systems.

486. The study also dealt with a number of points that were largely regulated by the EU Damages Directive, such as: the quantification of damages, ruling out the application of punitive damages; the need to move towards a more uniform approach in the EU on the binding effects of NCA decisions and to provide greater legal certainty and limit forum shopping. These include: the protection of leniency applicants by reducing the liability of applicants for immunity or reduction of fines; legislation on access to evidence and, in this context, limiting access to information held by the EC and the NCAs (especially with regard to leniency applications); and the obligation to send the NCA a copy of the initial application and all relevant documents, so that it can intervene in the proceedings (producing documents and evidence) within a set time limit, in the name of the public interest, i.e., the defence of the competitive structure, the defence of the competitive structure of the market and the effectiveness of the application of competition rules – *see* pp. 88-90.

3.3.6 The 2013 Recommendation and the 2018 Report by the European Commission

The European Commission ignored most of the conclusions of the Independent Study explored above and, in its 2013 Recommendation,[487] reaffirmed its preference for the *opt-in* model;[488] representative actions;[489] the prohibition on linking a lawyer's or third-party funder's remuneration to the amount of compensation awarded;[490] the prohibition of punitive damages;[491] and the application of the 'loser pays' principle.[492]

This Recommendation diverged from the earlier Green and White Papers,[493] as it extended beyond competition law infringements to address the broader framework of the EU law. It contributed to the ongoing debate on how to introduce a harmonised class action system within the EU, while efforts to promote the private enforcement of competition law continued in parallel - although this book contends that these two dimensions are inherently interconnected.

As previously mentioned,[494] the 2013 Recommendation coincided with the proposal for the EU Damages Directive and was met with several criticisms (particularly from European Parliament committees), regarding the perceived 'devaluation' of collective actions in competition matters. In response to questions about the relationship between these two instruments, the European Commission clarified that collective redress was not included in the Directive because it had already been addressed in the 2013 Recommendation. The Commission emphasised that the Recommendation was intended to complement the Directive and reiterated its position that any EU legislative initiative on collective redress should be general in scope, rather than limited to competition law. In support of this view, the Commission noted that the challenges faced by SMEs and consumers are common across various areas of EU law.[495]

Contrary to what the European Commission suggests, it is difficult to identify another branch of EU law where the imbalance between the parties is as pronounced as in competition law. This is a field marked by such complexity that injured parties

487. On the common principles that should govern Member States' collective redress mechanisms for injunctions and compensation for violations of rights guaranteed by EU law, *see* https://eur-lex.europa.eu/legal-content/PT/TXT/PDF/?uri=CELEX:52018DC0040&from=en.
488. *See* pt. 21.
489. *See* pt. 4.
490. *See* pts 30 and 32.
491. *See* pt. 31.
492. *See* pt. 13.
493. *See Commission Staff Working Paper, Annex to the Green Paper on Damages actions for breach of the EC antitrust rules*, COM(2005) 672 final, 2005, available at https://eur-lex.europa.eu/legal-content/EN/ALL/?uri=CELEX%3A52005DC0672.
494. *See* s. 3.3 above.
495. Specifically, the European Commission said that '[s]ince consumers and SMEs may face the same difficulties when enforcing their rights also in other fields of EU law, the Commission recommends that some form of collective redress should be available in all EU Member States to act against breaches of whatever EU rule, including breaches of the EU antitrust rules. This non-binding recommendation is thus a useful complement of the proposed Directive.', *see Memo Frequently Asked Questions: Commission proposes legislation to facilitate damage claims by victims of antitrust violations*, 11 June 2013, available at https://ec.europa.eu/commission/presscorner/detail/en/MEMO_13_531.

often remain unaware of the infringement itself. Moreover, although the preceding developments might suggest that competition rules would be included in a future EU legislative initiative on collective actions, this has not materialised. As will be discussed in the following section, competition law was ultimately excluded from Directive 2020/1828 on representative actions for the protection of the collective interests of consumers.

To further justify its decision to issue a general, non-binding Recommendation on class actions (rather than incorporating collective redress into the EU Damages Directive), the European Commission argued that, unlike individual actions, collective actions were not available in all Member States. In the view of this book, however, such reasoning supports the opposite conclusion. Precisely because of the disparity in procedural mechanisms across Member States, a binding legislative initiative at the EU level would be warranted to ensure a minimum standard of access to justice. Moreover, if consumers and SMEs already face significant obstacles in seeking redress for harm caused by competition law infringements through individual actions, how can the EU Damages Directive fulfil its objective of ensuring effective compensation without binding provisions on collective redress?

In 2018, the European Commission published a report on the implementation of the aforementioned Recommendation, which revealed that legislative developments in the area of collective redress remained limited across the Member States. Notably, nine Member States still had no provisions in place for bringing collective actions for damages in cases of mass harm.

Moreover, in many Member States that do provide for collective redress mechanisms, injured parties (particularly SMEs and consumers) rarely make use of them. This is often due to the rigidity of the procedures, the excessive duration of the proceedings, or the perception that the costs involved are likely to outweigh the potential benefits.

Finally, only seven Member States adopted measures after the 2013 Recommendation,[496] and even these reforms did not transpose it correctly.[497] These findings revealed a persistent divergence among Member States on the issue of collective redress and underscored the European Commission's failure to take the necessary legislative initiative in this area.

3.3.7 The Directive on Representative Actions to Protect the Collective Interests of Consumers (Apart from Fair Competition)

Also in 2018, the European Commission introduced the 'New Deal for Consumers'[498] which, as previously mentioned, included a proposal for a directive on representative

496. On or before the deadline, i.e., 26 July 2015.
497. *See* Philipp Kirst, *The Impact of the Damages Directive on the Enforcement of EU Competition Law: A Law and Economics Analysis*, Edward Elgar, 2021, p. 48.
498. *See* Review of EU Consumer Protection Legislation: New Deal for Consumers | European Commission (europa.eu).

actions aimed at protecting the collective interests of consumers.[499] As the name implies, the proposal focused on consumer protection and was limited to breaches of EU law listed in Annex I (such as unfair commercial practices and data protection), explicitly excluding competition law infringements.

In other words, although the European Commission took the initiative to explore collective actions in the context of competition law – through the Green and White Papers mentioned above – and has been working on the issue for over a decade, it has yet to establish a coherent approach that aligns the collective protection of consumer and competition rights. As Astrid Stadler aptly observes,[500] the Commission may still be influenced by (anecdotal) concerns about frivolous class actions in the US, often portrayed as being driven by opportunistic competition lawyers targeting large corporations and the perceived risk of such practices spreading to the EU. By excluding competition law from the current proposal for a directive on representative actions, it is sending a message that casts even greater uncertainty over the future of competition law class actions at the EU level – arguably more so than a few years ago, when a legislative initiative in this area still seemed likely.

The following reasons[501] put forward by the European Commission to justify this directive largely apply to competition law – a field in which, as repeatedly emphasised throughout this book, consumers face particular challenges in exercising their right to redress due to its specific legal and procedural complexities:

(1) '[e]ffective enforcement of EU rules matters to Europeans and affects their daily lives. That is why a robust, efficient and effective enforcement system is needed to ensure that Member States fully apply, implement and enforce EU law and provide adequate redress for citizens';
(2) 'the risk of infringements of Union law affecting the collective interests of consumers is increasing due to economic globalisation and digitalisation';[502]
(3) '[t]raders that infringe EU law may affect thousands or even millions of consumers';
(4) '[i]n light of increasing cross-border trade and EU-wide commercial strategies, these infringements increasingly also affect consumers in more than one Member State';
(5) 'the Collective Redress Report showed that a number of Member States still do not provide for collective compensatory redress mechanisms tailored for mass harm situations';

499. *See* Proposal for a Directive of the European Parliament and of the Council on representative actions for the protection of the collective interests of consumers and repealing Directive 2009/22/EC, Brussels, 11 April 2018, COM(2018) 184 final.
500. In *Are Class Actions Finally (Re)conquering Europe?: Some Remarks on Directive 2020/1828*, Juridica International, 30 March 2021, pp. 14 and 15.
501. *See* pp. 1 and 2.
502. *See* Vicente Bagnoli, *Designing Competition Policy in Digital Markets for Developing Economies: How the EU Can Contribute with the Digital Markets Act and Digital Services Act,* Revista de Defesa da Concorrência, Brasília, vol. 9, No. 2, 2021, pp. 133-158, available at https://revista.cade.gov.br/index.php/revistadedefesadaconcorrencia/article/view/957, p. 136.

(6) 'the European Parliament highlighted the need for a horizontal EU approach to collective redress, with focusing on infringement of consumers' rights'.

This book believes it is important to highlight the reasons cited above (just a few illustrative examples) as they underscore the lack of justification for excluding competition law from the scope of this directive. Both consumer protection and competition law share a common foundation: safeguarding the most vulnerable party in the economic relationship – the consumer. Moreover, it is difficult to conceive of another type of infringement that can simultaneously affect such a broad base of consumers and present such significant barriers to redress. Offences against competition rules are uniquely complex from both legal and economic perspectives, and the individual harm involved is often too small to justify stand-alone claims, making collective redress mechanisms particularly vital in this area.

Finally, as previously noted, the proposed directive addresses collective actions across a wide range of legal areas, including unfair commercial practices, tourism, product safety, energy, financial services, telecommunications, product liability, and data protection.[503] Against this backdrop, the exclusion of competition law is difficult to comprehend. Given its significant impact on consumers and the broader market, competition law would appear to be a natural fit within this directive's scope. Not least because, as previously discussed, it was the European Commission itself that initially emphasised the importance of collective redress specifically within the context of EU competition law.

This book argues that there are compelling reasons[504] to treat collective protection in competition law as a distinct matter at the EU level, given its unique characteristics. These include the significant imbalance in awareness and resources between the injured parties and the infringers, as well as the inherent difficulties in investigating and proving such violations. While these challenges apply across all types of competition law infringements (particularly in cartel cases, which is precisely why the leniency regime was introduced), they are not equally present in consumer law.

In fact, consumer protection may justify a more fragmented approach to collective redress. For instance, some consumer law violations, such as misleading advertising, are visible and broadly applicable, while others – like defective products – may involve highly individualised circumstances that are incompatible with collective procedures.

Moreover, this directive's inclusion of areas where the public interest is more pronounce – such as environmental or public health violations – suggests that a one-size-fits-all model for collective redress, particularly regarding the distribution of damages, may not be appropriate across such diverse legal domains.

503. *See* Frank Peters, Michelle Krekels and Louis Berger, *New European Directive Gives Teeth to Consumer Rights (and There Are Many ...!)*, 20 January 2021, available at New European Directive gives teeth to consumer rights (and there are many ...!) – Bureau Brandeis.
504. *See* s. 3.2 above.

Therefore, if combining competition law class actions with broader consumer law matters is already suboptimal, the complete absence of dedicated legislation for competition law collective redress is even more concerning.

Despite the European Commission's decision to include various areas of consumer law in its proposal for a directive while excluding competition law, it remains essential to examine the adopted legislation, Directive 2020/1828, for two key reasons. First, its relevance to this study is clear: it obliges Member States that previously lacked collective redress mechanisms to implement one, and it allows for the possibility of going beyond the Directive's scope (which, as will be discussed, provides only minimum harmonisation) by extending such mechanisms to competition law. Second, any legislative proposal this book puts forward must be aligned with, or at least not contradict, this recently adopted directive in order to be viable – particularly in areas concerning consumer protection.

Indeed, while competition law has its own specificities that must be carefully considered when designing a sector-specific collective redress regime at the EU level, EU legislation must nonetheless maintain a consistent and coherent framework, particularly with respect to its underlying principles.

Moreover, if the new regime proposed by the European Commission – and adopted by the European Parliament and the Council – were likely to be effective in the field of competition law, there would be no need to develop a parallel framework specifically for antitrust infringements. In that case, this book's final recommendation would simply be to amend Directive 2020/1828 to include competition law within its scope, or alternatively, to issue a recommendation encouraging Member States to extend the Directive's application to competition rules during transposition. However, this book will demonstrate below that this does not appear to be a viable solution.

The proposal for a directive introduced measures such as: (i) preserving Member States' existing rules on the allocation of procedural costs – typically based on the 'loser pays' principle, which, as previously noted, may discourage claimants due to the potential financial risks involved;[505] and (ii) restricting legal standing to bring representative actions to qualified entities.[506] These provisions aim to strike 'a balance between facilitating access to justice to safeguard consumers' interests and ensuring adequate safeguards from abusive litigation'.[507]

The legislative process concluded in December 2020 with the publication of Directive 2020/1828. While the final text diverged from the European Commission's original proposal in several respects – as will be discussed – it ultimately upheld the exclusion of competition law from its scope,[508] as previously noted.

Duncan Fairgrieve and Rhonson Salim highlight[509] the broad scope of Directive 2020/1828, which applies to sixty-six legal instruments across diverse areas such as

505. *See* Recital 4 and Articles 7.1 *in fine* and 15.2 *in fine*.
506. *See* Article 4.
507. *See* p. 4.
508. Available at https://eur-lex.europa.eu/legal-content/PT/TXT/PDF/?uri=CELEX:32020L1828&from=PT.
509. In *Collective Redress in Europe: Moving Forward or Treading Water?*, Cambridge University Press for the British Institute of International and Comparative Law, 2022, p. 468.

product liability and safety, data protection, financial services, travel and tourism, and sectors including chemicals, cosmetics, food, energy, telecommunications, health, and the environment. While the Directive covers several consumer-relevant legislative acts - such as those on tyre labelling for energy efficiency[510] and access to the activity of electronic money institutions[511] - the authors also acknowledge that it falls short of the ambitions set out in the 2013 Recommendation. That earlier instrument, although favouring the opt-in model for collective actions, was broader in scope, aiming to cover the entirety of EU law.[512]

As previously noted, Member States retain the discretion to extend the application of this directive beyond its defined scope.[513] Indeed, Article 1(2) of Directive 2020/1828 explicitly states that it 'does not prevent Member States from adopting or retaining in force procedural means for the protection of the collective interests of consumers at national level'. However, as confirmed in the 2013 Report on the Recommendation,[514] several Member States still lack collective redress mechanisms for harm caused by infringements of competition law. In this context, the exclusion of competition rules from the Directive makes it difficult to view this legislative act as a true paradigm shift in enabling consumers to effectively exercise their rights.

As for the type of collective action that Directive 2020/1828 provides for, it is essentially representative, i.e., an action to protect the collective interests of consumers brought on behalf of consumers by an entity qualified as a claimant with a view to obtaining an injunction, a remedy or both.[515] By broadly including these measures, Directive 2020/1828 goes beyond the EU Damages Directive, which is limited to a remedy (the action for damages).[516]

The qualified entities mentioned above are designated by the Member States. Unlike the European Commission's Proposal,[517] Directive 2020/1828 differentiates between national and cross-border class actions. To initiate a cross-border action (i.e., one brought by a qualified entity in a Member State other than the one in which it was designated), the following conditions[518] must be met:

(1) *Legal status and activity:* the entity must be a legal person that has engaged in effective public activity in the protection of consumer interests for at least twelve months prior to its request for designation.

510. *See* Regulation (EC) No. 1222/2009 of the European Parliament and of the Council of 25 November 2009 on the labelling of tyres with respect to fuel efficiency and other essential parameters (OJ L 342, 22 December 2009, p. 46): Articles 4, 5 and 6 - point 33 of Annex I to Directive 2020/1828.
511. Directive 2009/110/EC of the European Parliament and of the Council of 16 September 2009 on the taking up, pursuit and prudential supervision of the business of electronic money institutions amending Directives 2005/60/EC and 2006/48/EC and repealing Directive 2000/46/EC (OJ L 267, 10 October 2009, p. 7) - pt. 26 of Annex I to Directive 2020/1828.
512. *See* s. 3.3.6 above.
513. *See* Recital 18.
514. *See* s. 3.3.6 above.
515. *See* Article 3(5).
516. *See* s. 2.3.3.1 above.
517. *See* Articles 3 and 4.
518. *See* Articles 3(6) and (7) and 4(1) to (3).

(2) *Purpose alignment:* its statutory purpose must include a legitimate interest in protecting the consumer interests outlined in Annex I of Directive 2020/1828 (scope of application).
(3) *Non-profit nature:* the entity must operate on a not-for-profit basis.
(4) *Financial standing:* it must not be insolvent.
(5) *Independence and integrity:* the entity must be independent and free from influence by parties other than consumers, particularly professionals with an economic interest in initiating collective actions. This includes cases involving third-party funding. To safeguard this independence, the entity must have established procedures to prevent such influence and to avoid conflicts of interest between itself, its funders, and the consumers it represents.
(6) *Transparency:* the entity must make publicly available, namely on its website, information related to its independence (as described above), sources of funding, governance, organisational structure, objectives, and activities.

The legitimacy to bring this type of action is indeed a central issue. It is widely believed that the choice to entrust such actions to non-profit organisations, typically consumer associations, reflects a deliberate intention to prevent abusive litigation. This approach helps ensure that the action serves a public interest, rather than private or commercial motives.[519]

It is important to note that these types of organisations – typically non-profits such as consumer associations – often lack the financial resources or specialised expertise required to bring actions in complex areas like competition law, which is particularly relevant to our work. However, as highlighted above (point (5)), Directive 2020/1828 does allow for the use of private funding, provided that such funding does not compromise the independence of the representative entity. This represents, in our view, a positive shift away from the European Commission's earlier tendency to demonise the presence of economic interests in collective actions. By permitting third-party funding under strict safeguards, the Directive acknowledges the practical challenges faced by qualified entities while still aiming to prevent conflicts of interest and undue influence.[520]

Once designated, these qualified entities must be notified to the European Commission by each Member State,[521] being the list of designated entities publicly available.[522] Thereafter, as previously noted, these entities are authorised to bring actions in any

519. *See* Duncan Fairgrieve and Rhonson Salim, *Collective Redress in Europe: Moving Forward or Treading Water?*, Cambridge University Press for the British Institute of International and Comparative Law, 2022, p. 469.
520. *See* s. 3.3.6 above.
521. *See* Article 5.
522. *See* Cross-border Qualified Entities | EC-REACT, available at https://representative-actions-collaboration.ec.europa.eu/cross-border-qualified-entities.

Member State. In cases involving cross-border infringements, they may also collaborate and initiate a collective action in a single Member State, representing the collective interests of consumers across the affected jurisdictions.[523]

Despite the stricter criteria imposed for cross-border actions (as opposed to national actions, where the designation of qualified entities is left to the discretion of each Member State), such as the minimum requirement of twelve months of public activity, independence, and a non-profit purpose, the EU legislator's approach has faced criticism. Specifically, the option to allow qualified entities to bring actions in any Member State has been challenged for potentially encouraging forum shopping. Volker Herrmann, Donata Freiin von Enzberg, and Kerstin Bär[524] have argued that this framework creates a multiplicity of possible jurisdictions across Member States, thereby fostering competition for the most favourable forum in which to initiate representative actions.

This book takes the view that concerns over forum shopping – aligned with the European Commission's Proposal, which set out uniform criteria for all qualified entities regardless of whether they pursue national or cross-border actions (namely: (i) legal establishment in a Member State; (ii) a legitimate interest in ensuring compliance with EU legislation covered by the Directive; and (iii) a non-profit purpose) – may be premature. Given the still limited use of class actions within the EU, the fear of widespread forum shopping appears overstated.

That said, it is undeniable that the current framework creates incentives to select more favourable jurisdictions – such as Ireland.[525] However, the appropriate response to this risk is not to restrict access but to pursue greater harmonisation across Member States. Such harmonisation would strengthen the principle of effectiveness under EU law, particularly in the context of class actions concerning breaches of competition rules.

The above dual criteria (one for entities qualified to bring national class actions, determined at the discretion of each Member State, and another for those qualified to bring cross-border class actions,[526] governed by Directive 2020/1828) have also drawn criticism from Alexander Biard and Stefaan Voet,[527] for instance, arguing that a single,

523. *See* Article 6.

524. In *Die EU-Richtlinie über Verbandsklagen tritt in Kraft* (The EU Directive on representative consumer actions enters into force), 29 January 2021, available at tw-2021---die-eu-richtlinie-ber-verbandsklagen-tritt-in-kraft.pdf (taylorwessing.com). *See also* Duncan Fairgrieve and Rhonson Salim, *Collective Redress in Europe: Moving Forward or Treading Water?*, Cambridge University Press for the British Institute of International and Comparative Law, 2022, pp. 469 and 479.

525. *See* Peter Johnston, *Consumer Representative Actions: Floodgates Opening Soon?*, 27 July 2022, available at Consumer Representative Actions - Floodgates ... | Mason Hayes Curran (mhc.ie).

526. On the fact that Directive 2020/1828 does not regulate the jurisdiction of cross-border actions and resolve the conflicts that the interpretation of Regulation 1215/2012 has generated in this area, *see* Duncan Fairgrieve and Rhonson Salim, *Collective Redress in Europe: Moving Forward or Treading Water?* Cambridge University Press for the British Institute of International and Comparative Law, 2022, p. 474. *See also* Alexander Biard and Stefaan Voet, *Collective Redress in the EU: Will It Finally Come True? in Class Actions in Europe: Holy Grail or a Wrong Trail?*, Alan Uzelac and Stefaan Voet (eds), Springer, 2021, pp. 297 and 298.

527. In *Collective Redress in the EU: Will It Finally Come True? in Class Actions in Europe: Holy Grail or a Wrong Trail?*, Alan Uzelac and Stefaan Voet (eds), Springer, 2021, p. 295.

harmonised framework applicable to both national and cross-border actions would have simplified the legal landscape and enhanced legal certainty. However, the Council insisted on maintaining this distinction as a *sine qua non* condition for adopting the Directive.

While it is true that Member States could choose to apply the same criteria used for cross-border actions to the designation of qualified entities for national class actions, doing so could disproportionately burden smaller organisations that operate exclusively at the national level. These entities may lack the resources or institutional capacity to meet the more stringent requirements set out in Directive 2020/1828, potentially limiting their ability to represent consumer interests effectively within their own jurisdictions.[528]

A noteworthy aspect of Directive 2020/1828 is that it preserves the right of the National Court before which the representative action is brought to assess whether the statutory purpose of the qualified entity 'justifies its taking action in a specific case'.[529] This applies even when the entity is already included in the list submitted to the European Commission, which serves as proof of its active legal standing. This provision effectively grants defendants an additional opportunity to challenge the plaintiff's legitimacy, potentially leading to divergent interpretations across Member States (and even within the same Member State). Moreover, it risks perpetuating the bureaucratic delays[530] that have historically hindered the establishment of standing in such actions.[531] In this respect, the Directive may have opened a 'Pandora's box,' undermining its own objective of facilitating the effective functioning of class actions across the EU, irrespective of national procedural rules.[532] Had the EU legislator introduced a time limit for this preliminary assessment phase, the rationale behind this safeguard might have been more compelling and less disruptive to procedural efficiency.

With regard to the representative collective action model adopted by Directive 2020/1828, it is generally understood that the EU legislator left it to the discretion of Member States to choose between opt-in and opt-out[533] mechanisms. Indeed, Recital 43 of the Directive states that Member States should provide, in accordance with their legal traditions, for a mechanism of collective participation or exclusion - or a combination of both - and determine at which stage of the proceedings individual consumers may exercise their right to opt in or opt out of the action. However, we

528. *See* Duncan Fairgrieve and Rhonson Salim, *Collective Redress in Europe: Moving Forward or Treading Water?*, Cambridge University Press for the British Institute of International and Comparative Law, 2022, p. 470.
529. *See* Article 6(3).
530. In this regard, *see* Duncan Fairgrieve and Rhonson Salim, *Collective Redress in Europe: Moving Forward or Treading Water?*, Cambridge University Press for the British Institute of International and Comparative Law, 2022, pp. 473 and 479.
531. *See*, for example, the Portuguese case, in s. 3.4.3.6 below.
532. *See* Recital 12.
533. *See* Alexander Biard and Stefaan Voet, *Collective Redress in the EU: Will It Finally Come True? in Class Actions in Europe: Holy Grail or a Wrong Trail?*, Alan Uzelac and Stefaan Voet (eds), Springer, 2021, p. 295.

contend that the Directive's provisions are not as flexible or 'liquid' as they may initially appear.

In fact, this directive distinguishes between collective actions aimed at injunctions and redress measures,[534] with '[t]he consumers concerned by a representative action (...) entitled to benefit from [these] measures'.[535] With regard to injunctions, the model adopted is clearly opt-out, since individual consumers are not obliged to express their wish to be represented by the qualified entity.[536] As for redress measures, which include compensation (also redress itself, replacement, price reduction, cancellation of the contract or reimbursement of the amount paid),[537] the text of Directive 2020/1828 stipulates that Member States should establish 'rules on how and at which stage of a representative action for redress measures the individual consumers concerned by that representative action explicitly or tacitly express their wish'.[538]

This book maintains that an expressed will corresponds to the opt-in model, while a tacit will aligns with the opt-out model. However, we concur with Duncan Fairgrieve and Rhonson Salim[539] in questioning the clarity of the term 'tacitly'. As they rightly observe, its use significantly blurs the line between opt-in and opt-out mechanisms, creating ambiguity that may complicate both interpretation and implementation across Member States.

To summarise, the text of Directive 2020/1828 is ambiguous on this crucial point. Specifically, with regard to the class action model - an essential element for the effectiveness of the horizontal collective redress mechanism the Directive seeks to establish - the lack of clarity is problematic. The burden should not fall on National Courts to 'guess' the intention of the EU legislator. Given the importance of legal certainty in this area, we anticipate that preliminary references will be submitted by National Courts to the CJEU to clarify the scope and interpretation of these provisions.

In any case, with regard to redress measures, and based on the initial passage cited above, it appears that the EU legislator has effectively left it to the Member States to determine the appropriate model. As for consumer participation, the Directive provides that consent - whether expressed or tacit - must be given 'after that representative action has been brought'.[540] This marks a departure from the traditional opt-in model, which requires consumers to be identified in advance. While this shift may suggest greater procedural flexibility, it also raises questions about the clarity and consistency of implementation across jurisdictions.

It is worth noting that the European Commission's original proposal stated that Member States should be allowed to require a mandate from individual consumers prior to the issuance of a declaratory judgment or redress order. In this context, the shift introduced by Directive 2020/1828 - allowing the transfer of this 'mandate' to a

534. *See* Article 7(4).
535. *See* Article 7(6).
536. *See* Article 8(3).
537. *See* Article 9(1).
538. *See* Article 9(2) first part (emphasis added).
539. In *Collective Redress in Europe: Moving Forward or Treading Water?*, Cambridge University Press for the British Institute of International and Comparative Law, 2022, pp. 471 and 472.
540. *See* Article 9(2), second part.

point after the action has been filed – originates from the proposal itself. Importantly, this timing adjustment does not constitute a prerequisite for initiating the action but rather reflects a procedural evolution aimed at enhancing flexibility in collective redress mechanisms.

As for consumers who are not resident in the Member State where the representative action is brought, Directive 2020/1828 makes it compulsory for them to join the action in order to benefit from its outcome.[541] In other words, the Directive imposes an opt-in model for non-resident consumers, thereby introducing a territorial distinction in the application of participation mechanisms.

One provision from the European Commission's Proposal that was ultimately omitted from Directive 2020/1828 was the option to issue a declaratory decision – rather than a redress order – regarding the liability of the operator towards consumers harmed by infringements of EU law listed in Annex I, in 'duly justified cases where the quantification of the individual redress to be attributed to each of the consumer concerned by the representative action is complex'.[542] In such cases, consumers would be required to bring a subsequent individual action and quantify the damages themselves. The European Commission acknowledged this in its proposal, suggesting that Member States should ensure these individual actions follow a swift and simplified procedure. However, this appears to be more aspirational than realistic – a true utopia, one might say. In practice, individual consumers often have even fewer resources than representative entities to assess and quantify harm, and certainly far fewer than National Courts themselves.

The European Commission's Proposal made two exceptions to the general rule requiring a mandate from individual consumers. First, when the consumers harmed by the infringement are identifiable and have suffered comparable damage resulting from the same practice during the same period or related to the same purchase, redress should be directed to those consumers – even though obtaining a mandate from them would not be a prerequisite for bringing the action. Second, when the damage suffered by consumers is minor and distributing redress would be disproportionate, no mandate is required, and the redress is instead allocated to public interest purposes that serve the collective interests of consumers.[543] In other words, in such cases, consumers would receive no direct compensation.

In light of the above, the EU legislator was right to reject these elements of the European Commission's Proposal. The stated objective of Directive 2020/1828 is to 'achievement of a high level of consumer protection',[544] and this goal would be fundamentally undermined if consumers were left to shoulder the burden of initiating a second action to claim damages – especially when the calculation of such damages is already widely acknowledged as complex and resource-intensive.

Moreover, the fact that individual damages are typically small is a defining feature of this type of action. Retaining the provisions proposed by the European Commission,

541. *See* Article 9(3).
542. *See* Article 6(2) (emphasis added).
543. *See* Article 6(3).
544. *See* Article 1(1).

such as requiring consumers to bring individual follow-up actions, would have rendered Directive 2020/1828 largely ineffective. Recognising this, the EU legislator has even added a provision stating that 'Member States shall ensure that a redress measure entitles consumers to benefit from the remedies provided by that redress measure without the need to bring a separate action.'[545]

It is clear that the Directive requires any redress measure to describe – if not identify – the consumers covered, or at least the group or class to which they belong.[546] However, it does not provide for access to evidence prior to the filing of a class action. In fact, it only allows the National Court to order the disclosure of evidence by the defendant or a third party at the request of the qualified entity, and only once the latter has already 'provided reasonably available evidence sufficient to support a representative action, and has indicated that additional evidence lies in the control of the defendant or a third party'.[547]

What this book concludes from the above is that the burden of gathering the primary evidence necessary to support a collective compensation claim falls largely on the qualified entity itself. In practice, this means that the entity will often need to identify the affected consumers early on, as they are likely to possess much of the relevant evidence. This book finds this requirement deeply problematic, particularly in the context of competition law, which is the lens through which it assesses the adequacy of Directive 2020/1828. The evidentiary burden is not only substantial but also misaligned with the Directive's stated goal of facilitating access to justice. Without more robust mechanisms for early access to evidence, the effectiveness of collective redress in this domain remains seriously compromised.

This book therefore argues that parties should be allowed to request access to evidence held by the opposing party or a third party at any stage of the proceedings, particularly when the opt-in model is adopted. However, we respectfully disagree with Duncan Fairgrieve and Rhonson Salim[548] in their view that Directive 2020/1828 should have imposed a general obligation on both the defendant and the qualified entity to declare evidence (adverse or otherwise) that they have relating to what is at stake in the action. Such a declaratory obligation would risk conflicting with the principle against self-incrimination. While the proceedings are civil in nature, the underlying claims often stem from infringements that constitute administrative offences. This hybrid character of representative actions – civil in form but quasi-punitive in substance – demands a careful balance between transparency and the protection of fundamental rights.[549]

545. *See* Article 9(6).
546. *See* Article 9(5).
547. *See* Article 18 (emphasis added).
548. In *Collective Redress in Europe: Moving Forward or Treading Water?*, Cambridge University Press for the British Institute of International and Comparative Law, 2022, p. 478.
549. On the balance between the duty to cooperate with the EC and national authorities and companies' rights of defence, *see* Marta Campos, *De novo o direito à não autoincriminação em processos de contraordenação por práticas restritivas da concorrência contra pessoas colectivas*, Revista de Concorrência & Regulação, Lisbon, No. 36, 2018, p. 97.

With regard to the legal effects of final decisions by authorities or National Courts concerning infringements that harm the collective interests of consumers, Directive 2020/1828 falls short of the EU Damages Directive. It merely allows such decisions to be used as evidence, subject to national rules of evidence, without even establishing a rebuttable presumption.[550] On this point, the European Commission's Proposal was more ambitious: it recommended a rebuttable presumption for judgments issued in the Member State where the collective action is brought, and also - remarkably - for judgments from other Member States.[551] This latter provision would have gone beyond the EU Damages Directive, aligning with the approach taken by certain Member States in their transposition of that directive.[552]

With regard to costs, Directive 2020/1828 addresses three key aspects: (i) the loser pays principle,[553] (ii) private financing, and (iii) public financing. In doing so, it goes beyond the scope of the EU Damages Directive, which does not regulate cost-related matters (despite the fact that antitrust litigation is notoriously expensive).[554]

The retention of the loser pays principle was anticipated, as it aligns not only with the European Commission's proposal but also with a long-standing tradition in Europe, particularly within Roman-Germanic legal systems.[555] What raises concern, however, is the following provision: 'in exceptional circumstances, an individual consumer concerned by a representative action for redress measures may be ordered to pay the costs of proceedings that were incurred as a result of the individual consumer's intentional or negligent conduct'.[556] This is a vague and therefore dangerous provision, as it opens the door to a precedent, which is to make an individual consumer liable for the costs of a representative action, without fully clarifying the applicator and running the risk of discouraging consumers from expressly or tacitly expressing their intention to be covered by the action.

As for private third-party funding, Directive 2020/1828 leaves it to the discretion of Member States to determine whether such funding may be permitted in collective actions for redress.[557] While the Directive neither prohibits nor directly regulates this form of financing, it does require Member States to adopt safeguards against potential abuse. Specifically, it emphasises the need to prevent conflicts of interest by ensuring that the financial interests of third-party funders do not compromise the primary objective of protecting consumers' collective interests.[558]

More concretely, the Directive obliges Member States to ensure that: (i) '[t]the decisions of qualified entities in the context of a representative action, including decisions on settlement, are not unduly influenced by a third party in a manner that would be detrimental to the collective interests of the consumers concerned by the

550. *See* Article 15.
551. *See* Article 10(1) and (2).
552. *See* s. 2.3.1.4 above.
553. *See* Article 12(1).
554. *See* s. 2.3.3.3 above.
555. *See* s. 3.6.5.5 below.
556. *See* Article 12(3).
557. *See* Article 10(1) first part.
558. *See* Article 10(1), second part.

representative action'; and (ii) '[t]he representative action is not brought against a defendant that is a competitor of the funding provider or against a defendant on which the funding provider is dependent'.[559] The assessment of these aspects will be carried out by the National Courts, and qualified entities are required to submit a financial summary detailing the sources of funding used to support the class action.[560] In essence, while this directive does not regulate private funding directly, it imposes a transparency obligation regarding its existence. This effectively opens the door to private third-party funding within the EU – a significant development at a time when record levels of funding for collective actions have been reported in both the EU and the UK since 2023.[561]

With regard to public funding, Directive 2020/1828 follows the European Commission's proposal[562] by establishing the general principle that Member States must ensure procedural costs do not prevent qualified entities from effectively exercising their right to bring collective actions for redress.[563] To support this, the EU legislator encourages the creation of public funding mechanisms, which may take the form of: (i) structural support, (ii) limitations on legal costs, and/or (iii) legal aid.[564]

It is not clear what the legislator intended by structural support. Is it meant to be monetary? In other words, does the Directive suggest allocating public funds to finance this type of action, specifically compensation? If so, as discussed below,[565] this book believes such an approach could prove counterproductive.

Limiting legal costs, however, despite also implying a reduction in public revenue, appears to be a reasonable and justified measure. This is particularly true given the nature of the representative entities involved, often under-resourced, and especially in cases where an opt-out model is adopted. Such a model typically entails higher costs but also ensures broader consumer coverage and stronger protection of the right to redress. It is important to note, however, that the bulk of the financial burden in these actions does not stem from legal costs per se but rather from other litigation-related expenses specific to this type of complex and specialised procedure.

Finally, the provision of legal aid in this context appears to be incompatible with the legal frameworks of certain Member States. Extending this recommendation to the field of competition enforcement would likely exacerbate these incompatibilities, as further explored later in this book.[566]

What is more, the EU legislator suggests that Member States establish rules allowing 'qualified entities to require consumers who have expressed their wish to be represented by a qualified entity in a specific representative action for redress measures to

559. *See* Article 10(2).
560. *See* Article 10(3).
561. *See* Edward Turtle, *New EU Class Actions Mechanisms to be Implemented by Christmas*, 11 October 2022, available at New EU Class Actions Mechanisms to be Implemented by Christmas - Lexology.
562. *See* Article 15(1).
563. *See* Article 20(1).
564. *See* Article 20(2).
565. *See* s. 3.6.5.3 below.
566. *Ibid.*

pay a modest entry fee or similar charge in order to participate in that representative action'.[567]

This book understands the rationale behind the suggestion of a modest fee, as mentioned above. However, this should be accompanied by control mechanisms to verify whether the amount collected is actually used to fund the class action. Moreover, this approach appears compatible only with opt-in class actions, which inherently limit its scope. Given this limitation, we do not anticipate that such a fee would generate substantial revenue, certainly not enough to cover the full costs associated with this type of litigation.

The issue of funding is undeniably central in this area. As previously noted, qualified organisations lack the financial capacity to support this type of action, primarily due to their non-profit nature, as required by Directive 2020/1828. The costs associated with class actions are substantial, and such actions remain rare across the EU, largely due to the absence of adequate incentives, particularly financial ones. This funding gap affects not only the private enforcement of competition rules but also the broader enforcement of rights under the EU Treaties, as highlighted by Duncan Fairgrieve and Rhonson Salim.[568]

Finally, Directive 2020/1828 introduces a series of safeguards to prevent potential abuses of litigation in the context of collective redress. In addition to the measures already discussed - such as the requirements for representative entities, the loser pays principle, and safeguards against conflicts of interest in private funding - the Directive requires Member States to establish a preliminary control mechanism. This mechanism should allow for the early dismissal of manifestly unfounded actions, thereby preventing frivolous or abusive claims from proceeding.[569]

In the case of injunctions, the Directive further provides that Member States may require qualified entities to engage in a prior consultation process with the alleged infringer. This process would give the infringer a two-week period to voluntarily cease the infringement before formal proceedings are initiated.[570]

It is worth noting that several Member States already allow for the outright rejection of manifestly unfounded actions, and some even require prior certification of the action before it can proceed.[571] That said, concerns about abusive litigation in this area remain largely theoretical within the EU and, for now, do not appear to constitute a significant issue in practice.

The transposition deadline was 25 December 2022, although the provisions adopted by the Member States to transpose the Directive did not enter into force until 25 June 2023.[572] A large number of MS failed to notify the transposition of Directive 2020/1828 by the above date, and the European Commission announced on 27 January 2023 the

567. *See* Article 20(3).
568. In *Collective Redress in Europe: Moving Forward or Treading Water?*, Cambridge University Press for the British Institute of International and Comparative Law, 2022, p. 470.
569. *See* Article 7(7).
570. *See* Article 8(4).
571. *See* Table 3.1 - Comparison of Antitrust Class Actions in Selected European Jurisdictions, s. 3.4.7 above.
572. *See* Article 24(1).

sending of letters of formal notice.[573] These letters seem to have had an effect because, in the meantime, only Luxembourg has yet to report transposition measures.[574] The first Member State mentioned in the comparative analysis below[575] to take action in this regard was France.[576]

By 26 June 2027, and annually thereafter, Member States are required to report to the European Commission the number and types of class actions concluded within their jurisdiction. This includes details on the nature of the infringements, the parties involved, and the outcomes of those actions. The purpose of this reporting obligation is to enable the Commission to assess the effectiveness of Directive 2020/1828. Based on this assessment, the Commission must present its main findings to the European Parliament, the Council, and the EESC and may accompany the report with a legislative proposal, if deemed appropriate.[577]

Given the complexity of the issues involved and the wide divergence in national rules, as well as the absence of collective redress mechanisms in many Member States, it was anticipated that the transposition of Directive 2020/1828 would be challenging. For Member States that already had collective redress instruments in place, this directive demanded a degree of legislative 'gymnastics' to integrate the new provisions into existing, well-established procedures. For those without any prior framework for collective actions, Directive 2020/1828 entailed many legislative changes.

For those Member States that previously lacked collective redress mechanisms, the obligation to implement such systems under Directive 2020/1828 represented a significant advancement in consumer rights protection. Another key contribution of the Directive was its requirement for Member States to adopt anti-abuse safeguards in the context of private funding. This has compelled national legislators to address an area that was often underregulated, thereby introducing much-needed legal certainty.

While public funding remains a possible alternative, it may be adequate only for class actions concerning the specific consumer matters covered by this directive. In contrast, when it comes to competition law enforcement, given its complexity and the high costs typically involved, serious doubts remain as to whether public funding alone would be sufficient to ensure effective access to justice.[578]

At this point, it is important to recall that the primary objective of analysing the regime established by Directive 2020/1828 was to assess its suitability for the collective enforcement of competition law. If it were deemed appropriate, the logical course of action would be to advocate for the extension of this regime to antitrust rules, rather than proposing the creation of a separate, sector-specific framework. It is also worth noting that the inclusion of competition law within the scope of Directive 2020/1828

573. Namely: Belgium, Bulgaria, the Czech Republic, Denmark, Germany, Estonia, Ireland, Greece, Spain, France, Croatia, Italy, Cyprus, Latvia, Luxembourg, Malta, Austria, Poland, Portugal, Romania, Slovenia, Slovakia, Finland and Sweden – *see* Non-transposition of EU legislation: Commission takes action (europa.eu).
574. *See* https://eur-lex.europa.eu/legal-content/EN/NIM/?uri=CELEX:32020L1828.
575. *See* s. 3.4 below.
576. *See* Avis sur une proposition de loi relative au régime juridique des actions de groupe (conseil-etat.fr).
577. *See* Article 23.
578. *See* s. 3.6.5.3 below.

was even proposed by the IMCO (Committee on the Internal Market and Consumer Protection),[579] although this suggestion was ultimately not adopted.

Although Directive 2020/1828 undoubtedly represents progress in advancing the right to collective redress within the EU - particularly by moving away from the previously dominant preference, especially by the European Commission, for the opt-in model (except for consumers residing in other Member States) - it can still be regarded as a missed opportunity. This is not only because it explicitly excludes competition law, an area where collective redress may be the only viable path for consumers to obtain compensation for complex and widespread violations, but also because it fails to ensure legal certainty. The Directive's vague and ambiguous language, coupled with the broad discretion[580] granted to Member States, is likely to perpetuate the current fragmented landscape of collective action mechanisms across the EU (mechanisms that remain underutilised and of limited effectiveness).

In any case, while it is clear that, as in other areas covered by Directive 2020/1828, a single infringement in competition law can affect a large number of individuals - and experience shows that SMEs and consumers rarely pursue damages due to the disproportionate cost of legal action relative to the individual harm suffered - we acknowledge that competition law presents unique challenges. These include, in particular, the issues of awareness and the burden of proving the infringement, which are less prevalent in other areas of consumer protection.

Given that competition law has historically been the area where access to justice is most at risk, due to the persistent underdevelopment of private enforcement mechanisms, and considering that victims of antitrust infringements collectively bear estimated annual damages of around EUR 23 billion,[581] the EU legislator's decision to exclude collective redress from this domain is difficult to justify. This omission is particularly striking given that it was precisely the challenges of enforcing competition law that initially prompted the European Commission to explore collective redress at the EU level. It is no coincidence that much of the academic and policy discourse surrounding Directive 2020/1828 begins with references to antitrust damages actions and the Commission's foundational White and Green Papers on the subject.[582]

Moreover, the overarching framework of Directive 2020/1828 once again reflects a persistent apprehension about aligning too closely with the North American model of

579. In an opinion addressed to the CAJ on 23 November 2018, *see* Amendment 63 - PR_COD_1amCom (europa.eu).

580. *See* Alexander Biard and Stefaan Voet, *Collective Redress in the EU: Will It Finally Come True? in Class Actions in Europe – Holy Grail or a Wrong Trail?*, Alan Uzelac and Stefaan Voet (eds), Springer, 2021, p. 296.

581. *See Commission Staff Working Paper Document Executive Summary of the Impact Assessment Damages actions for breach of the EU antitrust rules Accompanying the proposal for a Directive of the European Parliament and of the Council on certain rules governing actions for damages under national law for infringements of the competition law provisions of the Member States and of the European Union (SWD/2013/0204 final)*, pt. 8.

582. *See*, for example, Diego Agulló, *Directive 2020/1828 on Representative Actions for the Protection of the Collective Interests of Consumers: An Overview*, UNIO – EU Law Journal, vol. 8, No. 1, December 2022, pp. 127-142, p. 128 https://doi.org/10.21814/unio.8.1.4521.

collective redress – an approach that has often been criticised by market actors[583] (a concern this book shares). This cautious stance continues to shape EU legislative choices, even at the expense of more robust and effective enforcement mechanisms.

Finally, as Alexander Biard and Stefaan Voet[584] rightly observe, Directive 2020/1828 also falls short in promoting coherence across the EU. It treats final decisions declaring violations of EU law merely as one piece of evidence among others, rather than granting them a presumptive effect. This stands in stark contrast to the approach adopted in the EU Damages Directive, which confers such decisions with a presumptive effect in follow-on actions. The inconsistency between these two legislative instruments underscores a missed opportunity to strengthen legal certainty and harmonisation in the field of collective redress.

In short, Directive 2020/1828 remains limited in scope and imposes restrictive safeguards on the availability of collective redress mechanisms, reflecting a persistent reluctance to adopt a model that might resemble the US system.[585]

As Nuno A. Pires Salpico aptly notes[586] regarding the financing of collective actions (an issue this book will explore in more detail below), it is not honest to talk about abusive litigation when there is a lack of consumer protection actions without litigation funding. Fear of the consequences of these mechanisms kills enforcement and empties the true content protected by the rules of competition law. This applies, with the necessary adaptations, to many of the restrictive measures discussed above. This book raises the question: what sense does it make to centre the legal solution on preventing abuse when the prevailing reality is one of scarcity?

Furthermore, the risks of leaving it to the discretion of Member States to either extend the transposition of Directive 2020/1828 or to introduce new collective action rules in the field of competition law are readily apparent. Chief among these are: (i) the risk of inaction and (ii) the emergence of fragmented and inconsistent legal frameworks, where consumer protection under general consumer law diverges significantly from that under competition law. Such divergence not only undermines the coherence of the EU legal order but also fails to account for the specificities of competition law, thereby jeopardising the EU principles of effectiveness and equivalence.

It should be noted that Articles 101 and 102 of the TFEU confer rights not only on consumers but also on businesses. This dual scope justifies greater protection for SMEs in this context, as they often resemble, to a certain extent, consumers in terms of financial capacity and the scale of harm suffered.

583. *See* Alexander Biard and Stefaan Voet, *Collective Redress in the EU: Will It Finally Come True? in Class Actions in Europe: Holy Grail or a Wrong Trail?*, Alan Uzelac and Stefaan Voet (eds), Springer, 2021, p. 288.
584. In *Collective Redress in the EU: Will It Finally Come True? in Class Actions in Europe – Holy Grail or a Wrong Trail?*, Alan Uzelac and Stefaan Voet (eds), Springer, 2021, p. 295.
585. *See* Christina Renner and Cécile Manong, *Collective Actions in the EU: The Past, the Present, the Future*, Thomson Reuters Practical Law, 1 March 2020.
586. In *The Effectiveness of Private Enforcement of Competition Law: Deterrent, Collective Actions and Third-party Ligation Funding*, Revista de Concorrência & Regulação, Lisbon, 45, 2021, p. 123.

As Barry Rodger, Miguel Sousa Ferro and Francisco Marcos have pointed out,[587] until quite recently, private enforcement in the EU aimed at securing compensation for damages resulting from competition law infringements, particularly those affecting consumers and SMEs, was virtually non-existent. More recently, Maria José Azar-Baud and Fabienne Jault-Seseke have also observed that,[588] in terms of access to justice, protection against mass harm, and the right to compensation, Europe is still in search of mechanisms that offer more (if not better) benefits to its citizens.

The reality is that even when the European Commission issues decisions declaring infringements of competition rules, very few are followed by damages actions. As David Ashon has clearly noted,[589] despite the current reluctance to adopt EU-level legislation, there is a direct correlation between the absence of class actions and the ineffective enforcement of EU competition law. This gap highlights a systemic weakness in ensuring that victims can effectively exercise their right to compensation.

For all the reasons outlined above – and without disregarding the important contribution of Directive 2020/1828, particularly in prompting Member States to legislate on collective actions and to reflect on the role of private litigation funding – this book contends that merely extending this directive's scope to include competition law would be insufficient. As currently formulated, its provisions fall short of the measures necessary to ensure the effective private enforcement of EU competition law, especially in relation to SMEs and consumers.

3.3.8 European Parliament Resolution on 'Responsible Private Funding of Litigation', the EPRS Study, and the 2025 Mapping Exercise

The importance of third-party litigation funding was formally acknowledged by the European Parliament on 13 September 2022, when it issued a set of recommendations to the European Commission on this matter. According to the Parliament, 'commercial third party litigation funding (TPLF) is a growing practice whereby private investors ("litigation funders") who are not a party to a dispute invest for profit in legal proceedings and pay legal and other expenses, in exchange for a share of any eventual award; whereas collective redress is only one type of litigation in which TPLF is currently used, with other examples being arbitration, insolvency proceedings, investment recovery, anti-trust claims and others'.[590]

587. In *The EU Antitrust Damages Directive: Transposition in the Member States*, Oxford University Press, 2018, pp. 320 and 321.
588. In *Private Enforcement of Competition Law in Europe: Directive 2014/104/EU and Beyond*, Rafael Amaro (ed.), Bruylant, 2021, p. 87.
589. In *Competition Damages Action in the EU: Law and Practice*, economics contribution from Frank Maier-Rigaud and Ulrich Schawalbe, Elgar, *Competition Law and Practice*, 2nd ed., 2018, p. 284.
590. European Parliament resolution of 13 September 2022 with recommendations to the Commission on responsible private funding of litigation (2020/2130(INL)), available at Texts adopted - Responsible private funding of litigation - Tuesday 13 September 2022 (europa.eu), Recital B. (emphasis added).

This Resolution was preceded by a study (with the same title)[591] conducted by the European Parliamentary Research Service (EPRS) and finalised in March 2021. The study examined the evolution of private litigation funding across the EU and its normative foundations, particularly in the context of ensuring access to justice. It employed a multidisciplinary approach, combining legal-normative analysis, comparative law, and qualitative research. The study concluded that there is a clear need for EU-level regulation of private litigation funding to ensure a balanced and coherent system – especially in the area of collective redress – by weighing its advantages and disadvantages.[592]

The question of whether private litigation funding should be regulated will be addressed in detail later;[593] nevertheless, this book concurs with the EPRS in recognising that the principal benefit of TPLF (third-party litigation funding) lies in its ability to enhance access to justice, particularly for consumers and SMEs, in collective redress cases. By assuming the financial burden of litigation, funders enable parties with legitimate claims to bring actions before National Courts that they would otherwise be unable or unwilling to pursue, either due to a lack of financial resources or because the expected monetary return does not justify the cost of litigation.

How can one be certain that the claims receiving funding are legitimate? As the EPRS Study rightly points out,[594] the due diligence conducted by litigation funders serves as a natural filter, ensuring that only cases with a reasonable prospect of success are selected for funding. Without such prospects, funders would have no incentive to invest, given the financial risks involved.

With regard to the potential risks associated with TPLF, the EPRS Study identifies four key concerns: (i) the risk of overwhelming the judicial system with excessive litigation; (ii) the possibility of conflicts of interest – particularly where there is a pre-existing relationship between the funder and the legal representatives of either party, or where the funder's control over legal fees may influence litigation strategy, including decisions on settlement, to the detriment of class members; (iii) the imposition of excessive remuneration by funders, which could deprive injured parties of a substantial portion of their compensation; and (iv) legal uncertainty surrounding the operation of TPLF in opt-out class actions, where class members are not individually identified in advance and have not explicitly agreed to share a portion of their compensation with the funder.[595]

In light of these risks, the study proposes a series of safeguards to ensure that TPLF operates in a fair, transparent, and balanced manner:

591. *See* Jérôme Saulnier, Klaus Müller and Ivona Koronthalyova, *Responsible Private Funding of Litigation*, European Parliamentary Research Service, European Added Value Unit, PE 662.612 – March 2021, available at EPRS_STU(2021)662612_EN.pdf (europa.eu).

592. *Ibid.*, pp. 90 and 91.

593. *See* s. 3.6.5.1.2 below.

594. *See* Jérôme Saulnier, Klaus Müller and Ivona Koronthalyova, *Responsible Private Funding of Litigation*, European Parliamentary Research Service, European Added Value Unit, PE 662.612 – March 2021, available at EPRS_STU(2021)662612_EN.pdf (europa.eu), pp. 88 and 90.

595. *Ibid.*, pp. 80 and 90.

(1) Incorporation of TPLF regulation into the Code of Conduct for European Lawyers.[596]
(2) Adoption of a legislative instrument at the EU level to prevent forum shopping by funders in cross-border disputes – particularly where national regimes differ in terms of funder establishment, applicable law, and procedural rules. This instrument should include:
   (i) clear definition of 'third-party funder' and 'third-party funding';
   (ii) requirements for insurance coverage and/or capital adequacy for funders established in the EU;
   (iii) measures to encourage transparency in funder remuneration rates, and potentially impose caps to balance private autonomy with the public interest in ensuring access to justice.
   (iv) a mandatory disclosure obligation, along with sanctions for non-compliance, requiring parties to inform both the National Court and the opposing party of the use of private funding and the identity of the funder.
   (v) a duty on funders not to interfere with the claimant's decision-making, including decisions regarding settlement.
   (vi) a provision allowing defendants, in the event of a successful defence, to seek recovery of legal costs directly from the funder if the funded party fails to pay.
   (vii) clarification of how funder remuneration should operate in opt-out class actions, for example, through the establishment of a common fund.
(3) Promotion of self-regulation mechanisms among litigation funders.[597]

Fundamentally, the EPRS Study appears to 'point in all directions', making it difficult to discern a coherent regulatory stance. On the one hand, it recommends the adoption of EU-level legislation; on the other, it simultaneously endorses self-regulation – an apparent contradiction that weakens the normative clarity of its proposals. Moreover, the study's emphasis on potential conflicts of interest between lawyers and their clients raises questions. It is, in fact, quite common for a pre-existing relationship to exist between the funder and the claimant's or defendant's legal representatives, as lawyers are typically the ones familiar with litigation funding mechanisms and are best positioned to connect clients with funders. Additionally, in the event of a settlement, it is both expected and reasonable that the remuneration of both the funder and the lawyer be proportionate to their respective investments in the case.

596. Adopted at the plenary session of the Conseil des Barreaux européens (CCBE) on 28 October 1988 and translated into Portuguese by Deliberação No. 2511/2007 OA (2.ª série), of 27 December 2007/Ordem dos Advogados. General Council, available at Code of Ethics for European Lawyers - Portuguese Bar Association (oa.pt).

597. *See* Jérôme Saulnier, Klaus Müller and Ivona Koronthalyova, *Responsible Private Funding of Litigation*, European Parliamentary Research Service, European Added Value Unit, PE 662.612 – March 2021, available at EPRS_STU(2021)662612_EN.pdf (europa.eu), p. 91.

The European Parliament endorsed most of the EPRS recommendations, including the call to regulate TPLF, to encourage its broader use across the EU while acknowledging the significant financial disparities that often exist between parties.[598]

As Kai Hüschelrath aptly observes,[599] the costs associated with the private enforcement of competition law must be justified by the benefits it yields. This book will delve deeper into this issue.[600] However, it is important to emphasise that, as previously noted, for injured parties with limited financial resources or whose individual damages are relatively minor, achieving a favourable cost-benefit balance is often unattainable, particularly in complex areas such as competition law.

This reflects the classic 'David versus Goliath' scenario.[601] Opt-out class actions can involve costs amounting to millions of euros – or dollars, as the United States remains the prime stage for this type of complex, lengthy, and highly expensive litigation.[602]

The aforementioned costs stem, as previously noted, from the high level of expertise required to enforce competition law through private actions, particularly given that private claimants lack the investigative powers available to public authorities. First and foremost, proving an infringement of competition law necessitates defining the relevant market, which demands not only specialised legal expertise but also economic and sector-specific knowledge. This typically involves engaging lawyers and expert consultants, whose fees are often substantial.

Depending on the nature of the case, thousands of documents may need to be produced and analysed. In terms of economic evidence, it is not uncommon for each party to submit its own expert report. Trials – especially the examination of witnesses and experts, who must respond to extensive documentation – can stretch over several months. When factoring in the time from the initial filing to final appeals, some antitrust cases can span years or even decades.

Beyond market definition, claimants must also establish the infringement, the harm suffered, and the causal link between the two. Even in follow-on actions, where the infringement has already been established by a public authority, claimants must still

---

598. Indeed, for the European Parliament, 'whereas TPLF could, if properly regulated, be used more often as a tool to support access to justice, especially in countries where legal costs are very high or for women and marginalised groups with additional funding barriers; whereas TPLF could also increasingly help to ensure that public interest cases are brought to court and to reduce significant economic imbalances that exist between corporations and those citizens seeking redress, and thereby ensure appropriate corporate accountability', *see* European Parliament resolution of 13 September 2022 with recommendations to the Commission on responsible private funding of litigation (2020/2130(INL)), available at Texts adopted - Responsible private funding of litigation - Tuesday 13 September 2022 (europa.eu), Recital C (emphasis added).
599. In *Is it Worth all the Trouble?: The Costs and Benefits of Antitrust Enforcement*, Discussion Paper No. 08-107, Centre for European Economic Research (ZEW) of Germany, available at DP 08-107 (zew.de), p. 22.
600. *See* s. 3.6.5 below.
601. *See* Jason Levine, *The Role of Litigation Finance in Antitrust Lawsuits*, 30 March 2022, available at The role of litigation finance in antitrust lawsuits (omnibridgeway.com).
602. *See* s. 3.4.1 below.

prove causation and quantify damages. These cases may also involve multi-jurisdictional or EU-level enforcement, which introduces additional complexity, including the need for translation of legal and evidentiary materials.

When large companies are on one side and SMEs, consumers, or consumer associations on the other, it becomes relatively easy for the former to deploy large-scale litigation strategies (often involving substantial financial resources) to pressure the injured party into withdrawing or settling the case.

Private financing thus emerges as a viable solution to enable the effective private enforcement of competition law in the context described above. Such arrangements can be mutually beneficial: the funder gains a return on investment, the lawyer is incentivised to pursue litigation, and the injured party is empowered to exercise their right to redress, despite the financial and procedural barriers that might otherwise prevent them from doing so.

This is why such funding agreements have seen exponential growth in Europe and are increasingly common in the US. However, their use remains limited. In the EU, private litigation funding is still largely unregulated. Existing regulatory frameworks and voluntary codes of conduct have not been widely adopted by funders, leaving claimants, particularly those with limited resources, significantly exposed and without sufficient safeguards.

Furthermore, this book shares the view of the EPRS and the European Parliament that leaving the regulation of TPLF entirely to the Member States risks creating fragmentation and regulatory imbalances across the EU.[603] At the same time, the provisions on funding set out in Directive 2020/1828 are limited in scope and do not extend to actions falling outside its framework, leaving significant gaps in oversight and protection.

Accordingly, the European Parliament has called on the European Commission to closely monitor and assess the development of TPLF across the Member States. Moreover, after 25 June 2023 and taking into account the practical effects of Directive 2020/1828, the Parliament has urged the Commission to present, on the basis of Article 114 of the TFEU, a legislative proposal establishing common minimum standards at the EU level for the TPLF.[604]

In response to the European Parliament's Resolution, the European Commission did not propose a directive (at least yet) but stated, on 30 November 2022, that TPLF is addressed within the Directive 2020/1828 framework.[605] Since Member States had until 25 December 2022 to transpose the Directive into national law, the Commission indicated it would only assess the need for further regulation of TPLF after this implementation period had ended. Following that, the Commission planned to initiate

603. *See* Litigation Funding: New Rules on the Way? (mccannfitzgerald.com).
604. European Parliament resolution of 13 September 2022 with recommendations to the Commission on responsible private funding of litigation (2020/2130(INL)), available at Texts adopted - Responsible private funding of litigation - Tuesday 13 September 2022 (europa.eu), pt. 14, part one.
605. *See* s. 3.3.7 above.

a mapping exercise to gather information on national regulations and practices, commission an external study, and conduct stakeholder consultations.[606]

The mapping exercise referred to above was published on 21 March 2025[607] and includes an analysis of the 'degree of compatibility of TPLF regulation with the European Parliament Resolution'. This assessment is based on reports from national experts evaluating whether their legal systems contain provisions that are similar or equivalent to the measures outlined in the draft directive annexed to the Resolution. The findings[608] revealed that, in most cases (an exception, for example, is the fact that Germany has imposed a 10% cap on the funder's share in redress actions),[609] no specific regulation on TPLF is in force across the Member States (without prejudice to the application of general contractual principles) - and Greece has even prohibited TPLF in representative actions.[610]

It is important to note that the European Parliament's Resolution was not driven by the intention to promote or simplify the use of TPLF through harmonised rules across Member States. On the contrary, the recommendation to propose a directive was rooted in MEP (Members of the European Parliament)'s concerns that, in the absence of regulation, litigation funders were engaging in abusive practices, such as withdrawing funding mid-proceeding or claiming disproportionate shares of awarded compensation. Additional concerns included a lack of transparency, where neither the National Court nor the opposing party was aware that a funding agreement had been concluded, as well as the potential implications of applying such agreements to opt-out collective actions.[611]

The concern regarding the need to clarify how third-party funding operates in the context of opt-out collective actions is well founded, given that the individuals represented in such actions are not parties to the funding agreements. However, it is important to note that this model of collective redress remains an exception within the EU.[612]

Furthermore, since litigation funding is closely linked to collective redress mechanisms, we respectfully disagree with Johanna Weißbach's view that it is positive for the European Parliament to focus on the risk of excessive litigation. In our assessment, the EU is far from facing such a scenario, and we anticipate that the practical impact of Directive 2020/1828 will remain limited.[613]

---

606. *See* https://www.europarl.europa.eu/legislative-train/theme-legal-affairs-juri/file-third-party-funding-of-civil-litigation.
607. *See* Final Report EC Mapping TPLF in the EU, 21 March 2025, available at https://commission.europa.eu/strategy-and-policy/policies/justice-and-fundamental-rights/civil-justice/civil-and-commercial-law/third-party-litigation-funding-tplf_en.
608. *See* pp. 9-11.
609. *See* p. 70.
610. *See* p. 692.
611. *See* Emilie Jones and Johanna Weißbach, *EU Plans to Regulate Third-Party Litigation Funders Meet Mixed Response*, 12 January 2023, available at EU plans to regulate third-party litigation funders meet mixed response | ICLG.com Briefings.
612. *See* s. 3.4.3 below.
613. *See* s. 3.3.7 above.

Building on the above, the European Parliament appended to its Resolution a set of recommendations in the form, as previously referred, of a draft directive,[614] aimed at ensuring TPLF facilitates meaningful access to justice for claimants and beneficiaries, while also holding funders accountable. This draft proposal outlines minimum standards applicable to commercial litigation funders and their authorised activities. It also introduces safeguards designed to prevent: (i) conflicts of interest, (ii) abusive litigation practices, and (iii) the disproportionate allocation of compensation to funders.[615]

A first positive point of this draft is that it applies to all types of actions, regardless of their nature.[616] While the text draws on certain concepts from Directive 2020/1828, such as the notion of 'qualified entity',[617] it distinguishes it from 'claimant', defined as any natural or legal person who initiates or intends to initiate proceedings before a National Court or an administrative authority.[618] It also differentiates the 'intended beneficiary', as a person entitled to a share in the outcome of the case, whose interests are represented by the funded claimant or the qualified entity bringing the action.[619]

The draft proposal for a directive also defines the concepts of: (i) 'litigation funder' as any for-profit company that enters into this type of agreement and acts in the respective proceedings in that capacity only (and is neither a party, nor a lawyer, nor a provider of regulated insurance services to one of the parties), with the main aim of receiving remuneration for the investment it makes by making funds available in relation to the proceedings or achieving a competitive advantage in a specific market; and (ii) 'third-party funding agreement', under which a litigation funder agrees to fund all or part of the procedural costs in exchange for part of the monetary amount awarded to the claimant or a success fee, in order to reimburse the litigation funder for the funding it has provided and, where appropriate, to cover its remuneration for the service provided, based in whole or in part on the outcome of the proceedings.

This book has outlined the above definitions because their inclusion significantly enhances legal certainty in an area that has long suffered from ambiguity. This uncertainty is largely rooted in the EU's cautious stance towards TPLF, often shaped by a near-demonisation of the North American model. As a result, this financing mechanism has been met with scepticism, sometimes even questioning its ethical foundations.

However, there is still a lack of clarity on what additional objectives the litigation funder might pursue beyond financial remuneration. Specifically, it remains unclear what the European Parliament meant by 'obtaining a competitive advantage in a specific market'. The underlying principle is that funders should remain at arm's length

614. European Parliament resolution of 13 September 2022 with recommendations to the Commission on responsible private funding of litigation (2020/2130(INL)), available at Texts adopted - Responsible private funding of litigation - Tuesday 13 September 2022 (europa.eu), pt. 14 part two.
615. *See* Article 1.
616. *See* Article 2.
617. *See* Article 3f).
618. *See* Article 3b).
619. *See* Article 3d).

from the litigation itself to prevent conflicts of interest and undue external influence on the judicial process. Notably, the Parliament acknowledges[620] that one of the key risks the proposed directive seeks to mitigate – based on experiences from other jurisdictions, particularly the US – is the possibility of third-party funders steering litigation to serve their own economic interests. This concern appears to contradict the notion of funders seeking competitive market advantages.

Moreover, the application of the concept of a success fee in this context raises questions within the EU framework. Traditionally, a success fee implies a remuneration agreed upon in advance – similar to how lawyers are compensated for their legal services.[621] While various business models exist for TPLF,[622] it is worth noting that, in a broader sense, lawyers have historically financed cases themselves, often by charging symbolic fees in anticipation of a success-based payment. In jurisdictions where contingency fees are permitted, such as the US, lawyers frequently act as the litigation funders or share the financial burden with dedicated funding companies.[623]

Still within the scope of definitions, it is worth noting that the draft proposal for a directive does not define 'defendant'. Moreover, its provisions appear to assume that litigation funding is exclusively available to claimants. While this may be more common (particularly in competition law, where defendants are typically economically robust companies), it is not unprecedented for defendants to receive third-party funding, as seen in jurisdictions such as the US. This implicit assumption introduces a bias in the draft. Indeed, this concern has been raised by the CCBE,[624] a criticism this book shares. The scope of the proposed directive should therefore be broadened to explicitly include defendants as potential recipients of TPLF.

The European Parliament ultimately leaves it to the discretion of Member States to determine whether such funding arrangements should be permitted.[625] However, as previously discussed, in the context of class actions, particularly those involving breaches of competition law, the issue of litigation costs presents a significant barrier to access to justice. Allowing each Member State to decide independently whether to permit private litigation funding risks creating disparities in access to justice across the EU.

---

620. *See*, for example, European Parliament resolution of 13 September 2022 with recommendations to the Commission on responsible private funding of litigation (2020/2130(INL)), available at Texts adopted - Responsible private funding of litigation - Tuesday 13 September 2022 (europa.eu), Recital 2.
621. *See* s. 3.6.5.4 below.
622. *See* Duarte Gorjão Henriques, *Third Party Funding or the Financing of Litigation by Third Parties in Portugal*, Revista da Ordem dos Advogados, vol. 75, No. 3 (2015), pp. 573-624, pp. 576 and 577.
623. *See* Christopher Hodges, John Peysner and Angus Nurse, *Litigation Funding: Status and Issues*, Oxford Legal Studies Research Paper No. 55/2012, September 2012, p. 116.
624. *See CCBE first comments on the European Parliament's recommendations to the Commission on Responsible private funding of litigation*, 13 May 2022, available at EN_DEON_20220513_CCBE-comments-on-the-European-Parliament-s-Recommendations-to-the-Commission-on-Responsible-private-funding-of-litigation.pdf, p. 3.
625. *See* European Parliament resolution of 13 September 2022 with recommendations to the Commission on responsible private funding of litigation (2020/2130(INL)), available at Texts adopted - Responsible private funding of litigation - Tuesday 13 September 2022 (europa.eu), Article 4(1).

To address potential ethical concerns – such as attempts by funders, either independently or in collaboration with lawyers, to influence the outcome of the litigation – the European Parliament proposes that Member States permitting this type of funding be required to implement an 'authorisation system'. This system would be overseen by an independent supervisory authority or department designated by the Member State, responsible for granting, suspending, or revoking authorisations for litigation funders and monitoring their activities.[626] Furthermore, once a funder is authorised by a supervisory body in one Member State, that authorisation must be mutually recognised by other Member States, thereby allowing the funder to operate across borders within the EU.[627]

An interesting note is that the European Parliament does not propose that litigation funders be prohibited from engaging in other activities, such as providing legal or economic services. This position is reflected in Article 4(3) of the draft directive: '[w]here litigation funders are also providers of other legal, financial or claims management services supervised by another authority within the Union, this Directive shall be without prejudice to any system of supervision and authorisation that exists in relation to those other services'. Once again, the European Parliament leaves it to the discretion of Member States to decide whether consultancies that provide legal services[628] – or even law firms – may simultaneously act as litigation funders.[629]

The European Parliament's decision to leave open the possibility for litigation funders to combine funding activities with the provision of other services (particularly legal and economic) is consistent with Directive 2006/123/EC.[630] Specifically, Article 25 of this directive allows Member States to determine whether to permit multidisciplinary practices (MDPs) in professions governed by specific deontological rules, as well as to regulate them accordingly.[631] This approach reflects a broader trend towards

626. *See* Article 4(2).
627. *See* Article 5(2).
628. *See* Paulo Castro Rangel, *Advocacia e Preconceito*, Revista da Ordem dos Advogados (ROA) Year 2002 Year 62, vol. II, April 2002: it was then that the auditing companies took over, with their armies of young economists, tax experts and lawyers. By the nature of things, auditing cannot be done without a legal component. The same goes for firms involved in investment, bankruptcy, property brokerage or architecture. As a result, these firms end up providing a whole host of typical legal services in a multidisciplinary, complementary way. On the brink of illegality, without these lawyers, legal advice would be left (as it so often is) in the hands of mere laymen.
629. In Portugal, for example, previously according to Article 213.7 of the Portuguese Bar Association Statute, available at https://portal.oa.pt/ordem/regras-profissionais/estatuto-da-ordem-dos-advogados/, law firms were not allowed to carry out their activity directly or indirectly in any type of association or integration with other professions, activities and entities whose corporate purpose is not the exclusive practice of law. This prohibition was repealed in 2024.
630. Of the European Parliament and of the Council of 12 December 2006 on services in the internal market.
631. This article states that '1. Member States shall ensure that providers are not made subject to requirements which oblige them to exercise a given specific activity exclusively or which restrict the exercise jointly or in partnership of different activities. However, the following providers may be made subject to such requirements: (a) the regulated professions, in so far as is justified in order to guarantee compliance with the rules governing professional ethics and conduct, which vary according to the specific nature of each profession, and is necessary in order to ensure their independence and impartiality; (...) 2. Where multidisciplinary activities

the progressive liberalisation of the EU framework for regulated professions, including the legal profession,[632] as driven by both the EU legislator and the case law of the ECJ.[633]

There are also voices within the legal profession advocating for multidisciplinary practices in contrast to the position of many professional bodies, particularly bar associations which they accuse of economic protectionism. These critics argue that appeals to values such as professionalism, independence, and the public interest often serve as rhetorical tools to defend entrenched interests, much like any trade union or lobbying group.[634] In response to these 'winds of change', several authors continue to emphasise that the legal profession's core foundation lies in its independence - not only from other actors in the justice system but also from political, economic, judicial, media, and even client influence.[635]

Focusing on the role of the financier or funding entity, we believe that it should not coincide with that of the lawyer or law firm, given the distinct functions and remuneration models of these two actors. It is important to recall that the Romano-Germanic legal tradition, followed by most EU Member States, prohibits *quota litis* agreements, unlike success fees, which are permitted under certain conditions. Whether lifting this prohibition is a necessary step to address the limited exercise of the right to redress for infringements of competition law by consumers and SMEs in the EU is a question this book will examine further below.[636]

Regarding the requirements for the authorisation of litigation funders mentioned above, the European Parliament, unlike Directive 2020/1828, does not differentiate between national and cross-border litigation. While Member States may impose additional conditions, the Parliament proposes that third-party funders must meet the following core criteria:

---

between providers referred to in points (a) and (b) of paragraph 1 are authorised, Member States shall ensure the following: (a) that conflicts of interest and incompatibilities between certain activities are prevented; (b) that the independence and impartiality required for certain activities is secured; (c) that the rules governing professional ethics and conduct for different activities are compatible with one another, especially as regards matters of professional secrecy.'

632. *See* George C. Nnona, *Multidisciplinary Practice in the International Context: Realigning the Perspective on the European Union's Regulatory Regime*, Cornell International Law Journal, vol. 37, No. 1, 2004, Article 4, pp. 129 et seq.

633. *See*, for example, *EC v. Republic of Austria*, supported by the Federal Republic of Germany, of 29 July 2019, Case C-209/18 (restriction of multidisciplinary activities for companies of civil engineers and patent agents) and *EC v. Kingdom of Belgium*, of 27 February 2020, Case C-384/18 (prohibition of the joint pursuit of the activity of accountant with that of insurance broker or agent, real estate agent or any banking or financial services activity). C-384/18 (prohibition on the joint pursuit of the profession of accountant with that of insurance broker or agent, real estate agent or any banking or financial services activity, as well as the joint pursuit of the profession of accountant with any craft, agricultural or commercial activity).

634. *See*, for example, Daniel R. Fischel, *Multidisciplinary Practice*, The Business Lawyer, vol. 55, No. 3, May 2000, pp. 951-974, p. 974.

635. *See*, for example, Vasco Marques Correia, *O Logro das Sociedades ditas Multidisciplinares*, available at https://www.oa.pt/upl/%7Bc7112026-0691-483e-8bc8-880eefd42049%7D.pdf, p. 6.

636. *See* s. 3.6.5.4 below.

(1) *Registered office:* maintain their registered office in the Member State where authorisation is sought.
(2) *Applicable law:* commit to concluding third-party funding agreements governed by the law of the Member State where the legal action is initiated, or, if different, the law of the Member State of the claimant or the beneficiaries.
(3) *Governance and compliance:* demonstrate the existence of appropriate procedures and governance structures to ensure continuous compliance with the Directive's provisions - particularly those concerning transparency and fiduciary duties - and establish internal mechanisms to prevent conflicts of interest with defendants.
(4) *Capital adequacy*: fulfil the capital adequacy requirements set out in the Directive.
(5) *Fiduciary oversight*: certify that they have the necessary governance frameworks and procedures in place to uphold and respect the fiduciary obligations established by the Directive.[637]

One particularly noteworthy requirement is point (4), which concerns capital adequacy.[638] After all, there is little value in seeking litigation funding if the funder lacks the financial capacity to support the case. Therefore, litigation funding organisations must consistently maintain sufficient liquidity to fully cover the foreseeable party costs in all the cases they choose to fund. This ensures that claimants are not left exposed to financial risk due to undercapitalised funders and reinforces the credibility and reliability of third-party financing arrangements.

To strengthen compliance with capital adequacy requirements, the European Parliament proposes that National Courts and administrative authorities be empowered, upon a claimant's request supported by specific and justified concerns, to require litigation funders to provide a financial guarantee covering the anticipated costs of proceedings.[639] In addition, the Parliament recommends that funders be obligated to confirm, or formally attest, that an insurance scheme is in place to fully cover, if necessary: (i) the financing of all stages of the legal process to which they have committed, including trial and any subsequent appeals; and (ii) the payment of all debts arising under the funding agreement as they become due and enforceable.[640]

Finally, the draft directive allows Member States to establish a 'specific insurance fund', managed and financed by the state through annual contributions from authorised litigation funders, to cover these costs in the event of a funder's insolvency during ongoing proceedings.[641]

---

637. *See* European Parliament resolution of 13 September 2022 with recommendations to the Commission on responsible private funding of litigation (2020/2130(INL)), available at Texts adopted - Responsible private funding of litigation - Tuesday 13 September 2022 (europa.eu), Article 5(1).
638. *See* Article 5(1)(d).
639. *See* Article 6.3.
640. *See* Article 6(1) and (2).
641. *See* Article 6(4).

This book acknowledges the importance of verifying the financial capacity of third-party funders, should the proposed authorisation system be adopted. While the idea of establishing a public fund to cover expenses in the event of a funder's insolvency may appear precautionary, it seems excessive, particularly given that funders would already be subject to rigorous economic assessments. Such a measure risks favouring[642] public intervention unnecessarily. A more proportionate and market-oriented approach would be to rely on private insurance mechanisms to ensure coverage of litigation costs in case of insolvency.[643]

Additional attention should be given to requirements (3) and (5), particularly regarding the fulfilment of the 'fiduciary duty'.[644] Article 7(2) of the draft directive states: '[w]here a claimant intends to take a claim on behalf of others in proceedings, such as where the claimant is a qualified entity representing consumers, the litigation funder shall be required to owe a fiduciary duty to such intended beneficiaries'.[645] This raises important questions. If the claimant is also a beneficiary, or if the action is brought individually, does the funder not owe a fiduciary duty in those cases? What exactly constitutes a fiduciary obligation in this context? And why does the European Parliament propose that such a duty should depend on the procedural posture of the claimant – whether acting on their own behalf or representing others? These ambiguities are concerning. As rightly noted by the CCBE,[646] the draft makes only a vague reference to the concepts of fiduciary duties and fiduciary relationships, without clarifying their necessity or intended function.

The fiduciary business is typically characterised by the transfer of an asset, from either the trustor or a third party to the fiduciary, who assumes full and exclusive ownership of that asset. This transfer is not for the fiduciary's benefit, but rather with the obligation to later transfer the asset to the trustor or to a party designated by the trustor. This transfer occurs either after a specified period or upon the occurrence of a defined event.[647]

According to the CCBE, '[t]he only constellation in which the concept of a fiduciary relationship applies, is when the assignment of the claim is made to a third party who, as plaintiff, at the same time brings about the enforcement of the claim and thus the assumption of the litigation risk. Conversely, if the third party finances the litigation, it is merely a matter of financing not a fiduciary relationship'.[648]

642. *See* s. 3.6.5.3 below.
643. *See* litigationsolutions (aon.com).
644. *See* Article 5(1)c) and e).
645. Our underlining.
646. *See CCBE first comments on the European Parliament's recommendations to the Commission on Responsible private funding of* litigation, 13 May 2022, available at EN_DEON_20220513_CCBE-comments-on-the-European-Parliament-s-Recommendations-to-the-Commission-on-Responsible-private-funding-of-litigation.pdf, p. 5.
647. *See*, for example, *Judgement* of the TRL, of 24 April 2018, in Case 1405/17.3YLPRT.L1-7, available at Judgement of the Lisbon Court of Appeal (dgsi.pt).
648. *See CCBE first comments on the European Parliament's recommendations to the Commission on Responsible private funding of* litigation, 13 May 2022, available at EN_DEON_20220513_CCBE-comments-on-the-European-Parliament-s-Recommendations-to-the-Commission-on-Responsible-private-funding-of-litigation.pdf, p. 6.

The connection between a 'fiduciary relationship'[649] and litigation funding remains conceptually unclear. While the draft directive introduces the notion of a fiduciary duty, it does not fully explain how this legal construct, traditionally associated with asset management, translates into the context of TPLF. The likely rationale lies in drawing a parallel between the funder and the lawyer in their respective relationships with the beneficiary.[650] This alignment aims to ensure that the funder's interests do not conflict with those of the funded party, and that the latter's interests are prioritised. The underlying concern is the potential for conflicts of interest, an issue this book will revisit in more detail later.

In addition to Article 7, the European Parliament addresses fiduciary obligations in Recital 7 of the draft, which recommends 'that litigation funders be obliged to respect a fiduciary duty of care requiring them to act in the best interests of a claimant'. This language suggests an intention to clarify that the control and interests pursued in TPLF must ultimately align with those of the beneficiary. However, despite this clarification, it is evident that Article 7 requires revision. In particular, the scope and applicability of the fiduciary relationship remain ambiguous, especially regarding the duties funders owe not only to claimants but also to other parties involved in the proceedings. Greater precision is needed to define the nature of these obligations and to ensure consistent protection against conflicts of interest across all types of claims.

One of the most frequently raised concerns by defendants in class actions, particularly as TPLF gains traction across Europe, is the legitimacy of the plaintiff's funding. The draft directive addresses this by allowing any natural or legal person to submit a complaint to the competent authority regarding 'the compliance of a litigation funder with its obligations'.[651]

In the context of ongoing proceedings, if such concerns are raised (most likely by the defendant), they will be handled by the National Court or administrative body designated by the Member State as competent in this area. Importantly, this review will take place in a separate procedure, distinct from the litigation in which the issue was raised.[652]

To reinforce this oversight mechanism, the European Parliament recommends that the supervisory authority for litigation funders be empowered to initiate investigations based on referrals from the National Court or administrative authority. These referrals would be triggered when doubts arise during a case about whether a funder has complied with the obligations or conditions tied to its authorisation.[653]

Consequently, each Member State would be required to designate not only a supervisory authority but also a National Court or administrative body with the competence to assess the compliance of third-party funding agreements, either upon a party's justified request or on its own initiative, pursuant to Article 17 of the draft directive.

649. *See* Article 7(1).
650. *See* Gian Marco Solas, *Third Party Funding: Law, Economic and Policy*, Cambridge University Press, 2019, p. 295.
651. *See* Article 8(1) and (2).
652. *See* Articles 8(3), 16 and 17.
653. *See* Article 9(3)iv).

In practice, if the defendant raises a preliminary objection regarding the legitimacy of the claimant's funding, how will this issue be addressed procedurally? More specifically, how will the responsibilities of the supervisory authority and the National Court or competent administrative authority be coordinated? Should the main proceedings be suspended pending a decision by the supervisory authority? These are crucial questions that remain unanswered in the current draft. Given the potential impact of such objections on the course of the main action, it is essential that the Directive provide clear guidance on how concerns about the legitimacy of litigation funding – particularly when raised by the defendant – are to be handled. The process should not only ensure legal certainty and procedural fairness but also avoid unnecessary bureaucratic complexity.

This issue is particularly significant because, as previously noted, challenges to the legitimacy of the claimant's funding (especially when raised by defendants) are not only common but can also substantially delay proceedings. If the EU legislator intends to regulate litigation funding, we agree that the framework must include transparency and oversight mechanisms that can be triggered either by the opposing party or ex officio. However, it is essential that these mechanisms are designed to be efficient and not susceptible to misuse. The regulation must not, in practice, allow these procedures to become tools for delay, particularly by defendants seeking to obstruct or undermine the claimant's right of access to justice – which litigation funding is meant to support or facilitate.

In the interest of transparency, the European Parliament recommends several key obligations. First, claimants or their representatives should be required to notify the National Court or competent administrative authority at an early stage of the proceedings about the existence of a third-party funding agreement and the identity of the funder. This aligns with the recommendations of the EPRS.[654] Upon request by the National Court, administrative authority, or the defendant, a full and unredacted copy of the funding agreement must be provided.

Second, defendants should have the right to be informed (via the competent administrative authority) of the existence of the funding agreement and the identity of the litigation funder. This is essential to enable the defendant to exercise their right to challenge the legitimacy of the funding arrangement, including through formal complaints.[655]

To support this framework, the identity of authorised litigation funders should be publicly accessible through the supervisory authority's website, which must maintain an up-to-date list of all authorisations and refusals.[656] These authorisations are subject to annual review,[657] and the list must also be submitted to the European Commission and updated as necessary.[658] This is particularly important given that funders

654. *See* s. 3.3.8 above.
655. *See* Article 16.
656. *See* Article 8(4)c) and d).
657. *See* Article 8(4)e).
658. *See* Article 10(4).

authorised in one Member State may operate in others, provided they can demonstrate valid authorisation.[659]

Given the proposed authorisation system and its public accessibility, along with the supervisory powers already outlined, the obligation to provide a full, unredacted copy of the litigation funding agreement appears excessive. While transparency is essential, this level of disclosure, especially to the opposing party, raises legitimate concerns about confidentiality that the European Parliament has not adequately addressed. Sensitive commercial terms, strategic considerations, and privileged information may be embedded in such agreements.

Finally, in its effort to mitigate the perceived risks of abusive litigation, the European Parliament has proposed a series of additional safeguards beyond the transparency and oversight mechanisms already discussed. These include: (i) setting minimum content requirements for third-party funding agreements to ensure clarity and accountability; (ii) requiring funders to implement internal procedures designed to prevent conflicts of interest; and (iii) establishing joint and several liability for costs, thereby ensuring that funders share financial responsibility for adverse outcomes.

(i) Content of the Agreement

According to the European Parliament, third-party litigation funding agreements should, at a minimum, include the following elements: a declaration by the funder affirming the absence of any conflict of interest; a clear specification of the costs and expenses covered by the funder; a detailed outline of the remuneration, fees, and other payments to be made by the claimants and/or beneficiaries to the funder; and a transparent explanation of the financial risks assumed by the claimants or beneficiaries.[660]

As for what should be excluded from third-party funding agreements, the draft directive sets[661] out a number of clauses that are to be considered null and void. While the list is relatively comprehensive, this analysis will highlight several particularly significant provisions. These include: (i) any clause granting the litigation funder the power to influence the allocation of resources in the proceedings – including financial resources – or to control decisions regarding settlement agreements; (ii) any clause guaranteeing the funder a minimum return on investment before the claimant or beneficiary receives their share; (iii) any provision entitling the funder to 40% or more of the total amount awarded by the National Court, including damages, costs, fees, and other recoverable sums; (iv) any clause limiting the funder's liability in the event of an adverse costs order; and (v) any provision allowing the funder to unilaterally withdraw funding.

---

659. *See* Article 10(7).
660. Including 'the scope for escalating costs in the litigation, and how that impacts the financial interests of the claimants, beneficiaries or both; ii. the strictly defined circumstances in which the third-party funding agreement can be terminated and the risks to claimants, beneficiaries or both in that scenario, and iii. any potential risk of having to pay adverse costs, including circumstances in which adverse costs insurance or indemnities may not cover such exposure', *see* Article 12a), b), e) and g).
661. *See* Article 14.

This book has selected the above clauses because they directly relate to the ethical concerns raised by the TPLF – concerns that legal scholarship has broadly categorised into three levels. First, those concerning the relationship between the funder and the funded party, including issues of control, influence, and financial fairness. Second, those affecting the administration of justice and the efficient allocation of judicial resources, particularly where funding arrangements may distort procedural balance or incentivise speculative claims. And third, those arising within the tripartite relationship between the funder, the funded party, and the lawyer, where conflicts of interest and divided loyalties may compromise the integrity of legal representation.[662]

Indeed, it is the first level of concern – the relationship between the funder and the funded party – that has generated the greatest apprehension. This is largely due to the risk that the vulnerable position of the injured party may be exploited to impose contractual terms that result in undue interference in the conduct of the proceedings or in the extraction of disproportionate benefits from the litigation. Such concerns underscore the need for robust safeguards to ensure that funding arrangements do not compromise the autonomy of the claimant or distort the fairness of the process.

There is, indeed, a growing perception that litigation funders are securing disproportionately high returns on their investments, often at the expense of plaintiffs who may receive unacceptably low reparations relative to the value of the claim.[663]

However, the European Parliament does not provide a clear justification for why it considers it inherently disproportionate – and therefore abusive – for litigation funders to receive a share of the award that reduces the claimant's or beneficiary's compensation to 60% or less.[664] While the intention may be to protect the injured party from exploitative funding arrangements, the threshold appears arbitrary in the absence of a detailed rationale or empirical basis.[665]

In Australia, where litigation funding has become a key enabler of collective redress by helping overcome the significant cost barriers associated with class actions,[666] a comprehensive enquiry into the industry was conducted.[667] In late 2020, Corporations and Financial Services released its report on litigation funding and the regulation of the

662. *See* Wayne Attrill, *Ethical Issues in Litigation Funding*, 16 February 2009, available at https://portal.omnibridgeway.com/docs/default-source/site-documents/ethical-issues-paper-imf09---globalaw-conference.pdf, p. 7.
663. Litigation Funding - Final PwC Report - March 2020 (omnibridgeway.com), p. 4.
664. *See* European Parliament Resolution of 13 September 2022, Article 14(4), according to which, '[i]n the absence of exceptional circumstances, where a litigation funding agreement entitles a litigation funder to a share in the outcome which reduces the share available to the claimant and the intended beneficiaries to 60% or less of the total amount awarded (including all amounts of damages, costs, fees and other expenses), that agreement shall have no legal effect'.
665. *See* Rémi Chevalier, *Recommendations for Responsible Private Funding of Litigation: European Parliament Resolution 2022/2130(INL)*, 6 March 2023, available at Recommendations For Responsible Private Funding Of Litigation: European Parliament Resolution 2022/2130(INL) - Trials & Appeals & Compensation - European Union (mondaq.com).
666. *See* Michael Legg, *The Rise and Regulation of Litigation Funding in Australian Class Actions*, Erasmus Law Review, vol. 14, No. 4, 2021, p. 223 https://doi.org/10.5553/elr.000213.
667. Litigation Funding and the Regulation of the Class Action Industry: Parliament of Australia (aph.gov.au).

class action industry.[668] Regarding the imposition of a cap on funders' remuneration, the report recommended a limit of 30%,[669] grounded in empirical analysis of domestic cases. This analysis considered both the funders' investment levels and the distribution of returns based on the gross proceeds of class actions.

The Australian Committee concluded that funders' profits should not unreasonably exceed their actual costs – a pattern that had become increasingly common,[670] often to the detriment of class members' compensation. Notably, in Australia, funders typically receive between 20% and 30% of the proceeds, but this percentage is calculated after reimbursement of costs, meaning the entire amount constitutes profit.[671]

In this context, a study conducted by a consultancy firm assessed the potential impact of three hypothetical caps on funders' gross returns: (i) 30%, as recommended by the Australian Committee; (ii) 40%; and (iii) 50%, as recommended by a litigation funding company.[672] The findings revealed that such caps could significantly affect the volume of funded litigation. Specifically, the percentages of cases that would not proceed as litigation costs are higher than the gross settlement (i.e., a negative return for the litigation funder) would be 36%, 18%, and 12%, respectively.

Moreover, the study estimated the percentage of cases affected (i.e., where the return to the litigation funder is reduced but remains above 0): 55%, 58%, and 33%[673] for the 30%, 40%, and 50% caps, respectively. These results illustrate the inherent trade-off in imposing limits on funder returns: while caps may protect claimants from disproportionate profit-sharing, they may also deter funders from supporting meritorious claims. Notably, the Australian Committee's recommendation of a 30% cap was not grounded in economic efficiency or return-on-investment analysis, but rather in considerations of proportionality and fairness in the distribution of litigation proceeds.[674]

Based on the calculations discussed above, one could argue that imposing a strict cap on the profits of third-party funders, intended to increase the share of compensation received by injured parties, may, paradoxically, result in lower or even no compensation at all. If the cap renders certain claims financially unattractive to funders, those claims may never be brought forward. In this light, it may be preferable

668. Litigation Funding and the Regulation of the Class Action Industry Report (pmc.gov.au).
669. *See* Recommendation 20: 'The committee recommends the Australian Government consult on: the best way to guarantee a statutory minimum return of the gross proceeds of a class action (including settlements); whether a minimum gross return of 70 per cent to class members, as endorsed by some class action law firms and litigation funders, is the most appropriate floor; and whether a graduated approach taking into consideration the risk, complexity, length and likely proceeds of the case is appropriate to ensure even higher returns are guaranteed for class members in more straightforward cases', *see* Litigation Funding and the Regulation of the Class Action Industry Report (pmc.gov.au), p. 28.
670. According to it, '[c]urrently, the difference between the capital a litigation funder has put at stake and the profit made is often unreasonable, disproportionate and unfair', *see* Litigation Funding and the Regulation of the class Action Industry Report (pmc.gov.au), p. 236.
671. *See* Michael Legg, *The Rise and Regulation of Litigation Funding in Australian Class Actions*, Erasmus Law Review, vol. 14, No. 4, 2021, p. 223 https://doi.org/10.5553/elr.000213.
672. Omni Bridgeway - Submission in response to - Guaranteeing a minimum return of class action proceeds to class members (treasury.gov.au), p. 3.
673. Litigation Funding - Final PwC Report - March 2020 (omnibridgeway.com), p. 16.
674. *Ibid.*, p. 4.

for claimants to receive a smaller portion of a successful award than to receive nothing due to the absence of funding. This trade-off highlights the need for a balanced regulatory approach – one that protects claimants from exploitative arrangements without disincentivising funders from supporting legitimate actions that would otherwise be inaccessible.

The Australian Committee anticipated this line of argument and responded by emphasising that it overlooks a key point: class members can still receive a higher proportion of compensation without denying litigation funders a reasonable, proportional, and fair return on their investment. The Committee attributed the excessive profits observed in recent years largely to the widespread use of percentage-based fee structures, which have enabled funders to secure windfall returns – often disproportionate to the actual costs and risks incurred.[675]

This regulatory debate finds a parallel in competition law through the concept of excessive pricing.[676] While this form of abuse is recognised under Article 102 of the TFEU, it is notably absent from US antitrust law. The US approach is shaped by three main arguments (widely debated in the literature) against intervening in cases of high pricing: (i) it incentivises innovation and investment, ultimately benefiting consumers; (ii) it is self-correcting, as excessive prices attract market entry and competition; and (iii) it is difficult to assess when a price becomes excessive, making enforcement uncertain and potentially counterproductive.

In the EU, precedents on excessive pricing remain limited, with no more than five landmark cases.[677] The foundational case is *United Brands*,[678] in which the ECJ established a two-part test, commonly referred to as the UB test. This test asks: (i) whether the difference between the price charged and the costs incurred is excessive; and (ii) if so, whether the price is unfair in itself or when compared to competing products or services. The ECJ has clarified that this test does not preclude the use of other valid methods, such as comparative pricing analyses. In subsequent years, both the European Commission and the CJEU have further developed the UB test, particularly in the pharmaceutical sector, where pricing abuses have raised significant regulatory concerns.[679]

In this book's view, imposing limits on the profits of funding organisations involves complex and sensitive considerations that warrant thorough economic analysis before any regulatory measures are adopted in the EU – especially given that the European context differs significantly from that of the United States or Australia.

675. Litigation Funding and the Regulation of the Class Action Industry Report (pmc.gov.au), p. 204.
676. *See* Liyang Hou, *Excessive Prices Within EU Competition Law*, European Competition Journal, vol. 7, pp. 47-70, *in Dominance and Monopolization*, vol. II, Rosa Greaves (ed.), 2012, p. 333.
677. *See General Motors*, of 13 November 1975, Case C-26/75; *United Brands*, of 14 February 1978, Case C-27/76; *Corinne Bodson*, of 4 May 1988, Case C-30/87; *Autortiesību*, of 14 September 2017, Case C-177/16; and, more recently, the UK case of *CMA v. Flynn Pharma*, of 12 May 2020, Case C3/2019/1293.
678. *See United Brands* judgment of 14 February 1978, Case C-27/76, pts 252 and 253.
679. *See* George Zacharodimos, *Excessive Pricing*, 21 October 2022, available at Guide to Life Sciences - Global Competition Review.

The European experience – particularly in the UK, Austria, and Switzerland – shows that litigation funding companies typically charge between 20% and 30% of the awarded compensation. Even in Germany, where funders initially demanded up to 50%, the standard has shifted a few years ago towards a 30% share driven by increased market competition (and remember that currently, in Germany, the cap is only 10%). This trend supports the notion of self-correcting pricing mechanisms in the litigation funding sector.[680]

In light of the above, setting a maximum remuneration cap of 39% does not appear unreasonable, particularly in light of the prevailing 20-30% range observed across the EU (especially in class actions involving competition law violations, where damages often reach several million euros). However, the core issue lies not in the percentage itself, but in the imposition of such a cap at this stage. The private litigation funding market in the EU remains relatively nascent or, at best, still maturing. As demonstrated by the German experience,[681] where initial rates of 50% have naturally adjusted to around 30% due to increased market competition, pricing mechanisms appear to be self-correcting. This suggests that regulatory intervention may be premature and potentially disruptive to a market that is still finding its equilibrium – contrary to the German legislator's view.[682]

(ii) Preventing Conflicts of Interest

The draft directive requires litigation funders to establish internal procedures to prevent conflicts of interest. According to the European Parliament, these procedures must be documented in writing, published on the funder's website, and attached to any funding agreement. Claimants and beneficiaries must be informed of any circumstances that could reasonably give rise to a conflict of interest, including: (i) pre-existing financial or other agreements between the funder and any party involved in the case (e.g., lawyers, claimants, or defendants); and (ii) any relevant connection between the funder and the defendant, particularly in competitive contexts.[683] While the Parliament was right to include safeguards against conflicts of interest in its recommendation, the treatment of the issue remains somewhat superficial and would benefit from further elaboration.

Conflicts of interest are typically identifiable on a case-by-case basis, depending on the identity and history of the parties involved (namely, the third-party funder, legal

680. *See* Marco de Morpurgo, *A Comparative Legal and Economic Approach to Third-Party Litigation Funding*, 11 January 2011, available at cejamericas.org, p. 366.
681. As Felix von Zwehl and Malte Stübinger point out, while a few years ago it was predominantly subsidiaries of insurance groups that offered funding services in Germany, presenting the service somewhat as an *ex post* alternative to legal expenses insurance, over the years more companies with different origins and global reach have entered the market. With this has come a diversification of offers, conditions and target markets, in *The Third Party Litigation Funding Law Review: Germany*, Simon Latham and Augusta Ventures (eds), 6th ed., The Law Reviews, 8 December 2022.
682. *See* Marco de Morpurgo, *A Comparative Legal and Economic Approach to Third-Party Litigation Funding*, 11 January 2011, available at cejamericas.org, p. 366.
683. *See* Article 13.

representatives, and the claimant) as well as the procedural stage of the case. It is therefore advisable to establish a disclosure framework among these parties at the outset of financing negotiations, at least in general terms. While such a system may be complex, it remains the most effective starting point for preventing conflicts of interest.[684] However, once a real or potential conflict is identified and deemed manageable (i.e., not requiring the replacement of any party), the specific resolution should be explicitly incorporated into the funding agreement.[685]

That said, certain potential conflicts of interest are inherent to the roles each party plays in the litigation process and are not, in themselves, problematic - provided that the 'correct interest'[686] ultimately prevails. Take, for example, lawyers' fees: under an hourly billing model, a lawyer may have an incentive to prolong proceedings, which runs counter to the interests of both the funder (who bears the cost) and the client, who seeks timely compensation. Conversely, under a fixed-fee arrangement, the lawyer may be incentivised to minimise time spent on the case.[687] Both incentives are legitimate, so long as they do not compromise the lawyer's duty of professional diligence.

A similar dynamic applies to litigation funders in the context of potential settlements between claimants and defendants - an area where conflicts of interest frequently arise. While funders, clients, and, in the case of success or contingency fees, lawyers all share a common interest in maximising compensation, their incentives may diverge when it comes to deciding whether to settle. Given the substantial costs associated with prolonged litigation (particularly legal fees and expert assessments), a funder may prefer an early settlement, even at a lower amount, if it ensures a quicker return on investment and potentially higher net profit. This interest in expediency and profitability may not align with that of the claimant, who may seek full compensation for the harm suffered, including for reasons of justice or principle. In such cases, the lawyer, who is ethically bound to act in the client's best interest, must uphold their professional duties. The funding agreement can reinforce this by explicitly stating that the lawyer represents only the client, even if the funder's interests are adversely affected. Moreover, the agreement may provide that any irreconcilable disagreement over settlement decisions be referred to the lawyer, who could be tasked with issuing a binding opinion for the funder.[688]

---

684. *See* Tian-Yu DU, *Research on Conflicts of Interest Arising from Third-Party Funding In International Investment Arbitration*, Advances in Social Science, Education and Humanities Research, vol. 281, 4th International Conference on Social Science and Contemporary Humanity Development (SSCHD 2018), p. 424.
685. *See* Mark Humphries, *The Ethics of Litigation Funding*, 17 September 2014, available at The_Ethics_of_Litigation_Funding_17.09.14.pdf (humphrieskerstetter.com), p. 6.
686. *See* Samia A. Hurst and Alex Mauron, *A Question of Method. The Ethics of Managing Conflicts of Interest*, EMBO Rep. February 2008, vol. 9 (No. 2), pp. 119-123.
687. *See* Mark Humphries, *The Ethics of Litigation Funding*, 17 September 2014, available at The_Ethics_of_Litigation_Funding_17.09.14.pdf (humphrieskerstetter.com), p. 6.
688. *See* Wayne Attrill, *Ethical Issues in Litigation Funding*, 16 February 2009, available at https://portal.omnibridgeway.com/docs/default-source/site-documents/ethical-issues-paper-imf09---globalaw-conference.pdf, p. 11.

In reality, when substantial investments are involved – as is typically the case in class actions for breaches of competition law – it is unrealistic to expect the funder to be entirely removed from the litigation process. The funder's involvement can, in fact, be pivotal to the direction and viability of the case. Recognising this, the European Parliament has rightly proposed that any contractual provision granting the funder decision-making authority over the strategic conduct[689] of the action should be deemed null and void. This safeguard aims to preserve the autonomy of the claimant and the integrity of the legal process, ensuring that strategic litigation decisions remain in the hands of those with a direct legal interest in the outcome.

(iii) Joint and Several Liability for Costs

The European Parliament proposes that litigation funders be held liable for costs, either jointly or severally with the claimants, if the action is unsuccessful. National Courts would be empowered to order funders to cover these costs, based on a set of criteria, including:

(1) the value of the funder's initial investment;
(2) the amount and proportion of compensation the funder would have received had the claim succeeded;
(3) the extent to which unpaid costs would otherwise burden the defendant, claimant, or beneficiary; and
(4) the funder's conduct throughout the proceedings, particularly its compliance with the forthcoming directive and whether its actions contributed to the overall cost of litigation.[690]

This recommendation is directly linked to the aforementioned nullity of clauses limiting the funder's liability[691] and aligns with a recent decision by the English High Court, which will be discussed in detail below.[692]

Once again, the European Parliament fails to clarify the legal basis for imposing joint and several liability on litigation funders for adverse costs. In our view, this provision (alongside the proposed fiduciary duty framework) warrants serious reconsideration. Litigation funders already assume substantial financial risk by supporting high-cost actions, particularly in the field of competition law class actions, without any guarantee of return. Imposing personal liability for costs on top of this risk could deter funders from entering the market altogether, ultimately undermining access to justice for injured parties.

689. *See* What You Need to Know About Third Party Litigation Funding - ILR (instituteforlegalreform.com).
690. *See* Article 18.
691. *See* Article 14(5) of the Proposal for a Directive annexed to the European Parliament Resolution of 13 September 2022, according to which 'Member States shall ensure that third-party funding agreements do not contain provisions that limit the liability of a litigation funder in the event of an order for adverse costs following unsuccessful proceedings.'
692. *See* s. 3.4.4.4 below.

Moreover, the rationale behind this liability appears inconsistent. The European Parliament's broader approach seeks to exclude funders from the litigation process entirely, in order to avoid conflicts of interest. It even recommends nullifying any clause that grants funders influence over cost management.[693] Yet, paradoxically, it proposes to hold them personally liable for those very costs, despite denying them any control over how those costs are incurred. This contradiction raises serious concerns about the coherence and fairness of the proposed framework.

This assessment would be different if the European Parliament had opted to grant funders a more active role in the proceedings – for example, by allowing the transfer of the claimant's position to the funder, as occurs in certain types of collective actions known as 'assigned action', which will be discussed below.[694] Alternatively, the amount agreed upon in the funding arrangement should already account for the payment of costs in the event the case is lost. However, those costs should remain the responsibility of the claimant. If the funder fails to pay them, the breach is against the claimant and constitutes a contractual violation.

At a minimum, this book would support the introduction of subsidiary liability, meaning that the defendant could only seek recovery of costs from the third-party funder if the claimant is unable to pay. This approach preserves a degree of financial accountability without disproportionately burdening funders or undermining the claimant's primary responsibility.

(iv) Overall Assessment

Broadly speaking, this book shares the concerns expressed by stakeholders[695] who view the European Parliament's Resolution with scepticism, for three main reasons. First, the European Commission has shown little interest in regulating litigation funding, having yet to adopt a legislative proposal that reflects the Parliament's recommendations on the matter.[696] Second, the Resolution is based on a flawed assumption that litigation funding inherently leads to abusive practices or a lack of transparency – despite the absence of evidence or reported issues of this kind in the Member States. Third, the process by which the Resolution was adopted lacked transparency and revealed a limited understanding of how the litigation funding market operates in practice, an issue that could have been mitigated through a public consultation.

---

693. *See* Article 14(2)(a) of the Proposal for a Directive annexed to the European Parliament Resolution of 13 September 2022, according to which, 'the grant of an explicit power to a litigation funder to take or influence decisions in the course of proceedings, such as with respect to specific claims pursued, settlement of the case, or <u>management of expenses associated with the proceedings</u>' (emphasis added).

694. *See* s. 3.6.1 below.

695. *See* Carmen Perales, *European Parliament Litigation Funding Resolution Criticised by Experts*, ION Analytics, 13 December 2022, available at European Parliament litigation funding resolution criticised by experts | ION Analytics Community.

696. *See* Juan Nascimbene and Olivia Anderson, *EU Plans To Regulate Third-Party Funding in Litigation and International Arbitration*, 3 April 2023, available at EU Plans To Regulate Third-Party Funding in Litigation and International Arbitration - Lexology.

With the caveats previously discussed, this Resolution nonetheless represents a step in the right direction, particularly at a time when TPLF is expanding across the EU. As reported, the global market for such funding is currently estimated to range between EUR 40 and EUR 80 billion.[697] Notably, a joint initiative by the UNIDROIT (International Institute for the Unification of Private Law) and the ELI (European Law Institute) has also recently advocated for the mandatory acceptance of TPLF, as part of their proposed Model European Rules of Civil Procedure.[698]

The decision to regulate TPLF also reflects a broader international trend. Several jurisdictions (despite the inherent complexities) are actively considering regulatory frameworks, as illustrated by the example of Australia mentioned earlier. In parallel, the United Nations has been examining[699] the possibility of regulating TPLF in other types of disputes, proposing measures that closely resemble those discussed above.[700] Although these efforts target different contexts, they underscore a growing global recognition of the need for structured oversight in this evolving market.

Finally, a 2021 study[701] on consumer perceptions in five Member States (France, Germany, the Netherlands, Poland, and Spain)[702] found that 83% of respondents support the introduction of safeguards[703] through formal regulation (rather than self-regulation) to ensure that the interests of litigation funders do not override those of claimants.[704] In this respect, the European Parliament's proposal is a positive development, as it goes beyond Directive 2020/1828. As previously noted,[705] that directive

697. Third Party Funding of Litigation (europeanlawinstitute.eu).
698. *See* Microsoft Word – ELI-UNIDROIT Rules 15 February 2021, p. 507.
699. *See* Third-party funding | United Nations Commission On International Trade Law.
700. United Nations Commission on International Trade Law, Working Group III (Investor-State Dispute Settlement Reform), Thirty-eighth session, Vienna, 14-18 October 2019, available at V1908390.pdf (un.org), p. 6.
701. *Consumer Attitudes to Third Party Litigation Funding and its Potential Regulation in the EU*, 27 September 2021, available at EU-Litigation-Funding-Survey-WEB.pdf (instituteforlegalreform.com).
702. Chosen because they represent a *spread of* different MS, in terms of size, location and date of accession, *see Consumer Attitudes to Third Party Litigation Funding and its Potential Regulation in the EU*, p. 1.
703. Nine safeguards have been tested to the effect that TPLF (*see Consumer Attitudes to Third Party Litigation Funding and its Potential Regulation in the EU*, p. 17): (i) must be licensed and authorised by a licensing agency before they can invest in lawsuits; (ii) must have to disclose their investments and their terms so that all parties involved in the case are aware of them; (iii) must have limitations on the fees they can charge in the event of a win; (iv) must not be able to control strategic litigation decisions (such as appointing lawyers, determining case strategy or negotiating a settlement with the other party), which are usually left to the discretion of the lawyers or the claimants themselves; (v) should subject their funding agreements to independent scrutiny, taking into account all relevant circumstances, to ensure that they are drafted fairly; (vi) should be responsible for paying costs arising during the proceedings if their party loses; (vii) must have a fiduciary duty; i.e., they must be obliged, both legally and ethically, to put the best interests of claimants before their own investment interests; (viii) must not abandon a case before it is concluded; (ix) must adopt their own codes of conduct (self-regulation).
704. *Consumer Attitudes to Third Party Litigation Funding and its Potential Regulation in the EU*, pp. 7 and 15.
705. *See* s. 3.6.1 below.

is limited not only in its scope of application but also in the substance of its provisions, including those relating to private funding[706] – a topic that will be revisited later in this book.

3.3.9 The European Commission's October 2022 Communication on the Application of EU Law and Second Preliminary Conclusion

On 13 October 2022, the European Commission adopted a Communication on the application of the EU law, aimed at promoting consistent compliance, to ensure that citizens enjoy the same rights across the Union.[707] According to Commission President Ursula von der Leyen, 'effective enforcement of EU law remains key for people and businesses to ensure that they can continue to enjoy the protection and legal certainty offered by EU law'.[708]

Competition rules are referenced as early as page 4 of the Communication, where the European Commission highlights the costs associated with the incomplete or incorrect application of the EU law. It emphasises that the robust enforcement of competition rules is essential for both businesses and consumers to fully benefit from the single market. A failure to apply these rules effectively undermines the level playing field for businesses – and, this book would add, for consumers as well.

Building on this foundation, the European Commission recalled – on the basis of the second subparagraph of Article 19(1) of the TEU and Article 47 of the CFREU – that when applying EU law, National Courts act as EU Courts. Accordingly, when the rights of EU citizens or companies are at stake, Member States are required to ensure access to effective judicial protection at the national level, in line with the principle of effective judicial protection. The Commission also invoked the principles of primacy and uniformity in the application of EU law,[709] noting that a stocktaking exercise is currently underway between the Commission and the Member States to assess whether the existing enforcement tools are adequate to ensure the practical effectiveness of EU legislation.

Despite the record-high fines imposed by public authorities, compensation for consumers and SMEs in the Member States for harm resulting from infringements of Articles 101 and 102 of the TFEU remains largely elusive. The initiatives of the European Commission and the European Parliament discussed above have yet to yield concrete measures capable of transforming this reality and ensuring effective collective redress under EU competition law.

706. *See* s. 3.6.5.1.2 below.
707. *See Communication from the Commission: Enforcing EU Law for a Europe That Delivers*, available at https://ec.europa.eu/info/sites/default/files/com_2022_518_1_en.pdf.
708. Enforcing EU Laws: Delivering the Benefits to Citizens (europa.eu).
709. *See Communication from the Commission: Enforcing EU Law for a Europe That Delivers*, available at https://ec.europa.eu/info/sites/default/files/com_2022_518_1_en.pdf, p. 7.

3.4 COMPARATIVE INSIGHTS: THE US EXPERIENCE AND PARADIGMATIC EUROPEAN CASES

Change has already begun - albeit slowly - even before the adoption of Directive 2020/1828. As noted in the 2018 Report,[710] several Member States still lacked any form of collective redress mechanism, whether through injunctive relief or compensation for damages. Moreover, significant disparities persist among national rules in this area, resulting in a fragmented and inconsistent landscape across the EU.[711]

Compounding this issue is the absence of binding EU legislation specifically addressing competition law class actions, as well as the lack of adequate funding mechanisms. These gaps continue to hinder the development of private enforcement in the EU, especially when contrasted with the US,[712] where even small antitrust victims benefit from an effective opt-out collective redress system that facilitates access to justice and compensation.[713]

In this context, the environment in the EU remains particularly unfavourable for SMEs and consumers seeking redress for competition law infringements, often encouraging forum shopping.[714] Against this backdrop, this book will now examine the US experience and then analyse paradigmatic European cases.

3.4.1 Class Actions in the US: A Tool for Justice or a Vehicle for Abuse?

US competition law is to a large extent, as mentioned above, enforced by class action[715] - a mechanism widely utilised across various legal areas[716] and particularly in antitrust

710. *See* s. 3.3.6 above.
711. *See* Diego Agulló, *Directive 2020/1828: A New Era for 'European Class Actions'?*, UNIO - EU Law Journal, 22 November 2021, available at https://officialblogofunio.com/2021/11/22/directive-2020-1828-a-new-era-for-european-class-actions/.
712. *See* Nuno Calaim Lourenço, *The European Commission's Directive on Antitrust Damages Actions*, Revista de Concorrência e Regulação, vol. 5, No. 18, 2014, pp. 65-87, p. 85.
713. *See* Mantas Pakamanis, *The Role of Class Actions in Ensuring Effective Enforcement of Competition Law Infringements in the European Union*, International Comparative Jurisprudence, vol. 2, No. 2, December 2016, pp. 122-130, p. 129 https://doi.org/10.1016/j.icj.2016.11.001.
714. As Žygimantas Juška points out, favouring countries such as Portugal, the Netherlands and the UK, in *The Effectiveness of Antitrust Collective Litigation in the European Union: A Study of the Principle of Full Compensation*, International Review of Intellectual Property and Competition Law, vol. 49, pp. 63-93, 2018, p. 85 https://doi.org/10.1007/s40319-017-0644-4.
715. *See* Eva W. Cole and Jeffrey J. Amato, *Collective or Class Actions and Claims Aggregation in the United States, in GCR's Private Litigation Guide,* Nicholas and Heaton and Benhamin Holt (eds), 3rd ed., 2021, *asset download - Global Competition Review*, p. 23.
716. *See* Margaret M. Zwiskler, Christopher S. Yates and William R. Sherman, *United States, in Class Actions: A Global Guide from Practical Law*, Omar Shah (ed.), Thomson Reuters, 2015, pp. 383-402, p. 387.

cases.[717] The modern form of class action litigation was established in 1966,[718] allowing one or more members of a class to sue or be sued as representative parties on behalf of all members,[719] provided the following conditions are met:[720]

(1) *Numerosity*: the class must be so large that joining all members individually would be impracticable. This is often the case in antitrust matters, where hundreds, thousands, or even millions of affected individuals can be identified (such as consumers who purchased a specific product in a supermarket).
(2) *Commonality*: there must be questions of law or fact common to the class. This is typically straightforward to demonstrate in antitrust cases, as the same anticompetitive conduct tends to produce widespread market effects.
(3) *Typicality*: the claims or defences of the representative parties must be typical of those of the class. This ensures alignment of interests (e.g., consumers who overpaid due to a price-fixing cartel share a common goal of recovering the overcharge).
(4) *Adequacy*: the representative parties must fairly and adequately protect the interests of the class. This requirement is closely linked to typicality and is not met when conflicts of interest exist among class members. A notable example is *Valley Drug Co. v. Geneva Pharm., Inc.* case, where the Court found that three large national distributors, who accounted for approximately 50% of the total damages, had actually benefited from the absence of a generic drug on the market, thereby undermining their adequacy as class representatives.[721,722]

While defence-side class actions are technically possible, they remain exceedingly rare – even in the United States.[723] In short, the fundamental principles that must be

717. Which originated, as already mentioned, in the *Sherman Antitrust Act of* 1890, amended by the Clayton Act of 1914. *See* s. 3.1 above. *See also* Mantas Pakamanis, *The Role of Class Actions in Ensuring Effective Enforcement of Competition Law Infringements in the European Union*, International Comparative Jurisprudence, vol. 2, No. 2, December 2016, pp. 122-130, p. 127 https://doi.org/10.1016/j.icj.2016.11.001.
718. Robert G. Bone, *The US Class Action from a Utilitarian Perspective: Balancing Social Benefits and Social Costs, in The Cambridge Handbook of Class Actions: An international Survey*, Brian T. Fitzpatrick and Randall S. Thomas (eds), Cambridge University Press, 2021, p. 3.
719. *See* Rule 23(a) of the Federal Rules of Civil Procedure, available at federal_rules_of_civil_procedure_-_december_2020_0.pdf (uscourts.gov).
720. J. Douglas Richards, Michael B. Eisenkraft and Abigail E. Shafroth, *Class Actions, Private Enforcement of Antitrust Law in the United States: A Handbook*, Albert A. Foer and Randy M. Stutz (eds), Edward Elgar, 2012, pp. 113 et seq.
721. *See United States Court of Appeals, Eleventh Circuit, Valley Drug Co. v. Geneva Pharm., Inc.*, No. 02-12091, 15 September 2003, available at https://caselaw.findlaw.com/us-11th-circuit/1330664.html.
722. *See* Kenneth M. Kliebard et al., *Class/Collective Actions in the United States: Overview*, 1 September 2020, available at Class/collective actions in the United States: overview | Practical Law (thomsonreuters.com).
723. *See* Margaret M. Zwiskler, Christopher S. Yates and William R. Sherman, *United States, in Class Actions: A Global Guide from Practical Law*, Omar Shah (ed.), Thomson Reuters, 2015, p. 387.

met in order to file a class action in the US and have it certified by the TN are the above explained (numerosity, commonality, adequacy and typicality).[724] Moreover, the US legal framework contains several features that actively encourage the use of class actions, particularly in antitrust enforcement:

(i) class members may be either individuals or legal entities;
(ii) the system generally follows an opt-out model, whereby all potential claimants are included in the class unless they explicitly choose to litigate independently;[725]
(iii) in addition to injunctive relief and compensatory damages, courts may award punitive damages. These can exceed compensatory damages by a ratio of up to 9:1. In antitrust cases, treble damages[726] (3:1)[727] are standard, reflecting the seriousness of the violation and the need for deterrence;
(iv) contingency fees aggregate – where attorneys are compensated only if the case is successful, typically as a percentage of the award – is not only permitted but also standard practice in class litigation;
(v) pre-certification discovery is generally allowed and often extensive, enabling plaintiffs to gather evidence before the class is formally certified; and
(vi) TPLF is permitted, with no federal cap on funding amounts and no requirement for court approval of funding agreements. While not federally regulated, some states (e.g., Maine and Ohio) have enacted specific rules. Common Law principles and ethical obligations – such as the prohibition against funder interference – continue to apply.[728]

The distinctive features of the US class action system help explain why the current debate in North America differs significantly from that in Europe. While European countries are still exploring ways to promote the use of class actions, particularly in the field of competition law, the US has long moved past this stage. Instead, the American legal discourse now focuses on striking a balance between the benefits and potential excesses of class actions, given their widespread and well-established use.

In this context,[729] various social pluses and minuses of class actions have been pointed out, of which this book has selected five costs (–) and benefits (+) illustrated above (Figure 3.1).

---

724. The additional requirements set out in Rule 23(b) of the Federal Rules of Civil Procedure must also be complied with.
725. This can substantially prolong the process and expose defendants to additional defence costs and liability, *see* Dee Bansal et al., *United States: Class Actions – Litigation, Policy and Latest Developments*, 2 December 2022, available at Class actions hub - Global Competition Review.
726. Some argue that, for this reason, these damages actions possess a quasi-criminal character. *See* Spencer Weber Waller, *The Incoherence of Punishment in Antitrust*, Chicago-Kent Law Review, vol. 78, No. 1, April 2003, Symposium: Private Law, Punishment, and Disgorgement, Article 8, p. 215.
727. *See* s. 4 of the Clayton Act (15 U.S.C. para. 15(a)).
728. *See* s. 3.3.8 above.
729. *See* Robert G. Bone, *The US Class Action from a Utilitarian Perspective: Balancing Social Benefits and Social Costs, in The Cambridge Handbook of Class Actions: An international Survey*, Brian T. Fitzpatrick and Randall S. Thomas (eds), Cambridge University Press, 2021, p. 7 ff. *See also* Bruno Deffains and Dominique Demougin, *Class Actions, Compliance, and Moral Cost, in*

Figure 3.1 Key Benefits and Costs of Class Actions in US Antitrust Law

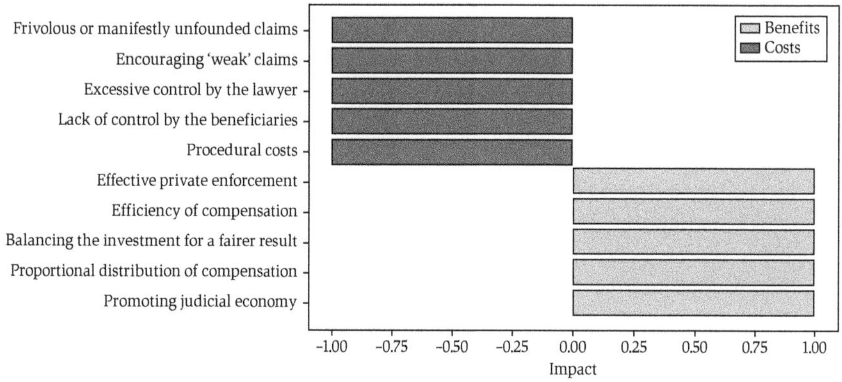

- *Frivolous or manifestly unfounded claims* (risk of encouraging frivolous claims to pressure defendants into settlements): there is a well-documented[730] concern that class actions (particularly in the US, where contingency fees can amount to a significant percentage of multi-million or even billion-dollar settlements) may incentivise the filing of frivolous or weak claims solely to pressure defendants into settling. One might ask: if a claim is unfounded, why would a defendant agree to settle? The answer lies in the high stakes involved. Faced with the prospect of a costly and high-profile lawsuit, where the outcome is binary - either complete exoneration or potentially ruinous damages - defendants may opt for a settlement as the 'lesser evil' to avoid reputational harm, business disruption, and financial risk. However, the US legal system includes safeguards to mitigate such risks. Class actions must undergo a rigorous certification process, and any proposed settlement must be approved by the Court. These mechanisms are designed to filter out unmeritorious claims and ensure that settlements are fair, reasonable, and in the best interest of the class.
- *Encouraging 'weak' claims* (lawyers may present poorly substantiated claims and propose high-value settlements): in class actions, attorneys may be tempted to 'hide their hand' by filing a poorly substantiated claim at the outset. This strategy, common in the US, is often used to avoid revealing too much information to the defendant early in the proceedings while simultaneously proposing a high-value settlement. Although defendants may anticipate this tactic, their ability to assess the claim is limited by the asymmetry of information that persists until the evidentiary phase of the trial. As a result,

Contract Governance: Dimensions in Law and Interdisciplinary Research, Stefan Grundmann, Florian Möslein and Karl Riesenhuber (eds), Oxford University Press, 1 July 2015, pp. 276 et seq.

730. *See* s. 3.3 above.

defendants may initially respond with a lower counteroffer but could ultimately agree to a higher settlement than warranted, simply to mitigate risk. While any such agreement must be reviewed and approved by the Court, judicial scrutiny is itself constrained by the limited information presented in a weakly substantiated claim. This can compromise the fairness of the outcome. Moreover, weak claims can dilute the strength of the class as a whole, potentially leading to under-compensation for members with strong claims or prompting them to opt out of the class action entirely.

- *Excessive control by the lawyer* (potential conflicts of interest between lawyers and beneficiaries, leading to unfair settlements): one of the key concerns in class actions is the potential for excessive control by the lawyer, especially when combined with the limited legal expertise of the beneficiaries. This imbalance can create conflicts of interest between the attorney and the class members. As previously noted in the context of the European Parliament's resolution on private funding,[731] lawyers may be incentivised to negotiate settlements that minimise their own workload and maximise their contingency-based compensation - particularly in the US, where legal fees are typically calculated as a percentage of the total award rather than on an hourly basis. While any settlement must be approved by the Court as advanced, once both parties have reached an agreement, there is often little motivation to alert the judge to potential opportunism or unfairness. Judges themselves may be inclined to approve settlements to expedite the resolution of lengthy and complex proceedings. This dynamic can also have broader implications. If settlements are consistently lower than what might be achieved through full litigation, it may reduce the deterrent effect of class actions and inadvertently encourage future infringements. Although unethical conduct can be reported (such as to the Bar Association), this is complicated by the significant information asymmetry between lawyers and clients, particularly in complex areas like antitrust law (this asymmetry is not unique to class actions and can also affect individual litigation).
- *Lack of control by the beneficiaries* (beneficiaries have limited control over the process and may not interact with the Court): In most class actions, beneficiaries have little to no control over the litigation process. Typically, they are not in direct contact with the Court and are only required to submit basic documentation, such as proof of purchase, to the designated body responsible for distributing compensation. This passive role may not be problematic for individuals with limited resources or minor claims, for whom class actions offer a practical path to redress. However, for beneficiaries with the financial means to litigate individually and whose damages are substantial, this lack of involvement can be a concern. In competition law, for instance, the same anticompetitive conduct can affect both individual consumers and large corporations, with damages varying accordingly. While class members do

731. *See* s. 3.3.8 above.

retain the right to intervene in the proceedings or opt out and pursue individual claims,[732] more active participation generally leads to more robust litigation and, potentially, fairer outcomes. That said, the contingency fee model (where lawyers are compensated only if the case is successful) provides a strong incentive for attorneys to invest in the case and pursue well-founded claims. This alignment of interests can help ensure that even passive beneficiaries are adequately represented.

- *Procedural costs* (high costs for both parties due to the burden of proof and certification requirements): class actions are often associated with substantial procedural costs for both plaintiffs and defendants. This is largely due to the dual burden of meeting the stringent requirements of the certification phase and proving the substantive claims. In the context of competition law, these challenges are amplified by the complexity and technical nature of the evidence typically involved. This extends to the Court as well, which must carefully assess each stage of the proceeding, from certification to final resolution. In practice, however, many class actions in the US do not proceed to trial. It is not uncommon for parties to reach a settlement even before the class is formally certified. Once approved by the Court, such settlements bind both current and future claimants. Nevertheless, this approval process still demands thorough preparation and judicial scrutiny to ensure fairness and legal compliance.

In addition, some critics question the legitimacy of class actions that represent a small number of claimants or result in large global settlements that may not appear proportionate to the actual harm caused. These concerns often centre on whether such actions truly reflect the scale of the damage or whether they risk distorting the principle of proportionality.

However, while other criticisms of class actions may hold merit, this particular concern seems less persuasive, especially in the US context. The legitimacy of a class action should not hinge solely on the size of the class or the magnitude of the settlement. If the mechanism enables injured parties to recover damages they would otherwise be unable to pursue individually, then the action serves a valid and necessary function.

As for the often-criticised million-dollar settlements and contingency fees, these should not be viewed as problematic per se. Provided that the rights of the injured parties are protected and that the attorney has fulfilled their ethical obligations, such outcomes are consistent with the goals of private enforcement. After all, class actions operate within the realm of civil justice – not public enforcement – and their legitimacy lies in access to redress, not in symbolic proportionality:

- *Effective private enforcement* (ensures redress for small individual damages, particularly in competition law cases): this is perhaps the most compelling benefit of class actions, particularly in the field of competition law. When

732. *See* Rule 23(b)(3) of the Federal Rules of Civil Procedure.

individual damages are small, pursuing a claim independently is often economically unviable. Class actions ensure that the right to redress is not lost simply because the harm is dispersed across a large number of victims. This rationale applies in both the EU and US contexts, but it is especially pronounced in the US, where contingency fee arrangements are standard. These allow lawyers to be compensated as a percentage of the total award, making it feasible to consolidate numerous small claims into a single, viable action. Without class actions, many victims would remain uncompensated, and infringers could be incentivised to continue their illegal conduct - so long as the individual harm remains low, even if the aggregate profit is substantial due to the scale of affected consumers. While public enforcement also plays a critical role in deterring anticompetitive practices, it may not be sufficient on its own. Even when fines reach the statutory maximum (e.g., 10% of the previous year's turnover), the economic gains from the infringement,[733] combined with the absence of private compensation, can still outweigh the penalties. Moreover, although reputational damage from a public conviction can be significant, it does not necessarily restore losses to the victims. In this light, class actions serve as a vital complement to public enforcement by ensuring that private harm is addressed and that deterrence is reinforced through financial accountability.

- *Efficiency of compensation* (allows global settlements, avoiding future litigation through a single compensation):[734] class actions enhance procedural efficiency by enabling global settlements that resolve all related claims in a single proceeding. This approach not only prevents the proliferation of individual lawsuits but also streamlines the compensation process. Typically, a designated body is appointed to evaluate the evidence submitted by each claimant and to distribute the compensation accordingly. This centralised mechanism ensures consistency, reduces litigation costs, and accelerates the delivery of redress to affected parties.[735]
- *Balancing the investment for a fairer result* (equalises the resources invested by plaintiffs and defendants, influencing the outcome): in litigation, particularly in competition law, defendants (often large companies) typically possess greater financial resources and are able to invest heavily in legal defence, including specialised lawyers and experts. When faced with multiple lawsuits on the same issue, this investment is naturally amplified. In contrast, an individual plaintiff may lack the means or incentive to match such resources,

733. Classical economic theory, for example, assumed that collusive companies were more profitable than those that complied with the rules - which should only make sense in the absence of competition law enforcement. *See* Dosoung Choi and George C. Philippatos, *The Review of Economics and Statistics*, vol. 65, No. 3, August 1983, pp. 501-506, p. 501.
734. However, it is a very expensive process, in which lawyers usually earn large fees/awards.
735. Also in this context, and despite the fact that this book focuses on compensation actions, it cannot fail to mention that in the case of complex injunctions, for example those that involve a major change in the organisation or *modus operandi* of that company, collective action avoids contradictory decisions and allows for the construction of more reasoned and effective measures, through the consultation of various interested parties.

especially when only a single claim is at stake. Class actions help level this imbalance. By consolidating numerous similar claims into one coordinated action, they allow plaintiffs to pool resources and share legal costs. This collective approach not only enhances the quality of representation but also increases the likelihood of a fair outcome, as it reduces the disparity in legal firepower between the parties.

- *Proportional distribution of compensation* (ensures fair distribution of available assets among all claimants): if the total compensation value of the various individual actions exceeds the defendant's assets or the limit of the insurance he holds, the first litigants will receive more than the plaintiffs of the subsequent actions, who may receive nothing. A class action ensures a proportional distribution of the available assets among the various holders of the right to compensation.
- *Promoting judicial economy* (reduces the likelihood of multiple lawsuits on the same issue, encouraging settlements): this is the most frequently mentioned benefit, although this book believes it is unlikely that there will be several lawsuits on the same issue. In fact, if the first lawsuit is unsuccessful, it is unlikely that lawyers will accept any more. However, if the first one is successful, it is likely that the defendant will try to reach a settlement in subsequent cases.

In addition, many of the criticisms directed at the US class action system can be addressed through existing safeguards. Rule 23 of the Federal Rules of Civil Procedure provides key control mechanisms, such as those already mentioned: the requirements for class certification and the judicial approval of settlements. Additionally, the opt-out model ensures that beneficiaries retain the freedom to leave the class at any time, preserving their autonomy and legal options.

Even the award of punitive damages, often cited as a controversial feature of the US system, is subject to judicial scrutiny. Courts assess such awards based on the specific circumstances of the case and in accordance with the principle of proportionality.[736] As emphasised by Francis E. McGovern,[737] US Supreme Court jurisprudence has consistently placed limits on punitive damages in class actions, reinforcing the system's built-in checks and balances.[738]

In response to growing criticism of the US class action system, Congress enacted the CAFA (Class Action Fairness Act)[739] in 2005. This legislation significantly expanded

736. *See* Michigan Law Review, *Class Actions for Punitive Damages*, Michigan Law Review, vol. 81, p. 1787 https://doi.org/10.2307/1288607, available at *'Class Actions for Punitive Damages' by Michigan Law Review (umich.edu)*, p. 1789.
737. In *Punitive Damages and Class Actions*, Louisiana Law Review, vol. 70, Number 2, Symposium on Punitive Damages, Winter 2010, p. 435.
738. *See* Daniel McClure and Matthew Dekovich, *Class and Group Actions Laws and Regulations: USA*, 9 November 2022, available at Class and Group Actions Laws and Regulations Report 2023 USA (iclg.com), pt. 5.3.
739. Available at https://www.congress.gov/109/plaws/publ2/PLAW-109publ2.pdf.

federal jurisdiction over class actions, aiming to enhance judicial oversight and consistency. CAFA was designed to address concerns about excessive contingency fee arrangements and disproportionate settlement awards, while also reducing the risk of conflicting decisions issued by state trial courts.[740] By centralising more class actions in federal courts, CAFA sought to ensure greater uniformity, transparency, and fairness in the handling of complex, multi-state litigation.

While increasing judicial oversight of class action settlements and fee arrangements is sensible in the US context, we respectfully disagree with Janet Cooper Alexander's proposal[741] to shift from an opt-out to an opt-in model as a way to curb lawyers' dominance under the contingency fee regime. Such a change would fundamentally undermine the effectiveness of class actions in the US legal system.

The reality is that most injured parties lack both the incentive and the resources to initiate litigation on their own. Requiring affirmative participation would drastically reduce the number of claimants, effectively 'killing' class actions as all know them in the US. Instead, the current opt-out model ensures broad participation and access to justice, particularly for those with small individual claims.

Concerns about financial barriers can be addressed through mechanisms such as success fees and TPLF. While these funding arrangements raise legitimate concerns about potential conflicts of interest between funders and lawyers, they also play a crucial role in enabling access to justice – especially when lawyers themselves act as funders, as is often the case in the US.[742] This issue is particularly relevant for the EU, where the development of private enforcement mechanisms is still evolving and where funding models will require careful consideration.[743]

Although the pace of class actions in the US may slow in the coming years due to policy efforts aimed at curbing excessive litigation,[744] it remains one of the most favourable jurisdictions for bringing such actions, particularly in the field of antitrust. Compared even to the UK, where the concept of class actions originated[745] and which serves as one of the national case studies in this book's comparative analysis,[746] the US system stands out for its procedural flexibility and distinctive features. These include the widespread use of contingency fees, the availability of punitive damages, and streamlined mechanisms[747] that facilitate collective redress. Together, these elements create a legal environment that strongly supports the initiation and resolution of class actions.

740. *See* Margaret M. Zwiskler, Christopher S. Yates and William R. Sherman, *United States, in Class Actions: A Global Guide from Practical Law*, Omar Shah (ed.), Thomson Reuters, 2015, p. 403.
741. In *Contingent Fees and Class Actions*, DePaul Law Review, vol. 47, No. 2, Winter 1998, Symposium – Contingency Fee Financing of Litigation in America, Article 7, pp. 350 and 360.
742. *See* s. 3.3.8 above.
743. *See* s. 3.6.5.4 below.
744. *See* Arthur R. Miller, *The American Class Action: From Birth to Maturity*, Theoretical Inquiries in Law, vol. 19, No. 1, 13 February 2018, p. 45 https://doi.org/10.1515/til-2018-0001.
745. *See* s. 3.2 above.
746. *See* s. 3.4.4 below.
747. *See United States (U.S.) Class Actions and United Kingdom (UK) Collective Actions (orrick.com).*

3.4.2 Rationale for the Selection of National Cases

The comparative analysis of national class action regimes is instrumental in shaping an effective EU-level framework. It enables the identification of successful elements, as well as the structural or procedural shortcomings that contribute to the underutilisation of collective redress mechanisms.

Given the significant diversity among Member States' legal systems in this area, it is essential to examine national collective action regimes in order to identify shared features that could serve as a foundation for EU-level harmonisation. This approach ensures that any proposed solution respects the legal traditions of individual Member States, which often reflect deeply rooted principles and serve important functions within their respective jurisdictions.

One of the common arguments against harmonising Member State rules on collective actions is that each Member State should retain the autonomy to determine what best serves its citizens. Moreover, the diversity of national approaches allows for experimentation, enabling some Member States to serve as models, highlighting both the strengths and weaknesses of different legislative options.[748] While this perspective is valid, it must be acknowledged that progress in developing effective collective redress mechanisms for competition law actions at the national level has been limited, and this may justify a horizontal, EU-wide solution. Given the significant disparities in national legislation, any harmonised approach will inevitably require substantial adjustments to existing legal frameworks. This makes it all the more essential to analyse national legal traditions and current practices in collective protection. Such analysis provides the foundation for designing a harmonised EU model that is both effective and respectful of the legal diversity across Member States.

Among the Member States that already had collective action mechanisms in place, this book selected Portugal, the UK, Belgium, and France for its comparative analysis. These countries were chosen because they represent contrasting approaches to collective redress, offering valuable insights for EU-level reflection. Notably: Belgium, France and the UK[749] have undergone significant reforms in recent years; Portugal and the UK have been cited as emerging success stories; and (in contrast) Belgium and France continue to face challenges that suggest the need for further intervention.[750]

The European Class Action Report 2024[751] recently categorised several jurisdictions using a 'high, medium and low' risk scale for class actions, based on national legislation and case law. The analysis considered factors such as the class action model (opt-in versus opt-out), procedural rules for filing and certifying claims, and access to litigation funding. Within this framework, Portugal and the United Kingdom were

748. *See* Eda Şahin, *Collective Redress and EU Competition Law*, Routledge, 2019, p. 58.
749. *See* Sofia Oliveira Pais, *Private Antitrust Enforcement: A New Era for Collective Redress?*, Yearbook of Antitrust and Regulatory Studies, vol. 8, No. 12, CARS, 2015 https://doi.org/10.7172/1689-9024.yars.2015.8.12.1, available at 3Private Antitrust Enforcement.pdf, p. 23.
750. *See* Žygimantas Juška, *The Role of Collective Redress Actions to Achieve Full Compensation for Violations of European Union Competition Law*, PhD thesis defended at Leiden University on 23 June 2019, available at view (universiteitleiden.nl), pp. 119, 125 and 157.
751. *See* european-class-action-report-2024 (cms.law), p. 18.

identified as hot jurisdictions, indicating a high level of class action activity and risk. Belgium was classified as medium, while France was the only large Member State (by population, France is currently the EU's second most populous country after Germany) to receive a low classification.

Portugal and the UK currently operate opt-out collective action mechanisms[752] and, although at different stages of development - with the UK further ahead, as will be discussed - they have both experienced a notable rise in such actions, particularly in the field of competition law. This makes them natural focal points for this analysis.[753] Žygimantas Juška previously observed that, at least until 2019, antitrust collective litigation had only been viable in three Member States: Portugal, the Netherlands, and the UK. However, he excluded Portugal from his analysis at the time, citing the existence of only one relevant case. Since then, as anticipated by Miguel Sousa Ferro[754] (who also highlighted the UK and Belgium, albeit to varying degrees), Portugal has seen a surge in competition law class actions, effectively propelling it to the forefront of this area.

Belgium, by contrast, currently employs a hybrid collective action model, allowing for either opt-in or opt-out mechanisms depending on the circumstances of the case, as determined by the Tribunal de Première Instance. France, however, maintains a strictly opt-in model.[755] Despite having collective action frameworks in place, both countries have seen limited practical outcomes.[756] This raises an important question: what is holding them back? The following analysis will attempt to address this by comparing their performance in the private enforcement of competition law - particularly in terms of the number of cases - with the more active jurisdictions discussed above.

When considering the development of a horizontal class action mechanism at the EU level, specifically for competition law disputes, it is essential to draw on the diversity of existing national models. A viable EU-wide solution must be compatible with the legal particularities of representative Member States, including those that employ opt-out, hybrid and opt-in collective action frameworks. This comparative approach ensures that any harmonised mechanism reflects the practical realities and procedural nuances already embedded in national legal systems.

---

752. *See* Till Shreiber and Martin Seegers, *Collective or Class Actions and Claims Aggregation in the EU: The Claimant's Perspective*, in *GCR's Private Litigation Guide*, Nicholas and Heaton and Benhamin Holt (eds), 3rd ed., 2021, *asset download – Global Competition Review*, p. 42.
753. The ease of gathering information for this work also contributed to this: Portugal is the author's jurisdiction, and the UK makes information on this matter publicly available, namely through the CAT *website*.
754. In *Collective Redress: Will Portugal Show the Way?*, Journal of European Competition Law & Practice, vol. 6, No. 5, 2015 https://doi.org/10.1093/jeclap/lpv031, available at Collective Redress: Will Portugal Show the Way? by Miguel Sousa Ferro:: SSRN, p. 299.
755. *See* Till Shreiber and Martin Seegers, *Collective or Class Actions and Claims Aggregation in the EU: The Claimant's Perspective, in GCR's Private Litigation Guide*, Nicholas and Heaton and Benhamin Holt (eds), 3rd ed., 2021, *asset download – Global Competition Review*, pp. 41 and 42.
756. *See* Alexander Biard and Stefaan Voet, *Collective Redress in the EU: Will It Finally Come True? in Class Actions in Europe: Holy Grail or a Wrong Trail?*, Alan Uzelac and Stefaan Voet (eds), Springer, 2021, p. 296.

Moreover, this book believes it is insufficient to focus solely on the most successful cases. A meaningful analysis must also consider their counterparts, i.e., jurisdictions where collective actions have yielded limited results. This comparative approach is essential to identifying the underlying factors that differentiate these scenarios. In this context, such contrasts can offer valuable insights into the structural, procedural, or cultural elements that either facilitate or hinder effectiveness. Indeed, these insights are crucial for informing the design of any future EU-level solution.

This book therefore adopts the comparative method advocated by Carlos Ferreira de Almeida and Jorge Morais Carvalho,[757] selecting States as the scope of analysis to examine emerging EU legislation through the lens of two distinct legal traditions: the Roman-Germanic and the Common Law families:

(i) On the one hand, this book considered Belgium particularly due to its hybrid collective action regime - and France, which, as the aforementioned authors note, is the 'head of the line' of the Roman-Germanic family (along with Germany - which was not included in our core comparison because it is 'halfway' in terms of innovation and effectiveness of the legal solutions adopted in this area; i.e., it is not a typical example to follow or reject in this book's view, although has made notable progress in recent years).[758,759]

(ii) On the other side are Portugal and the UK. As Charlotte Leskinen highlights,[760] Portugal represents the most prominent example of an opt-out class action regime within the EU. The UK, as the origin of the Common Law tradition (and the legal foundation from which US law evolved), also plays a central role in this comparative framework.[761]

Before proceeding with the comparative analysis itself, it is important to set out the three methodological phases guiding this book's approach: *(i) knowledge*, *(ii) understanding*, and *(iii) comparison*. Accordingly, this study will not only present factual information but also reflect critically on it, culminating in a synthesis of similarities and differences. These will be explained and contextualised to support meaningful conclusions,[762] particularly in light of the potential development of EU-level legislation.

The analysis is structured around the following framework:

(i) *Tertium comparationis (object of comparison):*
Collective action mechanisms applicable to competition law in *Portugal*, the *UK*, *Belgium* and *France*.

757. *In Introdução ao Direito Comparado*, Almedina, 3rd ed., 2017, pp. 37 and 41.
758. *See 2024 CMS European Class Action Report*, available at european-class-action-report-2024 (cms.law), p. 23.
759. *See*, for example, s. 3.6.5.4 below.
760. *In Collective Actions: Rethinking Funding and National Cost Rules*, The Competition Law Review, vol. 8, No. 1, December 2011, p. 91.
761. *See* s. 3.4.1 above.
762. *See* Carlos Ferreira de Almeida and Jorge Morais Carvalho, *Introduction to Comparative Law*, Almedina, 3rd ed., 2017, p. 30.

(ii) *Informative topics:*
 (1) Class action model.
 (2) Control.
 (3) Proceeding.
 (4) Limitations.
 (5) Class actions.
(iii) *Comparative grid (concrete comparative factors):*[763]
 (1) Class action model.
 (2) Specific rules for antitrust class actions.
 (3) Standing: who may initiate proceedings.
 (4) Class certification or need for court authorisation.
 (5) Pre-action disclosure of evidence.
 (6) Cost allocation.
 (7) Litigation funding.
 (8) Fee arrangements (*quota litis* agreements, conditional fees and success fees).
 (9) Punitive damages.
 (10) Antitrust class actions filed.
(iv) *Objective:*
The goal is not only to uncover what unites and distinguishes these four countries but also to spotlight how they contribute to shaping a more effective and coherent EU-wide framework for collective redress in competition law. By learning from both their strengths and shortcomings, this comparative analysis aims to inspire a more harmonised and impactful legal landscape for antitrust class actions across the EU.

3.4.3 Portugal

For several years, Portugal has been highlighted[764] as a promising model for collective redress within the EU, particularly in the enforcement of competition law. As will be detailed below, the country boasts a theoretically robust legal framework for such actions. However, until recently, the number of actual cases remained low, largely attributed to the absence of strong litigation funding mechanisms. That landscape has changed dramatically. Today, Portugal stands out for its growing volume of compensation claims related to competition law infringements, including class actions. This shift is clearly illustrated in the table provided in Appendix II – Survey of Recent

763. Although they may coincide with some of the above topics, these are stricter concepts.
764. *See* Sofia Oliveira Pais, *Private Antitrust Enforcement: A New Era for Collective Redress?*, Yearbook of Antitrust and Regulatory Studies, vol. 8, Nos 12f., CARS, 2015 https://doi.org/10.7172/1689-9024.yars.2015.8.12.1, available at 3Private Antitrust Enforcement.pdf, p. 30. *See also In Collective Redress: Will Portugal Show the Way?* Journal of European Competition Law & Practice, vol. 6, No. 5, 2015 https://doi.org/10.1093/jeclap/lpv031, available at Collective Redress: Will Portugal Show the Way? by Miguel Sousa Ferro:: SSRN, p. 299.

Competition Law Private Enforcement Cases in Portugal (annexed to this book as a complementary resource, enriching the broader analysis presented herein).[765]

3.4.3.1 Class Action Model

Portugal is one of the few Member States, as previously noted, that adopts an opt-out class action model - meaning actions are brought on behalf of an indeterminate group of individuals, without requiring their express consent to join. This contrasts with the opt-in model, which demands explicit participation. In Portugal, this form of collective redress is known as *actio popularis* or ação popular (popular action), designed to protect diffuse interests.[766]

As Paulo Otero eloquently puts it,[767] this mechanism offers a form of judicial protection for material legal positions that, while collectively held by all members of a given community, are not individually appropriable, meaning they cannot be effectively safeguarded through individual legal action. In the context of competition law, this captures the essence of diffuse interests that require collective redress to ensure meaningful enforcement.

This instrument remains rare within the EU, not only because it follows an opt-out model but also because it is constitutionally enshrined in Portugal.[768] In theory, it offers a highly effective mechanism for collective redress. However, in practice, several barriers have historically limited its use, particularly in the field of competition law.

---

765. This table was made possible by the author's registration as a lawyer with the Portuguese Bar Association, which grants privileged access to case information not readily available in other Member States. Specifically, the author was able to consult case files under Article 27 of Ministerial Order 280/2013 of 26 August, which regulates the electronic processing of court proceedings. Furthermore, the scope of the table extends beyond class actions strictly related to competition law infringements. For these reasons, the table focuses exclusively on Portugal.
766. Law No. 83/95, of 31 August.
767. In A *acção popular: configuração e valor no actual Direito português*, Revista da Ordem dos Advogados, vol. III, 1999, pp. 871-893, p. 872.
768. Article 52(3) of the Constitution of the Portuguese Republic: (1) All citizens have the right to present, individually or collectively, petitions, representations, claims or complaints to the organs of sovereignty, to the organs of self-government of the autonomous regions or to any authorities in defence of their rights, the Constitution, the laws or the general interest, as well as the right to be informed, within a reasonable time, of the outcome of the respective examination.

    (2) The law establishes the conditions under which petitions presented collectively to the Assembly of the Republic and the Legislative Assemblies of the autonomous regions are considered in plenary session.
    (3) Everyone has the right to take popular action, in person or through associations for the defence of the interests in question, in the cases and terms provided for by law, including the right to request the corresponding compensation for the injured party or parties, namely to:
    (a) promote the prevention, cessation or prosecution of offences against public health, consumer rights, quality of life, the preservation of the environment and cultural heritage;
    (b) ensure the defence of the assets of the state, autonomous regions and local authorities.

These include monetary constraints (notably litigation costs), legal complexities (such as the distribution of compensation) and social factors (like a limited culture of litigation). As a result, the number of cases brought under this mechanism remained low until recently. While the volume of actions has since increased, especially in competition law, the compensation outcomes have yet to reflect this substantial shift.

Portugal presents a compelling case study[769] in this context: despite having one of the few European collective redress mechanisms that closely resembles the American model - particularly in its use of the opt-out class action - why is it that only now are we beginning to see a meaningful rise in cases, especially in the field of competition law?

As we have seen,[770] although the EU Damages Directive does not explicitly address collective actions, Portugal went beyond the minimum requirements in its transposition law[771] to ensure the full realisation of the right to redress.[772] Notably, it extended standing to bring collective actions - not only for injunctions but also for compensation for damages suffered (excluding punitive damages) - to a broader range of entities. This includes not only consumer protection associations and foundations but also business associations, such as those representing SMEs, even when their statutory purpose does not include the protection of competition, provided their members have been harmed by the infringement. This legislative choice reflects Portugal's commitment to strengthening access to justice in competition law enforcement.[773]

Portugal has long been notably permissive regarding standing to bring popular actions - whose very name, rooted in Roman law, signifies 'open to all' or 'for the protection of all'.[774] This constitutional mechanism allows for the defence of diffuse interests, and its accessibility is one of its defining features. In fact, the right to initiate such actions has traditionally been recognised not only for all citizens enjoying their civil and political rights but also for local authorities (when acting in defence of interests within their territorial scope) and for associations or foundations that explicitly include the protection of those interests in their statutory objectives.[775] As

769. *See* Miguel Sousa Ferro, *Class Actions in Portugal: The Little Regime That Could, in Mass Claims*, No. 2, December 2021, available at Class Actions in Portugal - Mass Claims - Uitgeverij Den Hollander, p. 115.
770. *See* s. 2.3 above.
771. Law No. 23/2018.
772. *See* Sofia Oliveira Pais, *A First Look at the Portuguese Act 23/2018 Transposing the EU Damages Directive, in EU Competition Litigation: Transposition and First Experiences of the New Regime*, Magnus Strand, Vladimir Bastidas Venegas and Marios C. Iacovides (eds), Oxford Hart Publishing, 2019, pp. 63-76, available at untitled (ucp.pt), p. 73.
773. Article 19(2) of Law 23/2018.
774. *See* António Pedro Pinto Monteiro and José Miguel Júdice, *Class Actions & Arbitration in the European Union:– Portugal*, Estudos em Homenagem a Miguel Galvão Teles, vol. II, Almedina, 2012, pp. 189-205, p. 190.
775. *See* Articles 1(2), 2 and 3(b) of Law 83/95. In addition, the general requirements (Article 3 of Law 83/95) require associations/foundations to have legal personality and not to carry out any kind of professional activity in competition with companies or freelance professionals - no additional requirements are provided for, such as a minimum number of members.

Rita Lobo Xavier, Inês Folhadela, and Gonçalo Andrade e Castro aptly observe,[776] to be a legitimate party is to have a direct relationship with the object of the litigation.[777]

Nevertheless, as Sofia Oliveira Pais rightly points out,[778] not everyone is entitled to bring a popular action in Portugal. Despite the broad scope of this mechanism, the law explicitly excludes companies (even SMEs) from initiating such actions directly. In practice, SMEs may only seek redress through individual claims, as has traditionally been the case,[779] or indirectly through representation by legal entities such as associations or foundations, as outlined above.

In this book's view, the most significant driver behind the recent surge in class actions for breaches of competition law in Portugal has been the binding effect of national decisions[780] implementing the EU Damages Directive.[781] Prior to its transposition, National Courts were under no obligation to follow public enforcement decisions issued by national authorities.[782] This lack of binding force limited the practical utility of such decisions in private litigation. The Directive's implementation changed that dynamic, strengthening the legal foundation for claimants and enhancing the credibility and enforceability of collective redress mechanisms. This shift has played a pivotal role in unlocking the potential of Portugal's opt-out model, particularly in the competition law arena.

3.4.3.2 Control

It is important to note that THE popular action, unlike class actions in Common Law countries, does not have a class certification; i.e., there is no need for prior judicial authorisation of class representation by the National Courts.[783] Instead, the Portuguese

776. In *Elementos de direito procedual civil: Teoria geral – Princípios: Pressupostos*, Universidade Católica Portuguesa Editora – Porto, 2nd ed., 2018, p. 164.
777. Although legal standing may also arise indirectly, either through statutory provisions (as previously noted) or by virtue of a legal transaction. *See* Castro Mendes and Miguel Teixeira de Sousa, *Manual de Processo Civil*, vol. I, AAFDL, 2022, pp. 340-345.
778. In Sofia Oliveira Pais and Anna Piszcz, *Package on Actions for Damages Based on Breaches of EU Competition Rules: Can One Size Fit All?*, Yearbook of Antitrust and Regulatory Studies, vol. 7, No. 10, 2014, p. 216.
779. *See* Appendix II – Survey of Recent Competition Law Private Enforcement Cases in Portugal, which includes eight individual actions brought by companies. Of particular note is the decision of the *TCRS Transfrugal v. Daf Trucks*, in Case 71/19.6YQSTR, of 6 November 2022. This was the first ruling in the context of the 'trucks cartel' (AT.39824, available at https://ec.europa.eu/competition/elojade/isef/case_details.cfm?proc_code = 1_39824), in the sum of EUR 15,487.65. There are approximately hundred more individual follow-on actions like this one pending before the TCRS.
780. *See* s. 2.3.1.4 above.
781. *See* s. 3.4.3.6 below.
782. *See* Miguel Sousa Ferro, *Binding Effect of Public Enforcement Decisions, in Research Handbook on Competition Law Private Enforcement in the EU,* Barry Rodger, Miguel Sousa Ferro and Francisco Marcos (eds), Edward Elgar, 2023, p. 6.
783. *See* Miguel Sousa Ferro, *Ações populares cíveis em Portugal*, Revista de Direito Comercial, 23 February 2022, pp. 424 and 425.

system includes a specific procedural safeguard: the possibility of rejecting the initial application if the judge considers the claim manifestly unlikely to succeed.[784] In such cases, the National Courts must first consult the Public Prosecutor's Office (Ministério Público),[785] which plays a unique and active role in popular actions. The Public Prosecutor not only holds standing to initiate proceedings but also has powers of representation and procedural intervention. Notably, it may substitute the original plaintiff in the event of withdrawal, settlement, or any conduct deemed detrimental to the interests at stake.[786]

This control mechanism typically takes place before the defendant and the represented consumers are even formally notified. On this basis, Miguel Sousa Ferro argues[787] that the Portuguese regime offers robust safeguards against abuse. While we acknowledge the value of this early-stage filter, we would hesitate to describe it as extensive, particularly when compared to the class certification process conducted by the CAT, which will be examined later.[788] Notably, the Portuguese National Court does not assess the representativeness of the claimant as a prerequisite for proceeding.[789] Even so, considering the broader EU context and the litigation barriers already discussed, we regard this preliminary control mechanism as sufficiently balanced and appropriate for the Portuguese legal landscape.

Additionally, litigation conducted in bad faith[790] is subject to sanctions under Portuguese law. A party found to be acting abusively may be ordered to pay a fine and compensate the opposing party (if the latter requests it).[791] A litigant is considered to be acting in bad faith when, with intent or gross negligence, they:[792]

(1) submit a claim or opposition they could not reasonably believe to be valid;
(2) distort or conceal facts relevant to the case;
(3) seriously neglect their duty to cooperate with the Court; or

784. *See* Article 13 of Law 83/95.
785. The intention to grant legitimacy to the Public Prosecutor's Office in the context of popular action first appeared in Bill 465/V of 1990. On the long legislative process that led to the current law, *see* Margarida Sousa Lobo de Carvalho, *Tutela Coletiva Indemnizatória*, Master's dissertation, Lisboa, Universidade Católica Portuguesa, 2020, pp. 16 et seq.
786. *See* Article 16 of Law 83/95.
787. *See* Miguel Sousa Ferro, *Class Actions in Portugal: The Little Regime That Could, in Mass Claims*, No. 2, December 2021, available at Class Actions in Portugal - Mass Claims - Uitgeverij Den Hollander, p. 119.
788. *See* s. 3.4.4 below.
789. *See* Aloísio Bolwerk and José Eustáquio de Melo Júnior, *Considerações sobre a Tutela do Processo Coletivo no Brasil e em Portugal*, Revista Jurídica Luso-Brasileira, Year 7, No. 6, 2021, pp. 75-101, p. 86.
790. *See* João Alves, *Ação popular: a intervenção acessória do Ministério Público na jurisdição civil*, Revista do Ministério Público No. 160, October and December 2019, pp. 131-151, p. 133.
791. *See* Articles 20.4 of Law 83/95 and 542.1 of the Portuguese Code of Civil Procedure, approved by Law 41/2013 of 26 June.
792. *See* Marta Alexandra Frias Borges, *Algumas Reflexões em Matéria de Litigância de Má-Fé*, Master's dissertation, Coimbra University, 2014, p. 45.

(4) misuse procedural tools to pursue an unlawful objective, obstruct the discovery of truth, hinder the administration of justice, or unduly delay the final judgment.[793]

In this sense, concerns often raised at the EU level about the risk of abusive litigation under a collective redress model inspired by the US system would be mitigated if the Portuguese framework were adopted under the EU law. This is especially true given that Portugal also prohibits *quota litis* agreements – a safeguard explored in more detail below.[794]

3.4.3.3 *Proceeding*

Once the potential preliminary rejection mentioned above is overcome, the procedure unfolds across twelve key stages, following the general framework of popular actions and incorporating the specific provisions of competition law[795] introduced with the transposition of the EU Damages Directive:[796]

(1) Upon receipt of the petition for a popular action, the holders of the interests at stake (whether or not they are parties to the proceedings) are summoned through public announcements. These announcements may be disseminated via any form of mass communication or published in appropriate outlets, depending on whether the interests involved are general or geographically localised. There is no requirement to identify these individuals personally; it is sufficient to refer to them as the holders of the relevant interests and to identify the action by naming at least the first plaintiff (if there are multiple), the defendant(s), and by providing a concise description of the claim and its legal basis.[797]

(2) Within the time limit set by the judge in the aforementioned summons – typically sixty days[798] – the holders of the interests at stake may choose one of the following options: (i) intervene in the main proceedings,

793. *See* Article 542(2) of the Portuguese Code of Civil Procedure.
794. *See* s. 3.6.5.4 below.
795. There are more lex specialis, for example, on consumer law (Articles 10 to 13, 17 and 18, No. 1 of the Consumer Defence Law, approved by Law No. 24/96, of 31 July) and environmental protection (Articles 7 of Law No. 19/2014, of 14 April, as well as 10 and 11 of Law No. 35/98, of 18 July).
796. Previously there were no specific competition law rules in Portugal applicable to damages actions, *see* Sofia Oliveira Pais, *National Report: Portugal, XXVII FIDE Congress, Budapest,* Hungary, 18-21 May 2016, Private Enforcement and Collective Redress in European Competition Law – Congress Proceedings, Kluwer Law International, 2016, available at Microsoft Word - FIDE 2016 Topic 2.docx (apde.org.pt), p. 2.
797. *See* Article 15(1) and (2) of Law 83/95.
798. *See* Miguel Sousa Ferro, *Ações populares cíveis em Portugal,* Revista de Direito Comercial, 23 February 2022, p. 425.

accepting the case at its current stage; (ii) declare in the case file that they accept being represented by the plaintiff; or (iii) exclude themselves from such representation, by making an express declaration in the case file (this must be done no later than the end of the evidentiary stage or its equivalent).[799] Failure to take any of these actions within the prescribed period will be interpreted as tacit acceptance of representation by the plaintiff, and the resulting decisions will be binding upon them.[800]

(3) The proceedings follow the general rules applicable to civil actions, with particular emphasis on the preliminary hearing held after the initial written submissions. This hearing addresses any procedural or substantive objections raised in the defence – whether dilatory or peremptory – and may be replaced by a written decision at the judge's discretion.[801]

(4) Once the judgment has been issued and has become final, its effects extend to all holders of the rights or interests at stake who did not exercise their right to opt out of the representation. This general applicability is subject to two exceptions: (i) when the action is dismissed due to insufficient evidence, or (ii) when the judge determines otherwise based on case-specific considerations.[802]

(5) Final judgments must be published at the expense of the losing party and under penalty of contempt. The publication must reference the final decision and appear in two newspapers with national circulation that are likely to reach the affected audience. The judge selects the newspapers and may authorise publication in the form of an extract summarising the essential aspects of the judgment.[803]

(6) The judgment establishes the criteria for identifying the victims of the competition law infringement and for quantifying the damages suffered by each individually identified victim.[804]

799. As seen below, the effects of a final judgment handed down in the context of a popular action process cover all the holders of the rights or interests at stake in that action who have not exercised the right to opt out of representation. *See* Tiago Branco da Costa, *O sistema português da ação coletiva*, Dereito, Revista Xurídica da Universidade de Santiago de Compostela, vol. 28 No. 1, 2019, pp. 85-107, p. 96.

800. *See* Article 15, paras 1, 2 and 4 of Law 83/95.

801. As Miguel Sousa Ferro points out, these may include challenges to the active legitimacy of the plaintiff or the applicability of the popular action to the defence of the rights and interests in question. This is the moment when the Court confirms whether the action should proceed (as a popular action), in which case the representation of the class members is confirmed. A negative decision at this stage puts an end to the proceedings (in principle) and is subject to immediate appeal. There are many precedents of lower court decisions rejecting the admissibility of popular actions and then being overturned on appeal. It is not easy to identify an example of the opposite, in *Ações populares cíveis em Portugal*, Regista de Direito Comercial, 23 February 2022, p. 426.

802. Article 19(1) of Law 83/95.

803. Article 19(2) of Law 83/95.

804. Article 19(3) of Law 23/2018.

(7) If not all[805] injured parties are individually identified (which is expected to be the norm), the judge will determine a global amount of compensation.[806]

(8) If it is practically impossible or excessively difficult to accurately calculate the total damage suffered by the injured parties or the value of the harm passed on, based on the available evidence, the judge shall make this determination using an approximate estimate.[807] For this purpose, the judge may refer to the European Commission's Communication (2013/C 167/07) of 13 June 2013 on the quantification of damages in actions for damages based on infringements of Articles 101 and 102 of the TFEU.[808]

(9) If it is determined that the overall amount of compensation set is insufficient to fully redress the harm suffered by the injured parties identified in the meantime, that amount shall be distributed among them in proportion to the respective damage each has sustained.[809]

(10) The condemnatory judgment must designate the entity responsible for receiving, managing, and distributing the compensation owed to injured parties who have not been individually identified. This role may be assigned to the plaintiff, one or more of the identified injured parties, or another suitable entity, as determined by the National Court.[810]

(11) Following the judgment, injured parties may request their share of the compensation from the designated management entity.[811] Such requests must be submitted within a reasonable time limit set by the National Court and must include the necessary information to enable payment.[812]

805. In other words, as José Lebre de Freitas points out in *Regime da ação popular do art. 19 da Lei 23/2018*, Revista de Direito Comercial, 23 March 2022, pp. 557-594, p. 572, the wording of (special) Law No. 23/2018 differs from the wording of (general) Law No. 83/95. According to the latter, if there are identified and unidentified injured parties, the former are entitled to the corresponding compensation under the general terms of civil liability (verifying, for each, the causal link and the extent of the damage, under the terms of Articles 22(3) of Law 83/95 and 566 of the Portuguese Civil Code), while the latter have their compensation fixed globally. Despite this differentiation, the author excludes that, in practice, the regime applicable to competition law offences is different from the previous one. In other words, for the author the criterion to be followed in the event of a breach of competition rules is to compensate each injured party who is identified in the course of the proceedings, according to the criteria established by the condemnatory sentence, which may lead, taking into account the circumstances, to a distribution in equal instalments among the various injured parties or among predefined categories of injured parties. If not all the injured parties are identified, a global amount is fixed for those who are not identified (*see* p. 573).

806. *See* Article 19(4) of Law 23/2018.

807. *See* s. 2.3.1.5 above.

808. *See* Article 9(2) of Law 23/2018.

809. *See* Article 19(5) of Law 23/2018.

810. *See* Article 19.6 of Law 23/2018.

811. Paula Meira Lourenço, *Public Hearing on a Horizontal Instrument for Collective Redress in Europe*, Brussels, 12 July 2011, p. 8, points to practical difficulties in this process, due to the number of injured parties and the uncertainty regarding the division of the amount of compensation.

812. *See* Articles 20(2) and (3) of Law 83/95 and 19(7) of Law 23/2018.

(12) Any portion of the global compensation that remains unclaimed after the expiration of the Court-defined period will first be used to cover the plaintiff's costs, charges, fees, and other related expenses. The remaining balance will be transferred to the Portuguese Ministry of Justice, which will deposit it into a special account. These funds will be allocated to support the Public Prosecutor's Office and to facilitate access to justice and the courts for holders of the right to bring popular actions who can demonstrate financial need.[813]

Although this appears to be a claimant-friendly system,[814] it raises complex procedural challenges – particularly regarding the distribution of compensation to unidentified victims, as previously discussed. One such challenge concerns the distinction between identified and unidentified injured parties in the context of determining overall compensation or applying general civil liability principles. This book questions whether, as asserted by José Lebre de Freitas,[815] this duality still persists. The reason is that the special law, which takes precedence, does not draw a distinction between identified and unidentified victims when it comes to setting the amount of compensation.

On the one hand, it is reasonable to expect that, where victims are individually identified, compensation should reflect the actual harm they have suffered. On the other hand, as noted above, the legislator expressly allows for 'approximate compensation' when precise quantification is impractical. Ultimately, case law is decisive in clarifying how this issue is resolved in practice.

Moreover, while Law 23/2018 confirms the competence of the Portuguese National Court (TCRS) to establish the criteria for determining the quantum of compensation, doctrinal criticisms remain highly relevant. These include concerns over the broad discretion granted to judges in the absence of a legislated collective settlement mechanism,[816] as well as ongoing uncertainty about whether compensation should be calculated based on the actual harm suffered by victims or the total profit derived from the infringement.[817] These unresolved issues continue to raise important questions about consistency, fairness, and the effectiveness of the current legal framework.

Additionally, under Article 22(4) of Law 83/95, the right to compensation is subject to a three-year limitation period, starting from the date the judgment recognising that right becomes final. However, this general rule must be considered alongside the special rule discussed in point (11) above, which allows the judge to set a 'reasonable period' for injured parties to claim their share of compensation.

813. Articles 20(4) and (5) of Law 83/95 and Article 19(7) and (8) of Law 23/2018.

814. *See* Miguel Sousa Ferro, *Consumer antitrust private enforcement in Europe: as complete a survey as possible (extended version)*, 23 October 2022, available at https://ssrn.com/abstract=4223770, p. 17.

815. *See* fn. 843 below.

816. *See* Maria Elisabete Ramos, *Situação do 'private enforcement' da concorrência em Portugal, Revista de Concorrência e Regulação*, Year VII, No. 27/28, July/December 2016, p. 69.

817. *See* s. 3.6.4 below.

According to José Lebre de Freitas,[818] these two timeframes - the statutory three-year period and the judicially defined reasonable period - should coexist. He further argues that both groups of creditors, those who claim within the reasonable period and those who do so afterwards but within the three-year window, should be treated equally.

Yet this raises a fundamental question: what is the purpose of the reasonable period if it does not limit the right to claim compensation? Applying the principle of lex specialis *derogat legi generali*, one could argue that the special rule prevails, meaning that injured parties who fail to act within the judge's deadline may be barred from claiming compensation later.

Moreover, as noted in point (12) above, the law imposes a negative consequence for missing the National Court's deadline: unclaimed compensation may be redirected to cover litigation costs. This outcome contradicts the interpretation proposed by José Lebre de Freitas and highlights yet another inconsistency in the legal framework - one that contributes to significant legal uncertainty.

Another important question in this context concerns the entity to which injured parties must submit their claims - namely, who is responsible for receiving, managing, and distributing the compensation referred to in point (10) above. While it would seem logical for this role to be assigned to the representative,[819] Law 23/2018 once again leaves the decision to the TCRS, without establishing a default mechanism.

Equally unclear is what documentation injured parties must provide to substantiate their claims. It is reasonable to assume that proof of purchase - such as receipts, invoices, or contracts - would be required to demonstrate eligibility. However, the law remains silent on this point as well, leaving both claimants and the designated entity without clear procedural guidance.

One of the most significant challenges of the proceeding described above is its duration, which often spans several years.[820] This delay is not attributable solely to the slowness of the Portuguese National Courts. Rather, it stems from structural features of the Portuguese civil litigation system, which is heavily reliant on written submissions - unlike systems such as that of the US, where oral proceedings and settlements are more common and tend to expedite resolution.[821]

In addition, several procedural factors contribute to the length of these proceedings. Among the most time-consuming are the preliminary objections raised by defendants concerning the plaintiffs' standing, requests for access to evidence (which will be

818. In *Regime of the Popular Action of Art. 19 of Law 23/2018*, Commercial Law Magazine, 23 March 2022, pp. 557-594, p. 574.
819. *See* Sofia Oliveira Pais and Anna Piszcz, *Package on Actions for Damages Based on Breaches of EU Competition Rules: Can One Size Fit All?*, Yearbook of Antitrust and Regulatory Studies, vol. 7, No. 10, 2014, p. 218.
820. *See* Nuno Salazar Casanova and Madalena Afra Rosa, *The Class Actions Law Review: Portugal*, 21 April 2022, available at The Class Actions Law Review - The Law Reviews.
821. *See* s. 3.4.1 above.

addressed in more detail below),[822] and the frequency of appeals. In follow-on class actions, delays are further compounded by the need to suspend proceedings until the underlying infringement decision becomes final – as illustrated by the cases of *Ius Omnibus v. Super Bock and Ius Omnibus v. EDP*, discussed below.[823]

3.4.3.4 Costs

The assertion that Portugal is not a jurisdiction where the loser pays principle applies should not be conflated with the claim that litigation in Portugal is comparatively affordable – yet this distinction appears to be overlooked by Miguel Sousa Ferro.[824] Under the general rules of civil procedure, the party responsible for costs is the one who caused them, which typically means the losing party.[825] This interpretation has been upheld by the STJ (Supreme Court of Justice), which has confirmed that the losing party is liable for costs.[826]

In terms of what those legal costs entail – namely, court fees, charges, and party costs (including expenses borne by the prevailing party such as certificates, expert opinions, translations, postage, travel, and attorney's and enforcement officers' fees) – popular actions are exempt under the Portuguese Procedural Costs Regulation.[827]

Furthermore, while the general rule in popular actions aligns with the loser pays principle, the law provides that plaintiffs are exempt from costs if their claim is partially upheld.[828] In the event of total dismissal, the plaintiff may be ordered to pay between 10% and 50% of the costs that would ordinarily apply, with the amount determined by the National Court based on the plaintiff's financial situation and the grounds for dismissal.[829]

The apparent contradictions in Portuguese Law resulting from the above remain unresolved, largely because most current popular actions are still pending. Exceptions

822. *See* Miguel Sousa Ferro, *The Reality of Access in Antitrust Private Enforcement: Overview of 3 Years' Experience in Portugal*, Revista de Concorrência e Regulação, Year XIII, No. 46-47, Almedina, 2021, pp. 37-71, available at CR 46-47_Miguel Sousa Ferro.pdf (concorrencia.pt), pp. 48 and 58.
823. *See* s. 3.4.3.6 below and Appendix II – Survey of Recent Competition Law Private Enforcement Cases in Portugal.
824. In *Chapter 16: Portugal and Spain, in Research Handbook on Competition Law Private Enforcement in the EU*, Barry Rodger, Miguel Sousa Ferro and Francisco Marcos (eds), Edward Elgar, 2023, p. 11.
825. Article 527 of the Portuguese Code of Civil Procedure reads as follows: (1) The decision judging the action or any of its incidents or appeals shall condemn to costs the party who gave rise to them or, if the action is not successful, the party who profited from the proceedings. (2) The losing party shall be deemed to have given rise to the costs of the proceedings, in the proportion in which they do so. (3) In the event of a conviction for joint and several liability, solidarity shall extend to costs.
826. *See* STJ ruling of 9 October 2020, Case 1934/16.6T8VCT.G1.S1: The general rule of liability for the payment of costs is based, primarily, on the principle of causality and, subsidiarily, on the principle of procedural advantage or profit, the latter being indicated by the principle of succumbence, so the losing party must pay the costs, in the respective proportion.
827. Article 4(1)(b) of the Portuguese Procedural Costs Regulation, approved by Decree-Law 34/2008 of 26 February.
828. Article 20(2) of Law 83/95.
829. *See* Article 20(3) of Law 83/95.

include two settlements: one in the competition law case of *Ius Omnibus v. ANT*,[830] which will be discussed below;[831] and another in *DECO*[832] *v. Portugal Telecom*,[833] where the defendant agreed to compensate consumers with EUR 120 million in free calls following a National Court ruling[834] that activation fees were unlawful.[835] It is true that no court fee is due in this type of action. Also, as Miguel Sousa Ferro also notes,[836] the recovery of the plaintiff's costs, including financing costs, can be included in a transaction.

3.4.3.5 *Limitations*

Among the key limitations of the Portuguese system, the following stand out:

(i) the lack of standing for companies, particularly SMEs, to bring private enforcement actions directly. Ironically, these are often the entities most in need of such mechanisms. While the Portuguese legislator's decision to grant standing to associations representing companies was, in this book's view, one of the most significant innovations in the transposition of the EU Damages Directive,[837] it remains unclear why individual companies are excluded from initiating such actions;

(ii) the prohibition of *quota litis* agreements, which tie lawyers' fees exclusively to the outcome of the case. Although Portuguese law allows for success fees (where an additional amount is agreed based on the result), *quota litis* arrangements remain prohibited;[838] and

(iii) the absence of a clear legal framework for TPLF in this context – until the end of 2023, at the time of the transposition of Directive 2020/1828 on collective actions for the protection of consumers' interests, there was no specific rules governing third-party funding (other than by the plaintiffs themselves[839] or

830. *See* Appendix II – Survey of Recent Competition Law Private Enforcement Cases in Portugal.
831. *See* s. 3.4.3.6 below.
832. In fact, this Portuguese Association for the Defence of Consumers brought several class actions, at least between 1999 and 2015, based on violations other than competition law, *see Observatoire des Actions de Groupe et autres Actions Collectives*, 2021, available at Acoes_DECO-2021.pdf (observatoireactionsdegroupe.com).
833. *See* Appendix II – Survey of Recent Competition Law Private Enforcement Cases in Portugal.
834. *See* STJ ruling of 10 July 2003, Case 03A1243.
835. *See* Sofia Oliveira Pais, *Private Antitrust Enforcement: A New Era for Collective Redress?*, Yearbook of Antitrust and Regulatory Studies, vol. 8, No. 12, CARS, 2015 https://doi.org/10.7172/1689-9024.yars.2015.8.12.1, available at 3Private Antitrust Enforcement.pdf, p. 29.
836. In *Ações populares cíveis em Portugal*, Regista de Direito Comercial, 23 February 2022, p. 436.
837. *See* Article 19(2)(b).
838. Article 106 of the Statute of the Portuguese Bar Association, approved by Law No. 145/2015, of 9 September.
839. *See* Sofia Oliveira Pais, *National Report: Portugal, XXVII FIDE Congress*, Budapest, Hungary, 18-21 May 2016, Private Enforcement and Collective Redress in European Competition Law – Congress Proceedings, Kluwer Law International, 2016, available at Microsoft Word - FIDE 2016 Topic 2.docx (apde.org.pt), p. 4.

the state,[840] e.g., through legal aid). Now there is an article on funding class actions for redress measures that transposes Article 10 of the Directive,[841] but the transposition law[842] (as the Directive) only applies to class actions brought on the basis of laws referred to in its Annex I (meaning this does not apply to competition law).

Also remains undetermined whether the costs of such funding (including capital and remuneration of the funder) are recoverable from the residual compensation. This legal uncertainty[843] discourages the use of third-party funding mechanisms and may hinder the viability of collective redress.

Despite the absence of wide-ranging regulation on TPLF, there appears to be no compelling reason to consider such arrangements unlawful in any type of action, provided they do not contravene general legal principles. These include prohibitions against agreements that are contrary to law, public order, or good customs,[844] as well as those deemed usurious.[845] In particular, any arrangement that exploits a party's vulnerability – such as a situation of need, inexperience, dependence or mental incapacity – to secure excessive or unjustified benefits for the funder or a third party would be inadmissible.[846]

As advanced, the transposition of Directive 2020/1828 did not entail any changes to these limitations, not only because it did not apply to class actions based on competition law but also because it does not provide for the active legitimacy of companies, not even SMEs, in this matter and corroborates the prohibition of contingency fees.[847]

Furthermore, although the law permits requests for access to evidence held by the offender, the PCA, the TCRS, or even third parties prior to the initiation of proceedings, such access is rarely granted in practice.

Indeed, Portuguese civil and procedural law[848] already allowed for the possibility of requesting access to evidence prior to the filing of an action. While the EU Damages Directive requires that such requests be justified by facts and evidence reasonably

840. *See* Articles 6 of the Access to Law and Courts Regime, approved by Law 34/2004, of 29 July, and 3 of the Access to Justice in Cross-Border Disputes Regime, approved by Decree-Law 71/2005, of 17 March.
841. *See* s. 3.3.7 above.
842. Article 10 of Decree-Law No. 114-A/2023, of 5 December.
843. *See* Miguel Sousa Ferro, *Ações populares cíveis em Portugal*, Revista de Direito Comercial, 23 February 2022, pp. 435 and 436.
844. Articles 280 and 281 of the Portuguese Civil Code, approved by Decree-Law 47344/66 of 25 November.
845. Article 282 of the Portuguese Civil Code.
846. *See* Nuno A. Pires Salpico, *In Operacionalidade do Private Enforcement do Direito da Concorrência: dissuasão, ações coletivas e Third-Party Ligation Funding (The Effectiveness of Private Enforcement of Competition Law: Deterrent, Collective Actions and Third-party Ligation Funding)*, Revista de Concorrência & Regulação, Lisbon, No. 45, 2021, pp. 120 and 121.
847. *See* s. 3.3.7 above.
848. *See* Portuguese Civil Code, Articles 573 to 576, and Portuguese Code of Civil Procedure, Articles 1045 to 1047.

available to support the plausibility[849] of a damages action,[850] the Portuguese transposition went further by expressly permitting access to evidence even before the action is brought. However, even when such a request is made pre-litigation, the claimant must still demonstrate the plausibility of the damages claim based on the evidence already in their possession, an onerous requirement that significantly limits the practical utility of this mechanism.[851]

In practice, National Courts have frequently denied such requests,[852] and only recently has the first case of successful disclosure been reported: *Ius Omnibus v. Meliá,*[853] which will be examined in the following section.

3.4.3.6 Class Actions

There is currently no public database in Portugal that allows for the consultation of class actions brought to claim damages resulting from infringements of competition law. However, to appreciate the rarity of such actions in Portugal until recently, it is useful to consider the broader European context. For example, even in the UK – widely regarded as the most attractive jurisdiction in Europe for class actions across various legal domains, including competition law[854] – only between one and five such actions were filed between 2008 and 2012. Not all of these reached a final judgment or resulted in compensation.[855] This comparison underscores the historical scarcity of private enforcement actions in Portugal, a trend that has only begun to shift in recent years.

This scenario has changed significantly in recent years.[856] According to a 2024 report,[857] in the last five years Portugal has emerged as one of the European jurisdictions where class actions – broadly defined, not limited to competition law – have grown most rapidly, alongside countries as the Netherlands and, unsurprisingly, the

849. *See* Article 5(1) of the EU Damages Directive.
850. *See* s. 2.3.1.3 above.
851. *See* Article 13 of Law No. 23/2018: (1) Anyone who, under the terms and for the purposes of Articles 573 to 576 of the Civil Code, wishes to obtain information or the presentation of evidence, including that which the possessor does not wish to provide, may, upon justification of the need for the procedure and with the other limitations established in this chapter, request the competent court to summon the refuser to present it on the day, time and place that the judge designates, under the terms of Articles 1045 to 1047 of the Code of Civil Procedure. (2) To the requests for access referred to in the previous paragraph, the provisions of paras 2 to 9 of the previous article shall apply *mutatis mutandis*, which include the substantiation with facts and means of proof reasonably available and sufficient to corroborate the plausibility of the claim for damages or defence and indication of the facts to be proved (Article 12, para. 2 of the same law).
852. *See* Miguel Sousa Ferro, *In the Reality of Access in Antitrust Private Enforcement: Overview of 3 Years' Experience in Portugal,* Revista de Concorrência e Regulação, Ano XIII, Nos 46-47, Almedina, 2021, pp. 37-71, available at CR 46-47_Miguel Sousa Ferro.pdf (concorrencia.pt), p. 50.
853. *See* Appendix II – Survey of Recent Competition Law Private Enforcement Cases in Portugal.
854. *See* 2024 CMS European Class Action Report, p. 6.
855. *See Collective Redress in Antitrust*, available at https://ec.europa.eu/competition/antitrust/actionsdamages/study_legislative_action_collective_redress.pdf, p. 39.
856. *See* s. 3.4.2 above.
857. *See* 2024 CMS European Class Action Report, p. 12.

UK. It is worth noting that both the Netherlands and the UK operate under opt-out class action models, which may contribute to their higher volume of cases.

The report indicates that 11% of all class actions filed in Europe during the last five years were brought in Portugal.[858] However, only 19% of all European class actions related specifically to competition law, highlighting that while the overall use of collective redress mechanisms is increasing, competition-based claims still represent a small fraction of it.

Until 2019, class actions based on competition law infringements were virtually non-existent in Portugal.[859] The earliest class actions date back to the entry into force of Law No. 83/95 and were primarily rooted in consumer protection law. In those cases, allegations of competition law violations were often secondary and rarely succeeded.[860]

Moreover, as noted earlier, it was not until the recent settlement in *Ius Omnibus v. ANT,*[861] initiated in mid-2021, that a popular action for competition law infringements resulted in global compensation for mass harm. This case marks the first known instance in which such a claim 'saw the light of day' in terms of delivering tangible redress to affected parties.[862]

The first known class action in Portugal based on competition law was *OdC v. Sport TV,*[863] filed on 12 May 2015,[864] as previously mentioned.[865] This was a follow-on action[866] against the main Portuguese sports content broadcaster, based on the same decision by the PCA[867] that was at issue in the *Cogeco* ruling of 28 March 2019.[868] The claimant, OdC ('Observatório da Concorrência'), is a non-profit association composed of academics from various Portuguese universities.[869] It was established shortly before the action was filed, had a small membership base, and did not demonstrate financial capacity.

858. *Ibid.*, p. 16.
859. *Ibid.*, p. 8.
860. By way of example, in 1997, the STJ established for the first time, in Case No. 97B503, that ACOP (Associação de Consumidores de Portugal) had legal standing to bring a popular action seeking compensation from subscribers to a public telephone service contract for a breach of contract by the service provider. This legal standing was also recognised by DECO, as already mentioned, by the STJ, in Cases 97A725, 03A1243; and 08B3798.
861. *See* Appendix II – Survey of Recent Competition Law Private Enforcement Cases in Portugal.
862. *See* Miguel Sousa Ferro, *Ações populares cíveis em Portugal*, Regista de Direito Comercial, 23 February 2022, pp. 437 and 438.
863. *See OdC v. Sport TV*, of 12 May 2015, TJCL, 7074/15.8T8LSB.L.
864. *See* Maria Elisabete Ramos, *Situação do 'private enforcement' da concorrência em Portugal, Revista de Concorrência e Regulação*, Year VII, No. 27/28, July/December 2016, p. 68.
865. *See* s. 2.2 above.
866. *See* Appendix II – Survey of Recent Competition Law Private Enforcement Cases in Portugal.
867. *See* PRC/2010/2, available at https://extranet.concorrencia.pt/PesquisAdC/PRC_OR_INC_OR_PCC_Page.aspx?Ref=PRC_2010_2&isEnglish=False.
868. As mentioned above, the first preliminary ruling on the EU Damages Directive issued by the ECJ, declaring that the Portuguese limitation period was in conflict with the principle of effectiveness of the EU Law.
869. *See* Sofia Oliveira Pais, *Private Antitrust Enforcement: A New Era for Collective Redress?*, Yearbook of Antitrust and Regulatory Studies, vol. 8, No. 12, CARS, 2015 https://doi.org/10.7172/1689-9024.yars.2015.8.12.1, available at 3Private Antitrust Enforcement.pdf, p. 29.

On 4 December 2018, the TRL (Lisbon Court of Appeal) ruled[870] that OdC had standing to bring a class action (popular action) seeking recognition of the right to full compensation for harm caused by infringements of competition law – in this case, the abuse of a dominant position through the imposition of unfair trading conditions. The case remains pending at the pre-trial stage.[871]

Until 2024, at least[872] twelve more competition law class actions were filed[873] – it is true that five actions were filed at the beginning of 2024 alone, but as all concern the 'banking cartel', they will be grouped into one for this purpose. Specifically, two actions were initiated in 2020, five in 2021,[874] four in 2022,[875] one in 2023 and one (group of five actions on the same infringement) in 2024.

With the exception of the case brought by Fabrizio Esposito,[876] all the above were filed by Ius Omnibus, a non-profit association established in March 2020 to defend consumer rights within the European Union.[877] Another consumer association that is

870. *See* ruling of 2018-12-04 (Case No. 7074/15.8T8LSB.L1-1), of December 4, available at https://diariodarepublica.pt/dr/detalhe/acordao/7074-2018-190371575.
871. *See* ruling of 2022-09-26 (Case No. 7074/15.8T8LSB-D.L1-PICRS), of September 26, available at https://diariodarepublica.pt/dr/detalhe/acordao/7074-2022-209589275; and ruling of 2022-10-12 (Case No. 7074/15.8T8LSB-C.L1-PICRS), of October 12, available at https://diariodarepublica.pt/dr/detalhe/acordao/7074-2022-209581975.
872. As far as this study has been able to ascertain (it should be remembered that there is no public database in Portugal with all the competition law class actions).
873. *See* (i) *Ius Omnibus v. Mastercard*, of 2 December 2020, TCRS, 19/20.5YQSTR; (ii) *Ius Omnibus v. Super Bock*, of 14 December 2020, TCRS, 20/20.9YQSTR; (iii) *Ius Omnibus v. Meliá*, of 6 July 2020, TCRS, 6/21.6YQSTR; (iv) *Ius Omnibus v. Comcast/Universal Studios*, of 9 July 2021, TCRS, 21.4YQSTR, 8/21.2YQSTR, 9/21.0YQSTR, 10/21.4YQSTR, 11/21.2YQSTR, 12/21.0YQSTR, 13/21.9YQSTR and 14/21.7YQSTR; (v) *Ius Omnibus v. ANT*, of 12 July 2021, TCRS, 15/21.5YQSTR; (vi) *Ius Omnibus v. Apple* (iPhone), of 19 July 2021, TJCL, 17713/21.6T8LSB; (vii) *Ius Omnibus v. EDP*, of 6 September 2021, TCRS, 18/21.0YQSTR; (viii) *Apple* (AppStore), of 21 March 2022, TCRS, 3/22.4YQSTR; (ix) *Ius Omnibus v. Google* (PlayStore), of 21 March 2022, TCRS, 4/22.2YQSTR; (x) *Fabrizio Esposito v. Google* (PlayStore), June 2022, TCRS 61/22.1YQSTR; (xi) *Ius Omnibus v. Sony (PlayStation)*, of 3 August 2023, TCRS; and (xii) *Ius Omnibus v. Abanca and other 11 banks*, of 8 January 2024, 3/24.0YQSTR, 4/24.8YQSTR, 5/24.6YQSTR, 2/24.1YQSTR and 6/24.4YQSTR. *See* Appendix II – Survey of Recent Competition Law *Private Enforcement* Cases in Portugal.
874. *See* 2024 CMS European Class Action Report, p. 6.
875. Between 2021 and 2025, Ius Omnibus brought six more class actions for damages against Daimler/Mercedes-Benz, Stellantis/Fiat Chrysler Automobiles, Estée Lauder (Clinique), TikTok (two actions) and Flo Health, Inc., based exclusively on other branches of the law, involving unfair commercial practices, as well as personality rights, advertising, data protection and sector regulation. DECO also brought several popular actions, at least between 1999 and 2015, based on violations other than competition law, *see* Sofia Oliveira Pais, *Private Antitrust Enforcement: A New Era for Collective Redress?* Yearbook of Antitrust and Regulatory Studies, vol. 8, No. 12, CARS, 2015 https://doi.org/10.7172/1689-9024.yars.2015.8.12.1, available at 3Private Antitrust Enforcement.pdf, p. 29, and *Observatoire des Actions de Groupe et autres Actions Collectives*, 2021, available at Acoes_DECO-2021.pdf (observatoireactionsdegroupe.com). Of particular importance is the action brought against Portugal Telecom, which ended in a settlement (STJ decision of 10 July 2003, Case 03A1243, available at http://www.dgsi.pt/jstj.nsf/954f0ce6ad9dd8b980256b5f003fa814/1db6e4a1a7cadeed80256de5005292d4).
876. Assistant Professor of Private Law at the Nova University Law School.
877. *See* https://iusomnibus.eu/pt/.

very active in Portugal in this field is CITIZENS' VOICE, although more focused on consumer law (with dozens of actions filed in recent years).[878]

According to Esposito, large-scale lawsuits of this nature typically require investments of several hundred thousand euros. This financial barrier has historically prevented such actions in Portugal, where neither consumers nor consumer protection associations have had the resources to support them, and no public funding has been available. Ius Omnibus, for instance, addresses this gap by employing a relatively novel approach in Portugal: litigation funding.

Indeed, to the best of this book's knowledge, several of these actions – Mastercard, Super Bock, Sony (PlayStation), Banking Cartel, etc. – were financed through TPLF. The plaintiff estimates that millions of consumers were affected by the respective infringements.[879]

The 'new' class actions mentioned above are still ongoing, with the exception of the aforementioned *Ius Omnibus v. ANT* case.[880] The earliest of these is *Ius Omnibus v. Mastercard*,[881] filed on 2 December 2020 as a partial follow-on action – or mixed action – based on two European Commission decisions: one imposing sanctions and the other accepting commitments.[882] In this collective action, the plaintiffs expanded both the material and temporal scope of the alleged infringement.

The case concerns cross-border restrictions and intra-regional Multilateral Interchange Fees (MIFs), which stemmed from a decision by an association of undertakings. These practices were found to restrict cross-border trade, obstruct the functioning of the internal market, and constitute a breach of Article 101 of the Treaty on the Functioning of the European Union (TFEU).[883]

This proceeding is backed by a third-party funder, as previously mentioned. If the claim is successful, each consumer is expected to receive approximately EUR 40 in compensation, based on a total claim value of EUR 400 million. It exemplifies the rationale behind collective redress mechanisms. The potential individual compensation is too low to justify the high litigation costs – estimated in the hundreds of thousands of euros – making it highly unlikely that a single injured party would pursue such an action independently, even if financially capable. As the association argues,[884] without collective action, nearly EUR 1 billion in damages could remain uncompensated, despite being potentially owed.

878. *See* https://citizensvoice.eu/.
879. *See* Appendix II – Survey of Recent Competition Law Private Enforcement Cases in Portugal.
880. *Ibid.*
881. Case No. 19/20.5YQSTR. *See* Appendix II – Survey of Recent Competition Law Private Enforcement Cases in Portugal.
882. *See* Miguel Sousa Ferro, *Consumer Antitrust Private Enforcement in Europe: As Complete a Survey as Possible (Extended Version)*, 23 October 2022, available at https://ssrn.com/abstract=4223770, p. 18.
883. AT.40049 Mastercard II, available at https://ec.europa.eu/competition/elojade/isef/case_details.cfm?proc_code=1_40049.
884. *See* www.iusomnibus.eu/pt/ius-omnibus-v-mastercard-pt. *See* Appendix II – Survey of Recent Competition Law Private Enforcement Cases in Portugal.

One of the most eventful cases to date is *Ius Omnibus v. Super Bock*,[885] which was notably suspended at the beginning of 2023. This action, like *Ius Omnibus v. Mastercard*, seeks the same estimated total and individual damages and was filed on 14 December 2021 as a partial follow-on (or mixed) action. It is based on the PCA's decision of 24 July 2017, which sanctioned the company, along with one of its directors and an executive officer, with a total fine of EUR 24 million. The PCA found that Super Bock had engaged in anticompetitive practices by fixing minimum resale prices and other transaction conditions for its products sold through the HORECA channel (hotels, restaurants, and cafés) – a market in which Super Bock is one of the leading Portuguese players. These practices allegedly persisted for over a decade, from 2006 to 2017.[886]

The fine imposed in the *Super Bock* case – EUR 24 million – stands in stark contrast to the EUR 400 million in compensation being claimed. If awarded, this disparity would underscore how the alleged offenders may have 'profited' from the historical absence of private enforcement in competition law. Meanwhile, the affected consumers would have suffered a double harm: first, from the anticompetitive conduct itself and, second, from the lack of accessible legal remedies.

The progress of this popular action[887] was initially slow, primarily due to the defendant's challenge regarding the validity of the summons. On 20 February 2023, as previously noted, the TRL confirmed the suspension of the proceedings. This suspension followed the earlier suspension of the related administrative offence case,[888] which had been referred to the ECJ for a preliminary ruling. As the national decision was not yet final, the presumption of infringement established by the EU Damages Directive could not apply in this instance.[889] Meanwhile, on 12 September 2023, the infringement was confirmed by the TRL.[890]

Despite the suspension mentioned above, the National Court have already ruled on several key procedural issues that highlight the novelty of these types of proceedings in Portugal.[891] Over the past years:

(1) the TRL recognised the association's right to access the administrative offence file, with confidential elements redacted. This expanded upon an earlier decision by the TCRS, which had granted access only to the administrative process, appeal, and defence stages;[892]

885. *See* www.iusomnibus.eu/pt/ius-omnibus-v-super-bock-pt. *See* Appendix II – Survey of Recent Competition Law Private Enforcement Cases in Portugal.
886. *See* PRC/2016/4, available at https://extranet.concorrencia.pt/PesquisAdC/PRC_OR_INC_OR_PCC_Page.aspx?Ref = PRC_2016_4&isEnglish = False.
887. *See* Case No. 20/20.9YQSTR.
888. *See* Case No. 71/18.3YUSTR-M.L1.
889. *See* s. 2.3.1.4 above.
890. *See* https://www.concorrencia.pt/en/articles/lisbon-court-appeal-confirms-infringement-super-bock-sanctioned-adc.
891. *See* www.iusomnibus.eu/pt/ius-omnibus-v-super-bock-pt/.
892. *See* www.iusomnibus.eu/pt/relacao-de-lisboa-da-razao-a-ius-no-direito-de-acesso-a-processo-judicial.

(2) the TCRS confirmed the standing of Ius Omnibus as a legitimate consumer association entitled to bring popular actions seeking compensation for harm caused by anticompetitive practices;[893]
(3) the TRL annulled a judicial order concerning the preservation of evidence, citing a lack of reasoning and procedural error.[894] The plaintiff argued that the purpose of the request was to safeguard the evidence in question from being lost during the suspension period, i.e., while the National Court had yet to rule on the access request.[895]

Another case that was suspended before reaching the trial phase is *Ius Omnibus v. EDP Produção*.[896] This class action was filed on 6 September 2021 as a follow-on action based on a decision by the PCA dated 17 September 2019. In that decision, the PCA imposed a fine of EUR 38 million on EDP Produção for abuse of a dominant position in the secondary regulation band market in mainland Portugal. EDP Produção is the primary supplier of teleregulation services within the National Electricity System and holds the largest share of authorised capacity for such services. According to the PCA, between 2009 and 2013, the company manipulated the supply of secondary regulation band services by limiting the capacity offered through its plants operating under the Contractual Equilibrium Maintenance Costs regime. This capacity was instead redirected to plants operating under the market regime, allowing EDP Produção to benefit twice, at the expense of consumers.[897]

EDP contested the action on 21 December 2021. Subsequently, on 13 July 2022, the TCRS issued a Procedural Order addressing several key points:[898] (i) it rejected the objections raised concerning the admissibility of the action and the plaintiff's standing; (ii) it deferred the decision on the statute of limitations until after the evidentiary phase; and (iii) it suspended the proceedings pending the final outcome of the related administrative offence case.[899] The PCA decision was upheld by the TRL on 1 June 2022[900] and became final on 10 August 2022.[901]

Given the content of the Procedural Order, particular emphasis is placed on the application of Law No. 23/2018, especially in affirming the association's standing to bring this type of action. As the National Court noted, Law No. 23/2018 (implementing

893. *See* www.iusomnibus.eu/pt/super-bock-tribunal-da-concorrencia-confirma-legitimidade-ativa-da-ius.
894. *See* www.iusomnibus.eu/wp-content/uploads/2023/02/2023.02.20-Acordao-Super-Bock.pdf.
895. *See* Miguel Sousa Ferro, *Consumer Antitrust Private Enforcement in Europe: As Complete a Survey as Possible (Extended Version)*, 23 October 2022, available at https://ssrn.com/abstract=4223770, p. 20.
896. *See* www.iusomnibus.eu/pt/ius-omnibus-v-edp-pt. *See* Appendix II – Survey of Recent Competition Law Private Enforcement Cases in Portugal.
897. PRC/2016/5, available at https://extranet.concorrencia.pt/PesquisAdC/PRC_OR_INC_OR_PCC_Page.aspx?Ref=PRC_2016_5&isEnglish=False.
898. Available on 2022.07.13-Despacho-Saneador-2-1.pdf (iusomnibus.eu). Case No. 18/21.0YQSTR.
899. *See* www.iusomnibus.eu/pt/ius-omnibus-v-edp-pt.
900. Case No. 309/19.0YUSTR-F.L1, Judgment Available at TRL-2022-06-01-IDF_2019_4-PRC_2016_5.pdf (concorrencia.pt).
901. *See* www.iusomnibus.eu/pt/ius-omnibus-v-edp-pt.

the EU Damages Directive) explicitly allows for claims to be brought under the framework of popular actions (*see* Article 19). Accordingly, and in line with the principle of effectiveness, there should be no barriers to the full application of Law No. 83/95 (the Popular Action law) in this context, nor to the recognition of the legitimacy of associations and foundations to pursue such claims, provided they fall within the scope of the interests protected by that law.[902] This interpretation strengthens the legal basis for collective redress in competition law and confirms the role of consumer associations, such as Ius Omnibus, in representing affected consumers in actions for damages arising from anticompetitive practices.

Also, the National Court held that the defendant's objection regarding third-party funding does not undermine the plaintiff's legal standing. Legal standing is determined by the parties' positions in relation to the specific legal dispute as defined by the plaintiff, and in this case, there is no ambiguity. The Court further noted that any concerns arising from the funding arrangement might relate to a potential abuse of right of action, but such an assessment would be premature at this stage of the proceedings.[903] This reasoning reinforces the principle that third-party litigation funding, in itself, does not undermine the legitimacy of a claimant's standing, particularly in collective redress actions.

However, the right of action is only considered abusive when it is exercised in a way that clearly exceeds the boundaries set by good faith, accepted standards of conduct, or the social and economic purpose of the right itself. Legal standing belongs to the plaintiff – not the third-party funder.[904] It is important not to conflate the plaintiff's legitimate interest in pursuing the case with the funder's financial interest, which, in principle, is a lawful commercial activity. The only exceptions would be if the funding arrangement were contrary to the law, public order, or customs,[905] or if it involved exploitative or usurious practices.[906]

A proportionality assessment is also necessary, considering that without private funding, the already limited number of civil liability actions for competition law infringements – particularly class actions – could remain scarce. Unless alternative public funding mechanisms are introduced, private financing may be the only viable means to ensure access to justice in such cases.

The reality is that, as advanced, actions targeting this type of infringement are uniquely complex. Proving the offence is inherently difficult – even for NCAs, which are equipped with increasingly extensive powers of investigation, including search and seizure. The very existence of leniency programmes, designed to encourage offenders to confess, is a testament to these challenges. Even in the case of so-called hardcore infringements, such as cartels – which are considered restrictions of competition by object and do not require proof of actual anticompetitive effects – the evidentiary burden remains high. These practices are often concealed through secrecy and

902. *See* 2022.07.13-Sanctioning Order-2-1.pdf (iusomnibus.eu).
903. *Ibid.*
904. *See* Article 334 of the Portuguese Civil Code.
905. *See* Articles 280 and 281 of the Portuguese Civil Code.
906. *See* Article 282 of the Portuguese Civil Code.

supported by sophisticated technology, making detection and proof difficult. As a result, even public enforcers frequently rely on indirect or presumptive evidence and draw analogies with similar cases to demonstrate the harmful nature of the conduct.

When the infringement is not classified as a restriction by object, the burden falls on the plaintiff to prove its anticompetitive effects. This typically requires the involvement of expert witnesses - particularly economists - alongside specialised competition lawyers. In such cases, the evidentiary and procedural complexity significantly increases.

In this context, the rules introduced by the EU Damages Directive are essential. Without the legal effects attributed to final infringement decisions and the presumption of harm, private enforcement would be extremely limited in practice. This is reflected in the Portuguese antitrust class actions discussed here: only five[907] are stand-alone actions, and of those, three are based on investigations or decisions by the European Commission.[908]

Even in follow-on actions, as noted earlier,[909] the plaintiff must still establish both the causal link and the actual harm suffered - which, again, requires complex legal and economic analysis, often significantly increasing litigation costs. When the individual harm is as low as EUR 40 - as seen in some of the cases discussed here - it becomes practically unthinkable for a consumer to pursue legal action independently.

This book will return to this issue later,[910] but these examples also highlight the need to clarify the rules on TPLF - an initiative currently under consideration by the EU legislator.[911] Alternatively, public funding mechanisms could be introduced, as suggested by Directive 2020/1828 (albeit not applicable to competition law).[912] Either approach would enhance legal certainty and, more importantly, ensure effective access to justice for victims of competition law infringements.

Also in 2021 - and more recently in March and June 2022 - four stand-alone class actions were filed against the tech giants Apple and Google. The first of these was Ius *Omnibus v. Apple (iPhone)*,[913] which, although formally a stand-alone action, is grounded primarily in consumer protection law. It challenges Apple's alleged misleading advertising and failure to provide accurate information regarding the iPhone's resistance to liquids. Additionally, the claim includes an allegation of abuse of a dominant position.[914]

907. *See Ius Omnibus v. Apple* (iPhone), of 19 July 2021, ECJ, 17713/21.6T8LSB; *Ius Omnibus v. Apple* (AppStore), of 21 March 2022, TCRS, 3/22.4YQSTR; *Ius Omnibus v. Google* (PlayStore), of 21 March 2022, TCRS, 4/22.2YQSTR; *Fabrizio Esposito v. Google* (PlayStore), June 2022, TCRS 61/22.1YQSTR; and *Ius Omnibus v. Sony (PlayStation)*, of 3 August 2023, TCRS.
908. *See Ius Omnibus v. Apple* (AppStore), of 21 March 2022, TCRS, 3/22.4YQSTR; *Ius Omnibus v. Google* (PlayStore), of 21 March 2022, TCRS, 4/22.2YQSTR; and *Fabrizio Esposito v. Google* (PlayStore), June 2022, TCRS 61/22.1YQSTR. *See* Appendix II - Survey of Recent Competition Law *Private Enforcement* Cases in Portugal.
909. *See* s. 1.1 above.
910. *See* s. 3.6.5 below.
911. *See* s. 3.3.8 above.
912. *See* s. 3.3.7 above.
913. *See* ECJCL, 19 July 2021, Case 17713/21.6T8LSB.
914. *See* Appendix II - Survey of Recent Competition Law Private Enforcement Cases in Portugal.

The remaining actions, while described as mostly stand-alone private enforcement of competition law, are in fact closely linked to public enforcement proceedings initiated by the European Commission.[915] This illustrates the hybrid nature of many such actions, which, although not strictly follow-on, often rely on findings or investigations by public authorities to support their claims.

The second class action brought against Apple focuses[916] on the lack of alternatives available to Portuguese consumers since 2008 for using Apple's operating system (iOS) on the company's devices (namely iPhones, iPads, and iPod Touch). The claim also challenges the 30% commission agreed between Apple and third-party app developers, which was allegedly passed on to Portuguese consumers purchasing apps and in-app content through the Apple App Store.[917] This conduct has been the subject of damages actions in other jurisdictions, including the US, the UK, and the Netherlands.[918] Moreover, similar practices prompted the European Commission to open[919] an investigation into Apple's suspected abuse of a dominant position in the market for mobile wallets on iOS devices. The investigation concerns Apple's alleged restriction of access to Near-Field Communication (NFC) technology – used for contactless payments in physical stores – and formal charges were issued on 2 May 2022.[920]

With regard to the two class actions brought against Google,[921] the conduct in question has also been challenged in damages actions currently pending in other jurisdictions, including also the US, the UK and the Netherlands. Moreover, aspects of this behaviour have already been addressed in a European Commission decision, which was subsequently upheld by the EGC.[922]

In July 2018, the European Commission found Google guilty of abusing its dominant position since 2011 in the global markets for Android app stores and in national markets for general search services. The Commission identified several distinct but closely interrelated anticompetitive practices, which together constituted a single and continuous infringement of Article 102 of the TFEU. More specifically, Google was found to have imposed the following contractual restrictions on mobile device manufacturers and mobile network operators: (i) distribution agreements – these required manufacturers to pre-install Google Search and the Chrome browser as a condition for obtaining a licence to use the Google Play Store; (ii) anti-fragmentation agreements – these restricted manufacturers from selling devices running alternative, non-Google-approved versions of Android, as a condition for licensing Google Search and the Play Store; and (iii) revenue-sharing agreements – these made the sharing of Google's

915. *See,* for example, www.iusomnibus.eu/pt/ius-omnibus-v-google-play-store-pt.
916. *See* TCRS, of 21 March 2022, Case 3/22.4YQSTR. *See* Appendix II – Survey of Recent Competition Law Private Enforcement Cases in Portugal.
917. *See* https://iusomnibus.eu/pt/ius-omnibus-v-apple-app-store-pt/.
918. This book discusses some of these actions below.
919. *See* https://ec.europa.eu/commission/presscorner/detail/hr/IP_20_1073.
920. *See* Antitrust: Commission sends Statement of Objections to Apple (europa.eu) and AT.40452 Apple – Mobile payments, available at https://ec.europa.eu/competition/elojade/isef/case_details.cfm?proc_code=1_40452.
921. *See Ius Omnibus v. Google (PlayStore),* TCRS, of 21 March 2022, Case 4/22.2YQSTR and *Fabrizio Esposito v. Google (PlayStore),* TCRS, of June 2022, 61/22.1YQSTR.
922. *See* Appendix II – Survey of Recent Competition Law Private Enforcement Cases in Portugal.

advertising revenue conditional on manufacturers and operators refraining from pre-installing competing general search services on a predefined portfolio of devices.[923]

The European Commission ordered Google to cease the anticompetitive practices identified in its 2018 decision – specifically, to dismantle its control over the Android mobile ecosystem, which it had maintained through a network of interlocking agreements with mobile network operators and device manufacturers. In addition to this structural remedy, the Commission imposed a record-breaking fine of EUR 4.34 billion, the highest ever levied against a single company for a competition law violation.[924] On 14 September 2022, the EGC largely upheld the Commission's findings, confirming the abuse of dominance and reducing the fine only slightly to EUR 4.125 billion (less than a 5% reduction).[925]

According to Ius Omnibus, Portuguese consumers have had no effective alternative to using the Android operating system and related apps and in-app content since 2009, due to the restrictive contractual practices described above. These practices allegedly resulted in a 30% commission on each sale, which was ultimately passed on to consumers through higher prices.[926]

The most recent stand-alone class action was filed in August 2023 against Sony (PlayStation), targeting the company's alleged anticompetitive conduct aimed at restricting and controlling the production and distribution of both physical and digital PlayStation games, as well as add-on content, game library services, and online multiplayer features. According to the plaintiff, Sony, through agreements with game publishers, sets both wholesale and retail prices for all digital PlayStation games, including those of its competitors. It determines the final consumer price and retains a 30% commission. Additionally, Sony allegedly controls the number of physical game units that competitors can produce and dictates which manufacturers they may use. This action draws inspiration from similar proceedings brought in the UK.[927]

Although these actions are promising, their stand-alone nature presents significant evidentiary challenges – particularly in proving harm and causation – which may ultimately require the intervention of the National Court to determine damages. As such, they remain at an early procedural stage.

With regard to document disclosure, the first two class actions were filed in July 2021 against the Meliá hotel[928] chain and the Comcast/Universal group,[929] with the

923. AT.40099 Google Android, available at https://ec.europa.eu/competition/elojade/isef/case_details.cfm?proc_code = 1_40099.
924. *See* Thomas Höpágs.ner and Philipágs. Westerhoff, *EU General Court Confirms Landmark Google Android Decision with Strong Signal for Tougher Antitrust Enforcement in Digital Ecosystems*, 14 September 2022, available at EU General Court confirms landmark Google Android decision with strong signal for tougher antitrust enforcement in digital ecosystems - Lexology.
925. *See Google and Alphabet v. Commission*, 14 September 2022, Case T-604/18, available at https://curia.europa.eu/juris/documents.jsf?num = T-604/18.
926. *See* www.iusomnibus.eu/pt/ius-omnibus-v-google-play-store-pt.
927. *See* https://iusomnibus.eu/pt/ius-omnibus-v-sony-playstation-pt/.
928. *See* www.iusomnibus.eu/pt/ius-omnibus-v-melia-pt.
929. *See* www.iusomnibus.eu/pt/ius-omnibus-v-comcast-universal-studios-pt.

specific objective of compelling the defendants to submit documents.[930] Indeed, these actions aim to obtain access to evidence necessary to substantiate consumer harm resulting from anticompetitive practices previously sanctioned by the European Commission. As such, they qualify as follow-on actions, despite being focused on evidentiary access rather than immediate claims for damages.

In the first case, the European Commission found that the agreements in question restricted tour operators' ability to sell Meliá accommodations freely across the EEA (European Economic Area). This led to the artificial partitioning of the internal market along national borders and constituted a restriction of competition by object.[931]

On 7 April 2022, the TCRS issued its first ruling on the right to pre-filing discovery in this context. Specifically, it addressed whether a consumer association could initiate a popular action to compel a company to disclose evidence necessary to prepare a damages claim for competition law violations.[932]

In this case, Ius Omnibus filed a popular action in the form of a special declaratory procedure for document production.[933] The association requested that the National Court order the defendant to produce the documents listed in the initial application (subject to any proportionality safeguards the Court might find appropriate). Alternatively, it asked the Court to determine which of those documents, or any others it deems essential, are strictly necessary for the plaintiff to assess whether collective interests have been harmed, whether consumers in Portugal were affected by the alleged anticompetitive conduct, and to what extent they suffered damages.[934]

As previously noted, access to evidence before initiating a damages claim is governed by Article 13 of Law 23/2018, which refers to Articles 1045 to 1047 of the Portuguese Code of Civil Procedure. In this case, Meliá challenged the proceedings, arguing that Portuguese courts lacked international jurisdiction and that the plaintiff lacked standing. However, in a decision dated 13 July 2022,[935] the TRL upheld the applicability of Article 7(2) of the Brussels I Regulation.[936] This provision allows individuals domiciled in one EU Member State to be sued in another Member State in matters concerning torts, delicts, or quasi-delicts, specifically in the courts where the harmful event occurred or may occur. The TRL emphasised that the location of the documents or the fact that the defendant is based in Spain is irrelevant.[937] Ultimately,

---

930. *See Ius Omnibus v. Meliá*, of 6 July 2020, TCRS, 6/21.6YQSTR and *Ius Omnibus v. Comcast/ Universal Studios*, of 9 July 2021, TCRS, Cases 7/21.4YQSTR, 8/21.2YQSTR, 9/21.0YQSTR, 10/21.4YQSTR, 11/21.2YQSTR, 12/21.0YQSTR, 13/21.9YQSTR and 14/21.7YQSTR. *See* Appendix II - Survey of Recent Competition Law Private Enforcement Cases in Portugal.
931. AT.40528 Melia, available at https://ec.europa.eu/competition/elojade/isef/case_details.cfm ?proc_code=1_40528.
932. *See* www.iusomnibus.eu/pt/ius-omnibus-v-melia-pt.
933. Case No. 6/21.6YQSTR-A.
934. *See* Magistrate's Act opening a conclusion (iusomnibus.eu).
935. Rendered in Case No. 6/21.6YQSTR-A.L1, available at Ato de Magistrado com abertura de conclusão (iusomnibus.eu).
936. *See* Regulation 1215/2012.
937. For the National Court, the place of materialisation of the damage is considered to be located in the Member State where it allegedly occurred (the potentially affected consumers, represented by the plaintiff/appellant, being resident in Portugal), considering that the courts of the

it was not until 8 March 2023 that the TCRS ordered the disclosure of the requested documents – a ruling later upheld by the TRL.[938]

This judgment is significant not only because it is the first of its kind but also because it addresses a particularly delicate issue. On the one hand, the TCRS held that the requested information did not entail the creation of new documents. It reasoned that it was implausible for a sophisticated multinational company like the defendant not to possess any records reflecting the minimum, average, and maximum prices of its hotel units. And even if such documents did not already exist, the Court argued that the defendant had the ability to compile them, since the underlying data was already available, under its control, and could be processed without disproportionate effort.[939]

However, this presumption by the National Court raises concerns. If complying with the request requires gathering, aggregating, and linking data that had not previously been compiled in that form, then it effectively amounts to the creation of an *ex novo* document. Moreover, the Court confirmed that it is possible to order the production of newly created documents, provided the principle of proportionality is respected.[940] In doing so, the Court aligned itself with the interpretation of the ECJ in the *Paccar and DAF Trucks* case – an interpretation this book has previously criticised for exceeding the intent of the EU legislator.[941]

Comcast/Universal Studios is also a pre-filing discovery action. The case is against the companies named in the European Commission's decision of 30 January 2020[942,943] and aims to establish that consumers were harmed by the group's anticompetitive conduct in the licensing and merchandising of films and television programmes. Indeed, according to the Commission, these companies breached Article 101(1) TFEU by entering into and enforcing agreements and practices that restricted the sale of licensed merchandise across different territories and customer segments, both online and offline.[944] The TCRS has already ruled in favour of disclosing documents requested by the plaintiff on 2 June 2023.[945]

Member State in which the affected market is located are best placed to hear such actions, in the light of the case law of the CJEU indicated therein (*see* Case C-451/18) and the case law indicated by the appellee in Article 14 of the conclusions of the counterclaims (*see* Case C-30/20).

938. *See* ruling of 8 March 2023 in Case 6/21.6YQSTR.
939. *See* ruling of 23 October 2023 in Case 6/21.6YQSTR.L1-PICRS, available at https://www.dgsi.pt/jtrl.nsf/33182fc732316039802565fa00497eec/4bf89d6c451a296a80258a670036bac8?OpenDocument.
940. *Ibid.*, p. 53.
941. *See* s. 2.2 above.
942. *See* Miguel Sousa Ferro, *Consumer Antitrust Private Enforcement in Europe: As Complete a Survey as Possible (Extended Version)*, 23 October 2022, available at https://ssrn.com/abstract=4223770, p. 20.
943. *See* www.iusomnibus.eu/pt/ius-omnibus-v-comcast-universal-studios-pt.
944. AT.40433 Film merchandise, available at https://ec.europa.eu/competition/elojade/isef/case_details.cfm?proc_code=1_40433.
945. *See* https://iusomnibus.eu/wp-content/uploads/2023/06/Comcast-Universal-TCRS-Judgment_EN.pdf.

The first class action law settlement to be approved in Portugal and, based on this, the first compensation was *Ius Omnibus v. ANT*.[946] It addressed price-fixing practices in the market for surveying services. Notably, the related administrative offence proceedings also concluded with a settlement on 17 February 2021.[947] Under the terms of the class action settlement, ANT agreed to compensate affected consumers with an amount equivalent to 5% of the gross fees paid for the relevant services.[948]

The most recent competition law class action was filed at the beginning of 2024 against the so-called banking cartel.[949] This action is particularly significant: if the claims are upheld in full, the total compensation could amount to EUR 5.368 billion based on estimates by Ius Omnibus and calculated at the lowest threshold, covering only the period up to the end of 2022.

The case stems from a 2019 decision by the PCA, which fined fourteen banks operating in Portugal a total of EUR 225 million for engaging in a concerted practice of exchanging sensitive commercial information over more than a decade. According to the PCA, between 2002 and 2013, the banks involved shared confidential data related to retail banking credit products, including mortgage loans, consumer credit, and business loans.[950]

Twelve appeals were filed by the banks, prompting a preliminary reference to the ECJ.[951] On 20 September 2024, the TCRS upheld the PCA's decision, confirming the fine imposed on the banks involved.

Currently, the statute of limitations is under discussion. On 10 February 2025, the TRL declared the case time-barred. Appeals against this ruling were submitted by the PCA and the Public Prosecutor's Office to the Portuguese Constitutional Court. The judge assigned to the case was selected on 27 May 2025.

As for the class actions, public notices to potential injured parties were issued in June 2024. However, since these are follow-on actions, their progress depends on the final outcome of the administrative offence proceedings.

The wave of class actions filed in recent years and outlined above marks a pivotal test for the collective redress framework in Portuguese Competition Law (PCL). While these actions have already delivered meaningful outcomes, such as pre-filing access to evidence and a negotiated settlement, the true challenge lies ahead. The system's resilience will be tested in cases where no settlement is reached, particularly in stand-alone actions, where the complexity of quantifying total damages will be most acute.

---

946. *See Ius Omnibus v. ANT*, of 12 July 2021, TCRS, 15/21.5YQSTR. *See* Appendix II – Survey of Recent Competition Law Private Enforcement Cases in Portugal.
947. *See* PRC/2020/2, available at https://extranet.concorrencia.pt/pesquisAdC/PRC_OR_INC_OR_PCC_Page.aspx?Ref = PRC_2020_2&IsEnglish = False-.
948. *See* https://iusomnibus.eu/ius-omnibus-v-ant/.
949. *See* https://iusomnibus.eu/banking-cartel/.
950. *See* PRC/2012/9, available at https://extranet.concorrencia.pt/PesquisAdC/Page.aspx?Ref = PRC_2012_9&isEnglish = False.
951. *See Banco BPN/BIC Português SA and Others v. PCA*, 29 July 2024, Case C-298/22, available at https://curia.europa.eu/juris/document/document.jsf;jsessionid = DB21E35240B6F29B8BFAE862AF427E6E?text = &docid = 288834&pageIndex = 0&doclang = EN&mode = lst&dir = &occ = first&part = 1&cid = 217652.

3.4.4 United Kingdom

3.4.4.1 Class Action Model

The UK provides two main civil procedure mechanisms that allow claimants with similar claims to bring collective actions against defendants:

(1) *Group Litigation Order (GLO):*[952] under this procedure, claimants must initiate separate legal actions. The Court may then issue a GLO to manage these cases jointly if they involve common or related issues of fact or law. A group register is created, listing all individual claimants whose cases fall under the order.[953]

(2) *Representative Actions:*[954] this mechanism allows one or more individuals to represent others who share the same interest in a legal action. The Court may authorise the action to proceed on a representative basis, and any resulting judgment is binding on all represented parties – except for those who are not formal parties to the action, in which case enforcement requires court approval.[955]

The rule in both types of actions is that the individual claimants must be identified and must opt in. However, in the second type of action, the English legislature also allows for the representation of interested parties who cannot be identified in advance, provided that this is limited to specific types of claims (such as those involving the estate of a deceased person).

In addition to the general procedures outlined above, the UK was the first (former) Member State to establish a dedicated collective action mechanism specifically for competition law infringements, enabling the exercise of the right to compensation for breaches of antitrust rules. More precisely, this mechanism takes the form of a representative action before the CAT,[956] which alongside the High Court has jurisdiction over competition-related claims. However, class actions fall under the exclusive jurisdiction of the CAT, while claimants may choose between the CAT and the High Court for other types of competition law actions.[957]

---

952. *See* Part 19 s. III of The Civil Procedure Rules 1998, available at The Civil Procedure Rules 1998 (legislation.gov.uk).
953. *See* Gordon Blanke et al., *International Competition Litigation: A Multi-Jurisdictional Handbook, England and Wales*, Gordon Blanke and Renato Nazzini (eds) Kluwer Law International, 2012, p. 176.
954. *See* Part 19 s. II of The Civil Procedure Rules 1998.
955. *Ibid.*
956. *See Commission Staff Working Paper, Annex to the Green Paper on Damages actions for breach of the EC antitrust rules*, COM(2005) 672 final, 2005, available at https://eur-lex.europa.eu/legal-content/EN/ALL/?uri=CELEX%3A52005DC0672, p. 55.
957. *See* Nicholas Heaton and Paul Chaplin, *England & Wales Q&A, in GCR's Private Litigation Guide*, Nicholas Heaton and Benhamin Holt (eds), 3rd ed., 2021, *asset download – Global Competition Review*, p. 227.

The Enterprise Act 2002[958] introduced the possibility for designated bodies, i.e., organisations approved by the Secretary of State,[959] to bring representative actions before the CAT on behalf of two or more individual consumers, in cases involving breaches of competition law, with the aim of securing compensation for the affected individuals. However, only one such action was ever brought under this provision:[960] in 2007, the consumer association Which? filed a claim against JJB Sports plc on behalf of 130 consumers. These individuals, identified through the association's publicity efforts, had purchased replica football shirts (Manchester United and England national team) that, according to an investigation by the Office of Fair Trading, were subject to price-fixing agreements among retailers.[961] The case was ultimately settled, with each identified consumer receiving GBP 20 in compensation.[962]

In other words, the CAT has always had jurisdiction to adjudicate opt-in class actions,[963] and the majority of collective actions available in the UK continue to follow this opt-in model. However, contrary to the European Commission's expectations, these actions have not proven particularly successful, largely due to the challenges involved in identifying potential claimants and securing adequate funding.[964] These two factors – claimant identification and funding – are closely interlinked. Achieving a certain scale is essential to generate sufficient interest in initiating and financing this type of action, given the expected return. At the same time, scale also enhances the claimant group's leverage in negotiating legal settlements.

In 2015, the United Kingdom introduced new procedures for antitrust litigation[965] through the Consumer Rights Act, granting the CAT jurisdiction to hear opt-out class actions. As advanced, under this model, claimants are automatically included in the action unless they choose to opt out and pursue individual claims. This jurisdiction applies to both follow-on and stand-alone actions – whereas, prior to the 2015 reform, the CAT could only hear follow-on cases.[966]

958. Which introduced s. 47A and 47B of the Competition Act 1998.
959. *See* Sebastian Peyer, *Private Enforcement in England and Wales, in Private Enforcement of EU Competition Law: The Impact of the Damages Directive,* Pier Luigi Parcu, Giorgio Monti and Marco Botta (eds), Elgar, 2018, p. 112.
960. *See* Barry Rodger (also ed.), *Competition Law, Comparative Private Enforcement and Collective Redress Across the EU,* Kluwer Law International, 2014, p. 188.
961. *See* Sports Goods Retail Sector: Chapter I Investigation into Anti-competitive Practices – GOV.UK (www.gov.uk).
962. *See* Case 1078/7/9/07 – *The Consumers Association v. JJB Sports PLC,* available at 1078/7/9/07 The Consumers Association v. JJB Sports PLC | Competition Appeal Tribunal (catribunal.org.uk). *See also Settlement Reached in the First Representative Private Action for Damages under UK Competition Law: Mondaq United Kingdom – Blogs: VLEX* 35427196.
963. *See* pts 434 et seq. of the Consumer Rights Act 2015, available at https://www.legislation.gov.uk/ukpga/2015/15/contents/enacted.
964. *See* Matthew O'Regan, *United Kingdom: Consumer Rights Act 2015 Introduces New Procedures for Competition Litigation, Including Collective Follow-on Damages Actions,* Kluwer Competition Law Blog, 5 October 2015, available at http://competitionlawblog.kluwercompetitionlaw.com/2015/10/05/united-kingdom-consumer-rights-act-2015-introduces-new-procedures-for-competition-litigation-including-collective-follow-on-damages-actions/.
965. *See* Chapter 8 of the Consumer Rights Act 2015.
966. *See* Sebastian Peyer, *Private Enforcement in England and Wales, in Private Enforcement of EU Competition Law: The Impact of the Damages Directive,* Pier Luigi Parcu, Giorgio Monti and Marco Botta (eds), Elgar, 2018, p. 92.

These collective actions combine features of both class actions and representative actions. Specifically, the claimant must fall within the class of individuals protected by the competition rule allegedly infringed. However, the action may be brought either by the claimant themselves or by an approved representative body,[967] as will be discussed further below.

An important similarity between the UK regime and the Portuguese system - following Portugal's transposition of the EU Damages Directive - is the extension of protection beyond individual citizens[968]/consumers.[969] Both frameworks now allow for collective actions to be brought on behalf of other affected parties, including companies, with a particular emphasis on SMEs, in addition to consumers.[970]

With the major reform introduced by the Consumer Rights Act 2015, the UK's class action framework evolved from a purely opt-in model to a hybrid system, as noted by Rachael Mulheron.[971] Specifically, it now includes an opt-out mechanism applicable to competition law cases. Given this development - and the absence of EU legislation specifically addressing class actions in the field of competition law - the transposition of the EU Damages Directive in the UK (at the time still mandatory for this State) did not necessitate further legislative changes.

3.4.4.2 Control

As Rachael Mulheron aptly describes,[972] the UK's class action regime is a 'class action with brakes'. Indeed, class actions in the UK are subject to a rigorous certification process, similar in structure to that of the US[973] - though arguably more demanding.[974] This process includes a formal preliminary hearing to determine whether the minimum legal and procedural requirements are met before the action can proceed.

In order to act as a representative in collective proceedings, an individual must be authorised by the CAT. This authorisation is granted irrespective of whether the proposed representative is a member of the class described in the proceedings. Notably, in opt-in actions, if the representative is a class member and reaches an individual settlement with the defendant, the action may continue, either with the

967. *See* Jumana Rahman, Anna Hyde and Tanya Macrae, *UK: England & Wales, in* Class *Actions: A Global Guide from Practical Law*, Omar Shah (ed.), Thomson Reuters, 2015, pp. 383-402, p. 387.
968. *See* Article 2(1) of Law 83/95.
969. *See* Article 19, para. 2a) of Law 23/2018.
970. *See* Articles 19(2)(b) of Law 23/2018 and 47B(7)(a) of the Competition Act 1998.
971. In *Class Actions and Government*, Cambridge University Press, 2020, p. 7.
972. In *The United Kingdom's New Opt-out Class Action: The Unique Perspective of a 'Third Generation' Statute*, Oxford Journal of Legal Studies, Oxford University Press, vol. 37, No. 4, 2017, pp. 814-843, p. 820.
973. *See* s. 3.4.1 above.
974. *See* Rachael Mulheron, *The United Kingdom's New Opt-Out Class Action: The Unique Perspective of a 'Third Generation' Statute*, Oxford Journal of Legal Studies, Oxford University Press, vol. 37, No. 4, 2017, pp. 814-843, p. 831.

appointment of a new representative, under directions from the CAT, or be discontinued altogether.[975] However, any such continuation or discontinuation is subject to the CAT's assessment of whether it is fair and reasonable for the individual to act (or cease to act) as the representative in the specific case.[976]

In determining whether it is 'fair and reasonable' for a person to act as a representative in collective proceedings, the CAT considers five key criteria:

(1) *Fair and adequate representation* - whether the person has acted fairly and adequately in the interests of the class members.
(2) *Absence of conflict* - whether the person has any material interest that conflicts with the interests of the class in relation to the common issues.
(3) *Suitability* - whether the person is the most appropriate representative, particularly where multiple applicants seek approval.
(4) *Financial capacity* - whether the person has the financial resources to cover any costs recoverable by the defendant, if so ordered.
(5) *Ability to satisfy undertakings* - whether the person can meet any undertaking as to damages required by the CAT in the event that an interim injunction is sought.[977]

These English class actions are therefore subject to a process known as class certification, which is overseen by the CAT. The primary purpose of this procedural safeguard is to prevent frivolous or unmeritorious claims from proceeding. At this preliminary stage, the CAT not only assesses whether the action meets the minimum legal and procedural requirements but also determines the appropriate structure of the action - namely, whether it should proceed as an opt-in or opt-out model.[978]

In this area, the CAT enjoys broad discretion[979] and may[980] consider any factors it deems relevant when deciding whether to authorise a person to act as a class representative. The applicable legislation provides a non-exhaustive list of potentially relevant criteria, which are outlined below.

To grant a CPO (Collective Proceedings Order) and allow a collective action to proceed, the CAT must first be satisfied that three core requirements are met: (i) the claims are brought on behalf of an identifiable class of persons (with no maximum limit

975. *See* Articles 86 and 87 of the Competition Appeal Tribunal Rules 2015.
976. *See* s. 47B(8) of the Competition Act 1998.
977. *See* Article 79(2) of the Competition Appeal Tribunal Rules 2015.
978. *See* s. 47B of the Competition Act 1998.
979. *See* Richard Pike and Katherine Cousins, *Too Big, Too Small, Not Yet 'Just Right': UK Collective Actions Regime Still to Find Its Goldilocks*, Global Competition Litigation Review, No. 1, 2018, pp. 42-45, at p. 42.
980. *See* Kim Dietzel et al., *Collective or Class Actions and Claims Aggregation in the United Kingdom, in GCR's Private Litigation Guide,* Nicholas and Heaton and Benhamin Holt (eds), 3rd ed., 22 November 2021, available at Private Litigation Guide - Global Competition Review.

on class size);[981] (ii) the claims raise issues that are common to that class; and (iii) the claims are suitable to be brought in collective proceedings.[982]

In assessing the suitability of the action for collective proceedings, the CAT considers a range of factors, including the following:

- Whether collective proceedings are the appropriate means of resolving the common issues, in terms of fairness and efficiency.
- The costs and benefits of continuing the proceedings as a class action.
- Whether any individual actions have already been initiated by class members involving similar claims.
- The size and nature of the class.
- Whether it is possible to determine, for any given individual, whether they fall within the defined class.
- Whether the claims are suitable for an aggregate award of damages.
- The availability of alternative dispute resolution mechanisms or other means of redress, including voluntary redress schemes approved by the CMA (Competition and Markets Authority).[983]

English law includes a specific procedure that allows an individual - or a group submitting a joint application - who has infringed competition law to apply to the CMA for approval of a voluntary redress scheme,[984] in line with the official guidelines established for this purpose.[985]

In a second step, when determining whether the class action should proceed on an opt-in or opt-out basis, the CAT also considers: (i) the strength of the claims; and (ii) whether it is practicable to pursue the case under an opt-in model, taking into account the specific circumstances - particularly the estimated amount of damages that individual class members may recover.[986]

In short, the action may be initiated by a class representative, but it can only proceed if the CAT issues a CPO. This order must confirm that: (i) the claims are eligible for inclusion in collective proceedings; (ii) the proposed representative is authorised; (iii) the class of persons whose claims are eligible is properly defined; and (iv) the proceedings will follow either an opt-in or opt-out model.[987]

This book would argue that the most significant aspect of the CPO is point (iv) above - namely, the decision on whether the proceedings will follow an opt-in or opt-out

981. *See* Jumana Rahman, Anna Hyde and Tanya Macrae, *UK: England & Wales, in Class Actions: A Global Guide from Practical Law*, Omar Shah (ed.), Thomson Reuters, 2015, pp. 383-402, p. 389.
982. *See* Article 79(1) of the Competition Appeal Tribunal Rules 2015.
983. *See* Article 79(2).
984. *See* s. 49C of the Competition Act 1998.
985. *Guidance on the approval of voluntary redress schemes for infringements of competition law*, 14 August 2015, available at Guidance on the approval of voluntary redress schemes for infringements of competition law (publishing.service.gov.uk).
986. *See* Article 79(3) of the Competition Appeal Tribunal Rules 2015.
987. *See* Article 80.

model. As James Hennah and Haidee Barratt point out,[988] choosing the 'new' opt-out model means that class members domiciled in the UK are automatically included in the proceedings unless they actively opt out, and this choice carries several implications, particularly regarding the financial investment required for the action and the potential value of the claim.

The certification process has also raised important questions about its scope, which have led to key case law developments.[989] One notable example is *Merricks v. Mastercard*,[990] which addressed whether a CPO applicant must be able to roughly quantify damages at the time of the certification hearing.

More broadly, Rachael Mulheron observes that,[991] while the legislation sets a relatively low threshold for standing (i.e., broad active legitimacy), it imposes a more demanding standard when it comes to the preliminary merits of the class action.

In this book's view, since the certification does not constitute a decision on the merits of the case, it nonetheless requires a robust *fumus boni iuris*[992] – especially in opt-out actions. This threshold is generally more easily met in follow-on actions.

3.4.4.3 Proceeding

Once the previous stages have been successfully completed – namely: (i) the authorisation of the class representative, (ii) the certification of the class as eligible for inclusion in collective proceedings, and (iii) the issuance of the CPO – this proceeding largely mirrors the Portuguese model,[993] particularly when the CAT determines that the opt-out mechanism will apply.

It is the CPO that sets out, in particular, the timeframe and procedure for class members to opt in or opt out, depending on the nature of the collective action.[994] These details must be included in the notice published to inform potential class members.[995] Even in opt-out proceedings, individuals who are not domiciled in the UK must actively opt in.[996] After the deadline established by the CAT, it may still allow individuals to join or withdraw from the proceedings, taking into account factors such as whether the

988. In *United Kingdom: Class Actions – Litigation, Policy and Latest Developments*, 2 December 2022, available at Class actions hub - Global Competition Review.
989. *See* s. 3.4.4.6 below.
990. *See* Bill Batchelor, Bruce Macaulay and Sym Hunt, *UK Class Actions Update: Merricks Secures Uncontested CPO, But the Competition Appeal Tribunal Shows It Retains Significant Teeth to Narrow Claims*, 14 September 2021, available at UK Class Actions Update: Merricks Secures Uncontested CPO, But the Competition Appeal Tribunal Shows It Retains Significant Teeth to Narrow Claims | Insights | Skadden, Arps, Slate, Meagher & Flom LLP.
991. In *The United Kingdom's New Opt-out Class Action: The Unique Perspective of a 'Third Generation' Statute*, Oxford Journal of Legal Studies, Oxford University Press, vol. 37, No. 4, 2017, pp. 814-843, p. 831.
992. *See* Bill Batchelor et al., *European Union and Unite Kingdom: A New Dawn for Class Actions*, 24 June 2022, available at The European, Middle East and African Antitrust Review - Global Competition Review.
993. *See* s. 3.4.3.3 above.
994. *See* Article 80(1)(h) of the Competition Appeal Tribunal Rules 2015.
995. *See* Article 81.
996. *See* Article 82(1)(b)(ii).

delay was due to the class member's fault and whether the defendant would suffer substantial prejudice as a result.[997]

At any stage of the proceedings, the rules governing access to evidence - especially evidence held by the opposing party - are broad. The CAT has discretionary power to order the disclosure of such evidence.[998]

The CAT has the authority to issue a judgment awarding aggregate damages to the class as a whole, without the need to determine individual compensation amounts for each class member.[999] When such an aggregate award is made, the CAT must also provide directions for how individual entitlements are to be determined. These directions may include the following:[1000]

(1) A calculation method or formula to be applied.
(2) Provisions for interim payments where the final individual amounts have not yet been determined.
(3) The appointment of an independent or expert third party to assess any claims raised by represented persons regarding the quantification of their individual compensation - along with provisions for covering the costs of this third party.
(4) A requirement that the distribution of the aggregate award among class members be approved by the CAT.

The aggregate award is issued in favour of the class representative or any other person the CAT considers appropriate.[1001]

This phase of damage distribution[1002] also bears similarities to the Portuguese system, particularly in that it is the responsibility of the National Court to define the relevant criteria. However, as previously noted,[1003] Common Law systems like that of the UK are not based on codified statutes but rather on case law. This makes the UK's approach more contextually appropriate within its legal tradition.

Moreover, the English system tends to be more detailed at this stage. In our view, one particularly positive feature is the possibility of appointing an independent expert to assess disputes regarding the quantification of individual damages.

Any damages not claimed by represented persons within the period specified by the CAT must be paid either to a designated charity, as directed by the Lord Chancellor,[1004]

997. *See* Article 82(2)(3).
998. *See* Article 89.
999. *See* David Ashton, *Competition Damages Action in the EU: Law and Practice*, economics contribution from Frank Maier-Rigaud and Ulrich Schawalbe, Elgar, *Competition Law and Practice*, 2nd ed., 2018, p. 322.
1000. *See* Article 92(1)(2).
1001. *See* Article 93(1).
1002. *See* Elysia-Elena Stellakis, *5 Things We Learnt About Class Actions, Practical Law Dispute Resolution*, 8 March 2023, available at 5 things we learnt about class actions | Dispute Resolution blog (practicallaw.com).
1003. *See* fn. 1051 below.
1004. *See* ss 47C(5) of the Competition Act 1998 and 194(8) of the Legal Services Act 2007, available at Legal Services Act 2007 (legislation.gov.uk).

or to the class representative (or another party) to cover the costs incurred in the action, as determined by the Court.[1005] It could be argued that this provision delays the recovery of investments made by third-party funders until after the distribution phase. However, this would imply that funders are only reimbursed if there is a surplus - i.e., when the total compensation awarded exceeds the amount claimed - which would run counter to both the spirit of the English legislator and, as we will see, the case law of the CAT.[1006] In this book's view, the legislator's intention was not to establish a rigid rule on post-event cost recovery, but rather to clarify that the CAT has the discretion to allocate unclaimed damages towards covering litigation costs where appropriate.

The UK legal framework also provides that, if a collective settlement is approved by the CAT, it will apply to all class members unless they choose to opt out within the period specified by the Tribunal. For individuals not domiciled in the UK, inclusion in the settlement requires an active opt-in.[1007] Finally, while proceedings before the High Court typically take two to three years, cases before the CAT tend to progress more quickly. According to a UK Competition Collective Actions Report from 2022,[1008] time elapsed between the registration of an application and the hearing of the CPO fell to an average of 0.8 years (9.5 months), compared to the average of 1.8 years recorded before 2020. Just in 2023 alone, fifteen CPO applications were registered.[1009]

It is true that, although the CAT previously only dealt with follow-on actions,[1010] its consistent decision-making demonstrates a high level of specialisation. Notably, the Court has firmly upheld the CPO regime as outlined above, even while acknowledging that it may compromise procedural efficiency and hinder early settlements.

This stance was clearly illustrated in the 2022 case of *Mark McLaren v. MOL*,[1011] where the CAT unanimously ruled that defendants could not communicate directly with class members unless authorised by the Court or agreed upon by the parties. This decision followed an incident in which, during the opt-out period (which lasted nearly three months), lawyers for most defendants sent letters to class members. These letters warned that failure to opt out could result in obligations to disclose potentially confidential documents, incurring time and costs. The CAT viewed this as an attempt to dissuade participation and took a protective stance in response.

1005. *See* ss 47C(6) of the Competition Act 1998 and 93(4) of the Competition Appeal Tribunal Rules 2015.
1006. *See* Adrian Render and Sebastian Peyer, *Are Cases Too Good to Litigate? Cost Recovery in Antitrust Collective Actions in the UK*, European Competition Law Review, vol. 41, No. 1, 2020, pp. 3-12, available at Are cases too good to litigate? Cost recovery in antitrust collective actions in the UK - UEA Digital Repository, p. 6.
1007. *See* Article 97(9) of the Competition Appeal Tribunal Rules 2015.
1008. Prepared by Peter Davis, February 2022, available at 2022 UK Competition Collective Actions Report (brattle.com).
1009. *See* 2024 CMS European Class Action Report, p. 28.
1010. *See* Jumana Rahman, Anna Hyde and Tanya Macrae, *UK: England & Wales, in Class Actions: A Global Guide from Practical Law*, Omar Shah (ed.), Thomson Reuters, 2015, pp. 383-402, p. 391.
1011. *See* Case 1339/7/20 - *Mark McLaren Class Representative Limited v. MOL (Europe Africa) Ltd and Others*, available at https://www.catribunal.org.uk/cases/13397720-mark-mclaren-class-representative-limited.

This study addresses the case referred to above in this section (rather than in the class actions' section) because it exemplifies the CAT's protective approach towards class members throughout the proceeding. While Sarina Williams, Jason Shardlow-Wrest, and Alice Chung have criticised this position[1012] – arguing that allowing such communications might foster settlement – this book does not fully share this view. First, class members are not responsible for managing the proceedings; that role lies with the representative, who is best placed to negotiate a potential settlement. Second, any communication of this nature should be reviewed by legal counsel. Third, such communications should be subject to scrutiny not only by the opposing party but also by the CAT itself. Indeed, the communication at issue in *McLaren v. MOL* was unacceptable, as it risked undermining the collective action by discouraging participation.

3.4.4.4 Costs

In the UK, Courts have discretion[1013] over the allocation of costs, which may include not only court fees and legal/expert fees but also a conditional fee arrangement – commonly referred to as a 'success fee' – which adds a premium to the lawyer's standard fees. In some cases, a party may be ordered to pay 100% of both their own costs and those of the opposing party.[1014]

Despite this discretion, the prevailing rule is the 'loser pays' principle: the losing party is typically ordered to cover the winning party's costs.[1015]

Importantly, class members are generally not liable for costs. Exceptions may apply, for instance, if a class member also acts as the class representative or the costs in question relate specifically to individual issues.[1016]

3.4.4.5 Limitations

Compared to the limitations already identified in the Portuguese system,[1017] these representative actions – specifically designed to compensate for damages arising from competition law infringements – are even less.

It is true that, once again citing concerns over a potential culture of abusive litigation (particularly involving lawyers and third-party litigation funders), the English legislator has refrained from fully regulating the role of these funders, including whether they

1012. *In a Little Less Conversation: CAT Restricts Defendants' Communications with Actual or Potential Class Members*, 21 February 2023, available at Class actions hub - Global Competition Review.

1013. *See* Vincent Smith, Anthony Maton and Scott Campbell, *The International Handbook on Private Enforcement of Competition Law: England and Wales*, Albert A. Foer and Jonathan W. Cuneo (eds), Edward Elgar Publishing, 2012, p. 310.

1014. *See* Nicholas Heaton and Paul Chaplin, *England & Wales Q&A*, *in GCR's Private Litigation Guide*, Nicholas Heaton and Benhamin Holt (eds), 3rd ed., 2021, *asset download – Global Competition Review*, pp. 249 and 250.

1015. *Ibid.*, p. 259.

1016. *See* Article 98 of the Competition Appeal Tribunal Rules 2015.

1017. *See* s. 3.4.3.5 above.

may profit from the compensation awarded.[1018] As previously noted,[1019] this regulatory gap persists despite the growing relevance of TPLF in collective actions.

According to Sebastian Peyer,[1020] with whom this book agrees, this lack of clarity risks weakening opt-out actions in the UK. Drawing from the US experience, it is evident that such actions not only are high risk but also entail significant financial costs.

Nevertheless, these funding agreements are permitted in the UK and are subject to the general principles of Common Law.[1021] In practice, they have become widespread and are often cited as one of the key drivers behind the exponential growth of class actions in the country.[1022]

So much so that the litigation funding industry has taken steps to self-regulate. Most funders operating in the UK are now members of the Association of Litigation Funders of England and Wales,[1023] which has adopted a Code of Conduct for Litigation Funders.[1024] This framework sets out standards of transparency, capital adequacy, and ethical conduct, helping to build trust in the use of third-party funding in collective proceedings.

The English legislature has also taken steps to regulate TPLF, proposing the Litigation Funding Agreements (Enforceability) Bill.[1025] Specifically, it seeks to clarify - following the case law below - that litigation funding agreements (LFAs) are not to be treated as damages-based agreements (DBAs, addressed later in this section), thereby ensuring their enforceability across all types of proceedings. However, following the announcement of a general election on 4 July 2024, the UK Parliament was dissolved on 30 May, halting progress on this Bill.

Indeed, UK courts have addressed this issue in the past several times and, as Adrian Render and Sebastian Peyer have observed,[1026] most of the rulings were favourable. These have confirmed[1027] that funders may recover their costs before compensation is distributed to class members, even if only partially. This approach helps ensure that funders are not left uncompensated in cases where the total damages awarded are fully

1018. The only references to the reimbursement of *fees* are in the aforementioned Articles 47C(6) of the Competition Act 1998 and 93(4) of the Competition Appeal Tribunal Rules 2015.
1019. *See* s. 3.4.4.3 above.
1020. In *Private Enforcement in England and Wales, in Private Enforcement of EU Competition Law: The Impact of the Damages Directive,* Pier Luigi Parcu, Giorgio Monti and Marco Botta (eds), Elgar, 2018, p. 92.
1021. *See* Jumana Rahman, Anna Hyde and Tanya Macrae, *UK: England & Wales, in Class Actions: A Global Guide from Practical Law*, Omar Shah (ed.), Thomson Reuters, 2015, pp. 383-402, p. 393.
1022. *See* Martin Davies, Oliver Middleton and Tom Watret, *The Increasing Prevalence of Class Actions in the UK*, Business Law Review, vol. 42, No. 4, 2021, pp. 168-174, p. 168 https://doi.org/10.54648/bula2021024.
1023. *See* https://associationoflitigationfunders.com/.
1024. *See* https://associationoflitigationfunders.com/code-of-conduct/documents/.
1025. *See* https://bills.parliament.uk/bills/3702.
1026. *In Are Cases Too Good to Litigate? Cost Recovery in Antitrust Collective Actions in the UK*, European Competition Law Review, vol. 41, No. 1, 2020, pp. 3-12, available at *Are cases too good to litigate? Cost recovery in antitrust collective actions in the UK – UEA Digital Repository*, p. 13.
1027. *See* s. 3.4.4.3 above.

allocated to claimants, leaving no surplus. In doing so, the Courts have acknowledged the practical need to safeguard the financial viability of third-party funding in collective actions.

Nevertheless, there have also been rulings that take a more cautious stance towards private litigation funding. Notably, in the 2020 High Court case *Sharp and others v. Blank*, the Court held that a third-party funder could be held jointly and severally liable for the costs of a group litigation order (GLO).[1028] In that case, the claimant had relied on both private funding and after-the-event (ATE) insurance but ultimately lost. As a result, both the claimant and the funder were ordered to cover the legal costs.[1029]

Also, *quota litis* agreements (where a lawyer's fee is calculated as a percentage of the amount recovered only in the event of success) are not valid in opt-out actions – under the Competition Act 1998, such arrangements are classified as DBAs, which are expressly prohibited in opt-out collective proceedings.[1030]

In this context, more recently (July 2023), the UK Supreme Court issued its decision in the *PACCAR* case,[1031] interpreting section 58AA of the Courts and Legal Services Act 1990. The ruling held that litigation funders provide 'claims management services', which can bring their agreements within the scope of the above-mentioned DBAs. Since, as advanced, DBAs are prohibited in opt-out competition class actions, this raised serious concerns about the enforceability of many existing LFAs, particularly those where funders' returns were tied to a percentage of damages awarded.

In response, many funders began restructuring their agreements to calculate returns based on a multiple of the capital invested, rather than a percentage of damages, in an effort to avoid classification as DBAs. The CAT subsequently upheld these revised agreements in several cases – for example, in the *Commercial and Interregional Card Claims I Limited v. Mastercard*[1032] – ruling that they did not breach section 58AA. However, these decisions are currently under appeal, and legal uncertainty remains – that is why the UK government introduced the Bill mentioned above: to restore the pre-PACCAR position by amending the definition of DBAs to exclude LFAs, with retrospective effect.

The above-mentioned legislative initiative on this regard is still out of the new government's agenda; however, the Civil Justice Council has launched a formal review of litigation funding, whose final report was published on 2 June 2025.[1033]

1028. *See* Kenny Henderson, Lee Gluyas and Jonathan Scrine, *Funder Liable to Pay Substantial Adverse Costs in Group Litigation*, 20 July 2020, available at Funder liable to pay substantial adverse costs in group litigation (cms-lawnow.com).
1029. *See* Nicholas Heaton and Paul Chaplin, *England & Wales Q&A*, *in GCR's Private Litigation Guide*, Nicholas Heaton and Benhamin Holt (eds), 3rd ed., 2021, *asset download – Global Competition Review*, p. 251.
1030. *See* s. 47C(8) of the Competition Act 1998.
1031. *See* https://supremecourt.uk/cases/uksc-2021-0078#case-summary.
1032. *See* https://www.catribunal.org.uk/cases/14417722-commercial-and-interregional-card-claims-i-limited-cicc-i.
1033. *See* Review of Litigation Funding Final Report, Civil Justice Council, 2 June 2025, available at https://www.judiciary.uk/wp-content/uploads/2025/06/CJC-Review-of-Litigation-Funding-Final-Report-2.pdf.

That 2025 report recommends a series of reforms aimed at ensuring fair, proportionate, and accessible litigation funding in the UK. It confirms the intention of reversing the PACCAR ruling through retrospective legislation to distinguish TPLF from contingency fees arrangements and calls for light-touch statutory regulation tailored to the type of claimant – more robust for consumers and collective actions, and minimal for commercial parties. Key proposals include capital adequacy requirements, transparency on funders' identities, conflict of interest safeguards, and independent legal advice for funded parties. The report also suggests standardising litigation funding agreements, introducing mechanisms for dispute resolution, and enhancing Court oversight of funding arrangements. Additional recommendations cover contingency fee reform, regulation of crowdfunding and portfolio funding, and the creation of an Access to Justice Fund. Implementation would follow a twin-track approach: immediate legislative reversal of PACCAR, followed by broader primary legislation to embed the remaining reforms.[1034]

Regarding conditional fees arrangements, i.e., agreements that establish a condition for the payment of part or all of the lawyer's fees (usually the successful outcome of the action) and the aforementioned after-the-event (ATE) insurances,[1035] i.e., insurance that protects the litigant against the costs of losing the action, they are permitted under British law.

The key distinction between conditional fees arrangements or CFAs and contingency fee agreements (or *quota litis* agreements, also referred to as DBAs under the Competition Act 1998) lies in how the lawyer is compensated. In a CFA, the lawyer may charge their standard fee plus a success-related uplift if the case is won, and a reduced or no fee if it is lost. In contrast, DBAs involve the lawyer receiving a percentage of the damages recovered, and these are not allowed in opt-out collective actions, as previously discussed. Indeed, the UK Government noted during a 2013 public consultation, banning DBAs in such cases was seen as a crucial safeguard to prevent the emergence of a 'litigation culture'.

The UK Government has acknowledged that prohibiting DBAs in opt-out collective actions serves as an important safeguard. Allowing such agreements (where lawyers are paid a percentage of the damages recovered) could encourage speculative litigation, impose disproportionate costs on defendant companies, and incentivise lawyers to pursue only high-value cases. Instead, 'no win, no fee' CFAs and ATE insurance remain available for these types of claims (as mentioned above) – subject to the reforms introduced by the Legal Aid, Sentencing and Punishment of Offenders (LASPO) Act 2012.[1036]

1034. *See* pp. 7 et seq.
1035. *See* Nicholas Heaton and Paul Chaplin, *England & Wales Q&A, in GCR's Private Litigation Guide*, Nicholas Heaton and Benhamin Holt (eds), 3rd ed., 2021, asset download – Global Competition Review, p. 259.
1036. *See Private Actions in Competition Law: A Consultation on Options for Reform – Government Response*, available at https://assets.publishing.service.gov.uk/government/uploads/system/uploads/attachment_data/file/70185/13-501-private-actions-in-competition-law-a-consultation-on-options-for-reform-government-response1.pdf, pt. 5.62.

The reality is that, due to the high risks associated with competition law class actions, it remains challenging – despite growing interest, specially in the UK – to find financing and insurance companies willing to assume the roles described above (and specially the decision in the *PACCAR* case did not help at all). Their involvement typically hinges on the perceived strength of the case.

Compounding the above is the application of the 'loser-pays' principle, which has been enforced even in private opt-out actions for competition law infringements, in order to prevent such frivolous or clearly unmeritorious cases.[1037]

Finally, litigation costs in the UK are significantly higher than in Portugal for this type of action, largely due to the disparity in hourly rates charged by legal and economic experts in both jurisdictions. As noted by Miguel Sousa Ferro,[1038] the UK may well be the most expensive European jurisdiction for litigation, with funding requirements estimated to be '20 to 30 times higher' than those in Portugal for comparable cases.

3.4.4.6 Class Actions

Unlike individual actions brought by consumers – which remain virtually non-existent to date – the UK stands out as the European jurisdiction with the highest number of collective[1039] competition law actions initiated by consumers.[1040] The earliest of these dates back to 2007 with the landmark case of *Which v. JJB Sports plc*, which notably preceded the 2015 legislative reforms that introduced the opt-out model for class actions involving breaches of competition law.

After the *JJB Sports* case, at least sixty other actions have been brought under section 47B of the Competition Act 1998 (collective action) – all of which are currently active with the exception of two and emphasis for the *Dorothy Gibson v. Pride Mobility Products Limited* case.[1041]

In that case, the claimant relied in part on a 27 March 2014 decision by the Office of Fair Trading (OFT), which found that Pride Mobility Products Limited had engaged in anticompetitive vertical agreements with its retailers. These agreements restricted the online advertising of prices below the Recommended Retail Price (RRP) for certain mobility scooters in the UK.[1042]

1037. *Ibid.*, pt. 5.59.
1038. In *Consumer Antitrust Private Enforcement in Europe: As Complete a Survey as Possible (Extended Version)*, 23 October 2022, available at https://ssrn.com/abstract=4223770, p. 11.
1039. It should be noted that *common law* tends to be *uncodified*, which means that cases take on a distinct, precedential importance. In other words, similar cases will, in principle, be decided in the same way. *See* Sebastian Lewis, *Precedent and the Rule of Law*, Oxford Journal of Legal Studies, vol. 41, No. 4, Winter 2021, pp. 873-898, p. 873 https://doi.org/10.1093/ojls/gqab007.
1040. *See* Miguel Sousa Ferro, *Consumer Antitrust Private Enforcement in Europe: As Complete a Survey as Possible (Extended Version)*, 23 October 2022, available at https://ssrn.com/abstract=4223770, p. 11.
1041. *See* Case 1257/7/16 – *Dorothy Gibson v. Pride Mobility Products Limited*, available at https://www.catribunal.org.uk/cases/12577716-dorothy-gibson.
1042. *See* OFT Decision No. CE/9578-12 of 27 March 2014, https://assets.publishing.service.gov.uk/media/54522051ed915d1380000007/Pride_Decision_Confidential_Version.pdf.

Gibson sought compensation not only for consumers who purchased scooters from the eight implicated retailers but also for those who bought from other retailers – arguing that they too suffered harm due to an umbrella pricing effect. The proposed class would have encompassed approximately 32,000 consumers.

However, the UK's first opt-out competition law class action ultimately did not proceed. The claim was withdrawn by the claimant, who was subsequently ordered to pay Pride Mobility Products Limited GBP 308,997.64 in legal costs.[1043]

Nonetheless, the CAT issued a ruling on Dorothy Gibson's application for class certification on 31 March 2017. Among other preliminary findings, the Court concluded that the statement of claim required amendment to adequately substantiate the alleged harm. This was particularly necessary given that the claim relied heavily on the umbrella effect, i.e., the impact of the alleged anticompetitive conduct on prices charged by other Pride retailers and for other Pride scooter models.

According to the CAT, it would not be sufficient for the claimant to merely demonstrate a drop in prices following the end of the alleged infringements. Instead, the claimant must provide a credible basis to show that such a price change is causally linked to the cessation of the anticompetitive conduct, rather than to unrelated market factors. As the CAT noted, '[i]t may turn out that even an amended Claim Form and supported by expert evidence putting the claims on a revised basis still faces considerable difficulties'.[1044]

In adopting this position, the CAT emphasised the need for a rigorous approach to class certification. However, it deliberately distanced itself from the more demanding US model, which typically involves extensive disclosure, production of evidence, and adversarial expert testimony at the certification stage. Instead, the Court aligned itself with the Canadian approach, requiring that the claimant's expert present a credible and realistic methodology for establishing harm on a class-wide basis, without necessitating full evidentiary proceedings at this preliminary phase.[1045]

Following the *Gibson* case, several collective actions were filed, namely against Mastercard, and the most notably one is the landmark *Merricks v. Mastercard* case,[1046] initiated in September 2016. Indeed, this case earned recognition as the largest class action in British legal history and represented the first major test of the CPO regime, introduced under the Consumer Rights Act 2015 to facilitate access to justice by enabling consumers and small businesses to seek damages for competition law infringements through opt-out collective actions.[1047]

1043. *See* Order of the President (Withdrawal of claim) of 25 May 2017, available at https://www.catribunal.org.uk/sites/cat/files/1257_Dorothy_Gibson_Order_250517.pdf.
1044. *See* Judgment (CPO Application) of 31 March 2017, available at https://www.catribunal.org.uk/sites/cat/files/1257_Dorothy_Gibson_Judgment_CPO_CAT_9_310317.pdf, pt. 118.
1045. *See* David Ashton, *Competition Damages Action in the EU: Law and Practice*, economics contribution from Frank Maier-Rigaud and Ulrich Schawalbe, Elgar, *Competition Law and Practice*, 2nd ed., 2018, p. 324.
1046. *See* Case 1266/7/16 – *Walter Hugh Merricks CBE v. Mastercard Incorporated and Others*, available at https://www.catribunal.org.uk/cases/12667716-walter-hugh-merricks-cbe.
1047. Richard Crump, *The Biggest UK Antitrust Class Action Cases to Watch*, 9 March 2020, available at https://www.law360.com/articles/1250361.

In fact, the remaining collective actions were suspended pending the UK Supreme Court's ruling on the class certification stage of the *Merricks v. Mastercard* case, which was delivered on 11 December 2020. As will be discussed below, this judgment proved pivotal in clarifying the standard of scrutiny that the CAT must apply when assessing applications for CPOs, i.e., during the class certification phase.

The *Merricks v. Mastercard* action is a follow-on claim based on the European Commission's decision of 19 December 2007, which found that the payment organisation MasterCard – along with its affiliated entities, MasterCard Incorporated, MasterCard International Incorporated, and MasterCard Europe S.p.r.l. – had infringed Article 101 of the TFEU. The infringement involved the imposition of a minimum price that merchants were required to pay to their acquiring banks for accepting card payments within the EEA. This was implemented through the application of cross-border interchange fees on MasterCard-branded credit and single-payment cards, as well as MasterCard and Maestro-branded debit cards.[1048]

Following the European Commission's infringement decision, Walter Merricks, acting as class representative, filed a collective action against Mastercard on behalf of approximately 46 million UK consumers aged 16 or over. The claim covers individuals who purchased goods or services from UK businesses that accepted Mastercard payments between May 1992 and June 2008. Merricks argues that, absent the infringement, consumers would have paid lower prices during this period due to reduced merchant service charges. The total compensation sought amounts to approximately GBP 14 billion – making it, as advanced, the largest damages claim ever brought in the UK.

Initially, the CAT rejected[1049] Walter Merricks' application for a CPO, primarily on the grounds that the claim lacked sufficient data and methodology to determine the extent to which the interchange fees were passed on to consumers, and to calculate individual losses in a way that would support a fair distribution of any aggregate damages.[1050] This refusal was met with criticism in academic[1051] and was subsequently appealed. On 16 April 2019, the Court of Appeal overturned the CAT's decision, establishing several key principles:[1052]

(1) *Establishing common issues*: demonstrating consumer harm generally satisfies the requirement for common issues in class certification. A

1048. AT.34579 MasterCard I, available at https://ec.europa.eu/competition/elojade/isef/case_details.cfm?proc_code = 1_34579.
1049. *See* Neil Andrews, *English Systems of Multiparty Litigation, in The Cambridge Handbook of Class Actions: An International Survey,* Brian T. Fitzpatrick and Randall S. Thomas (eds), Cambridge University Press, 2021, p. 173.
1050. Judgment (CPO Application) of 21 July 2017, available at https://www.catribunal.org.uk/sites/cat/files/2.1266_Walter_Hugh_Judgment_CAT_16_210717.pdf.
1051. *See,* for example, Sebastian Peyer, *Has the CAT's MasterCard Decision Killed Off Opt-out Class Actions by Indirect Purchasers?,* Centre for Competition Policy, 10 August 2017, available at Has the CAT's MasterCard decision killed off opt-out class actions by indirect purchasers? | Centre for Competition Policy.
1052. Judgment of the Court of Appeal (CPO Application appeal) of 16 April 2019, available at https://www.catribunal.org.uk/sites/cat/files/2019-05/1266_Walter_Judgment_Court_of_Appeal_EWCA_Civ_674_160419.pdf.

detailed individual-level analysis of consumer impact is not necessary at this stage.

(2) *Methodological threshold*: at the certification phase, the CAT needs to only assess whether the proposed methodology is capable of establishing loss on a class-wide basis.

(3) *No premature merits assessment*: the CAT should not engage in a detailed evaluation of the evidence or its probative value at this preliminary stage.

(4) *Ongoing Nature of Certification*: Certification is not static; under section 47B(9) of the Competition Act 1998, a CPO can be amended or revoked as the case progresses.

(5) *Focus on suitability, not distribution*: the CAT's role at this stage is limited to determining whether the claim is suitable for an aggregate award of damages under Rule 79(2) of the Competition Appeal Tribunal Rules 2015. It is not required to decide how compensation will be distributed among class members.

Mastercard, in turn, appealed to the UK Supreme Court, which, on 11 December 2020, largely upheld the conclusions reached by the Court of Appeal.[1053] Following this Supreme Court's decision, a remittal hearing on the CPO took place in March 2021, with the CPO ultimately granted on 18 May 2022.

Following the certification, the CAT addressed several preliminary issues, including causation, limitation, and exemption. The Court ruled that claims predating 20 June 1997 were time-barred, as there was no deliberate concealment to justify extending the limitation period. Also, the Court found that Mastercard's EEA fees did not significantly affect UK fees and barred exemption arguments, prompting Mr Merricks to drop claims related to debit and Solo cards. These rulings substantially reduced the claim's value (by approximately 95%) and narrowed the class size by around 2 million individuals. In light of these setbacks, Mr Merricks and Mastercard reached a proposed settlement on 3 December 2024, under which Mastercard agreed to pay GBP 200 million without admitting liability. A joint application for a Collective Settlement Approval Order (CSAO) was filed in January 2025. The proposed distribution included GBP 100 million to be shared equally among claimants (subject to a per-person cap), GBP 45.57 million reimbursing the litigation funder Innsworth Capital, and GBP 54.53 million allocated either to enhance claimant compensation or provide additional return to the funder. Mastercard also waived its right to recover adverse costs. However, the funder opposed the settlement, initiating arbitration against Mr Merricks and intervening in the CSAO hearing. In the end, the Court approved the CSAO (on 21 February 2025).[1054]

Merricks v. Mastercard was the first contested settlement approval in UK opt-out collective proceedings and subjected the proposed agreement (and the CPO) to an exceptional degree of judicial scrutiny.

1053. *See* Neal Ross Marder et al., *UK Supreme Court Hands Down New Guidance for Collective Claim Certification, Thomson Reuters Wesrlaw,* 25 January 2021, available at pi_marder.pdf (akingump.com).

1054. *See* https://mastercardconsumerclaim.co.uk/Home/Timeline.

According to David Ashton[1055] – and in line with this book's view – the *Gibson v. Pride Mobility Products and Merricks v. Mastercard* cases illustrate the CAT commitment to conducting a thorough and rigorous review, even at the early certification stage. Both cases revealed challenges similar to those seen in Portugal, particularly around class definition, methodology, and the calculation of aggregate and individual damages.[1056]

Despite these hurdles, the UK remains one of the most attractive jurisdictions for private enforcement of competition law.[1057] Since the introduction of the UK's opt-out collective proceedings regime in 2015, over five hundred million class members have been represented in competition class actions – a striking figure that underscores the scale of this mechanism. Indeed, before the Mastercard settlement highlighted above, other two relevant settlements have been approved: the first in the McLaren roll-on/roll-off car delivery case, where the CAT approved a GBP 1.5 million settlement in December 2023, and the second in the Boundary Fares claim, where on 10 May 2024 the CAT approved a GBP 25 million settlement with South Western Trains, plus GBP 4.75 million in costs and GBP 750,000 for advertising. Part of the cost award will go to the litigation funder, and if claims fall below GBP 10.2 million, the class representative may request that unclaimed funds be reallocated to cover further costs or funder returns.[1058]

These developments are largely due to the presence of a specialised Court (the CAT), flexible procedural rules[1059] – including broad access to evidence[1060] – and cost-related mechanisms such as the discretion of English courts, contingency fee arrangements under the Damages-Based Agreements Regulations 2013 for opt-in actions, conditional fee arrangements for opt-out actions,[1061] and the availability of alternative litigation funding models.[1062]

Nevertheless, Brexit (the UK's withdrawal from the EU following the 2016 referendum) has impacted the legal landscape, particularly because infringement decisions issued under EU competition law after the end of the transition period in December 2020 are no longer binding on UK Courts.

1055. *Competition Damages Action in the EU: Law and Practice*, economics contribution from Frank Maier-Rigaud and Ulrich Schawalbe, Elgar, *Competition Law and Practice*, 2nd ed., 2018, p. 325.
1056. For further developments, *see* Barry Rodger, Miguel Sousa Ferro and Francisco Marcos, *The EU Antitrust Damages Directive: Transposition in the Member States*, Oxford University Press, 2018, pp. 402 and 403.
1057. *See* Kim Dietzel et al., *Collective or Class Actions and Claims Aggregation in the UK, in GCR's Private Litigation Guide*, Nicholas and Heaton and Benhamin Holt (eds), 3rd ed., 2021, *asset download – Global Competition Review*, p. 93.
1058. *See* 2024 CMS European Class Action Report, p. 26.
1059. *See* Elizabeth Morony, Ben Jasper and Oliver Carroll, *England & Wales, Private Antitrust Litigation 2020*, ed. by Francesca Richmond, July 2019.
1060. *See* Giles Warrington and Tim Riisager, *United Kingdom, Cartels 2020*, Nigel Parr and Euan Burrowns (eds), Global Legal Group, 8th ed., 17 February 2020, https://www.globallegalinsights.com/practice-areas/cartels-laws-and-regulations/united-kingdom.
1061. *See* 47C(8) of the Competition Act 1998.
1062. *See* Barry Rodger, Miguel Sousa Ferro and Francisco Marcos, *The EU Antitrust Damages Directive: Transposition in the Member States*, Oxford University Press, 2018, p. 404.

Prior to 2 January 2021, the European Commission held jurisdiction – under Article 11 of Regulation 1/2003 – to investigate and rule on breaches of EU competition law within the UK,[1063] working in coordination with the CMA, with Commission proceedings taking precedence. For instance, in 2012, the UK's Office of Fair Trading closed its investigation into suspected cartels among commercial vehicle manufacturers after the Commission launched its own enquiry into the same conduct.[1064] However, following Brexit, the Commission no longer has authority over competition law infringements occurring within the UK – unless it can demonstrate that the conduct in question meets the qualified effects test, meaning it is likely to produce immediate and substantial effects within the EU.[1065] Consequently, claimants seeking to bring follow-on actions, particularly collective ones, can only rely on CMA decisions issued after 31 December 2020, unless the European Commission had already initiated its investigation before that date.

With the disapplication of Regulation 1/2003 in the UK as of 1 January 2021, decisions issued by the European Commission after that date no longer carry binding authority for UK national authorities. However, decisions adopted before that date may still be relied upon in follow-on actions, as permitted by *The Competition (Amendment etc.) (EU Exit) Regulations 2019.*[1066]

As Edward Coulson and Ben Blacklock observe,[1067] this shift has a potential upside: assuming the CMA continues active and current, its decisions are likely to contain more detailed insights into the UK market – particularly useful for claimants seeking to establish causation and quantify damages.

Moreover, the UK had already diverged from the EU's preferred approach to collective redress when it introduced opt-out collective actions for competition law breaches in 2015, contrasting with the EU's general preference for opt-in models. While class actions in the UK have surged in recent years, they still fall short of the scale and maturity seen in the US system, where opt-out class actions are the norm across all areas of law. In the UK, by contrast, the opt-out model is currently limited to competition law. Additionally, the UK is no longer bound to implement new EU legislation, such as Directive 2020/1828 or any future EU rules on TPLF. Nonetheless, growing momentum from legal practitioners, economists, and academics suggests that opt-out collective actions in the UK will continue to expand, reinforcing the country's position as a leading forum for private enforcement of competition law.

1063. *See* Articles 7 and 20 to 22 of Regulation 1/2003 and s. 25 of the Competition Act 1998.
1064. *See* CE/9349-10, available at Commercial vehicle manufacturers: civil cartel investigation - GOV.UK (www.gov.uk).
1065. *Intel* ruling of 6 September 2017, Case C-413/14 P, pt. 49.
1066. Available at The Competition (Amendment etc.) (EU Exit) Regulations 2019 (legislation.gov.uk).
1067. *In Brexit and Its Impact on Competition Litigation in the UK, in GCR's Private Litigation Guide,* Nicholas and Heaton and Benhamin Holt (eds), 3rd ed., 2021, *asset download – Global Competition Review*, p. 160.

3.4.5 Belgium

3.4.5.1 Class Action Model

Until a decade ago, Belgium lacked a mechanism for collective redress. Injured parties were required to file individual civil liability actions. However, if the cases were closely related, they could later be joined (join actions)[1068] to avoid contradictory rulings and to promote procedural efficiency. As a result, only the principle of 'personal interest' applied.[1069]

In 2013, the *Cour de Cassation* - Belgium's highest Court in civil and commercial matters - recognised, for the first time, the possibility of a form of class action. In the absence of specific Belgian legislation on collective redress, the Court relied on laws concerning access to justice and environmental protection, such as the Law of 12 January 1993, which grants environmental associations the right to bring legal actions. Based on this framework, the Court accepted that environmental organisations could seek injunctions to defend the collective interests they represent. This marked the first instance of a class action in Belgium, framed as an action for the protection of collective (not individual) interests. Initially limited to environmental matters, the scope of such actions was later expanded by the Law of 21 December 2018 to include the defence of human rights and fundamental freedoms.

The landscape changed with the adoption of the Law of 28 March 2014, which introduced a collective redress mechanism in the form of a representative action, i.e., actions brought by designated entities. This marked a departure from the previous near-absence of collective action tools. The new mechanism applied to breaches of specific legal provisions, including competition law, provided they occurred after 1 September 2014.[1070] As noted by Stefaan Voet,[1071] its scope was limited to consumer-to-business (C2B) disputes.

In 2017, the Belgian legislator introduced a provision stating that, without prejudice to the Title dedicated to collective actions, the provisions of the subsequent Title - transposing the EU Damages Directive - would also apply to collective redress actions for infringements of competition law.[1072] However, this cross-reference alone does not appear sufficient to establish a distinct and comprehensive collective redress regime for competition law in Belgium.

In 2018, the collective redress mechanism was extended to cover disputes between SMEs (represented by the plaintiff) and infringing companies. Like consumers, SMEs often lack the scale and resources to pursue individual legal actions, particularly in the field of competition law. Nonetheless, this extension faced criticism from some

1068. *See* Articles 30, 701 and 856 of the Belgian Judicial Code of 10 October 1967, available on LOI - WET (fgov.be).
1069. *See* Articles 17 and 18 of the Belgian Judicial Code.
1070. *See* Title 2 of Book XVII of the Code of Economic Law of 23 February 2013 (which entered into force on 1 September 2014), available at LOI - WET (fgov.be).
1071. In *Class Actions in Belgium: Evaluation and the Way Forward, Class Actions in Europe: Holy Grail or a Wrong Trail?*, Alan Uzelac and Stefaan Voet (eds), Springer, 2021, p. 133.
1072. *See* Article XVII.70 of Title 2 and Title 3 of Book XVII of the Code of Economic Law.

quarters, with concerns that it might encourage abusive litigation.[1073] In practice, however, these fears have proven unfounded; quite the opposite has occurred.[1074]

The most recent developments came with the adoption of the Act of 21 April 2024,[1075] which transposed Directive 2020/1828 into Belgian law and applies to actions initiated since 10 June 2024. In certain respects, Belgium's collective redress mechanism has a wider scope than that set out in this directive – particularly, it covers the competition law (and the representation of SMEs, as mentioned above).

The specific entities authorised to bring collective actions in Belgium depend on the interests being protected.[1076] For actions seeking compensation for harm caused to consumers, the competent entities include the following:

(1) *Belgian legal entities authorised by the Minister of Economic Affairs* – to get this authorisation, the organisation must:
   - be a Belgian non-profit with at least twelve months of experience in consumer protection;
   - have consumer protection as part of its official mission;
   - not be bankrupt or in insolvency proceedings;
   - be independent from non-consumer interests;
   - clearly publish information about:
     - how it meets these requirements,
     - its funding sources,
     - how it is structured and managed,
     - its mission and activities.

   Once authorised, the status is permanent, but the Minister must regularly check that the organisation still meets all conditions.
(2) *Entities authorised in another Member States* – if an organisation is already authorised in another EU country, it can act as a group representative in Belgium. Proof must come from the European Commission's official list of such entities.
(3) *Ad Hoc representatives* – if an organisation does not fall into the two categories above, it can still act as a group representative for a specific case. In that situation, the National Court will decide if it meets the necessary criteria.
(4) *The Belgian Consumer Ombudsman* – this public body can also act as a group representative, but only during the early stages of a case (admissibility and negotiation). If no settlement is reached, another representative must take over for the rest of the process.

1073. *See*, for example, Emmanuel Plasschaert, *Les PME et les indépendants ont désormais accès à l'action en réparation collective*, 7 June 2018, available at https://www.lecho.be/opinions/carte-blanche/les-pme-et-les-independants-ont-desormais-acces-a-l-action-en-reparation-collective/10018844.html.
1074. *See* s. 3.4.5.6 below.
1075. *See* Law of 21 April 2024 amending Books I, XV and XVII of the Code of Economic Law, and transposing Directive 2020/1828, available at https://www.ejustice.just.fgov.be/eli/loi/2013/02/28/2013A11134/justel#LNK0745.
1076. *See* https://practiceguides.chambers.com/practice-guides/collective-redress-class-actions-2024/belgium.

In cases involving harm suffered by a group of SMEs, the action can be brought by an *interprofessional organisation for the protection of SMEs* that has legal personality and is either represented on the Higher Council for the Self-Employed and SMEs or recognised by Ministerial Decree.

Additionally, the following entities can represent both consumers and SMEs if:

- be a Belgian legal entity with at least twelve months of real experience in consumer/SMEs protection;
- have consumer/SMEs protection as one of its official goals;
- operate as a non-profit;
- not be undergoing insolvency or bankruptcy;
- be independent from any non-consumer/member of the group represented influence;
- publicly share clear, accessible information about:
  - how it meets these requirements.
  - its funding sources.
  - its structure, leadership, membership.
  - its mission and activities.[1077]

As for the model of collective action, until 2024 it was (*see* next paragraphs) to the National Court to decide,[1078] after the action is filed, whether to proceed under an opt-in or opt-out model. However, the opt-in model was still mandatory in two cases:

(1) when the harm involves physical or moral damage; or
(2) when the affected consumers or SMEs are not domiciled in Belgium.

After 2024, the Belgian legislator decided to change the rule on the class action model, making opt-in the default option.[1079] The opt-out model now is only permitted in rare cases – specifically, when both parties agree to settle and the Court approves the use of an opt-out mechanism (and the two limitations referred to above still apply, i.e., cases involving physical or moral harm and consumers or SMEs based outside Belgium).

3.4.5.2 Control

Belgian law[1080] provides for a preliminary judicial review to assess the admissibility of a collective redress action. This review focuses on whether, in the specific case,

1077. *See* Article XVII.39 of Title 2 of Book XVII of the Code of Economic Law.
1078. *See* Stefaan Voet, *Class Actions in Belgium: Evaluation and the Way Forward, Class Actions in Europe: Holy Grail or a Wrong Trail?*, Alan Uzelac and Stefaan Voet (eds), Springer, 2021, p. 137.
1079. *See* https://www.aoshearman.com/en/insights/new-law-expands-belgian-class-actions-framework.
1080. *See* Article XVII.36 of Title 2 of Book XVII of the Code of Economic Law.

pursuing the claim collectively would be more effective than through individual proceedings. In making this determination, the National Court assesses if:

- the claim involves a possible violation of one of the specific laws listed in Article XVII.37 of the Belgian Code of Economic Law (including competition law);
- the plaintiff meets the requirements referred above and has a mission that directly relates to the subject of the collective action;
- a collective redress procedure is likely to be more effective than pursuing the matter through regular legal channels - importantly, the amount of damage is not a decisive factor in this assessment.[1081]

The fact that the law significantly restricts standing to the specific entities mentioned above (selected based on their objectives or areas of interest), while excluding other natural or legal persons from bringing such actions, also serves as a safeguard. This limitation is intended to prevent frivolous or abusive lawsuits.[1082]

3.4.5.3 Proceedings

The Belgian class action procedure is relatively general[1083] and comparable to the proceedings aforementioned.[1084] It relies on the rules set out in the Belgian Judicial Code.[1085] Jurisdiction is exclusively assigned to the Brussels Court of First Instance, the Brussels Commercial Court, and the Brussels Court of Appeal for cases under the class action regime introduced in 2014.[1086]

Once the National Court declares a collective redress action admissible, this decision is published on the Ministry of Economic Affairs' website and in the Belgian official journal. This marks the start of the negotiation phase, which lasts for a period set by the Court. During this phase, the parties are encouraged to reach a settlement, and a mediator can be appointed. If no settlement is reached, or if the Court rejects the proposed agreement, the case moves to the merits phase.

At the conclusion of the proceedings, the National Court must appoint an administrator responsible for distributing individual compensation to confirmed class members, under the Court's supervision. This administrator is chosen from an official list of eligible professionals, such as lawyers, public officials, or Court agents. If someone who opted in (or did not opt out) is left off the list because the administrator believes they do not meet the criteria, they can file a short appeal. After the appeal period ends, the Court finalises the list of class members.

1081. *See* Hakim Boularbah, *Belgium, in Class Actions: A Global Guide from Practical Law*, Omar Shah (ed.), Thomson Reuters, 2015, p. 65.
1082. *Ibid.*, p. 68.
1083. *See* https://economie.fgov.be/fr/themes/protection-des-consommateurs/action-en-reparation.
1084. *See* s. 3.4.3.3 above.
1085. *See* Articles 30 and 701 of the Belgian Judicial Code of 10 October 1967, available on LOI - WET (fgov.be).
1086. *See* Article XVII.35 of Title 2 of Book XVII of the Code of Economic Law and Article 633ter of the Belgian Judicial Code.

3.4.5.4 *Costs*

Each party is responsible for covering its own legal costs. The only way to recover these expenses is through the 'loser pays' principle. However, even in that case, reimbursement is capped - currently at EUR 15,000. Given the high financial stakes often involved in collective actions, especially in competition law, this cap is widely seen as insufficient. If the case ends in a settlement, the parties can agree on how to divide the costs between them.[1087]

3.4.5.5 *Limitations*

One of the key strengths of the Belgian class action regime is that SMEs are represented - an important feature, as SMEs are often the most vulnerable to competition law violations and typically lack access to effective collective redress mechanisms. However, several limitations remain.

First, with the transposition of Directive 2020/1828, the Belgian legislator opted for the opt-in model, restricting opt-out actions to very exceptional cases. This is particularly problematic when combined with a second limitation - there is no specific rule allowing claimants to request access to documents held by the opposing party or third parties before the action begins.

In exceptional cases, if there is reason to believe that a party is withholding a key document, the Court may order its disclosure during the proceedings. If the party fails to comply without a valid reason (such as confidentiality), it may face a fine, and the Court may draw negative inferences from the refusal.

The aforementioned hypothesis was extended by the Law of 6 June 2017, which transposed the EU Damages Directive.[1088] Nevertheless, it should be remembered that, according to the Directive, National Courts should be able to order the defendant or a third party to disclose the relevant evidence under their control, in actions for damages for breaches of competition rules, if the plaintiff provides 'a reasoned justification containing reasonably available facts and evidence sufficient to support the plausibility of its claim for damages'.[1089] The Belgian legislator, when transposing this article, removed the reference to damages, ending with claim,[1090] which may be considered to refer to the request for access to documents, but no relevant practical consequences can be drawn from this difference,[1091] from the point of view of the moment of access to evidence. What is more, the rules on disclosure of evidence laid down in the EU Damages

1087. *See* Hakim Boularbah, *Belgium, in Class Actions: A Global Guide from Practical Law*, Omar Shah (ed.), Thomson Reuters, 2015, p. 72.
1088. *See* Caroline Cauffman, *Belgium*, in *The EU Antitrust Damages Directive: Transposition in the Member States*, Barry Rodger, Miguel Sousa Ferro and Francisco Marcos (eds), Oxford University Press, 2018, p. 66.
1089. *See* Article 5(1).
1090. *See* Article XVII.74 of Title 3 of Book XVII of the Code of Economic Law.
1091. *See* Caroline Cauffman, *Belgium*, in *The EU Antitrust Damages Directive: Transposition in the Member States*, Barry Rodger, Miguel Sousa Ferro and Francisco Marcos (eds), Oxford University Press, 2018, p. 67.

Directive were not designed for class actions, let alone opt-in ones, where the requirements of proof, starting with the identification of beneficiaries, are more demanding.

There are also three previously noted cost-related limitations. One key issue is the 'loser pays' rule, which in Belgium is further weakened by a cap on recoverable legal costs. This cap – especially in the context of large-scale collective actions – is clearly disproportionate and fails to reflect the true financial burden of such proceedings.

Another key limitation of the Belgian collective redress system is the lack of regulation and practical use of TPLF. Under current rules, each party must bear its own legal costs, and there is no established framework to support external financing of claims.

Associations seeking to bring collective actions must demonstrate, above all, that they have the financial capacity to represent multiple claimants and act in their best interests.[1092] While third-party funding is not explicitly prohibited, it is rarely used – mainly because existing rules make it impractical. For example, funders are not entitled to receive any portion of the compensation distributed by the Court-appointed administrator unless a prior agreement is in place before distribution.

Moreover, as in other jurisdictions, transparency is essential: any use of TPLF must be disclosed to the National Court, particularly to assess potential influence on the proceedings.

There is also no public funding available for these actions in Belgium, and group representatives are not allowed to profit from the outcome of the case.

Another significant limitation of the Belgian collective redress system is the prohibition of *quota litis* agreements (arrangements where lawyers are paid a percentage of the compensation awarded). This restriction adds to the financial burden of bringing such actions, making them less attractive and accessible, particularly in competition law cases.

That said, Belgian law does allow for success fees, meaning lawyers can agree to an increased fee in the event of a favourable outcome. However, these fees must comply with strict standards of reasonableness, transparency, and proportionality, taking into account the complexity of the case and the financial stakes involved.

Additionally, punitive damages are not permitted under Belgian law, further limiting the financial incentives for initiating collective actions.[1093]

3.4.5.6 *Class Actions*

As far as this book has known, since the legislative changes of 2014 and of 2024, around twelve actions have been brought (most by Test-Achats, the country's leading consumer protection organisation), but none in competition law.

In fact, as far as consumers and antitrust rules are concerned, this book only has knowledge of one individual follow-on action, filed by a consumer in the mid-2000s

1092. *See* Hakim Boularbah, *Belgium, in Class Actions: A Global Guide from Practical Law*, Omar Shah (ed.), Thomson Reuters, 2015, p. 71.
1093. *Ibid.*, pp. 70 and 74.

against an architects' association, for setting a fixed-fee scale.[1094] The consumer won the case and was awarded EUR 4,289 in compensation by the Belgium Court.[1095] However, this amount would barely cover the preliminary costs of a typical class action.

That example highlights the broader issue: Belgium has seen very few or no competition law class actions. And the fact that it practically abandoned the hybrid class action model does not help to change this landscape. As noted by Sofia Oliveira Pais, the lack of private funding remains one of the main barriers to the development of such actions.[1096]

3.4.6 France

3.4.6.1 Class Action Model

When France introduced class actions, it adopted a sector-specific approach, allowing different types of collective actions depending on the area of law involved. While this model aimed to tailor procedures to specific legal contexts, it has been criticised for three main reasons:[1097]

(1) Proliferation of legal norms, making the system overly complex.
(2) Difficulty in applying the rules consistently across sectors.
(3) Lack of coherence in how actions are coordinated and decided.

One of the forms of collective redress introduced in France in 2014 was the class action, established by the Law of 17 March 2014,[1098] which amended the French Consumer Code and came into effect in October of that year.[1099] Under this framework, authorised consumer associations could bring class actions on behalf of injured parties to seek compensation for harm caused by violations of various legal provisions, including competition law.

Indeed, in France, class actions on behalf of consumers for violations, particularly of competition law, could only be brought by nationally accredited and representative consumer associations.[1100] These actions target infringements committed by

1094. *See* Miguel Sousa Ferro, *Consumer Antitrust Private Enforcement in Europe: As Complete a Survey as Possible (Extended Version)*, 23 October 2022, available at https://ssrn.com/abstract=4223770, p. 32.
1095. *See Arrest de la Cour d'appel de Gand du 15 février 2008, Consumer/De Schepágs.er.*
1096. *See* Sofia Oliveira Pais, *Private Antitrust Enforcement: A New Era for Collective Redress?*, Yearbook of Antitrust and Regulatory Studies, vol. 8, No. 12, CARS, 2015 https://doi.org/10.7172/1689-9024.yars.2015.8.12.1, available at 3Private Antitrust Enforcement.pdf, p. 24.
1097. *See* Maria José Azar-Baud and Véronique Magnier, *Class Action à la Française, in The Cambridge Handbook of Class Actions: An International Survey*, Brian T. Fitzpatrick and Randall S. Thomas (eds), Cambridge University Press, 2021, p. 262.
1098. *See* French Consumer Code of 13 March 2014, available at LOI n° 2014-344 du 17 mars 2014 relative à la consommation (1) - Légifrance (legifrance.gouv.fr).
1099. *See* Articles L.623-1 et seq. of the French Consumer Code.
1100. Which have the monopoly of active legitimacy in this area, as stated by Maria José Azar-Baud and Alexandre Biard, *The Drawn of Collective Redress 3.0 in France?*, *Class Actions in Europe: Holy Grail or a Wrong Trail?*, Alan Uzelac and Stefaan Voet (eds), Springer, 2021, p. 78.

professional entities, meaning those acting within the scope of their economic activity. Notably, the consumer association does not require an express mandate from the consumers it represents, nor must it identify a specific number of consumers to the National Court. However, individual cases still needed to be submitted to substantiate the claim.[1101] Accreditation was granted at the government level, and the list of authorised associations – currently numbering fourteen[1102] – was published and regularly updated on the website of the French Ministry of the Economy.

Beyond that, France recognised two additional forms of collective action in the competition law domain:

(1) Action in the collective interest of consumers (*action exercée dans l'intérêt collectif des consommateurs*): this allowed authorised consumer associations to seek compensation for harm caused by criminal offences affecting the collective interest of consumers.[1103] Historically, French competition rules originated in the Penal Code of 1810.[1104] Although these provisions have since been largely decriminalised, the French Commercial Code still provides for criminal sanctions against natural persons who play a personal, decisive, and fraudulent role in organising or executing certain practices – such as cartels, abuse of dominance, or economic dependency.[1105]
(2) Collective actions by professional organisations: these allowed professional bodies to claim damages for harm, direct or indirect, caused to the collective interests of their profession or sector by price-fixing agreements or acts of unfair competition (though the latter fall outside the strict scope of competition law).[1106]

All of these collective actions followed an opt-in model (beneficiaries must explicitly declare their intention to be covered by the decision through a formal application).[1107]

Recently, France has restructured[1108] its class action framework as part of the implementation of Directive 2020/1828. This culminated in the adoption of a law on 30 April 2025,[1109] which not only transposes the Directive's requirements but also introduces broader reforms to the French collective redress system.[1110]

1101. *See* Article L.811-1 and R.811-1 of the French Consumer Code.
1102. *See* https://www.economie.gouv.fr/dgccrf/Liste-et-coordonnees-des-associations-nationales.
1103. *See* Article L.621-1 of the French Consumer Code.
1104. *See* Fabienne Siredey-Garnier, *Sanctions pénales*, Dictionnaire de droit de la concurrence, Concurrences, Article No. 88941.
1105. *See* Article L.420-1 and L.420-2 of the French Code of *Commerce*, available at *Code de commerce (Mise à jour du 2023-04-19) (droit.org)*.
1106. *See* Article L.490-10 of the French Commercial Code.
1107. *See* Maria José Azar-Baud and Véronique Magnier, *Class Action à la Française, in The Cambridge Handbook of Class Actions: An International Survey,* Brian T. Fitzpatrick and Randall S. Thomas (eds), Cambridge University Press, 2021, p. 260.
1108. *See* https://www.lw.com/en/insights/france-reforms-class-actions-regime.
1109. Law No. 2025-391, enacted on April 30, 2025, available at https://www.legifrance.gouv.fr/jorf/id/JORFTEXT000051538879.
1110. *See* https://www.gide.com/wp-content/uploads/2025/04/2025.05.02_New-French-Legal-Framework-for-Class-Actions-post-publication-ENG.pdf.

Indeed, the new legislation replaces the previous fragmented referred to above, but as it is very recent, it was important to keep the reference to the old model, in order to understand the scenario of a lack of active actions in this area until today. Also, from a procedural standpoint, the current framework largely builds on the foundation laid by Law No. 2014-344 of 17 March 2014 on consumer affairs.

The most notable developments of the 2025 reform of the French class action system include the following:

(1) A unified legal structure that has replaced the previous sector-specific approach.
(2) Certified associations – and in some cases, trade unions or qualifying non-profits – can continue to represent groups affected by similar breaches of legal or contractual obligations, including competition law.
(3) The Public Prosecutor's Office is now authorised to act as the main claimant in actions aimed at halting unlawful practices.
(4) The French legislator has maintained the opt-in model, which sets the system apart from the opt-out approach used in the US and aligns it closely with the Belgian model, already discussed.
(5) The introduction of special jurisdiction for certain Courts to hear class actions.
(6) The express indication that the plaintiffs receive third-party funding, provided it does not influence the initiation or conduct of the action in a way that harms the interests of the represented parties. Such funding must be publicly disclosed under conditions set by decree.[1111]

This applies to all class actions filed after 30 April 2025. Transitional provisions ensure continuity for actions already underway and allow eligible entities to initiate new actions under the previous rules for a limited period.

3.4.6.2 Control

First, all the class actions referred to above went through a first phase, in which the National Court decided on the admissibility of the action and, where appropriate, defined the group of people affected and how the decision will be publicised.

Specifically with regard to class actions, which are the most recent type and, theoretically, the most applicable, the Civil Court judge with territorial jurisdiction had to determine: (i) whether the association is representative at national level and has been accredited by the government for this purpose; and (ii) whether the class action is appropriate to the specific case, more specifically, whether it involves damage caused to consumers by the same infringement of competition rules.

When determining publicity, the judge was subject to strict rules, which only allowed it if the defendant's liability had already been established.[1112]

1111. *See* Article 16 I, D of Law No. 2025-391 of 30 April 2025.
1112. *See* Article L.623-7 of the French Consumer Code.

In practice, the judge ended up scrutinising both the admissibility and the merits of the case at the very first stage.[1113] This was likely the main reason why the legislator decided, following the 2025 reform, that plaintiffs are no longer required to issue prior notice for a class action to be admissible.

3.4.6.3 Proceeding

As previously mentioned, the proceedings framework of the French regime remains largely unchanged. Once the action is admitted, the National Court first determines the defendant's liability and only after this ruling does it define the group of individuals eligible for compensation. In other words, the beneficiaries have the opportunity to opt in to be covered by the class only at an advanced stage of the proceeding and only if the Court considers that compensation is indeed due.[1114]

The National Court then orders the decision to be publicised, inviting eligible individuals to join the group within a specified period, which can range from two months to five years (typically between two and six months).[1115] Following this, the Court will determine the amount of compensation due to each class member, effectively distributing the award. Depending on the conditions established by the Court, consumers may opt in by contacting the company responsible, the association, or another entity designated by the judge, such as the association's lawyer.

3.4.6.4 Costs

As a general rule, the losing party is ordered to bear the court fees and to contribute, albeit modestly, to the other expenses incurred by the prevailing party. More specifically, for chargeable costs related to the proceedings (such as expert fees and document production), the loser pays principle applies.[1116]

In contrast, non-taxable incidental costs, such as lawyers' fees, are subject to judicial discretion. The judge may decide whether the losing party should cover these costs, and to what extent, in favour of the winning party.[1117]

3.4.6.5 Limitations

When balancing access to justice against the risk of excessive litigation, France ultimately leaned towards the latter. It kept a rigid class action framework[1118] that prolongs the proceedings and only allows beneficiaries to opt in at a relatively late stage.

1113. *See* Maria José Azar-Baud and Véronique Magnier, *Class Action à la Française, in The Cambridge Handbook of Class Actions: An International Survey,* Brian T. Fitzpatrick and Randall S. Thomas (eds), Cambridge University Press, 2021, p. 264.
1114. *Ibid.*
1115. *Ibid.*, p. 261.
1116. *See* Articles 695 et seq. of the Code of Civil Procedure, available at Code de procédure civile (Mise à jour du 2023-02-19) (droit.org).
1117. *See* Article 700 of the French Code of Civil Procedure.
1118. *See* Maria José Azar-Baud and Véronique Magnier, *Class Action à la Française, in The Cambridge Handbook of Class Actions: An International Survey,* Brian T. Fitzpatrick and Randall S. Thomas (eds), Cambridge University Press, 2021, p. 264.

Beyond the evidentiary challenges inherent in the opt-in model, the French system also faces the typical cost-related constraints of this type of litigation. These actions are generally financed by the claimant associations themselves. While third-party funding is permitted, it remains unregulated and, in practice, virtually non-existent in France.[1119] Even with the 2025 reform, the legal framework still (at least for now, although it is planned)[1120] does not address key aspects of TPLF – such as how funders are to be compensated – leaving the practice in a legal grey area. Moreover, associations must comply with specific rules regarding their sources of funding.

Compounding these financial limitations, contingency fees are explicitly prohibited by French law. Even success fees must be strictly complementary, agreed upon in advance, and formalised in writing.

On the evidentiary front, French legislation does not provide for pre-trial access to documents held by the opposing party or third parties. However, during the proceedings, if a party suspects that relevant documents are being withheld, it may request the Court to order their production. The Court may also appoint an expert to provide technical clarification if such input is deemed to strengthen the requesting party's position.

3.4.6.6 Class Actions

Based on the information available, between 2014 and 2020, only fourteen class actions were filed under the 2014 French collective redress regime in consumer law matters. However, as in Belgium, none were based on competition law.[1121] It remains to be seen what the 2025 regime will bring.

Under the previous regimes, only one notable class action can be identified: a follow-on action brought in the early 2000s by the consumer association UFC Que Choisir, following a decision by the *Autorité de la concurrence* that confirmed the existence of a cartel in the telecommunications sector.[1122] Although approximately 20 million consumers were affected, only 12,521 opted into the action, each eligible for compensation of up to EUR 60. Despite this low participation rate – just 0.06 % – the association reportedly incurred substantial costs: around 2,000 hours of work, 550

1119. *See* David Bosco, *Le financement par les tiers de l'action collective: l'exemple* de *l'Union européenne,* Bulletin de Droit Économique, 2015, 1/2, available at http://www.droit-economique.org/wp-content/uploads/2015/11/DB-Le-financement-par-les-tiers-final-29-oct-15.pdf, p. 3.

1120. The French legislator provides that the funding conditions will be detailed in a forthcoming decree – *see* Article 16 I, D of Law No. 2025-391 of 30 April 2025.

1121. *See* Rapport No. 3085 de l'Assemblée nationale sur le bilan et les perspectives des actions de groupe, 11 June 2020, pt. I.C.1.a, available at *Rapport d'information déposé en application de l'article 145 du règlement, par la commission des lois constitutionnelles, de la législation et de l'administration générale de la République, en conclusion des travaux d'une mission d'information sur le bilan et les perspectives des actions de groupe (M. Philipdgs.e Gosselin et Mme Laurence Vichnievsky) (assemblee-nationale.fr).*

1122. *See* Miguel Sousa Ferro, *Consumer Antitrust Private Enforcement in Europe: As Complete a Survey as Possible (Extended Version),* 23 October 2022, available at https://ssrn.com/abstract=4223770, p. 31.

kilograms of paper, and EUR 500,000 in management costs.[1123] The case was ultimately dismissed, with the National Court ruling that the association lacked legal standing. To compound matters, the plaintiff was ordered to pay the defendants' legal costs, which included approximately EUR 6,000 in lawyers' fees.[1124]

As noted by Maciej Gac,[1125] France's struggle with collective redress spans at least three decades, marked by deep-rooted scepticism on legal, ethical, economic, and political grounds. Yet, this scepticism has analytical value: it forces a confrontation with the core questions that any effective collective redress system must address. In this sense, the French experience offers a valuable case study for shaping EU-level solutions.

This book shares the above perspective. This analysis of the French system aimed both to understand the causes of its shortcomings and to identify the legal traditions that might support a more effective model. This is particularly relevant given the European Commission's long-standing endorsement of the opt-in model – precisely the model that has still underperformed in France.

From this analysis, two structural issues emerge as key obstacles to the development of collective redress in France, particularly in the field of competition law:

(i) the opt-in model of collective action; and
(ii) the absence of a specific regulated framework for TPLF.

3.4.7 Comparative Analysis

This book will now undertake a macro-level comparison of legal systems through a structured comparative grid, focusing on key elements relevant to the effectiveness of collective redress mechanisms for breaches of competition law,[1126] based on the data presented in the preceding sections.[1127]

1123. *See* Action de groupe – 99.94% of the victims of the clash between mobile operators will not be compensated! – Action UFC-Que Choisir – UFC-Que Choisir.
1124. Arrêt de la Cour de Cassation du 26 mai 2011 (10-15.676), *UFC Que Choisir v. Bouygues Telecom*, available at Cour de cassation, civile, Chambre civile 1, 26 mai 2011, 10-15.676, Publié au bulletin – Légifrance (legifrance.gouv.fr).
1125. In *Group Litigation as an Instrument of Competition Law Enforcement: Analysis Based on European, French and Polish Experience*, Centre for Antitrust and Regulatory Studies, University of Warsaw, Faculty of Management, Eighty third Publication of the Publishing Programme, Series: Textbooks and Monographs (25), Prof. Dr. Tadeusz Skoczny (Series ed.), 2017, available at CARS 25 - Group litigation-Gac.indd (uw.edu.pl), pp. 335 and 336.
1126. *See* Carlos Ferreira de Almeida and Jorge Morais Carvalho, *Introduction to Comparative Law*, Almedina, 3rd ed., 2017, pp. 22 and 23.
1127. This table was compiled based on the subject matter and jurisdictions selected for comparison in this book, as well as the analytical factors outlined in s. 3.4.2 above. While similar tables exist that examine this type of information across various Member States, they differ from the present one in both the number of jurisdictions covered and the criteria analysed. For instance, the report *Collective Redress in Antitrust*, p. 10, available at https://ec.europa.eu/competition/antitrust/actionsdamages/study_legislative_action_collective_redress.pdf, includes twelve tables, each dedicated to a specific factor. Some of these overlap with this table, such as the model of collective action, while others, like judicial cooperation, do not. That report also includes all EU Member States, whereas this table focuses on paradigmatic cases.

Table 3.1 Comparison of Antitrust Class Actions in Selected European Countries

Country	*Class Action Model*	*Antitrust Specific*	*Standing*	*Class Certification/ Court Authorisation*	*Pre-Filing Evidence Disclosure*	*Costs*	*Funding*	*Fee Arrangements*	*Punitive Damages*	*Antitrust Class Actions Filed*
Portugal	Opt-out	Yes	Citizens; Consumer associations and foundations; Company associations (even if not competition-focused)	No formal certification, but manifestly unfounded claims can be dismissed and bad faith is penalised	Yes (recent cases)	Loser pays	Court fee exemption (public); TPLF (unregulated but applied in practice)	Only success fees arrangements are permitted	No	13
UK	Hybrid (opt-out by default)	Yes	Any person (member or not), subject to CAT approval	Yes	Yes	Court discretion, but loser pays is typically applied	No public funding; TPLF is widely used (self-regulated under Common Law); ATE insurance allowed	*Quota litis* arrangements are permitted in opt-in; conditional fees generally permitted	No	61

Belgium	Hybrid	No	Entities authorised by Minister of Economic Affairs; Interprofessional SME organisations	Yes	No	Loser pays (with cap)	No public funding; TPLF not regulated or used	Only success fees arrangements are permitted (must be reasonable/proportional)	No	0
France	Opt-in	No	Certified consumer associations; Trade unions or qualifying non-profits; Local authorities; Public Prosecutor; Consumer Ombudsman; Ad hoc representatives; Entities authorised in other Member States	No	No	Loser pays	No public funding; TPLF lightly regulated but unused	Success fees arrangements are permitted if complementary and pre-agreed in writing	No	1

To enhance visual clarity, Figure 3.2 presents the number of antitrust class actions across the selected European countries above.

Figure 3.2 Antitrust Class Actions Filed over Time

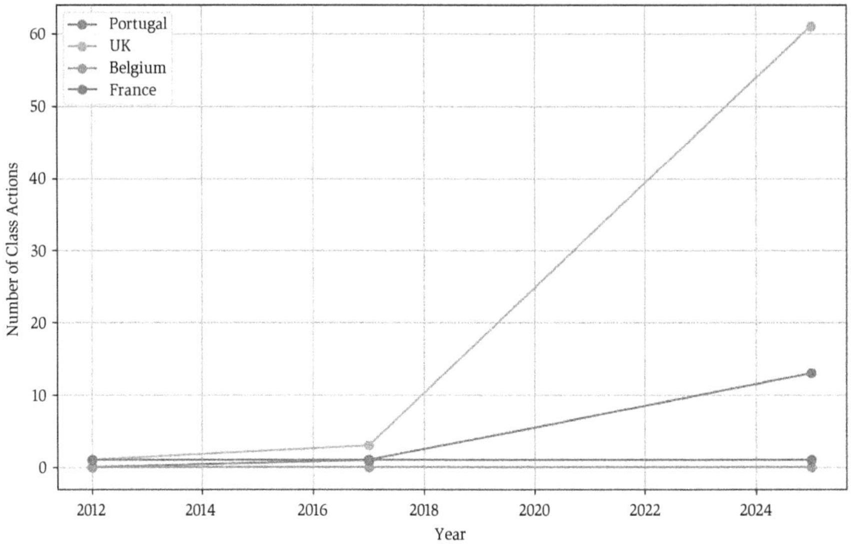

Over the past decade, the number of competition law class actions has surged in Portugal and the UK, while remaining almost absent in Belgium and France. What explains this divergence? Below is a comparative summary of the key similarities and differences between these two groups of European States.

I Common Features in Portugal and the UK

Portugal and the UK share several structural and procedural elements that likely contribute to the higher volume of competition law class actions:

- *Opt-out class action mechanisms* are in place.
- *Dedicated rules for competition law class actions* provide procedural clarity.
- *Legal standing for companies* to be represented in class actions.
- *Pre-action access to evidence*, facilitating case preparation.
- *Use of TPLF*, which lowers financial barriers to entry.

Despite these shared features, the UK has seen five times as many antitrust class actions as Portugal. This may be attributed to additional factors unique to the UK:

- *Broad standing rules*, allowing any person (not necessarily a class member) to bring an action, subject to Court authorisation.
- *Extensive evidence disclosure rules*, making access to it more practical.
- *Flexible cost allocation by the Court*, though the loser pays principle is typically applied.

- *Greater legal certainty in TPLF,* supported by Common Law principles and self-regulation (even with the *PACCAR* case and the bill yet to be adopted).
- *A more entrenched litigation culture,* including the use of ATEs.
- *Permissibility of quota litis agreements* in certain cases, along with conditional fee arrangements.

II Common Features in Belgium and France

In contrast, Belgium and France share characteristics that may help explain the scarcity of antitrust class actions in these countries:

- *No specific rules for competition law class actions,* leading to procedural uncertainty.
- *Lack of pre-action access to evidence,* which hinders case development.
- *Absence of public or private litigation funding,* increasing financial risk for claimants (although it is permitted).
- *Strict limitations on lawyers' fee arrangements,* including a prohibition on *quota litis* agreements.

III Key Levers for Effective Competition Law Class Actions

From the comparative data above, four key factors emerge as critical to enabling robust private enforcement of competition law through class actions:

(1) *Opt-out mechanisms,* which eliminate the need to individually identify and enrol class members.
(2) *Extended legal standing,* particularly to companies.
(3) *Financial risk mitigation,* especially through TPLF.
(4) *Early access to evidence,* which strengthens the foundation of claims.

These elements will be explored in greater detail in Chapter 5, where it will be designed this book's legislative proposal.

3.5 IS THE SOLUTION TO CREATE HORIZONTAL MECHANISMS FOR COLLECTIVE ACTION?

The creation of a collective redress mechanism common to all MS in the field of consumer rights was based mainly on the following facts: (i) 'the procedural means of collective action, both for injunctions and for redress measures, vary throughout the Union and provide a different level of protection for consumers; and (ii) there are also Member States that currently do not have procedural means for collective actions for redress measures'.[1128]

1128. Recital 6 of Directive 2020/1828.

Indeed, according to the Directive on representative actions for the protection of the collective interests of consumers, '[t]his situation diminishes the confidence of consumers and businesses in the internal market and their ability to operate in it. It distorts competition and hampers the effective enforcement of Union law (...) This Directive therefore aims to ensure that, at Union and national level, there is at least one effective and efficient class action procedure for injunctive and redress measures available to consumers in all Member States. Having at least one legal remedy available would increase consumer confidence, empower consumers to exercise their rights, contribute to fairer competition and create a level playing field for traders operating in the internal market'.[1129]

If this is true for consumer law, it is even more so for competition law. Infringements of competition rules have the capacity to affect a vast number of consumers and SMEs, even if the individual damage may be residual. However, they are complex offences and justify special rules, such as the leniency regime. Moreover, only the UK has a specific collective mechanism for *antitrust* rules.

Even if there is an increase in collective mechanisms beyond the scope of the 2020/1828 Directive, due to its transposition, and since it does not limit MS from going further and covering competition rules, this type of mechanism will remain, if it obeys the principles of that directive, unsuited both to the particularities of competition rules and to reality, which denounces the difficulty of having a sufficient number of individuals identified and *opting* in to a competition law collective action.

There is therefore an urgent need for a Community response to the lack of incentives to bring collective actions for infringements of competition rules in the EU. But what shape should this solution take?

3.6 OUTLINES OF THE PROPOSED SOLUTION

By way of introduction, as has been mentioned, any proposed solution must respect the common values and legal traditions[1130] of the Member States. These are very different from the US, which has more than a hundred years of litigation culture, in general, and competition culture, in particular, which translates into very particular figures such as the existence of punitive damages or *contingence fees.*[1131] And, of course, it must be framed in EU law and, in particular, in the principles contained in the *Private Enforcement* Directive. It is on this basis that we will address the issues *below.*

1129. Recitals 6 and 7.

1130. *See* Albert A. Foer, *The Ideal Model for Private Enforcement of Competition Law, in Private Enforcement of Competition Law,* Jürgen Basedow, Jörg Philipágs. Terhechte, Lubos Tichý (eds), Nomos, 2011, pp. 203 and 204.

1131. *See* s. 3.4.1 above. *See also Albert* A. Foer, *The Ideal Model for Private Enforcement of Competition Law, in Private Enforcement of Competition Law,* Jürgen Basedow, Jörg Philipágs Terhechte, Lubos Tichý (eds), Nomos, 2011, p. 206.

3.6.1 Type and Model

While there is no doubt that the existence of a mechanism allowing companies and consumers to collectively exercise their right to compensation for damage caused by violations of competition rules is necessary to fulfil the principle of effectiveness of Articles 101 and 102 of the TFEU, it is first important to determine the ideal type and models.

As Christopher Hodges points out,[1132] 'if there is more than one mechanism available, all options should be compared and evaluated'. Arianna Andreangeli[1133] also pointed out, with regard to the discussion on the appropriate *blueprint* for collective litigation in the EU, that 'as the Commission and a number of national authorities have recognised, *keeping an open mind* with regard to the different options to be considered is vital if the goal of effective EU competition law is to be achieved'.

Below, we will identify the different types of collective action according to the criterion of who brings the action. We are referring to this concept broadly, bearing in mind that, as we have seen, there are national regimes with characteristics of more than one type.[1134]

3.6.1.1 Collective Action in the Strict Sense

In the strict sense, collective action consists of bringing a single action on behalf of everyone. Depending on the specific regime of the State in question, the individuals covered by the action may be identified or identifiable (opt-in or opt-out), but the compensation will be awarded globally and then distributed.[1135]

3.6.1.2 Class Action

Similar to the above, this is an action that can follow the opt-in or opt-out model (which this study will revisit later). It is brought by one or more members on behalf of the entire previously identified class to which they belong. Compensation is allocated to the class as a whole, with each member entitled to a percentage of it.[1136] Thus, this type of action is characterised by two stages: the first stage defines the class, and the second

1132. In *Redress: Models, Evidence, Outcomes and Policy in Class Actions in Europe – Holy Grail or a Wrong Trail?*, Alan Uzelac and Stefaan Voet (eds), Springer, 2021, p. 27.
1133. In *Private Enforcement of Antitrust: Regulating Corporative Behaviour Through Collective Claims in the EU and US*, Edward Elgar, 2014, p. 191.
1134. *See* David Ashon and David Henry, *Competition Damages Action in the EU: Law and Practice*, economics contribution from Frank Maier-Rigaud and Ulrich Schawalbe, Elgar, Competition *Law* and Practice, 2013, p. 128 and Horacio Vedia Jerez, *Competition Law Enforcement and Compliance Across the World: A Comparative Review*, Wolters Kluwer, 2015, pp. 258 et seq.
1135. *See*, for example, Article 2 of Law 83/95.
1136. *See*, for example, Rule 23 of the US Federal Rules of Civil Procedure, available at federal_rules_of_civil_procedure_-_december_2020_0.pdf (uscourts.gov).

stage gives the injured parties the opportunity to choose whether to be covered or excluded from the action according to the chosen model.[1137]

3.6.1.3 *Representative Action*

The action is not brought by the rightsholders themselves, but by an organisation representing them, such as an association or foundation. The representative may also be a public body. Only the latter will benefit if they are ordered to pay compensation for damage suffered.

The action is not brought by the holders of the right to compensation, but by an organisation representing those holders,[1138] such as an association or foundation. The representative can also be a public body. Only the rightsholders will benefit in the event of a compensation order.[1139]

3.6.1.4 *Group Action*

This is an action that brings together a considerable number of individuals, or several actions that are managed as a group. It should not be confused with the grouping together of related individual actions, such as those based on the same offence or brought against the same company by the Court in a single case for purely economic procedural reasons. Some argue that joining actions together is also a form of collective action.[1140]

3.6.1.5 *Public Interest Action*

The action is brought by a representative body for the benefit of the general public. Thus, any damages awarded will also revert to the public. For example, if a consumer association wins the case, it will receive the damages and should use them to promote consumer protection.[1141] As Steven Van Uytveldt noted,[1142] the interests in this context are difficult to establish, and alongside the individual, collective and common interests,

1137. *See* Steven Van Uytsel, *Collective Actions in a Competition Law Context: Reconciling Multi-player Interests to Enhance Access to Justice, Collective Actions – Enhancing Access to Justice and Reconciling Multilayer Interests?*, Stefan Wrbka, Steven Van Uytsel and Mathias Siems (eds), Cambridge University Press, 2012, p. 78.

1138. *Ibid.*, p. 76.

1139. *See*, for example, s. 47B of the Competition Act 1998.

1140. *See* Steven Van Uytsel, *Collective Actions in a Competition Law Context: Reconciling Multi-player Interests to Enhance Access to Justice, Collective Actions – Enhancing Access to Justice and Reconciling Multilayer Interests?*, Stefan Wrbka, Steven Van Uytsel and Mathias Siems (eds), Cambridge University Press, 2012, p. 75.

1141. *See*, for example, Article 82 of the Brazilian Consumer Defence Law, available at L8078compiled (planalto.gov.br).

1142. In *Collective Actions in a Competition Law Context: Reconciling Multiplayer Interests to Enhance Access to Justice, Collective Actions – Enhancing Access to Justice and Reconciling Multilayer Interests?*, Stefan Wrbka, Steven Van Uytsel and Mathias Siems (eds), Cambridge University Press, 2012, pp. 57-91, p. 71.

there is the public interest, which benefits all stakeholders and society in general, in the non-occurrence, cessation or non-repetition of infringements of competition rules, so that the market functions correctly.

3.6.1.6 Assigned Action

This action is brought by a third party who is commissioned by those entitled to compensation. The third party litigates on its behalf using its own resources, in order to receive a predetermined percentage of the compensation.

This has been the case in Germany, where it was widely accepted for several years that this type of action was permitted as long as the incumbent held a state permit for extrajudicial debt collection under the *Rechtsdienstleistungsgesetz* (RDG, German Legal Services Act).[1143] However, in 2020, this understanding was contradicted by a Munich Regional Court, which rejected the action on the grounds that the plaintiff had no jurisdiction.[1144] The following year, in the *AirDeal* case,[1145] the German Supreme Court clarified that the assigned action is permitted under German law,[1146] thereby legitimising the contractual transfer of compensation claims from several victims of the same infringement to a specialised third party for the purposes of grouping, analysing and jointly executing these claims. This prompted the 2021 reform of the RDG.[1147]

Since then, German courts have permitted entities such as the CDC (Cartel Damages Claims),[1148] which was created for the sole purpose of bringing damages actions, to do so within an outsourced litigation regime. For the Advocate General Niilo Jääskinen, '[t]he emergence of layers on the judicial scene (...) [such as CDC] whose aim it is to combine assets based on claims for damages resulting from infringements of EU competition law, seems to me to show that, in the case of the more complex barriers to competition, it is not reasonable for the persons adversely affected themselves individually to sue those responsible for a barrier of that type'.[1149]

1143. *See* Carsten Krüger, *Revival of the 'Claims Assignment Class Action' in German Private Antitrust Enforcement (and Beyond)*, 8 May 2021, available at Revival of the 'claims assignment class action' in German private antitrust enforcement (and beyond) - CDC (carteldamageclaims.com).
1144. *See* Till Shreiber and Martin Seegers, *Collective or Class Actions and Claims Aggregation in the EU: the Claimant's Perspective, in GCR's Private Litigation Guide*, Nicholas and Heaton and Benhamin Holt (eds), 3rd ed., 2021, *asset download – Global Competition Review*, p. 50.
1145. *See the AirDeal* judgment of the German Supreme Court, available at http://juris.bundesgerichtshof.de/cgi-bin/rechtsprechung/document.py?Gericht=bgh&Art=en&sid=988087d1ccd21eb83d0d35e876892356&nr=120886&pos=0&anz=1.
1146. *See* Alex Petrasincu and Christopher Unseld, *Collective Redress in Germany for Cartel Damages Claims*, Lexology, 24 August 2022, available at Collective redress in Germany for cartel damages claims - Lexology.
1147. *See* Act on Out-of-Court Legal Services (Rechtsdienstleistungsgesetz – RDG) (gesetze-im-internet.de).
1148. *See* CDC – pioneer and leader in antitrust damage recovery in Europe (carteldamageclaims.com).
1149. Conclusions presented on 11 December 2014, in the case of *CDC Hydrogen Peroxide*, Case C-352/13, pt. 29.

In addition to the typical benefits of class actions already mentioned,[1150] this type of action saves the injured parties from having to deal directly with the offender, which can be particularly important if they are business partners.[1151] Moreover, these actions allow for even greater economies of scale in terms of resources and costs, generating significant synergies.

3.6.1.7 Parens Patriae *Action*

This is a collective action brought on behalf of specific individuals by a public authority, such as a Public Prosecutor or an NCA, reducing the costs of bringing this type of action. For example, there are no court fees. Furthermore, in the case of an NCA, it has investigative powers and economic experts on its staff.

Generally speaking, Christopher Hodges[1152] refers broadly to regulatory redress, including in this concept both actions where the public authority has the power to bring a collective action[1153] on behalf of the injured parties, and cases where these authorities themselves have the power to sentence the infringer under a collective redress mechanism or can influence him to join a voluntary mechanism of this type.[1154]

The EU Damages Directive does not define collective action, but it does define an action for damages: 'an action under national law by which a claim for damages is brought before a national court by an alleged injured party, or by someone acting on behalf of one or more alleged injured parties where Union or national law provides for that possibility, or by a natural or legal person that succeeded in the right of the alleged injured party, including the person that acquired the claim'.[1155] This definition seems to cover all of the above types of action, up to and including the action awarded through this final part. In addition, Article 7(3) *in fine* of the EU Damages Directive states that the use in damages actions of evidence obtained exclusively through access to the file of a competition authority is permitted to those who have acquired the claim.

Directive 2020/1828 defines collective action in a more restrictive way: 'an action for the protection of the collective interests of consumers that is brought by a qualified entity as a claimant party on behalf of consumers to seek an injunctive measure, a redress measure, or both'.[1156] In other words, if on the one hand it limits the concept

1150. *See* s. 3.2 above.
1151. *See* Carsten Krüger, *Revival of the 'Claims Assignment Class Action' in German Private Antitrust Enforcement (and Beyond)*, 8 May 2021, available at Revival of the 'claims assignment class action' in German private antitrust enforcement (and beyond) - CDC (carteldamageclaims.com).
1152. In *Collective Redress: The Need for New Technologies*, Journal of Consumer Policy, vol. 42, Nos 59-90, 2019, pp. 59-90, p. 63 https://doi.org/10.1007/s10603-018-9388-x.
1153. In support of this approach in Portugal – particularly given the legislative precedent in consumer law – Miguel Sousa Ferro and Nuno Salpico argue that granting regulators standing to bring popular actions could influence corporate behaviour and promote settlements. In *Consumer Compensation as a Priority for Regulators*, Revista da Faculdade de Direito da Universidade de Lisboa, vol. LXII, No. 2, 2021, pp. 407-445, available at Miguel-Sousa-Ferro-Nuno-Salpico.pdf (ulisboa.pt), p. 444.
1154. As in the case with the CMA, *see* s. 3.4.4.2 above.
1155. *See* Article 2(4), emphasis added.
1156. *See* Article 3(5), emphasis added.

to representative actions, on the other it only protects consumers. However, as mentioned above,[1157] this directive does not apply to the enforcement of competition rules and, in any case, it states that '[t]his Directive should not replace existing national procedural mechanisms'.[1158]

As mentioned above, existing collective action mechanisms, particularly in Europe, vary and combine references in an attempt to find an efficient mechanism. The disparity of solutions in States where such mechanisms exist makes it difficult for consumers and SMEs to obtain compensation for damage caused by infringements of competition rules, creating legal uncertainty. Nevertheless, a frequent feature is that the collective action can be brought by a representative organisation, usually a consumer association.

Traditionally, representative actions are designed for injunctive relief.[1159] In fact, the private application of competition law, as well as being individual[1160] or collective, can be used either to claim compensation for the damage caused (the objective this study has been focusing on) or to obtain a declaration of nullity of an anticompetitive agreement, or a revindication of an injunction, abstention or adoption of certain behaviour,[1161] as mentioned above.

As developed below,[1162] this book argues that legal standing (the criterion used above to distinguish between the various types of collective action) should be interpreted broadly in the context of competition law. This broader approach is essential to address the persistent lack of access to redress for both SMEs and consumers.

However, this book is caution against assigning powers of representation or the design of compensation mechanisms to the same entities responsible for public enforcement, particularly in competition law. Concentrating both punitive and compensatory functions within a single authority risks creating conflicting mandates – balancing collective public interests with individual redress – which could lead to what might be described as a 'schizophrenic' institutional mission.

Consider the challenge National Courts face when deciding whether to grant access to documents held in the files of NCA, particularly leniency statements, which are typically shielded from disclosure. How could an NCA, acting simultaneously as both a public and private enforcer of competition law, reconcile the competing interests of

1157. *See* s. 3.3.6 above.
1158. *See* Recital 11.
1159. *See* Simon Vande Walle, *Private Antitrust Litigation in the European Union and Japan*, Maklu, 2013, p. 177.
1160. The most paradigmatic example at the moment is Spain, where multiple individual private enforcement actions have been brought, in particular to claim damages caused by the so-called trucks cartel. For further information, *see* Miguel Sousa Ferro and Francisco Marcos, *Chapter 16: Portugal and Spain, in Research Handbook on Competition Law Private Enforcement in the EU*, Barry Rodger, Miguel Sousa Ferro and Francisco Marcos (eds), Edward Elgar, 2023.
1161. *See* Horacio Vedia Jerez, *Competition Law Enforcement and Compliance Across the World: A Comparative Review*, Wolters Kluwer, 2015, pp. 289 et seq.
1162. *See* ss 3.6.2 and 5.5. below.

injured parties seeking redress and the need to preserve the effectiveness of public enforcement and the integrity of the leniency regime?

The answer is: it could not - at least not without undermining one of these objectives. Such a dual role would be institutionally unworkable. Therefore, this book argues that the contribution of NCAs in private enforcement should be limited to *non-stricto sensu* private enforcement,[1163] namely in follow-on actions. Even in such cases, it would be highly unusual, and arguably inappropriate, for an NCA to enforce its own decision within the realm of private law.

3.6.1.8 Opt-Out Versus Opt-In

As previously discussed, class actions can follow either an opt-out or opt-in model. In opt-out systems, companies, consumers, or other class members are automatically included in the proceedings and bound by the outcome unless they explicitly choose to withdraw. In contrast, opt-in models require individuals to actively join the proceedings in order to benefit from any resulting decision.

The choice between these models remains a contentious issue and is central to defining common principles for collective redress within the EU. It also has a significant impact on the practical effectiveness of collective actions.

In this regard, variation across Member States is relatively limited, with opt-in models prevailing across much of Europe - including in Spain, Belgium, France, Italy, Greece, Austria, Poland, Croatia, Hungary, Lithuania, Romania, Malta, Ireland, Sweden and Finland. This trend reflects a deliberate effort to distance European systems from the more expansive US opt-out regime. Consequently, EU policy has also leaned towards endorsing the opt-in approach.

The opt-in model offers several important advantages. First, it *preserves the decision-making power of the beneficiaries,*[1164] allowing them to actively choose whether to participate in the action. This voluntary engagement increases the likelihood that they will ultimately pursue individual compensation.

Second, because class members are identified from the outset, the action can be conducted in a *more realistic and practical* manner. Knowing the size of the class in advance provides clarity on the potential scope of compensation, which is particularly useful when assessing the viability of settlement negotiations.

Third, the opt-in model helps *prevent excessive or vexatious litigation*, as only those with a genuine interest are likely to join the proceedings.

Finally, as noted by the EPRS,[1165] opt-in mechanisms *facilitate private funding arrangements*. Identified class members can commit in advance to sharing a portion of

1163. *See* Luís Silva Morais, *Integrating Public and Private Enforcement of Competition Law in Europe: Legal and Jurisdictional Issues,* available at https://papers.ssrn.com/sol3/papers.cfm?abstract_id=2657570, pp. 17 et seq.

1164. *See* David Ashton, *Competition Damages Action in the EU: Law and Practice,* economics contribution from Frank Maier-Rigaud and Ulrich Schawalbe, Elgar, *Competition Law and Practice,* 2nd ed., 2018, p. 287.

1165. *See* s. 3.3.7 above.

their compensation with funders, thereby enhancing the predictability and attractiveness of funding such actions.

Despite its advantages, the opt-in model presents several significant drawbacks:

(i) *Low participation rates*: one of the most critical limitations - particularly relevant to the scarcity of collective actions in Europe, and in competition law specifically - is the low rate of adherence by potential beneficiaries. According to the European Consumer Organisation BEUC,[1166] experience in Europe with the opt-in procedure in consumer complaints has shown that the participation rate is very low (less than 1%). In contrast, in opt-out schemes, the rates are typically very high (97% in the Netherlands and almost 100% in Portugal). This discrepancy is largely due to the fact that most consumers are unaware of their rights, and the cost of participating often exceeds the compensation they might receive. A striking example is the French case brought by the consumer association UFC-Que Choisir in the telecommunications sector: although 20 million consumers were affected, only 0.06% opted in. The case cost the association approximately EUR 500,000, required 2,000 hours of work, and generated 550 kg of paperwork[1167] - all for a potential individual compensation of EUR 40, which may not even cover the opt-in costs. In such cases, the opt-in model effectively undermines the viability of class actions, even when the total harm amounts to millions or billions of euros.

(ii) *Procedural and evidentiary hurdles*: the opt-in model also creates significant challenges at the early stages of litigation. Identifying and recruiting claimants and securing funding are both more difficult when participation is voluntary. These obstacles were among the reasons why, in 2015, the UK reformed its system to allow the CAT to certify opt-out collective actions.[1168]

(iii) *Insufficient finality*: As noted by Samuel Issacharoff and Geoffrey P. Miller,[1169] the opt-in model offers less legal certainty regarding the resolution of disputes. Class members who do not opt in retain the right to initiate separate proceedings, which prolongs litigation and undermines the goal of comprehensive settlement. While opt-out models also allow members to exclude themselves, the number who do so is typically negligible. In the US, for example, defendants often insist that settlements extinguish all liability, with agreements becoming void if too many members opt out. This uncertainty affects not only defendants but also plaintiffs, who may be forced to accept lower settlements - or none at all - due to the risk of ongoing litigation.

1166. *See* https://www.beuc.eu/sites/default/files/publications/2008-00394-01-e.pdf, p. 6.
1167. *See* s. 3.4.5.6 above.
1168. *See* s. 3.4.3.1 above.
1169. *In Will Aggregate Litigation Come to Europe?*, Vanderbilt Law Review, vol. 62, 2019, p. 177, available at https://scholarshipág.law.vanderbilt.edu/cgi/viewcontent.cgi?article=1448&context=vlr, p. 206.

Until relatively recently, only Portugal, the Netherlands, and Denmark had collective opt-out mechanisms in place in the EU (although quite limited).[1170] In fact, Portugal can be considered one of the first European countries to adopt a collective redress mechanism that closely resembles the US model – even though it does not permit the use of *quota litis* agreements, which are widely accepted in the US

In addition to these three countries, several others have since introduced opt-out or hybrid collective action regimes, including the UK, Belgium, Slovenia, Bulgaria, Norway, and Hungary (though in Hungary, opt-out actions are available only to the national competition authority).[1171] These systems vary in design and scope, often combining opt-in and opt-out features depending on the nature of the case or the parties involved.

In opt-out actions, the claim is typically initiated based on a broad estimate of the class size. Class members are not required to take any action to be included in the proceedings. They only become actively involved at the stage of damage quantification and compensation distribution (if they wish to receive their share).[1172]

In contrast to the limitations of the opt-in model, the opt-out model offers several compelling advantages:

(i) *Scale and inclusiveness*: opt-out mechanisms ensure broad class representation, as individuals are automatically included unless they explicitly choose to withdraw. This is particularly relevant in competition law cases, where the affected population is typically large. The scale achieved through opt-out actions is essential to attract interest from legal representatives and funders, given the potential for a meaningful return on investment.

(ii) *Enhanced negotiating power*: a larger, unified class strengthens the claimants' bargaining position in settlement discussions. The certainty of a substantial claimant base increases pressure on defendants and encourages more favourable outcomes.

(iii) *Greater likelihood of compensation*: since class members are included by default, the probability of actual compensation being distributed is significantly higher. Individuals only need to come forward after the judgment, once the total damages have been quantified and publicised. In competition law cases, such publicity is often amplified by media coverage, unlike the more discreet notifications required in opt-in systems.

Importantly, opt-out models still preserve individual autonomy, as class members retain the right to opt out if they so choose.

1170. *See* Simon Vande Walle, *Private Antitrust Litigation in the European Union and Japan*, Maklu, 2013, p. 178.

1171. *See* Part 5 Act LVII of 1996 on the Prohibition of Unfair and Restrictive Market Practices, available at file (gvh.hu).

1172. David Ashton, *Competition Damages Action in the EU: Law and Practice*, economics contribution from Frank Maier-Rigaud and Ulrich Schawalbe, Elgar, *Competition Law and Practice*, 2nd ed., 2018, p. 288.

Empirical data supports the effectiveness of opt-out systems. In a 2008 study submitted to the Civil Justice Council of England and Wales, Rachael Mulheron reported opt-out participation rates of approximately:

- USA: 99.8%
- Canada: 60%-100%
- Australia: 59%-98%
- Portugal: nearly 100%
- Netherlands: 97%.

In contrast, opt-in participation rates were significantly lower:

- UK: 0.8%-100%
- USA: 27%-61%
- Europe: less than 0.03%.

As Miguel Sousa Ferro has noted,[1173] the 'opt-in is rarely used, is resource intensive (for parties and courts), and never leads to compensation of more than 2,5% of consumers harmed by a mass infringement (even in cases with relatively high damages)'. He further observes that the only notable examples of competition law private enforcement under opt-in regimes in France and Italy failed to reach a decision on the merits.[1174]

However, the opt-out model has been criticised, mainly by the European Commission, which since the White Paper[1175] has showed a clear preference for 'a combination of two complementary mechanisms of collective redress to address effectively those issues in the field of antitrust:

- representative actions, which are brought by qualified entities, such as consumer associations, state bodies or trade associations, on behalf of identified or, in rather restricted cases, identifiable victims. These entities are either (i) officially designated in advance or (ii) certified on an ad hoc basis by a Member State for a particular antitrust infringement to bring an action on behalf of some or all of their members; and
- opt-in collective actions, in which victims expressly decide to combine their individual claims for harm they suffered into one single action'.[1176]

The adoption of the representative action model aligns with the approach taken in Directive 2020/1828 on collective redress in other areas of EU law. This model offers two key advantages: (i) it simplifies the procedural mandate by authorising designated

1173. In *Consumer Antitrust Private Enforcement in Europe: As Complete a Survey as Possible (Extended Version)*, 23 October 2022, available at https://ssrn.com/abstract=4223770, p. 3.
1174. *Ibid.*, p. 9 (our translation).
1175. *See* s. 3.3.2 above.
1176. White Paper, p. 4.

entities to act on behalf of claimants and (ii) it helps mitigate concerns about frivolous or abusive litigation by limiting standing to vetted organisations.[1177]

However, this expresses reservations regarding the representative action model as defined in Directive 2020/1828. Under this directive, the entities eligible to bring representative actions are typically non-profit organisations,[1178] and their scope of representation excludes SMEs. This exclusion raises concerns about equitable access to justice, particularly in competition law, where SMEs are often among the most affected. Moreover, the non-profit nature of these entities introduces a significant challenge in securing adequate funding – these topics are addressed in more detail below.[1179]

Criticism of the opt-out model generally centres on five key concerns:

(i) *Higher costs*: opt-out procedures tend to be more expensive due to the broader scope of notification, administration, and potential compensation.
(ii) *Lack of individual participation*: critics argue that it deprives beneficiaries of their day in court, as individuals are included in the proceedings without actively choosing to participate.
(iii) *Risk of overcompensation*: if a portion of the class does not come forward to claim their share of the compensation, the representative entity may retain a disproportionate amount, raising concerns about fairness and accountability.
(iv) *Agent–principal conflict*: the model can create conflicts between the interests of the representative (agent) and those of the class members (principals), particularly when it comes to settlement decisions or the distribution of funds.[1180]
(v) *Incentive for unmeritorious claims*: there is a risk that opt-out actions may be used strategically to pressure defendants into settlements, even in weak or speculative cases.

A particularly important concern relates to due process and legal certainty. As highlighted in the 2012 Independent Study commissioned by the European Commission on legislative action in the field of antitrust collective redress,[1181] '[t]he opt-out system requires that a deliberate action is taken to withdraw from a judicial action. Therefore uninformed people may find themselves bound by a judgment they did not even know was about to be issued. This element is rather important in the light of the right of access to the courts under Article 6 of the European Convention for Human

1177. *See* Charlotte Leskinen, *Collective Antitrust Damages Actions in the EU: The Opt-in v. Opt-out Model*, Working Paper IE Law School, 2010, available at http://ssrn.com/abstract=1612731, p. 25.
1178. *See* s. 3.3.6 above.
1179. *See* s. 3.6.5 above.
1180. David Ashton, *Competition Damages Action in the EU: Law and Practice*, economics contribution from Frank Maier-Rigaud and Ulrich Schawalbe, Elgar, *Competition Law and Practice*, 2nd ed., 2018, p. 289.
1181. *See* s. 3.3.4 above.

Rights (ECHR), which would probably prevent the introduction of a pure opt-out system in the EU (see Hodges 2012)'.[1182]

Criticism (iii) (risk of overcompensation) can be addressed through control mechanisms within the opt-out system, such as regulations governing the destination of unclaimed compensation. These safeguards can ensure that any surplus is redirected appropriately, for example, to public interest funds or consumer protection initiatives.

Criticism (iv) (agent–principal conflict) has already been addressed in the context of the Green Paper.[1183] In Europe, such concerns are mitigated by ethical obligations imposed on legal professionals, which require them to act in the best interests of their clients. Moreover, contingency fees are rare, and the broader the class action, the greater the investment required from legal representatives – aligning their incentives with the effective enforcement of victims' rights. As David Ashton has noted,[1184] there is no evidence of agent–principal problems in European jurisdictions where opt-out models are used.

Criticisms (i) and (v) (higher costs and unmeritorious claims) lose much of their relevance, in this book's view, when weighed against the alternative: *leaving up to 99% of injured parties without compensation.*

Finally, criticism (ii) (lack of individual participation) raises a fundamental concern that, in this book's view, deserves closer attention. In opt-out systems, class members do not actively participate in the trial unless they choose to opt out or later claim compensation. This raises the question: does such passive inclusion violate the right to a fair trial under Article 6 of the ECHR?

As previously noted and highlighted by Charlotte Leskinen,[1185] most opt-out systems include procedural safeguards to address this concern. Class members are typically duly informed of the action, either at its initiation or when a settlement is proposed, giving them the opportunity to opt out. Moreover, representative organisations and lawyers are bound by duties to act in the best interests of the class, ensuring that the rights of absent members are protected throughout the proceedings.

In addition, modern communication technologies, such as digital notifications, public registries, and targeted outreach, can significantly enhance the visibility of class actions, increasing the likelihood that affected individuals are aware of their rights and options.

Even in the worst-case scenario, where a beneficiary remains unaware of the action, they are not placed in a worse position than if the class action had never been brought. They neither opt out nor claim compensation, but their legal status remains unchanged. Meanwhile, others in the class may still benefit from the collective redress, advancing the broader goal of access to justice.

1182. *See* p. 65 of the Independent Study.
1183. *See* s. 3.3.1 above.
1184. *In Competition Damages Action in the EU: Law and Practice*, economics contribution from Frank Maier-Rigaud and Ulrich Schawalbe, Elgar, *Competition Law and Practice*, 2nd ed., 2018, p. 290.
1185. *In Collective Antitrust Damages Actions in the EU: The Opt-in v. Opt-out Model*, Working Paper IE Law School, 2010, available at http://ssrn.com/abstract=1612731, p. 44.

In addition, the ECtHR addressed the issue of unauthorised representation as early as 1986 in the landmark case of *Lithgow v. United Kingdom*.[1186] The case concerned the expropriation of a company under the UK's Expropriation Act of 1977, which provided for the appointment of a representative to claim compensation on behalf of shareholders before an arbitral tribunal. Notably, this mechanism was mandatory – shareholders could not opt out.

Among other claims, the applicants argued that this arrangement violated their right to a fair trial under Article 6 of the ECHR. In its judgment, the ECtHR acknowledged that the right to a fair trial is not absolute and may be subject to implied limitations, provided they pursue a legitimate aim and maintain a reasonable relationship of proportionality between the means employed and the objective pursued.

The Court found that the limitation on individual shareholders' direct access to the tribunal served a legitimate purpose: namely, to avoid a proliferation of individual claims in the context of a large-scale expropriation. Furthermore, although shareholders could not opt out, they had appointed the representative themselves, and the law included mechanisms to oversee and control the representative's conduct, thereby safeguarding their interests.[1187]

The above understanding was confirmed in the case of *Wendenburg and Others v. Germany*,[1188] where the ECtHR stated that it is not always required or even possible for every individual concerned to be heard before the Court.

However, in the opt-out model, the action is subject to public notice, as previously discussed, and potential beneficiaries are given the opportunity to opt out and pursue individual claims if they so choose. Therefore, in most cases, this system does not violate Article 6 of the ECHR, as it preserves the essential elements of procedural fairness – namely, the right to be informed and the freedom to decide whether or not to participate.

As Csongor István Nagy rightly observes,[1189] 'while the right of disposition is constitutionally protected, access to justice is equally a constitutional fundamental right. The purpose of collective litigation is to make practically unenforceable rights a reality'. The keyword here is indeed 'feasible'. And this is where the opt-in model has consistently failed.

Why has it failed? Because, *when weighing the pros and cons, the opt-out class action model emerges as the most efficient* – not only in terms of outcomes but also in terms of resource allocation. It requires fewer resources from both the claimant and the Court, while offering a realistic path to redress for a large number of injured parties.

In practice, the evidentiary burden in collective actions is already high. Under opt-in regimes, it becomes even more onerous, as claimants must first identify and reach out

1186. Case Nos 9006/80; 9262/81; 9263/81; 9265/81; 9266/81; 9313/81; 9405/81 *Lithgow v. United Kingdom*, 8 July 1986, available at https://hudoc.echr.coe.int/.
1187. *See* pts 194 to 197 of the judgment.
1188. Case 71630/01, *Wendenburg and Others v. Germany*, 6 February 2003, available at https://hudoc.echr.coe.int/.
1189. *In Collective Actions in Europe: A Comparative, Economic and Transsystemic Analysis*, Springer Open, 2019, available at https://link.springer.com/content/pdf/10.1007/978-3-030-24222-0.pdf, p. 26.

to potential victims. Even in jurisdictions with pre-filing discovery, typically available in Common Law systems,[1190] accessing the personal data of injured parties is complex and often impractical.[1191] And realistically, how many consumers retain proof of purchase for something as trivial as a shirt bought years ago? Most people only keep receipts for high-value items like electronics.

So why does the European Commission favour the opt-in model? The oft-cited concern about abusive litigation, drawn from the US experience, simply does not apply in the EU context. On the contrary, collective actions in Europe remain rare, concentrated in a few Member States, and have yet to yield significant compensation outcomes. To speak of abuse in a landscape marked by scarcity is, frankly, incomprehensible. In the absence of compelling justification, there is no reason not to embrace opt-out class actions as the more effective and equitable model for class actions.

Not least because, as previously discussed, national control mechanisms already exist – such as the English class certification process and the Portuguese prohibition of bad faith litigation[1192] – which could be incorporated into any future EU legislation on collective redress to safeguard against abuse.

Moreover, as already noted and further developed below, the US legal features most often cited as problematic – such as punitive damages and contingency fees[1193] – have no equivalent in most European jurisdictions. The fear of importing a US-style litigation culture is therefore largely unfounded.

This raises a fundamental question: should an ideological preconception continue to obstruct the development of effective private enforcement of competition rules in the EU – at the cost of denying access to justice for the vast majority of injured parties? The current preference for opt-in models, despite their proven inefficiency, risks doing just that. Indeed, it is time to shift the focus from theoretical concerns to practical outcomes and to recognise that opt-out mechanisms, when properly regulated, offer a more realistic and equitable path to collective redress.

3.6.2 Holders of the Right to Compensation and Legal Standing

As mentioned above and previously stated by Horacio Vedia Jerez,[1194] infringements of competition law usually have a very wide-ranging effect on the market and, as a result,

---

1190. *See* Simon Vande Walle, *Private Antitrust Litigation in the European Union and Japan*, Maklu, 2013, p. 181.
1191. In compliance, in the case of MS, with the provisions of Article 6 of the General Data Protection Regulation (Regulation (EU) 2016/679 of the European Parliament and of the Council of 27 April 2016): '1. Processing shall be lawful only if and to the extent that at least one of the following situations applies: (...) (c) processing is necessary for compliance with a legal obligation to which the controller is subject; (d) processing is necessary for the protection of the vital interests of the data subject or of another natural person; (e) processing is necessary for the performance of a task carried out in the public interest or in the exercise of official authority vested in the controller.'
1192. *See* ss 3.4.4.2 and 3.4.3.2 above.
1193. *See* Benjamin Holt, *United States Q&A*, *in GCR's Private Litigation Guide*, Nicholas and Heaton and Benhamin Holt (eds), 3rd ed., 2021, *asset download – Global Competition Review*, p. 397.
1194. *In Competition Law Enforcement and Compliance across the World: A Comparative Review*, Wolters Kluwer, 2015, p. 255.

such infringements can cause damage to a variety of market participants. It is therefore crucial that victims have adequate mechanisms to exercise their right to compensation, and this implies broad legal standing.

The rationale for the collective exercise of the right to compensation for damage caused by violations of competition rules, explored above, is particularly applicable to three groups of victims:

(i) injured people with limited economic resources, who are unable to invest in a complex and therefore expensive process such as the one in question;
(ii) injured parties who suffered minor damages, having no incentive to make the aforementioned investment in order to receive comparatively derisory individual compensation;
(iii) indirect purchasers, since their burden of proving the existence and extent of passing-on has traditionally been high – however, Article 14 of the EU Damages Directive has eased this burden by establishing a rebuttable presumption under certain conditions. Specifically, the Directive provides that an indirect purchaser is deemed to have established the passing-on of overcharges if they can demonstrate that: (a) the defendant committed an infringement of competition law; (b) the infringement of competition law resulted in an additional cost for the direct purchaser from the defendant; and (c) the indirect purchaser acquired the goods or services that are the subject of the infringement of competition law or acquired goods or services derived from or containing the goods or services that are the subject of the infringement.

These categories often include SMEs and consumers, both of whom face significant barriers to accessing justice individually. While the EU Damages Directive refers to SMEs only in the context of limiting their joint and several liability,[1195] Directive 2020/1828 similarly excludes them from the scope of representative actions. This exclusion is problematic, as SMEs – like consumers – are precisely the type of actors for whom collective redress mechanisms are most needed.

By design and according to EU legislator, collective actions aim 'to overcome the obstacles faced by consumers [and SMEs] in individual actions, such as those relating to uncertainty about their rights and about which procedural mechanisms are available, psychological reluctance to take action and the negative balance of the expected costs relative to the benefits of the individual action'.[1196] As such, excluding SMEs from collective redress undermines the very rationale of these mechanisms, which is to make enforcement of rights both effective and accessible for those who would otherwise be left without remedy.

1195. *See* Article 11(2).
1196. Recital 9.

3.6.3 Disclosure of Evidence

Disclosure of evidence - whether held by the competition authority, the opposing party, or third parties - is a critical issue in competition law litigation, even in follow-on actions. While any party injured by a breach of EU competition rules has the right to seek compensation before National Courts, the practical exercise of that right is often constrained by limited access to key documents.

The EU Damages Directive introduced important limitations, particularly through its so-called black list of documents that are exempt from disclosure - most notably, leniency statements. These documents are essential to public enforcement, as competition authorities often rely on them to uncover and prove anticompetitive conduct. Without access to such evidence, injured parties are left at a disadvantage.

Although Article 14 of the Directive has eased the burden of proof for indirect purchasers, claimants must still wait for the public enforcement decision to become final. Even then, they bear the burden of proving both causation and the quantification of damages - a task made significantly more difficult without access to the underlying evidence that supported the authority's findings.[1197]

In class actions, especially opt-in models, in which it is necessary to identify the beneficiaries, the aforementioned need for access to evidence, particularly at a preliminary stage of the case, when preparing the initial petition, is even more pronounced.

As far as access to evidence is concerned, the impact of the division between Common Law and Roman-Germanic systems is particularly marked,[1198] with the first being more permissive. Indeed, we can observe clear differences between jurisdictions such as the USA[1199] and the UK,[1200] on the one hand, and Belgium[1201] and France,[1202] on the other, in terms of access to evidence.

Portugal,[1203] however, stands out as something of an exception. Its legal framework provides for broad access to documents, including those held by the opposing party, and crucially, even before an action is formally brought. This comprehensive approach to disclosure significantly enhances the ability of injured parties to prepare their claims - particularly in complex competition law cases where evidentiary asymmetry is a major barrier to effective redress.

The principle of disclosure of evidence was born in the UK in 1873, according to which someone should not be able to avoid the fulfilment of an obligation just because

1197. *See* s. 3.1 above.
1198. *See* David Ashton, *Competition Damages Action in the EU: Law and Practice*, economics contribution from Frank Maier-Rigaud and Ulrich Schawalbe, Elgar, *Competition Law and Practice*, 2nd ed., 2018, p. 88.
1199. *See* s. 3.4.1 above.
1200. *See* s. 3.4.4 above.
1201. *See* s. 3.4.5 above.
1202. *See* s. 3.4.6 above.
1203. *See* s. 3.4.3 above.

only they had access to the document proving the existence of that obligation.[1204] As a result, Common Law countries have long provided for the obligation to disclose evidence, even if it is not favourable to the person in possession of it.

In Romano-Germanic legal systems, the burden of proof in civil cases is more often completely on the plaintiff, who must present the evidence available to them. Access to evidence held by the opposing party or third party is subject to limitations and, as a rule, only becomes possible at a later stage of the proceedings and not before the initial application.

Following the transposition of the EU Damages Directive, the rules governing access to evidence have been harmonised across Member States. It should be remembered that Articles 5 and 6 of the Directive establish the right of access to evidence, even when the evidence is part of the file of a competition authority. In such cases, access is subject to the limitations set out in Articles 6 and 7, the most significant being the prohibition – under Article 6(6)(a) – on disclosing leniency statements and settlement submissions.

However, as highlighted in the Belgian case concerning the extension of disclosure rules following the transposition of the EU Damages Directive,[1205] it is important to emphasise that this directive does not deal with class actions. Consequently, the disclosure rules it establishes are not tailored for such proceedings. Even in opt-out class actions, it is necessary to identify the class, which inherently requires additional evidence. The Directive appears to anticipate disclosure occurring at a later stage of individual proceedings – proceedings that do not involve preliminary control mechanisms or, in some jurisdictions, certification procedures (typical of class actions). This interpretation is supported by Article 5(3)(a), which requires National Courts to limit disclosure to what is proportionate, taking into account 'the extent to which <u>the claim</u> or defence is supported by <u>available</u> facts and evidence justifying the request to disclose evidence'.[1206]

However, as has also been highlighted,[1207] Directive 2020/1828, which applies to class actions in various matters other than competition law, provides that the party requesting the Court to disclose evidence must already have 'provided reasonably available evidence sufficient to support a representative action'.[1208]

It is evident that the current rules are inadequate when it comes to meeting the evidentiary requirements of class actions concerning competition law infringements. National case law has illustrated these shortcomings, even in individual actions. As previously noted, the persistent difficulty in accessing necessary evidence has long

1204. *See* David Ashton, *Competition Damages Action in the EU: Law and Practice*, economics contribution from Frank Maier-Rigaud and Ulrich Schawalbe, Elgar, *Competition Law and Practice*, 2nd ed., 2018, p. 893.
1205. *See* s. 3.4.5.5 above.
1206. Our underlining.
1207. *See* s. 3.3.7 above.
1208. *See* Article 18.

been identified by potential claimants as a major obstacle to the effectiveness of private enforcement in the EU.[1209]

To address this, a horizontal solution at the EU level should be considered – one that enables and harmonises class actions for competition law violations. Such a framework should include a mechanism for pre-action access to evidence. While this access would be subject to limitations, it is essential where the absence of such evidence would prevent claimants from establishing the basic facts necessary for class certification. Importantly, this preliminary evidentiary phase should be distinct from the proceedings on the merits of the case.

3.6.4 Punitive Damages

This form of compensation is characteristic of the US legal system, as previously noted.[1210] In fact, punitive damages in the US can reach up to nine times the amount of compensatory damages. Unlike compensatory damages – which aim to restore the injured party to the position they would have been in had the harm not occurred – punitive damages are intended to penalise the defendant by significantly increasing the award,[1211] particularly in cases involving wilful misconduct or aggravating circumstances.[1212]

In the context of antitrust damages actions, compensation may include up to three times the actual harm suffered – commonly referred to as treble damages – along with reasonable legal fees and post-judgment interest.[1213] Treble damages are a specific form of punitive damages designed to deter anticompetitive behaviour and encourage private enforcement.[1214]

Punitive damages were also born in the UK, in the 18th century, as a private penalty in response to the abusive behaviour of King George III's officials.[1215] In modern times,

1209. *See Commission Staff Working Paper Document Executive Summary of the Impact Assessment Damages actions for breach of the EU antitrust rules Accompanying the proposal for a Directive of the European Parliament and of the Council on certain rules governing actions for damages under national law for infringements of the competition law provisions of the Member States and of the European Union* (SWD/2013/0204 final), available at EUR-Lex - 52013SC0204 - EN - EUR-Lex (europa.eu), pt. 6.
1210. *See* s. 3.4.1 above.
1211. *See* Kent S. Bernard, *On Judgments and Settlements in Antitrust Litigation: When Should Damages Be Trebled?*, St. John's Law Review, vol. 56, No. 1, Fall 1981, available at https://scholarshipág.law.stjohns.edu/cgi/viewcontent.cgi?article = 2259&context = lawreview, p. 8.
1212. *See* John Y. Gotanda, *Charting Developments Concerning Punitive Damages: Is the Tide Changing?*, Villanova University Charles Widger School of Law Digital Repository, 2006, available at https://digitalcommons.law.villanova.edu/cgi/viewcontent.cgi?params = /context/wps/article/1065/&path_info = , p. 4.
1213. *See* s. 4 of the Clayton Act.
1214. *See* International Chamber of Commerce (ICC), *Compendium of Antitrust Damages Actions*, 2021, available at https://www.slcm.pt/xms/files/NOTICIAS/AT_Damage_Claims_SLCM.pdf, pt. 783.
1215. Paula Meira Lourenço, *A Indemnização Punitiva e os Critérios para a sua Determinação*, Colloquium organised by the Supreme Court of Justice, on the subject of Civil Liability – New

this figure has raised doubts about its constitutionality, even in the US, as Júlio Gomes points out.[1216] This is because, in the case of civil liability, it amounts to the application of a double penalty (in addition to the criminal or misdemeanour penalty), offending the general principle of law[1217] *ne bis in idem* (or double jeopardy), which prohibits the repetition of criminal proceedings after a first acquittal or conviction or the doubling of penalties. Furthermore, punishment under civil law would operate without the application of other general principles of law specific to criminal and administrative law, such as the presumption of innocence, due process and the prohibition of self-incrimination.[1218]

This is why most countries within the Romanesque-Germanic legal tradition prohibit punitive damages, viewing punishment as a function reserved for criminal or administrative proceedings. Even some Common Law jurisdictions impose limits on the amount of such damages.[1219] Nevertheless, the incorporation of preventive and punitive elements into the traditionally reparative function of civil liability is gaining broader acceptance. This shift is driven not only by the recognition of irreparable harm (where reparation alone may be insufficient) but also by evolving interpretations in legal doctrine and case law.[1220]

Moreover, civil penalties are not entirely foreign to Romanesque-Germanic systems. For example, the penalty clause, which predetermines a compensation amount and allows for its enforcement without requiring proof of actual damage, is legally valid in many such jurisdictions. However, National Courts have drawn important distinctions. The Portuguese STJ, for instance, has clarified that this clause cannot be identified with the institute of so-called punitive damages, a figure specific to other legal systems (Common Law), the aim of which is to punish the offender and not to repair the damage or exert coercion on the debtor.[1221]

Perspectives, held on 13 and 14 March 2008, available at https://www.academia.edu/37199605/MEIRA_LOURENCO_P_A_indemniza%C3%A7%C3%A3o_punitiva_e_os_crit%C3%A9rios_para_a_sua_determina%C3%A7%C3%A3o_03_2008_, p. 2.

1216. *In Uma função punitiva para a responsabilidade civil e uma função reparatória para a responsabilidade penal?*, Revista de Direito e Economia, Universidade de Coimbra, 1989, pp. 110 and 138.

1217. *See* Pierpaolo Rossi-Maccanico, *A Reasoned Approach to Prohibiting the Bis in Idem Between the Double and the Triple Identities*, Associations for European Criminal Law and the Protection of Financial Interests of the EU, No. 4, 2021, pp. 266-273, available at https://eucrim.eu/media/issue/pdf/eucrim_issue_2021-04.pdf#page=72, p. 266.

1218. *See* Sara Monteiro Pinto Ferreira da Silva, *Danos Punitivos: Problemas em relação à sua admissibilidade no ordenamento jurídico português*, UCP, 2012, dissertation available at https://repositorio.ucp.pt/entities/publication/6ce1156d-85b2-4e5c-9c01-bc469ad265db, pp. 16 and 17.

1219. *See* John Y. Gotanda, *Charting Developments Concerning Punitive Damages: Is the Tide Changing?*, Villanova University Charles Widger School of Law Digital Repository, 2006, available at https://digitalcommons.law.villanova.edu/cgi/viewcontent.cgi?params=/context/wps/article/1065/&path_info=, p. 2.

1220. *See* Luís Miguel Caldas Ribeiro Silva Amorim, *A Função Punitiva da Responsabilidade Civil, Coimbra*, 2014, dissertation available at https://eg.uc.pt/bitstream/10316/34853/1/A%20Funcao%20Punitiva%20da%20Responsabilidade%20Civil.pdf, p. 12.

1221. *See* ruling of 11 October 2020 in Case 2004/08.6TVLSB.L2.S1, available at http://www.dgsi.pt/jstj.nsf/954f0ce6ad9dd8b980256b5f003fa814/70071acfa36fd4e68025863400327d5a?OpenDocument.

In this light, one could argue that punitive damages serve a dual purpose: they are both punitive and reparative in nature.

With regard to the relationship between this type of 'compensation' and collective protection, Henrique Sousa Antunes[1222] stated that the relevance of the collective dimension of the injury allowed the legislator to test a new approach to the duty to compensate, in order to obtain an optimal level of prevention, welcoming the possibility of setting a global quantification. The author goes further, arguing in favour of extending the discussion on the introduction of private penalties to individual actions on the basis of prevention needs, as there are, in his opinion, practices that escape collective protection. Miguel Teixeira de Sousa[1223] also argues that the calculation of global compensation is based on the offender's gain and not the damage caused, and that its distribution cannot ensure the restoration of the individual situation of each injured party, which would exist in the absence of the violation.

Given that the total compensation expected in class actions for competition law violations can reach millions or even billions, it is easy to understand why the possibility of awarding punitive damages, i.e., multiplying the total compensation, makes such actions significantly more attractive. This applies not only to the beneficiaries, who see their individual awards increase, but also to lawyers, particularly where contingency or success fees are permitted, as their remuneration becomes a percentage of the overall compensation.[1224] Additionally, litigation funders are incentivised by the prospect of a multiplied return on their investment, further fuelling interest in bringing these actions.

However, the award of punitive damages is not recognised by international law,[1225] and the *ne bis in idem* principle is enshrined in Articles 4 of Protocol Nos 7 to the ECHR and 50 of the CFREU. To this extent, the ECtHR has issued judgments in which it has expressly opposed the application of punitive damages.[1226]

Some scholars, as Paulo Pinto de Albuquerque and Anne van Aaken,[1227] argue that the Court has, at times, implicitly endorsed punitive elements in its reasoning. They also point to socio-legal justifications for their use. As they note, '[w]herever the enforcement might be weak, e.g. because victims tend not to bring claims for different

1222. *In Das Funções Reconstitutivas e Punitiva da Responsabilidade Civil: Propostas de Reforma do Código Civil Português, in Novos Desafios da Responsabilidade Civil: Atas das II Jornadas Luso-Brasileiras de Responsabilidade Civil, Mafalda Miranda Barbosa,* Nelson Rosenvald and Francisco Muniz (eds), University of Coimbra, June 2019, pp. 121 and 144, p. 135.
1223. *In A Legitimidade Popular na Tutela dos Interesses Difusos,* LEX, 2003, p. 169.
1224. *See* s. 3.6.5.4 below.
1225. *See* Veronika Fikfak, *Changing State Behaviour: Damages Before the European Court of Human Rights,* The European Journal of International Law, vol. 29, No. 4, Oxford University Press, 2019, p. 1095 https://doi.org/10.1093/ejil/chy064.
1226. *See Acs. Akdivar v. Turkey,* Porc. 21893/93, 16 September 1996; and *Selçuk and Asker v. Turkey,* Case 30451/96, 25 September 2001, available at http://hudoc.echr.coe.int/.
1227. Paulo Pinto de Albuquerque and Anne van Aaken, *12 Punitive Damages in Strasbourg, in The European Convention on Human Rights and General International Law,* Anne van Aaken and Iulia Motoc (eds), Oxford University Press, 2018, pp. 230-248, p. 230.

reasons, "punitive damages" can set the correct incentives for following the law'. This argument persists despite Article 41 of the ECHR expressly referring only to 'just satisfaction to the injured party' and only where national law fails to provide even partial redress for the consequences of a violation.

Paulo Pinto de Albuquerque further contends[1228] that the inadequacy of national remedies often results in a failure to meet the preventive and punitive needs of justice. He advocates for the use of punitive damages by Courts, grounded in the principle of proportionality – taking into account the objective seriousness of the violation, the degree of intent or negligence, the impact of the conduct, and the likelihood that the right in question will remain unenforced.

The European Commission itself has questioned whether compensatory damages alone provide sufficient incentive for victims of competition law infringements to pursue damages claims, even in individual actions. In its 2005 Public Consultation, the Commission explored the possibility of introducing punitive damages for breaches of EU competition law. This proposal, however, met with significant opposition, primarily on the grounds of the *ne bis in idem* principle.[1229]

Moreover, punitive damages remain prohibited in nearly all Member States with the exception of the Republic of Ireland – and, more broadly in Europe, the UK. They are often viewed as encouraging abusive litigation.[1230]

This book's position is that, although European legal culture and history suggest a low risk of abusive litigation, the solution to the scarcity of competition law actions should not lie in rejecting one of the most harmonised legal principles across Member States. Indeed, the real barrier is not the absence of punitive damages, but rather the procedural and structural difficulties in bringing such actions – particularly the lack of effective collective redress mechanisms for both consumers and SMEs, and the absence of adequate funding models.

The final straw is the EU Damages Directive, which, as previously mentioned,[1231] ruled out[1232] in its Article 3(3) punitive, multiple or other types of compensation that go beyond the value of the damage suffered, as it leads to 'overcompensation'.[1233] In this

1228. *In Comentários do Regime Geral das Contraordenações à luz da Constituição da República e da Convenção Europeia dos Direitos do Homem*, Paulo Pinto de Albuquerque, Gabriel Mateus de Albuquerque (ed.), Universidade Católica Editora, 2022, pp. 33 and 36.
1229. *See* W.B. van. Bockel, *The Ne Bis In Idem Principle in EU Law: A Conceptual and Jurisprudential Analysis*, Meijers-reeks, 16 June 2009, available at https://scholarlypublications.universiteitleiden.nl/access/item%3A2875411/view, p. 112.
1230. *See* Christina Renner and Cécile Manong, *Collective Actions in the EU: The Past, the Present, the Future*, Thomson Reuters Practical Law, 1 March 2020.
1231. *See* s. 3.3 above.
1232. This was not the case, for example, with Directive 2004/48/EC of the European Parliament and of the Council of 29 April 2004 on the enforcement of intellectual property rights.
1233. *See* Pieter Van Cleynenbreugel, *Private Damages Actions in EU Competition Law and Restorative Justice: Towards a More Streamlined Institutional Framework?*, Market and Competition Law Review, vol. 3, No. 2, pp. 15-49 https://doi.org/10.7559/mclawreview.2019.1826, p. 23.

context, Henrique Sousa Antunes has acknowledged[1234] that there may be grounds to consider punitive damages contrary to EU public policy.[1235]

Directive 2020/1828 reinforces this stance, referencing punitive damages twice in its recitals to emphasise their prohibition.[1236] It states that: '[t]o prevent the misuse of representative actions, the awarding of punitive damages should be avoided and rules on certain procedural aspects, such as the designation and funding of qualified entities, should be laid down'.[1237] In essence, the EU legislator recognises the disproportionate relationship between the costs and benefits of collective redress mechanisms, but chooses to address this imbalance through funding solutions rather than through the introduction of punitive damages.

3.6.5 The Costs Barrier

Although the EU Treaties guarantee victims the right to compensation for infringements of competition law - and Member States are obliged to ensure this right is effectively enforced - the first question that often arises for victims, particularly consumers or SMEs facing relatively minor harm, is: 'how much is this going to cost me?'

As Nuno A. Pires Salpico explains,[1238] a litigant typically weighs three key elements: fixed or non-refundable costs (Fc), potentially recoverable costs (Rc), and expected gains (G), the latter two being contingent on a favourable outcome. The decision to litigate is rational if the following inequality holds:

$$(G \times Fa) - Fc + (Rc \times Ua) > 0$$

where Fa and Ua represent the probabilities of a favourable or unfavourable outcome, respectively.

This cost-benefit calculation highlights why access to funding is essential - particularly in competition law damages actions, which often require extensive preliminary investigation and the production of complex economic evidence. Even in follow-on actions, claimants must address intricate issues such as causation, damage quantification, and passing-on, all of which demand expert analysis and legal support. Therefore, beyond court fees, the costs of legal representation and economic expertise must be

1234. *In Das Funções Reconstitutivas e Punitiva da Responsabilidade Civil: Propostas de Reforma do Código Civil Português, in Novos Desafios da Responsabilidade Civil: Atas das II Jornadas Luso-Brasileiras de Responsabilidade Civil, Mafalda Miranda Barbosa,* Nelson Rosenvald and Francisco Muniz (eds), University of Coimbra, June 2019, pp. 121 and 144, p. 135.

1235. *In Intellectual Property Rights: Infringement and Calculation of Damages – A Comment on the Judgment of the Court of Justice of the European Union (Fifth Chamber) Stowarzyszenie 'Olawska Telewizja Kablowa' v. Stowarzyszenie Filmowców Polskich, 25 January 2017 (Case C-367/15)104,* Católica Law Review, vol. I, No. 2, May 2017, pp. 95 to 109, available at 1983_article_4255_1_10_20191020.pdf (ucp.pt), p. 104.

1236. *See* Recitals 10 and 42.

1237. *See* Recital 10.

1238. *In The Effectiveness of Private Enforcement of Competition Law: Deterrent, Collective Actions and Third-party Ligation Funding,* Revista de Concorrência & Regulação, Lisbon, No. 45, 2021, p. 115.

considered. Moreover, under the prevailing loser pays principle, an unsuccessful claimant may also be liable for the defendant's legal costs, further raising the financial stakes.[1239]

3.6.5.1 Third-Party Litigation Funding

TPLF, where a professional funder covers the costs of legal proceedings in exchange for a percentage of the recovered amount,[1240] is closely tied to class actions for breaches of competition law. These cases are typically complex, lengthy, and high risk, requiring substantial legal and economic expertise, as well as significant upfront investment. For plaintiffs - especially for consumers and SMEs - access to funding is often a prerequisite for pursuing such claims.

Historically, the financing of lawsuits by private third parties was considered contrary to public policy, even in Common Law jurisdictions.[1241] However, this perception has shifted. TPLF is now an increasingly accepted and widespread practice, and its encouragement by the EU legislator is both timely and necessary - particularly in the context of competition law enforcement. Provided that appropriate safeguards are in place, TPLF can play a vital role in ensuring access to justice.

This is especially true given the financial burden plaintiffs face. Beyond court fees, they must often cover lawyers' and experts' fees, the cost of producing complex economic evidence, translation services (especially in follow-on actions based on European Commission decisions), and travel expenses. These costs are disproportionately borne by the plaintiff, who must pay court fees in advance, provide retainers to legal and technical experts, and carry the burden of proof - even in follow-on actions, where issues such as causation, damage quantification, and passing-on remain highly technical and contentious.

It is important to bear in mind that, in this type of litigation, the opposing party will almost certainly be one or more companies with substantial financial resources and a strong incentive to resist liability - particularly in class actions, where the stakes are significantly higher. These defendants are often willing and able to deploy extensive legal and economic resources to challenge claims at every stage. It is not uncommon for them to present multiple, highly specialised economic analyses to contest causation, damage quantification, or market impact. This imbalance in resources further underscores the need for accessible funding mechanisms and procedural support for claimants, especially consumers and SMEs, to ensure a fair and effective enforcement of competition law.

1239. *See* Gordon Blanke et al., *International Competition Litigation: A Multi-jurisdictional Handbook, England and Wales*, Gordon Blanke and Renato Nazzini (eds) Kluwer Law International, 2012, p. 161.

1240. *See* Gian Marco Solas, *Third Party Funding: Law, Economic and Policy*, Cambridge University Press, 2019, p. 293.

1241. *See* Gordon Blanke et al., *International Competition Litigation: A Multi-jurisdictional Handbook, England and Wales*, Gordon Blanke and Renato Nazzini (eds) Kluwer Law International, 2012, p. 162.

3.6.5.1.1 *Risk or Remedy?*

Given the prohibitive cost of this type of litigation for consumers and SMEs, the involvement of companies that specialise[1242] in funding class actions for competition law infringements plays a crucial role in overcoming one of the main barriers to the effective enforcement of Articles 101 and 102 of the TFEU. It is therefore difficult to understand the persistent reluctance of the European Commission and some Member States to TPLF, often viewed as a driver of abusive litigation.

This concern appears misplaced. Since litigation funding is the core business of these companies, they have a strong financial incentive to avoid unmeritorious claims – they simply cannot afford to 'lose money'. Two key factors further undermine the argument that private funding encourages abuse:[1243]

(1) *Legal safeguards in the EU Damages Directive*: Article 9 establishes the binding effect of final infringement decisions in follow-on actions, while Article 17(2) introduces a presumption that cartels cause harm. These provisions significantly reduce the evidentiary burden on claimants and discourage frivolous claims.
(2) *The Loser Pays Principle*: present in most Member States, this rule ensures that an unsuccessful claimant not only receives no compensation but must also bear the legal costs of the opposing party. This creates a strong disincentive for speculative litigation.

As a result, litigation funders typically conduct rigorous due diligence before committing to a case. This includes a thorough legal and economic assessment of the claim's merits, potential risks, and likelihood of success. Far from promoting abuse, TPLF – when properly regulated – can be a powerful tool for enabling access to justice in complex and high-cost areas such as competition law enforcement.

3.6.5.1.2 *Regular or Non-regular? And in What Terms?*

TPLF is already a reality in Europe, even in the absence of substantive regulation. In practice, principles such as transparency are often observed, even voluntarily – for example, parties frequently disclose funding agreements and the identity of funders to the National Courts. This raises the question: is formal regulation necessary, or is self-regulation, as seen in the UK until now, sufficient?[1244]

Like Gian Marco Solas,[1245] this book leans towards the view that regulation is indeed necessary. It would professionalise the litigation funding sector and provide legal

1242. *See* Horacio Vedia Jerez, *Competition Law Enforcement and Compliance Across the World: A Comparative Review*, Wolters Kluwer, 2015, p. 314.
1243. *See* Till Shreiber and Martin Seegers, *Collective or Class Actions and Claims Aggregation in the EU: The Claimant's Perspective, in GCR's Private Litigation Guide ...*, p. 52.
1244. *See* s. 3.4.4.5 above.
1245. *In Third Party Funding: Law, Economic and Policy*, Cambridge University Press, 2019, p. 291.

certainty – particularly for beneficiaries – by ensuring funders meet minimum standards of financial capacity and ethical conduct, including the avoidance of conflicts of interest and the protection of confidential information. In this regard, we welcome the European Parliament's initiative to propose a Directive on the matter.[1246] Given that litigation funders often operate across borders, EU-level regulation would also promote harmonisation and coherence.

This book disagrees, however, with the current approach that leaves it to Member States to decide whether to permit litigation funding. This discretion risks undermining the principles of effectiveness and equivalence enshrined in the EU Treaties, especially considering the essential role that funding plays in enabling access to redress in complex areas such as competition law.

That said, while regulation is needed – primarily for legal certainty – overregulation could deter funders and, by extension, hinder access to justice. Directive 2020/1828 has already been criticised[1247] for discouraging private funding by imposing restrictive rules, and the European Parliament's draft proposal goes even further.

The choice of the regulatory model is, therefore, crucial. Should the EU adopt a conservative approach, as the European Parliament suggests, where funders remain third parties with no control over the litigation? Or should it allow 'active funding',[1248] as practised by entities like CDC in Germany, where the funder assumes the claimant's position and litigates in their own name in exchange for a share of the compensation?

While the conservative model offers greater protection for claimants – ensuring their interests are not subordinated to those of funders who are not bound by legal ethical duties – it must also ensure that funders' liability is limited to what is contractually agreed. Funders should not be held personally or jointly liable for litigation costs unless they breach the funding agreement, in which case contractual and possibly disciplinary consequences should follow. On this point, we support the European Parliament's proposal to establish a supervisory authority with sanctioning powers, to which injured parties can report non-compliance.

However, complaints raised by defendants regarding plaintiffs' funding arrangements must be handled with care. There is a risk that such objections could be used strategically to delay proceedings. The legislator must ensure that any challenges to the legitimacy of funding are resolved swiftly and do not obstruct the claimant's right to redress.

In conclusion, while EU-level legislation on TPLF is advisable, it should be proportionate. Regulation should focus on setting minimum standards for funders and their platforms, defining the essential terms of funding agreements, and safeguarding the rights and obligations of both parties. This includes ensuring financial capacity,

1246. *See* s. 3.3.8 above.
1247. *See* Octávio Viana, *Class Actions, Third-Party Litigation Funding, and Private Enforcement*, 2022, available at Class actions, third-party litigation funding, and private enforcement (associacaodeinvestidores.com).
1248. *See* Gian Marco Solas, *Third Party Funding: Law, Economic and Policy*, Cambridge University Press, 2019, p. 293.

preventing conflicts of interest, and maintaining confidentiality. Since both funders and claimants benefit from a strong case, it is already common practice for both sides - particularly the claimant's legal counsel - to conduct due diligence before proceeding.

It is also essential to distinguish clearly between the roles of funders and lawyers. Funders may operate on a no-win-no-fee basis in many jurisdictions, whereas lawyers are often prohibited from doing so. This distinction must be preserved in any future regulatory framework - something the European Parliament's proposal does not yet fully guarantee, as it leaves room for funders to engage in other activities.

Finally, as Gian Marco Solas notes,[1249] litigation funding extends beyond third-party funding of individual claims. It also includes investments in law firms - an area not covered by the Directive proposal but equally in need of regulation to ensure legal certainty, transparency, and the prevention of abuse. However, such models are more viable in jurisdictions that allow contingency fees, which remain restricted in most EU Member States.

3.6.5.2 Compensation for Representatives or Third-Party Funders

One of the key questions the legislator - particularly the EU legislator - must address is how to regulate the remuneration of representative entities and third-party funders. This issue becomes especially relevant if the European Parliament's recommendation to distinguish between passive funders and representative claimants is adopted.

Under Directive 2020/1828, qualified entity is defined as a non-profit organisation, which in practice often includes consumer associations, particularly in competition law cases. However, these entities still require financial resources to carry out their representative functions in collective actions. The challenge lies in ensuring they are adequately funded without compromising their non-profit status or independence.

For third-party funders, who operate for profit, the solution appears more straightforward. The European Parliament has proposed[1250] that funders may receive up to 39% of the compensation awarded to injured parties. While this figure is not explicitly justified, it does not seem unreasonable. However, the draft directive fails to resolve a critical issue - how funders are to be remunerated in opt-out class actions. In such cases, the beneficiaries are not individually identified during the proceedings and therefore cannot consent to a funding agreement that allocates a portion of their compensation to the funder.

If the European Parliament intends to empower National Courts or administrative authorities to order funders to cover litigation costs, it would be consistent to also allow them to allocate a portion of the awarded compensation to the funder. However, we believe this approach risks blurring the line between funder and claimant - roles that should remain distinct to preserve the integrity of the process.

1249. In *Third Party Funding: Law, Economic and Policy,* Cambridge University Press, 2019, p. 296.
1250. *See* s. 3.3.8 above.

A more balanced solution could be the creation of a common fund. This mechanism would allow the third-party funder to recover its agreed share of the compensation from a collective pool, regardless of whether individual class members have signed the funding agreement. Such a fund could also be used to compensate the representative plaintiff, particularly in the event of a loss, since they bear the procedural burden of the case - even if supported by external funding.

This approach would preserve the separation between funder and claimant, ensure fair remuneration, and maintain procedural safeguards. It would also align with the broader goals of access to justice and effective enforcement of competition law, particularly for consumers and SMEs.

3.6.5.3 Public Funding

Another potential solution to address the high costs of collective actions, particularly in competition law, is the creation of a public funding mechanism. While this approach has the clear drawback of relying on public resources, and private funding is generally preferable when it functions effectively, it is essential to recognise that the current lack of accessible funding undermines the principles of effectiveness and equivalence enshrined in EU law. This deficit disproportionately affects consumers and SMEs, who are often unable to exercise their right to redress for competition law violations.

The key advantage of public funding lies in its alignment with the public interest. Unlike private funders, whose decisions are driven by return on investment, public funders can support meritorious claims regardless of their economic value. For instance, if a class is too small to generate a high compensation total, private funders may decline to support the case - even if the legal claim is strong and socially relevant. Public funding, by contrast, can ensure that such claims are not excluded from the justice system.[1251]

This mechanism could be implemented either at the EU level, using the EU budget,[1252] or at the national level, through an EU legislation requiring Member States to establish dedicated funding schemes. To ensure efficient allocation of resources, the EU legislator could adopt a merit-based selection criterion, prioritising actions with a high likelihood of success - such as follow-on actions where an infringement has already been established. Additional criteria could include the broader public interest and the potential for systemic impact. Partial funding could also be considered to stretch limited resources further.

However, allocating substantial public funds to litigation remains politically sensitive.[1253] There has been resistance at the EU level to using public money for civil claims, even when sourced from fines imposed on competition law violators. An alternative proposal is to earmark a portion of the global compensation awarded in collective

1251. *See* Gian Marco Solas, *Third Party Funding: Law, Economic and Policy*, Cambridge University Press, 2019, p. 312.
1252. *See* Eda Şahin, *Collective Redress and EU Competition Law*, Routledge, 2019, p. 159.
1253. *See* Gian Marco Solas, *Third Party Funding: Law, Economic and Policy*, Cambridge University Press, 2019, p. 312.

actions to fund future claims brought by consumer associations.[1254] Yet this raises similar concerns to those associated with third-party funding: compensation belongs to the beneficiaries, and diverting part of it requires their consent – ideally through a transparent, opt-out-compatible funding agreement. A common fund model could again be adapted here to facilitate this.

While most Member States already provide legal aid to individuals lacking sufficient resources (in order to guarantee access to justice for all, in fulfilment of Article 47 of the CFREU), this traditional model is often ill-suited to the specific demands of competition law collective actions. Four key limitations highlight the need for a tailored EU-level solution:

(1) *Subject matter*: in some Member States, legal aid is not available for competition law cases.[1255]
(2) *Cost structure*: the expenses involved – especially for expert economic analysis – are significantly higher than in typical civil cases.
(3) *Eligibility*: legal aid is often unavailable to legal persons, or only to certain types of entities, excluding many SMEs.[1256]
(4) *Choice of lawyer*: in some jurisdictions, legal aid recipients cannot freely choose their lawyer, which is problematic in highly specialised areas like competition law.[1257]

Indeed, these cases often involve complex legal and economic issues that require specific expertise. If the assigned lawyer lacks expertise in antitrust litigation or class actions, the claimant may be disadvantaged from the outset. This not only affects the quality of representation but can also undermine the overall effectiveness and fairness of the action.

1254. *See* Eda Şahin, *Collective Redress and EU Competition Law*, Routledge, 2019, p. 159.
1255. Like Spain and Italy, according to Horacio Vedia Jerez, *Competition Law Enforcement and Compliance across the World: A Comparative Review*, Wolters Kluwer, 2015, p. 312.
1256. Portugal, for example, only allows non-profit organisations to apply for legal aid: associations, foundations, cooperatives, trade unions and religious institutions. *See* How can I apply for legal aid (justica.gov.pt). In the UK, legal aid is not available to legal persons, and in the Netherlands they have to fulfil certain conditions – *See* Horacio Vedia Jerez, *Competition Law Enforcement and Compliance Across the World: A Comparative Review*, Wolters Kluwer, 2015, p. 312.
1257. This is also the case in Portugal. According to Rodolfo Lavrador, *in O Apoio Judiciário*, VI Congresso dos Advogados Portugueses, 2005, available at https://portal.oa.pt/ordem/orgaos-da-ordem/congresso-dos-advogados-portugueses/vi-congresso/relatorios-conclusoes-e-discursos/relatorios-e-comunicacoes/1-seccao/o-apoio-judiciario/, the fact that it is not possible to choose a lawyer under the Portuguese Legal Aid Scheme is bad for those who need support, and it is bad for the lawyer (trust, which is essential for the fulfilment of our mission, begins with the initiative of the client or sponsored person in choosing their representative or patron), and it benefits no one.

3.6.5.4 Quota Litis *or Contingency Fee Agreements*

Agreements under which a lawyer is only paid in the event of success - typically as a percentage of the awarded compensation (known as *quota litis* or contingency fee arrangements) - are prohibited in most Member States.[1258]

However, a 2004 study revealed that this prohibition was more strictly observed in the 'old' Member States, while several newer Member States, particularly in Eastern Europe (e.g., the Czech Republic, Estonia, Hungary, Latvia, Lithuania, Malta, and Slovakia), tended to allow such agreements.[1259]

More recently, even Germany - a founding Member State with a strong Romano-Germanic legal tradition - has permitted these agreements, albeit as exceptions.[1260] The UK, with its Common Law heritage and closer alignment to US legal practices, goes further. In opt-in class actions, it allows damages-based agreements (contingency fees), and in both opt-in and opt-out actions, it permits conditional fee arrangements,[1261] where a lawyer's fee may depend, fully or partially, on the outcome. These mechanisms can incentivise lawyers to reduce fixed fees and align their interests with those of their clients.

The prohibition of *quota litis* agreements has deep historical roots, dating back to the Constitution of Constantine in AD 325.[1262] The main justifications are to preserve the: (i) independence and (ii) remuneration of the lawyer.[1263] If a lawyer were to tie their remuneration to the outcome of a case, they would risk becoming an interested party, thereby compromising their impartiality. Moreover, assuming such risk at a stage when the scope of work and actual costs remain uncertain - and when the result is entirely contingent on the case's outcome - could undermine the dignity of the legal profession.

This rationale underpins the continued prohibition in countries like Portugal.[1264] However, Portuguese jurisprudence has clarified that not all success-based remuneration is prohibited. The SCJ has upheld the validity of success fees or result bonuses - additional payments agreed upon after the fact, based on the outcome, and not tied to a pre-agreed percentage of the compensation. These are not considered *quota litis* because they are not random, predetermined, or variable in the same way.

1258. *See* Simon Vande Walle, *Private Antitrust Litigation in the European Union and Japan*, Maklu, 2013, p. 182.
1259. *See Study on the conditions of claims for damages in case of infringement of EC competition rules*, prepared by Denis Waelbroeck, Donald Slater and Gil Even-Shoshan, 31 August 2004, available at comparative_report_clean_en.pdf (europa.eu), pt. 93.
1260. *See* Kim Lars Mehrbrey, Lisa Hofmeister and Sophia Jaeger, *Germany Q&A, in GCR's Private Litigation Guide,* Nicholas and Heaton and Benhamin Holt (eds), 3rd ed., 2021, *asset download - Global Competition Review*, p. 284.
1261. *See* s. 3.4.4.5 above.
1262. *See* Susana Neto, *Quota Litis: da Evidência da sua Proibição*, Revista da Ordem dos Advogados, Lisbon, A.61, No. 2, April, 2001, pp. 1121-1140, available at https://portal.oa.pt/publicacoes/revista-da-ordem-dos-advogados/ano-2001/ano-61-vol-ii-abr-2001/temas/susa
na-neto-quota-litis-da-evidencia-da-sua-proibicao/, p. 1122.
1263. *Ibid.*, pp. 1125 et seq.
1264. Article 106 of the Statute of the Portuguese Bar Association.

From a policy perspective, prohibiting agreements between two informed and consenting parties – particularly when such arrangements can be mutually beneficial – should not be taken lightly. The presumption that a lawyer's financial interest would necessarily compromise their ethical duties is, arguably, more damaging to the profession's dignity than the agreements themselves. Moreover, existing legal safeguards (e.g., rules against abusive or usurious contracts, and public order principles) can address the risks that justify the prohibition.[1265] Alternatively, a cap on the permissible percentage could be introduced to strike a balance.

That said, this book does not believe that lifting the ban on *quota litis* agreements is the key to solving the under-enforcement of competition law by consumers and SMEs in Europe. Such a move would challenge one of the oldest traditions of the Romano-Germanic legal system, which seeks to avoid conflating the lawyer's economic interest with their role as a guarantor of justice.

Instead, the more pragmatic and culturally compatible solution lies in the possibility – already permitted in some jurisdictions like Portugal and the UK – of awarding a performance-based premium. This can be calculated as a percentage of the compensation and serves to incentivise lawyers while preserving the integrity of the profession.

Still, the financial burden of bringing such actions – especially for indirect purchasers[1266] – is so high relative to the individual harm suffered that maintaining the ban on *quota litis* agreements only reinforces a broader conclusion: access to funding is essential to unlocking the potential of class actions for competition law infringements.

3.6.5.5 *Each Party or Losers Pays*

The question of how the costs of class actions are allocated is inseparable from the question of how such actions are financed. Two primary models can be identified:

(1) Each party pays: under this model, each party bears its own legal costs, regardless of the outcome.
(2) Loser pays:[1267] this model requires the losing party to cover not only their own costs but also those of the prevailing party.

The former model is predominant in the US, while the latter is deeply rooted in the legal traditions of Member States and the UK.[1268] Indeed, even in jurisdictions where Courts have discretion (such as the UK's CAT), the loser pays principle is generally upheld.

1265. *See* s. 3.4.3.5 above.
1266. *See* Caroline Cauffman and Niels Philipsen, *Who Does What in Competition Law: Harmonising the Rules on Damages for Infringements of the EU Competition Rules?*, Maastricht European Private Law Institute Working Paper No. 2014/19, 7 November 2014, p. 26.
1267. *See* s. 3.3.3 above.
1268. *See* s. 3.4.3.4 above.

There is a wide gulf between the US and the European approaches to collective redress. The US system is designed to encourage private enforcement by minimising financial risk for plaintiffs, whereas the European model is more cautious, viewing litigation less as a commercial tool and more as a mechanism of justice.[1269] The EU's preference for the loser pays rule is grounded in the belief that it promotes settlement, deters frivolous claims, and encourages only meritorious actions. However, in practice, this has not translated into a high volume of litigation in competition law.

The European Commission has consistently emphasised the importance of preserving the loser pays principle. As early as its internal communications[1270] preceding the 2013 Recommendation[1271] and the 2012 European Parliament Resolution,[1272] the Commission warned against importing US-style litigation incentives, citing the risk of abusive claims. It explicitly identified the loser pays rule as a safeguard aligned with European legal traditions.[1273]

Nonetheless, this principle significantly increases the financial risk for plaintiffs. As Damien Geradin notes,[1274] the potential liability for the defendant's costs must be factored into any funding arrangement, making it more difficult to initiate collective actions in the EU. This is especially true in competition law, where defendants are often large corporations capable of producing extensive economic evidence. Alexander Stöhr[1275] argues that while plaintiffs should consider this risk, the costs are not necessarily prohibitive. However, given the complexity and scale of these cases, the financial exposure can be substantial.

Despite the deterrent effect of the loser pays rule, there is no conclusive empirical evidence that it effectively filters out unmeritorious claims. Still, this book believes that attempting to abolish this principle at the EU level would lack political support and would conflict with a deeply embedded legal tradition. While this book does not advocate for the imposition of contingency fees across the EU, we also do not support abandoning the loser pays principle, which remains a cornerstone of the Romano-Germanic legal framework.

That said, the continued application of this principle reinforces the need to promote private litigation funding. Without accessible funding mechanisms, the financial risks imposed by the loser pays rule will continue to suppress the number of collective

1269. *See* p. 73 of the Independent Study.
1270. *See* Viviane Reding, Joaquín Almunia and John Dalli, *Strengthening the Coherence of the European Approach to Collective Redress: Next Steps, note* presented to the other members of the EC on 12 October 2010, available at https://www.skadden.com/-/media/files/publications/2018/09/quarterly-insights/new-era-of-collective-actions-in-europe/fn1article1commission2010informationtowardseuropea.pdf.
1271. *See* s. 3.3.3 above.
1272. *Ibid.*
1273. *See* pt. 17.
1274. In *Collective Redress for Antitrust Damages in the European Union: Is This a Reality Now?*, George Mason University Law Review, 2015, pp. 13 and 18.
1275. In *The Implementation of Collective Redress: A Comparative Approach*, German Law Journal, vol. 21, 2020, pp. 1606-1624, p. 1621 https://doi.org/10.1017/glj.2020.95.

actions, particularly in the field of competition law, where the costs are high and the imbalance of power between parties is significant.[1276]

3.6.5.6 *After-the-Event Insurance*

As previously discussed in relation to the UK regime,[1277] ATE (after-the-event insurance) is a specific type of legal expense insurance that covers the risk of losing a lawsuit. It compensates the insured party for litigation costs - typically including the opponent's costs under the loser pays rule - in exchange for a one-off premium. This premium usually ranges between 30% and 45% of the amount covered.[1278]

If the case is lost, the premium is not recoverable, effectively adding to the claimant's financial loss. Perhaps for this reason, despite being available in most Member States, ATE insurance is rarely used in competition law actions.[1279]

According to BEUC,[1280] ATE insurance is primarily employed in a few jurisdictions such as Austria, the Netherlands, and the UK, although it is increasingly recognised as a potential solution to the broader challenge of litigation funding. Indeed, it has emerged as an alternative to TPLF, particularly in contexts where private financing is difficult to secure.[1281] It offers a potentially less complex and more transparent mechanism, as it does not involve a third party with a financial stake in the outcome of the case. However, ATE insurance typically only covers adverse costs (i.e., the opponent's costs if the claimant loses), while the claimant's own legal and expert fees - often substantial in competition law cases - must still be paid upfront.

Moreover, the high risk associated with competition law litigation, combined with the potentially significant financial exposure under the loser pays rule, makes ATE insurance a less attractive option for insurers unless premiums are set very high. This, in turn, may render the product unaffordable or unattractive to claimants, particularly consumers and SMEs.[1282]

In sum, while ATE insurance presents a promising tool for mitigating litigation risk, its practical utility in competition law class actions remains limited. Its effectiveness will depend on the development of more affordable and tailored products, as well as broader reforms to reduce the financial barriers to collective redress.

1276. *See* Table 3.1 - Comparison of Antitrust Class Actions in Selected European Jurisdictions, s. 3.4.7 above.
1277. *See* s. 3.4.3.5 above.
1278. *See*, for example, https://www.pinsentmasons.com/out-law/guides/litigation-costs-insurance#:~:text=The%20level%20of%20premium%20payable%20depends%20on%20the,successfully%20concluded%20by%20negotiation%20and%2For%20in%20court%20proceedings.
1279. In Germany, for example, the ATE cannot be used when the dispute concerns competition law - *See* Horacio Vedia Jerez, *Competition Law Enforcement and Compliance Across de World: A Comparative Review*, Wolters Kluwer, 2015, p. 314.
1280. *See* https://www.beuc.eu/sites/default/files/publications/2012-00074-01-e.pdf, p. 6.
1281. *See* Sarah-Jane Dobson Paula Margolis and Ed Gibson, *Collective Redress & Class Actions 2021: UK*, 2021, available at https://chambers.com/downloads/gpg/814/collective_redress__and__class_actions_2021.pdf, p. 272.
1282. *See* Eda Şahin, *Collective Redress and EU Competition Law*, Routledge, 2019, p. 160.

CHAPTER 4

Back to Basics and Global Positioning

Let us go back to the beginning: George Cumming, Brad Spitz, and Ruth Janel point out[1283] two fundamental principles govern the enforcement of EU law in general - and competition law in particular - by the Member States.

The first is the *principle of primacy*, which establishes that EU law takes precedence over conflicting national law. However, this does not necessarily require Member States to overhaul their legal systems; rather, they must ensure that national provisions do not obstruct the application of EU law.

The second is the *principle of effectiveness*, closely linked to the *principle of equivalence*. These were firmly established in the landmark *Courage v. Crehan* judgment and reaffirmed in subsequent rulings such as *Manfredi*, *Pfleiderer*, and *Otis I and II*.[1284] Under the principle of effectiveness, Member States must ensure that rules governing actions for damages arising from breaches of competition law do not render the exercise of the right to redress practically impossible or excessively difficult. The principle of equivalence requires that such actions be treated no less favourably than similar domestic claims.[1285]

Together, these principles form the legal foundation for the obligation of Member States to provide effective and non-discriminatory mechanisms for enforcing EU competition law rights, particularly in the context of private enforcement.

The latter principles (of effectiveness and equivalence in the national application of the EU law) have been developed by the CJEU, as Hanns Ullrich observes,[1286] not only to ensure the primacy and full effect of EU law within the Member States but also to

1283. *In Civil Procedure used for Enforcement of EC Competition Law by the English, French and German Civil Courts*, Kluwer Law International, 2007, p. 2.
1284. *See* ss 1.1, 1.2 and 2.2 above.
1285. *See* pt. 29.
1286. *In Private Enforcement of the EU Rules on Competition: Nullity Neglected*, Max Planck Institute for Innovation & Competition Research Paper No. 21-09, pp. 606-635, available at https://link.springer.com/content/pdf/10.1007/s40319-021-01054-w.pdf, p. 619.

support a functional division of responsibilities between the EU and national legal systems, in the shared interest of the EU as a whole.

In particular, the principle of effectiveness derives from Article 4(3) TEU and requires that Member States ensure the full and effective implementation of EU law within their national legal systems.[1287] This foundational principle gives rise to several key sub-principles, including direct effect, primacy (as previously discussed), uniformity of application, conforming interpretation, and state liability.[1288]

Since the right to compensation for damages resulting from infringements of competition law - specifically Articles 101 and 102 of the TFEU - is governed by EU law and further detailed in the EU Damages Directive, Member States are required to apply both the Directive and their national transposition measures in a manner that is complete, appropriate, and non-discriminatory. However, national legal traditions and principles, which have been developed for valid historical and constitutional reasons, must also be respected. How can national legal heritages be reconciled with the EU law principles?

The reconciliation of national 'touchstones' with the requirements of EU law is achieved through a balancing exercise: national rules may be maintained insofar as they are compatible with the EU law, in accordance with the principle of primacy.

Importantly, while the principles of effectiveness and equivalence do not demand uniformity of national rules applying EU law (principle of autonomous procedural application), they do require that national regimes enable EU law to produce its full effects and achieve its objectives.[1289] In this context, Member States must ensure that their legal systems provide mechanisms, even if they differ, that allow for the effective enforcement of Articles 101 and 102 TFEU. These provisions have direct effect and confer upon individuals the right to seek compensation for harm caused by anticompetitive conduct.

In short, the principles of effectiveness and equivalence under EU law establish what may be described as a *minimum standard of procedural application of EU law by national legal systems.*[1290] As Walter van Gerven aptly puts it,[1291] these principles require not merely minimal compliance, but adequate judicial protection - specifically, mechanisms that enable individuals to obtain reparation proportionate to the nature and severity of the interference with their EU rights.

1287. *See* Fausto de Quadros, *in Tratado de Lisboa: Anotado e Comentado*, Manuel Lopes Porto and Gonçalo Anastácio (eds) Almedina, 2012, p. 35.

1288. For further developments, *see* Miguel Gorjão-Henriques, *Direito da União, História, Direito, Cidadania, Mercado Interno e Concorrência*, Almedina, 7th ed., 2014, pp. 344 and following.

1289. Hanns Ullrich, *Private Enforcement of the EU Rules on Competition: Nullity Neglected*, Max Planck Institute for Innovation & Competition Research Paper No. 21-09, pp. 606-635, available at https://link.springer.com/content/pdf/10.1007/s40319-021-01054-w.pdf, p. 619.

1290. *See* George Cumming, Brad Spitz and Ruth Janel, *Civil Procedure used for Enforcement of EC Competition Law by the English, French and German Civil Courts*, Kluwer Law International, 2007, p. 11.

1291. In *Of Rights, Remedies and Procedures*, Common Market Law Review, vol. 37, No. 3, 2000, pp. 503 and 530 https://doi.org/10.54648/263877.

While the procedural autonomy of Member States in implementing EU law - particularly in private enforcement actions - remains a contentious issue,[1292] the CJEU has consistently limited this autonomy. As Constantinos Kakouris notes,[1293] the Court does not recognise procedural autonomy as a reserved domain of the Member States, but rather treats national procedural rules as ancillary instruments that must serve the overarching goal of ensuring the effectiveness of EU law.

This position was firmly established in *Costa v. ENEL*,[1294] where the Court held that the effectiveness[1295] of EU law cannot vary from one State to another on the basis of domestic legislation without jeopardising the achievement of the objectives of the Treaty and without causing prohibited discrimination. Similarly, in *Foto-Frost*,[1296] the Court emphasised that the uniform[1297] application of EU law is particularly imperative when the validity of an EU act is at stake.

In *Zuckerfabrik Süderdithmarschen*,[1298] the ECJ addressed the suspension of administrative acts based on EU regulations, warning that divergent national rules on interim relief could undermine the uniform application of EU law. It held that while national procedural rules govern the submission and examination of such requests, the conditions for granting suspension must be uniform across Member States.

Finally, in *Brasserie du Pêcheur*,[1299] the ECJ ruled that the exercise of the right to compensation for damage caused by breaches of EU law cannot depend on domestic rules alone, as this would compromise the uniform application of EU law.

Together, these rulings underscore that while Member States retain procedural discretion, it is strictly bounded by the need to ensure effective judicial protection and uniform application of EU law. This is particularly relevant in the context of competition law enforcement, where national rules must enable individuals to fully exercise their right to redress under Articles 101 and 102 TFEU.

Indeed, as previously noted, the right to redress for any individual harmed by a breach of competition rules stems from Articles 101 and 102 of the TFEU and is governed by the EU law through the EU Damages Directive. However, this framework overlooks a critical component for the effective private enforcement of competition law: *collective redress*.[1300]

1292. *See*, for example, Alvaro Águila-Real, *Contra la armonización positiva; la Propuesta de la Comisión para reforzar el private enforcemente del Derecho de la Competencia, in Indret 3/2009*, pp. 11 et seq.
1293. In *Do the Member States Possess Judicial Procedural 'Autonomy'*, Common Market Law Review, vol. 34, No. 6, 1997, p. 1390 https://doi.org/10.54648/157323.
1294. *Costa v. ENEL*, 15 July 1964, Case 6/64, pt. 13.
1295. *See* s. 2.1 above.
1296. *Photo-Frost* judgment of 22 October 1987, Case C-314/85, pt. 15.
1297. *See* Walter van Gerven, *Of Rights, Remedies and Procedures*, Common Market Law Review, vol. 37, No. 3, 2000, p. 502 https://doi.org/10.54648/263877.
1298. *Zuckerfabrik Süderdithmarschen*, 21 February 1991, Case C-143/88, pts 25 and 26.
1299. *Brasserie du pêcheur*, of 5 March 1996, Case C-46/93, pt. 33.
1300. *See* Barry Rodger, Miguel Sousa Ferro and Francisco Marcos, *The EU Antitrust Damages Directive: Transposition in the Member States*, Oxford University Press, 2018, p. 484.

For SMEs and consumers, pursuing individual claims is often economically unfeasible, even in follow-on actions. Maria Elisabete Ramos aptly describes[1301] this phenomenon as 'rational apathy'. Addressing this challenge requires a stronger emphasis on collective redress mechanisms, as advocated by Julian Nowag and Liisa Tarkkila.[1302]

While some Member States have implemented collective action tools tailored to competition law (e.g., the UK), and others have expanded the Directive's scope during transposition (e.g., Portugal), several countries either lack such mechanisms or have not adapted them to the specificities of competition law enforcement (e.g., Belgium and France).

Directive 2020/1828, which aims to ensure that consumers across the EU have access to at least one effective and efficient collective action mechanism for injunctive and redress measures, notably excludes competition law from its scope.[1303] This omission is particularly problematic during periods of health or economic crisis, when the number of affected consumers tends to rise - especially in cases involving widespread competition infringements. In such scenarios, individual redress is rarely effective or even viable. Furthermore, due to the divergent legal interpretations and implementations of collective redress across Member States, establishing a unified EU legal framework is essential to ensure consistent access to justice throughout the EU.[1304]

Indeed, this fragmented legal landscape across Member States in the area of collective redress undermines access to justice and the uniform application of Articles 101 and 102 TFEU. It risks violating the principles of effectiveness and consistency in EU law. For SMEs and consumers, the right to access justice - enshrined in Articles 6 and 13 of the ECHR - may be compromised. As previously emphasised, individual actions are not a realistic option for these victims due to the lack of economic rationality.

The establishment of a collective redress mechanism for competition law at the EU level is not only justified by the foundational principles of EU law but also promises at least four substantial benefits - both for SMEs and consumers, and for the broader effectiveness of private enforcement within the EU:

(1) *Effective judicial protection*: given the complex and far-reaching nature of competition law infringements, only a robust EU-level collective redress mechanism can address the current scarcity of class actions and the resulting lack of compensation for harmed SMEs and consumers. Such a

1301. In *Private Enforcement and Opt-out System Risks, Rewards and Legal Safeguards*, Yearbook of Antitrust and Regulatory Studies, vol. 11, No. 18, 2018, pp. 85-114, available at https://doi.org/10.7172/1689-9024.yars.2018.11.18.4, p. 90.

1302. In *How Much Effectiveness for the* EU *Damages Directive?: Contractual Clauses and Antitrust Damages Actions*, Common Market Law Review, vol. 57, No. 2, 2020, p. 32, available at https://doi.org/10.54648/cola2020033.

1303. *See* Recital 7.

1304. *See* Verica Trstenjak and Petra Weingerl, *Collective Actions in the European Union: American or European Model?*, Beijing Law Review, vol. 5, 2014, pp. 155-162, available at https://doi.org/10.4236/blr.2014.53015, p. 161.

mechanism would ensure a minimum standard of access to justice and help reverse the prevailing under-enforcement.

(2) *Legal certainty and prevention of forum shopping*: harmonising collective redress procedures across Member States – especially for cross-border cases – would encourage legitimate claims by SMEs and consumers while reducing the risk of duplicative or contradictory litigation. It would also prevent the strategic concentration of cases in jurisdictions perceived as more favourable to plaintiffs, thereby enhancing procedural fairness and predictability.

(3) *Enhanced effectiveness of EU Competition Law*: private enforcement complements public enforcement by deterring violations, enabling victims to seek redress, and reinforcing the consistent application of Articles 101 and 102 TFEU. A collective redress mechanism would significantly strengthen this dual enforcement model.

(4) *Efficiency gains for all stakeholders*: a harmonised class action framework would streamline litigation, reducing costs and resource burdens for plaintiffs, defendants, and Member States alike. It would allow SMEs and consumers to pursue claims more affordably, enable defendants to consolidate their defence strategies, and help National Courts manage resources more efficiently.

This book is, however, aware of the significant costs associated with collective redress mechanisms, which can amount to thousands of euros. In this regard, the recent EU initiative to regulate the TPLF of such actions is welcome, as it represents a step towards making collective enforcement more accessible and sustainable.

At the same time, the creation of a harmonised EU mechanism for collective redress must be carefully balanced with the legal traditions of the Member States. Any new legislation should, as far as possible and without contradicting the EU law, respect national legal frameworks to ensure both legitimacy and practical implementation.

In designing a horizontal EU-level solution for collective redress in competition law, the positive experiences of countries like Portugal and the UK should serve as foundational models. The mechanism should be inclusive – capable of covering not only consumers but also SMEs, which are currently excluded under Directive 2020/1828. Moreover, it should adopt an opt-out or at least a hybrid model. Leaving the choice of model entirely to Member States, or maintaining the current ambiguity under EU law, risks perpetuating inequalities in access to justice (an especially serious concern in competition law, where anticompetitive practices often affect millions).

Experience has shown that opt-in models are generally ineffective. They suffer from low participation rates among injured parties and are ill-suited to large, diffuse classes of victims. The evidentiary burden, financial costs, and time demands make opt-in procedures impractical for many, thereby undermining the very purpose of collective redress.[1305]

1305. *See* Eda Şahin, *Collective Redress and EU Competition Law*, Routledge, 2019, p. 148.

However, concerns about excessive litigation in the EU context are largely unfounded, for three key reasons:

(1) *Misplaced comparisons with the US*: the abuses observed in the US class action system are not attributable solely to the opt-out model. If that were the case, similar issues would have arisen in Member States that have adopted opt-out mechanisms. Instead, the US experience is shaped by a unique combination of factors, including the permissibility of contingency fee arrangements, punitive damages (which are prohibited in the EU) and a deeply embedded litigation culture – that do not apply in the European legal landscape.
(2) *Under-enforcement, not over-enforcement*: the European reality is the opposite of the US scenario. There is a notable scarcity of class actions in the field of competition law, resulting in limited access to redress for victims of anticompetitive practices.[1306]
(3) *Existing safeguards against abuse*: some Member States already have procedural tools to prevent frivolous or excessive litigation, such as class certification and preliminary dismissal mechanisms. These safeguards can ensure that only well-founded claims proceed.

However, simply adopting an opt-out or hybrid model is not sufficient. The goal must go beyond declaratory judgments or injunctive relief. The experiences of Portugal and the UK demonstrate that a litigation-friendly environment, combined with TPLF, has led to a significant increase in class actions seeking compensation for competition law infringements.[1307]

To ensure legal certainty and build trust in the system, we support the regulation of private funding at the EU level, as proposed by the European Parliament. However, such regulation should be minimal and focused. It should define:

- the eligibility criteria for funders and legal tech platforms;
- the essential terms of funding agreements;
- the rights and obligations of both funders and claimants;
- measures to prevent conflicts of interest;
- requirements to ensure funders' financial capacity and the confidentiality of sensitive information.

Importantly, this regulation must be clear and practical. Ambiguity would undermine its purpose and further erode confidence among potential users – a shortcoming already evident in the European Parliament proposal.

1306. *See* David Ashton, *Competition Damages Action in the EU: Law and Practice*, economics contribution from Frank Maier-Rigaud and Ulrich Schawalbe, Elgar, *Competition Law and Practice*, 2nd ed., 2018, p. 283.
1307. *See* Miguel Sousa Ferro, *Consumer Antitrust Private Enforcement in Europe: As Complete a Survey as Possible (Extended Version)*, 23 October 2022, available at https://ssrn.com/abstract=4223770, p. 11.

Finally, in light of the information asymmetry that typically characterises competition law disputes - especially to the detriment of injured parties - there must be a robust EU-level mechanism for pre-trial access to evidence. This is particularly critical if the EU ultimately adopts an opt-in model. Such a mechanism should allow claimants to obtain essential evidence needed for class admissibility, even before the merits of the case are addressed, while being subject to appropriate safeguards.

Complementing this, public funding, as envisaged in Directive 2020/1828, should be extended to all class actions, regardless of subject matter. This would ensure broader access to justice and reinforce the effectiveness of collective redress mechanisms across the EU.

CHAPTER 5

Proposal Design: What Is New?

The effective exercise of the right to redress by individuals harmed by infringements of competition law, enshrined in Articles 101 and 102 of the TFEU, depends fundamentally on the availability of effective enforcement mechanisms.[1308] Yet, despite the EU's long-standing strategic commitment to promoting private enforcement,[1309] there is little evidence[1310] that the collective action mechanisms currently available in Member States have meaningfully improved access to justice or compensation for victims of competition law violations.

This reality underscores the urgency of implementing a more robust and harmonised proposal. Importantly, this book is not alone in this call. For over a decade, stakeholders have consistently advocated for a horizontal approach to antitrust collective redress, aimed at reducing the persistent asymmetries in national legislation - or, in some cases, the complete absence of such frameworks.[1311]

As Christopher Hodges has observed,[1312] the political momentum in Europe towards collective redress is driven not only by legal principles but also by commercial incentives. However, the European Commission has deliberately distanced itself from the US model, beginning with the terminology shift - from class actions to collective

1308. *See* Michal S. Gal and Rivi Dahan, *Legal Obstacles to Private Enforcement of Competition Law*, Market and Competition Law Review, vol. 3, No. 2, pp. 133-152 available at https://doi.org/10.7559/mclawreview.2019.1835, p. 136.

1309. *See* Lia Athanassiou, *Collective Redress and Competition Policy, in Cross-Border Class Actions*, Arnaud Nuyts and Nikitas E. Hatzimihail (eds), Otto Schmidt and De Gruyter European Law Publishers, 2013, p. 145.

1310. *Collective Redress in Antitrust*, available at https://ec.europa.eu/competition/antitrust/actionsdamages/study_legislative_action_collective_redress.pdf, p. 40.

1311. *See* REPORT on 'Towards a Coherent European Approach to Collective Redress' | A7-0012/2012 | European Parliament (europa.eu) and s. 3.3 above. *See also Business Europe Position Paper on Collective Redress*, 17 August 2017, available at 2017-08-17_collective_redress_-_2017_public_consultation.pdf (businesseurope.eu).

1312. *In Current Discussions on Consumer Redress: Collective Redress and ADR*, ERA Forum, j Springerlink, June 2012, pp. 12 and 15.

actions, and ultimately to collective redress – to reflect a more restrained and context-sensitive approach.

As previously discussed,[1313] the European Commission's omission of collective actions in the field of competition law (and its inconsistent messaging on the matter) has drawn considerable criticism. Some observers have attributed this gap to a lack of political will, which may explain why collective actions were excluded from the EU Damages Directive.[1314]

In response to these concerns, ECON commissioned the 2012 study Collective Redress in Antitrust, which strongly advocated for a horizontal, sector-specific EU legal solution for competition law. The study recommended that the appropriate legal instrument should be a regulation, rather than a directive, to avoid compatibility issues with existing national laws and to reduce the risk of continued fragmentation in collective redress mechanisms across Member States.

The Independent Study proposed that this EU-level mechanism should apply to all competition law disputes – whether domestic or cross-border – involving the application of Articles 101 and 102 of the TFEU. Crucially, it emphasised that the mechanism should be accessible to both consumers and SMEs.

The study outlined several key features for the proposed legal instrument:

- Hybrid model: it should allow for opt-out procedures in cases where injured parties are unlikely to act individually, particularly when the harm suffered is of low individual value.
- Commonality requirement: actions should be limited to claims arising from the same facts and infringement, enabling the judge to issue a decision based on shared evidence.
- Flexible standing: both representative and collective actions should be permitted, including the possibility for an injured SME to bring a claim on behalf of a broader group.
- Fee arrangements flexibility: the mechanism should accommodate contingency and conditional fee arrangements to support access to justice.[1315]
- Loser pays principle: this principle should be preserved to deter frivolous claims.[1316]
- Access to evidence and passing-on: rules should be established to facilitate access to evidence and allow for the use of passing-on arguments, which are essential in competition law cases.[1317]

The creation of a sector-specific collective action mechanism for competition law at the EU level has also been supported in academic literature, albeit with some variations from the model previously outlined. Notable contributions include those of Charlotte

1313. *See* ss 1.3 and 3.3.6 above.
1314. *See* Eda Şahin, *Collective Redress and EU Competition Law*, Routledge, 2019, p. 59.
1315. *See* s. 3.6.5.4 above.
1316. *See* s. 3.6.5.5 above.
1317. *Collective Redress in Antitrust*, available at https://ec.europa.eu/competition/antitrust/actionsdamages/study_legislative_action_collective_redress.pdf, pp. 89 and 90.

Leskinen (2010, 2011),[1318] Žygimantas Juška (2014, 2019),[1319] and Eda Şahin (2019).[1320] Other valuable perspectives can be found, such as in the work of Maciej Gac (2017)[1321] – although this book respectfully diverge from his position on minimum harmonisation, as will become clear in the design chapter below.

These scholars generally agree that the EU should adopt a sectoral collective redress mechanism specifically for competition law. However, they propose that this should be implemented through a directive, rather than a regulation. Importantly, they also argue that the opt-in model should not be the default, given its limitations in ensuring broad and effective participation by injured parties.

For Charlotte Leskinen, incorporating an opt-in model into a directive increases the likelihood of effective implementation, as it offers flexibility and allows Member States to preserve their legal traditions.[1322] However, she also acknowledges the limitations of opt-in class actions, particularly in cases involving minor harm.[1323] In such instances, these actions are often unattractive and impractical.[1324]

Žygimantas Juška similarly supports the adoption of an EU legislative initiative through a directive, citing the principles of subsidiarity and proportionality, and the need to respect Member States' procedural autonomy.[1325] Regarding the model of collective action, he argues that opt-out mechanisms are more suitable, especially given the typically low participation rates of injured parties and the lack of funding. Nonetheless, he remains open to a hybrid regime as a viable alternative.[1326]

More recently, Eda Şahin has also advocated for the adoption of a directive, emphasising the importance of allowing Member States to align new rules with their existing legal frameworks.[1327] On the question of the action model, she strongly supports the inclusion of opt-out mechanisms, which she views as essential for

1318. In *Collective Antitrust Damages Actions in the EU: The Opt-in v. Opt-out Model*, Working Paper IE Law School, 2010, available at http://ssrn.com/abstract=1612731 and *in Collective Actions: Rethinking Funding and National Cost Rules*, The Competition Law Review, vol. 8, No. 1, December 2011, pp. 87-121.
1319. In *Obstacles in European Competition Law Enforcement: A Potential Solution from Collective Redress*, European Journal of Legal Studies, vol. 7, No. 1, 2014, pp. 125-153 and *in The Role of Collective Redress Actions to Achieve Full Compensation for Violations of European Union Competition Law, PhD* thesis defended at Leiden University on 23 June 2019, available at view (universiteitleiden.nl).
1320. *See* Eda Şahin, *Collective Redress and EU Competition Law*, Routledge, 2019.
1321. In *Group Litigation as an Instrument of Competition Law Enforcement: Analysis Based on European, French and Polish Experience*, Centre for Antitrust and Regulatory Studies, University of Warsaw, Faculty of Management, Eighty third Publication of the Publishing Programme, Series: Textbooks and Monographs (25), Prof. Dr. Tadeusz Skoczny (Series ed.), 2017, available at CARS 25 - Group litigation-Gac.indd (uw.edu.pl), p. 441.
1322. In *Collective Actions: Rethinking Funding and National Cost Rules*, The Competition Law Review, vol. 8, No. 1, December 2011, p. 115.
1323. In *Collective Antitrust Damages Actions in the EU: The Opt-in v. Opt-out Model*, Working Paper IE Law School, 2010, available at http://ssrn.com/abstract=1612731, p. 29.
1324. In *Collective Actions: Rethinking Funding and National Cost Rules*, The Competition Law Review, vol. 8, No. 1, December 2011, p. 88.
1325. In *Obstacles in European Competition Law Enforcement: A Potential Solution from Collective Redress*, European Journal of Legal Studies, vol. 7, No. 1, 2014, pp. 147 and 148.
1326. *Ibid.*, pp. 151 and 152.
1327. *See* Eda Şahin, *Collective Redress and EU Competition Law*, Routledge, 2019, p. 59.

realistically compensating consumers harmed by competition law violations. Given the large number of affected individuals, she argues that opt-in actions are too resource-intensive, costly, and time-consuming. Instead, she favours a hybrid approach that allows for case-by-case determination of the most appropriate model. Şahin also highlights that consumers typically present fewer risks of conflicts of interest or individual complexities that would hinder collective adjudication.[1328]

Both Leskinen and Şahin go further by addressing two central issues: the need for adequate incentives and the question of who is best positioned to initiate and represent the group. These are critical considerations, as – regardless of the legal instrument or model adopted – collective actions in the field of competition law are inherently complex and costly. Without meaningful financial incentives, such actions are unlikely to be pursued, leaving victims without effective redress.

According to Charlotte Leskinen, the introduction of a collective redress mechanism for EU competition law disputes should be accompanied (at a minimum) by an obligation for Member States to ensure adequate funding. She argues that this would allow each Member State to develop a funding model aligned with its civil procedure system, incorporating tools such as contingency fees, private funding, and insurance. In fact, Leskinen suggests that the European Commission should initially recommend the adoption of contingency fees, subject to safeguards such as judicial oversight and adjustment by National Courts. In a more advanced phase, once collective action practices are more established, she proposes that the Commission consider mandating contingency fees through national legislation if voluntary incentives prove insufficient. Furthermore, Leskinen advocates for binding EU rules on cost capping and exceptions to the loser pays principle to enhance access to justice. She notes that cost capping already exists in EU intellectual property law, which could make Member States more receptive to similar provisions in the competition law context.[1329]

Eda Şahin, by contrast, does not challenge the continued application of the loser pays principle. However, she emphasises that for competition law class actions to function effectively under this rule, robust funding mechanisms must be in place. These include ATE insurance, special funds financed by undistributed damages, private funding, and conditional or contingency fee arrangements. Şahin highlights the critical role of lawyers in this ecosystem, arguing that they are best positioned – in terms of both expertise and financial capacity – to initiate and lead such actions. She contends that incentivising legal professionals, particularly in conjunction with an opt-out model, would significantly improve the likelihood of securing compensation for consumers harmed by competition law infringements.[1330]

As for this book's own proposal for a collective action mechanism in EU competition law, it has been developed throughout the previous chapters. This study will now summarise its key features – highlighting both points of alignment and divergence from

1328. *Ibid.*, pp. 126, 136, 148 and 149.
1329. In *Collective Actions: Rethinking Funding and National Cost Rules*, The Competition Law Review, vol. 8, No. 1, December 2011, pp. 120 and 121.
1330. *See* Eda Şahin, *Collective Redress and EU Competition Law*, Routledge, 2019, p. 195.

the doctrinal proposals discussed above, as well as the innovations this book introduces to the debate.

Our proposal diverges significantly from earlier doctrinal contributions, primarily because those proposals predate key legal and institutional developments – such as Directive 2020/1828 and the European Parliament's Resolution on responsible private litigation funding. Notably, the Independent Study even predates the EU Damages Directive. As a result, those earlier models do not reflect the current legal landscape or the evolving needs of collective redress in competition law.

Moreover, this book's proposal addresses several critical dimensions that were either overlooked or treated differently in previous frameworks. These include empirical insights and legal design elements substantiated by the innovative comparative analysis presented in this study – specifically, the data summarised in the tables and graph above. That analysis spans more than a decade (2012-2024) and compares key parameters across paradigmatic Member State legal systems, offering a robust foundation for the refinements this study propose.[1331]

5.1 LEGISLATIVE INSTRUMENT: DIRECTIVE

From a coherence standpoint, it may appear that a collective action mechanism for competition law does not necessarily require adoption through a regulation – especially considering that both the general collective redress framework and the action for damages for breaches of competition rules were introduced via directives, in line with the principle of proportionality. In fact, the experience of transposing the EU Damages Directive partially contradicts the Independent Study's claim that harmonisation through a Directive would be ineffective. As discussed earlier, the limited impact of that directive stems not from the instrument itself, but from the selective and ambiguous nature of its harmonisation.[1332]

Specifically, the EU Damages Directive suffers from vague terminology, excessive discretion granted to Member States, and an overreliance on recitals to address substantive issues that should have been codified in the main legislative text. These factors have undermined the Directive's ability to achieve its objectives uniformly across the EU.[1333]

Nevertheless, considering the procedural nature of collective redress, the diversity of national legal systems, and the variety of possible funding models, we argue that a directive remains the most appropriate legislative instrument. It allows for necessary flexibility and adaptation to national contexts while still requiring Member States to actively engage in the pursuit of EU-level objectives through transposition.

This book does not dispute the need for Member State discretion in this area. However, also Directive 2020/1828 goes too far in this regard, to the point of

1331. *See* s. 3.4.7 above.
1332. *See* s. 2.2 above.
1333. *See* s. 2.3.1 above.

jeopardising its effectiveness. The Directive's minimum harmonisation approach – marked by a lack of clarity and excessive national leeway – has led to a fragmented landscape of collective action mechanisms across Europe, with limited practical impact.[1334]

This is particularly problematic in the context of competition law, where the effects of infringements are widely dispersed and often difficult for victims to perceive or quantify. Directive 2020/1828 leaves critical elements entirely to Member State discretion, including the following:

- The model of collective action (opt-in, opt-out, or hybrid), with ambiguous language such as consumers 'tacitly' expressing their will.[1335]
- The funding framework, where even public funding provisions are framed as non-binding recommendations.[1336]

These shortcomings raise the question of whether Directive 2020/1828 functions more as a recommendation than a true harmonisation instrument – precisely the issue this book aims to address with a proposed directive for competition law collective actions.

In conclusion, while this book disagrees with the Independent Study's preference for a regulation, we align with other scholars in asserting that a well-crafted directive, i.e., one that provides sufficient legal certainty and addresses the shortcomings of previous instruments, can effectively establish a collective redress mechanism for competition law at the EU level. This approach would also remain consistent with the EU's legislative tradition, as exemplified by both the EU Damages Directive and Directive 2020/1828.

5.2 SCOPE: COMPETITION LAW INFRINGEMENTS

As explored in detail above, competition law disputes possess distinct characteristics – particularly in terms of the complexity of detecting infringements, the evidentiary burden, and the widespread and diffuse nature of their effects, which often result in a large and scattered group of victims.

The comparative analysis of States above[1337] confirms this: those with specific rules on collective redress for competition law infringements – namely Portugal and the UK – have seen a significantly higher number of class actions in this area. In contrast, countries like Belgium and France, which lack such tailored mechanisms, have virtually no record of competition law collective actions.

The Independent Study, as previously noted, rightly advocated for the application of collective redress mechanisms to all disputes involving the enforcement of Articles 101

1334. *See* s. 3.3.7 above.
1335. *See* s. 3.3.7 above.
1336. *Ibid.*
1337. *See* s. 3.4.7 above.

and 102 TFEU, whether domestic or cross-border. This approach aligns with the broader logic of EU legislative instruments. For instance, the EU Damages Directive applies not only to EU competition law but also to national provisions that pursue the same objectives and are applied in parallel proceedings.[1338] In practice, all Member States have extended the scope of their transposing legislation to cover purely internal disputes as well.[1339]

Similarly, Directive 2020/1828 – although it excludes competition law – applies to both national and cross-border infringements of EU law, including national rules transposing such law.[1340] It also introduces distinct procedural rules for national and cross-border collective actions, depending on whether the qualified entity is designated in the same Member State or in another.[1341]

Indeed, the Independent Study's recommendation to apply collective redress mechanisms to both national and cross-border competition law disputes remains valid and consistent with the trajectory of EU legislative developments. The only notable exception is the artificial distinction introduced by Directive 2020/1828. In our view, a more coherent and effective approach would involve establishing common rules for representative entities, regardless of their Member State of origin. This would enhance both legal certainty and procedural efficiency in cross-border enforcement.

5.3 CLASS ACTION MODEL: OPT-OUT OR HYBRID

As previously discussed, this book aligns with the doctrinal consensus that the opt-in model is insufficient for ensuring effective collective redress in competition law. On this point, this study largely agrees with the proposals cited above. Notably, the European Commission itself appears to have retreated from its earlier preference for the opt-in model, as expressed in its 2013 Recommendation. Directive 2020/1828, while ambiguous, no longer mandates this model. Instead, it leaves the choice to Member States, stating that injured parties may express their will either 'expressly or tacitly'. However, the Directive fails to clarify whether 'tacit will' equates to an opt-out model[1342] – an omission that is particularly troubling given that the choice of model is the backbone of any collective redress system.

Recital 43 of Directive 2020/1828 further complicates the matter by referring to the right to opt in or out of the procedure, suggesting a shift in the Commission's stance. If the recital is not in conflict with the operative text, it may serve as an interpretative aid.[1343] This reflects a broader structural issue in EU legislative drafting, where recitals

1338. *See* Articles 1(1) and 2(1) and (3).
1339. *See* s. 2.3.1.1 above.
1340. *See* Article 2(1).
1341. *See* Article 3(6) and (7). *See* s. 3.3.7 above.
1342. *See* s. 3.3.7 above.
1343. In this regard, *see* Llio Humphreys et al., *Mapping Recitals to Normative Provisions in EU Legislation to Assist Legal Interpretation*, Legal Knowledge and Information Systems: JURIX 2015: The Twenty-Eighth Annual Conference, 9 January 2015, p. 4.

often contain substantive policy choices that were not formally adopted in the binding provisions.[1344]

In this book's view, the Directive's approach – based on minimum harmonisation and leaving critical design elements to Member State discretion – is inadequate for competition law. While this book acknowledges the Commission's step back from mandating opt-in, the sectoral collective redress mechanism this book proposes should adopt an opt-out model, or at the very least, a hybrid one.

Why Opt-Out Is Preferable

This book believes the opt-out model is the most appropriate for EU-level collective redress in competition law, for three main reasons:

(1) *For injured parties*: opt-out is the only model that offers a realistic chance of compensation for SMEs and consumers, especially in cases involving large numbers of victims and low individual damages – typical of competition law infringements. The cost and complexity of such actions make opt-in models practically inaccessible.
(2) *For representatives, funders, and lawyers*: the ability to represent a broad class of victims increases the attractiveness of these actions for those who must invest time and resources. Private funders require a return on investment, and even representative bodies and lawyers are more likely to engage if they can recover a portion of the compensation or gain reputational benefits.
(3) *For infringers and National Courts*: consolidating all claims into a single proceeding avoids duplicative litigation, reduces the risk of conflicting judgments, and promotes procedural efficiency.

The importance of incentives cannot be overstated. The UK's decision to empower the CAT to hear opt-out class actions (both follow-on and stand-alone) was driven by the recognition that opt-in models failed to attract claimants or funders.[1345] Opt-out also enhances legal certainty by reducing the risk of inconsistent rulings.

Empirical Support

This book's comparative analysis (*see* tables and graph)[1346] shows that Member States with opt-out or hybrid regimes – *Portugal and the UK* – have seen *seventy-four competition law class actions over the past decade*, compared to just one in France. Belgium, despite having a hybrid model until 2024, recorded zero such actions (and made opt-in the default option now) – underscoring that a theoretically favourable regime is not enough.[1347] Incentives and cost structures matter.

1344. *See* Maarten den Heijer, Teun van Os van den Abeelen and Antanina Maslyka, *On the Use and Misuse of Recitals in European Union Law*, Amsterdam Law School Research Paper No. 2019-31, 3 September 2029, p. 19.
1345. *See* s. 3.4.4.1 above.
1346. *See* s. 3.4.7 above.
1347. *See* s. 3.6.5 above.

Legal Tradition and Misconceptions

The opt-out model is not alien to European legal traditions. Several Member States already employ it. Moreover, fears of litigation abuse, often cited by the European Commission, are unfounded. The EU's legal safeguards, including judicial oversight and the absence of punitive damages, make US-style excesses unlikely.[1348]

While this book agrees with the Independent Study and other scholars on the need to include opt-out mechanisms in the sectoral solution, it views the hybrid model as a pragmatic compromise. If political realities make a pure opt-out model unfeasible, a hybrid regime - where National Courts determine the appropriate model based on the characteristics of the case - could still deliver meaningful redress.

Indeed, while maintaining an opt-in model for class actions may appeal to certain stakeholders and facilitate political approval - particularly given that any EU-level initiative on competition law collective redress will require the support of Member States - this book remains unconvinced by the assumption, implicit in some of the proposals discussed above, that small-scale victims of competition law infringements are likely to initiate or even join such actions voluntarily. Experience suggests otherwise.

Given the added value of a comprehensive collective redress model, we also question the legal basis on which a National Court could reasonably insist on applying an opt-in approach in such cases. More fundamentally, we strongly disagree with the suggestion - such as that advanced by Eda Şahin - that courts should be granted discretion to determine the applicable model. If discretion is to be permitted at all, the criteria guiding such decisions must be clearly and explicitly defined in legislation.

This book's proposal, therefore, aligns with the view that national legal systems should not only be required to establish mechanisms for collective redress in competition law but also be obliged to adopt an opt-out model as the default. This model offers the greatest likelihood of delivering effective compensation to victims. That said, we acknowledge that in certain circumstances, an opt-in process may be appropriate as a subsidiary option.

Considering the European Commission's evolving stance - initially distancing itself from the US class action model, then recommending opt-in, and more recently leaving the choice of model to Member States - this book recognises that a legislative push for a single, EU-wide opt-out model may be politically unfeasible, even if it would be the most effective solution.

If, as seems more plausible and constructive, a hybrid system is adopted - requiring each Member State to implement a collective redress mechanism that allows for both opt-in and opt-out models - then National Courts will need to conduct a structured analysis, akin to the certification process currently employed by the UK's CAT.[1349] This would involve the following.

1348. *See* s. 3.3.1 above.
1349. *See* s. 3.4.4.2 above.

Role of the National Court in Hybrid Models

In a hybrid system, the National Court should assess the following:

- The definition of the class (based on shared elements: infringement, harm, and causality).[1350]
- The absence of conflicting interests within the group.[1351]
- The feasibility of identifying and mobilising claimants.

Opt-in should be reserved only for small, easily identifiable groups with high individual damages. In such cases, opt-in may even enhance participation and control. But for large, diffuse groups, opt-out is essential to avoid excessive burdens on claimants and ensure access to justice.

Final Position

In conclusion, while this book recognises the political and legislative complexities involved, it firmly advocates for a *mandatory opt-out model for competition law collective actions at the EU level*. If that proves unattainable, a *hybrid model – anchored in clear legal criteria and judicial discretion – should be the minimum standard*. What must be avoided is the continuation of a fragmented, underperforming system that fails to deliver compensation to victims or deterrence to infringers.

5.4 ACCESS TO EVIDENCE: PRE-FILING PHASE

Access to evidence has long been identified as one of the principal barriers to the effective private enforcement of competition law. While the EU Damages Directive introduced the binding effect of final infringement decisions and restricted access to certain documents - such as leniency statements - it did not resolve the broader evidentiary challenges. These issues are even more pronounced in the context of class actions. As previously discussed,[1352] opt-in models require the identification of individual claimants, which is only feasible with sufficient access to evidence. Even in opt-out actions, National Courts must still define the class, which similarly depends on early evidentiary access.

Neither the EU Damages Directive nor Directive 2020/1828[1353] provides mechanisms for accessing evidence at the pre-litigation stage. This omission is particularly problematic in collective redress, where the complexity and scale of competition law infringements demand early access to key information to substantiate claims.

Therefore, any proposal for a directive establishing a sector-specific collective action mechanism in competition law must include a provision for pre-filing access to

1350. *Ibid.*
1351. *See* Steven Van Uytsel, *Collective Actions in a Competition Law Context: Reconciling Multiplayer Interests to Enhance Access to Justice, in Collective Actions: Enhancing Access to Justice and Reconciling Multilayer Interests?*, Stefan Wrbka, Steven Van Uytsel and Mathias Siems (eds), Cambridge University Press, 2012, p. 71.
1352. *See* s. 3.6.3 above.
1353. *Ibid.*

evidence. This mechanism should be subject to appropriate safeguards - such as requiring a demonstration that, without such access, it would be impossible to substantiate the essential facts of the claim, particularly those necessary for a class certification.

5.5 ELIGIBLE APPLICANTS: ANY INJURED PARTY AUTHORISED BY LAW OR NATIONAL COURT

One of the reasons existing national collective redress mechanisms - and Directive 2020/1828 in particular - have focused primarily on consumers is the potential for conflicts of interest among injured parties.[1354] For example, in a cartel scenario where the final retail price of a product or service is inflated due to anticompetitive conduct, consumers who purchase directly from the infringers suffer equivalent harm. However, the situation becomes more complex when direct purchasers (e.g., distributors) pass on part of the overcharge to indirect purchasers (e.g., consumers). In such cases, the interests of direct purchasers (who seek compensation for the portion of the overcharge they absorbed) may not align with those of indirect purchasers (who seek compensation for the portion passed on).[1355]

Despite this complexity, both groups have a legitimate interest in being compensated. While US Courts generally do not certify indirect purchaser class actions,[1356] the European approach - particularly in the UK, whose regime is closest to the US model - does not distinguish between direct and indirect purchaser claims.[1357] Nor does Directive 2020/1828. In fact, even in the US, as Gary A. Winters has noted,[1358] combining direct and indirect purchaser claims in a single proceeding is often the most efficient approach in terms of time, cost, and judicial resources.

It is worth recalling the European Commission's earlier proposal - ultimately excluded from the final text of Directive 2020/1828 - for a purely declaratory class action in cases where quantifying individual compensation would be too complex.[1359] This would have allowed consumers to pursue individual claims for damages after a collective declaration of liability. While we support the removal of this proposal, it illustrates the EU legislator's concern about overly individualised analysis in collective actions. However, this concern is less justified when actions are brought by qualified

1354. *See* Eda Şahin, *Collective Redress and EU Competition Law*, Routledge, 2019, p. 146.
1355. *See* Steven Van Uytsel, *Collective Actions in a Competition Law Context: Reconciling Multi-player Interests to Enhance Access to Justice, in Collective Actions: Enhancing Access to Justice and Reconciling Multilayer Interests?*, Stefan Wrbka, Steven Van Uytsel and Mathias Siems (eds), Cambridge University Press, 2012, p. 71.
1356. *See* US Supreme Court, *Illinois Brick Co. v. Illinois*, Case 431 U.S. 720 (1977).
1357. *See* Michael D. Hausfeld and Irving Scher, *Can U.S. Class Action Law Serve as Guidelines for the UK Indirect Purchaser Mastercard Case?*, Hausfeld Competition Bulletin, 18 August 2020, available at Hausfeld | Can U.S. class action law serve as guidelines for the UK indirect purchaser Mastercard case?.
1358. *Trial Issues in Consolidated Direct and Indirect Purchaser Cases: Lessons from the Sram Litigation*, ABA Antitrust Trial Practice Newsletter, Spring 2011, available at trialissues.pdf (mayerbrown.com), p. 4.
1359. *See* s. 3.3.7 above.

entities, typically consumer associations, where internal conflicts of interest are unlikely.[1360]

What seems essential is that any person – whether or not a member (ideological claimant)[1361] of the injured class – should be able to bring a collective action in competition law, provided they are either:

- *legally empowered*, as in Portugal, where not only consumer protection associations and foundations but also business associations (e.g., representing SMEs) may bring actions on behalf of their members;[1362] or
- *judicially authorised*, as in the UK, where the CAT assesses whether it is fair and reasonable for a proposed representative to act, based on objective criteria.[1363]

While this book agrees with Eda Şahin that consumer-only groups are less prone to internal conflicts, this should not preclude SMEs from initiating collective actions. As the Independent Study rightly argues, SMEs are also victims of competition law infringements and face similar barriers to individual redress. Excluding them would undermine the effectiveness of Articles 101 and 102 TFEU.

Limiting standing to SME representative organisations is also insufficient. Belgium, for instance, grants standing to the Interprofessional Organisation for the Protection of SMEs, yet no competition law class actions had been filed by the end of 2024.[1364] This may reflect a lack of legal or financial capacity within such organisations.

Finally, while some have suggested granting NCAs powers to represent injured parties or engage in private enforcement (akin to a *parens patriae* model),[1365] we believe this would raise serious and likely insurmountable conflicts of interest. NCAs are public enforcers and should not simultaneously act as private claimants.

5.6 INCENTIVES: COMPENSATION FOR LAWYERS AND PRIVATE FUNDERS

In the US,[1366] the modus operandi for class actions is predominantly lawyer-driven. Typically, it is the lawyer who identifies a potential cause of action – such as an infringement or a decision confirming a breach of antitrust law – and then seeks out a

1360. *See* Articles 3 and 4.
1361. *See* Eda Şahin, *Collective Redress and EU Competition Law*, Routledge, 2019, p. 153.
1362. *See* Article 19(2) of Law 23/2018. *See* s. 3.4.3.1 above.
1363. If such a person: (i) has acted fairly and properly in the interests of the members of the class; (ii) does not have, in relation to matters common to the members of the class, a material interest conflicting with the interests of the members of the class; (iii) is the most suitable, in the event that there is more than one applicant for approval to act as representative of the class in question; (iv) has the financial capacity to pay the costs recoverable by the defendant, if ordered to do so; and (v) will be able to satisfy any undertaking as to damages required by the CAT where an interim injunction is sought. *See* ss 47B(8) of the Competition Act 1998 and 79(2) of the Competition Tribunal Rules 2015. *See* s. 3.4.4.1 above.
1364. *See* s. 3.4.7 above.
1365. *See* s. 3.6.1.7 above.
1366. *See* s. 3.4 above.

willing individual to serve as the lead plaintiff representing the class. Lawyers also play a central role in locating other injured parties who meet the criteria set out in Rule 23, often through public outreach methods like newspaper or television advertisements. A notable example is the Norplant breast implant case,[1367] where women were encouraged to join the action via media campaigns.

This approach is largely incentivised by the contingency fee structure: the larger the class, the greater the potential payout for the lawyer in the event of a successful outcome. This is especially significant in the US context, where damages (particularly in competition law cases) can be punitive and are commonly tripled.[1368]

Ethical rules governing lawyers vary significantly across jurisdictions,[1369] particularly with respect to fee arrangements and advertising practices. As previously discussed, the permissibility of *quota litis* agreements or contingency fees differs across Europe.[1370] Advertising is another area where national regulations diverge. While the general prohibition on lawyer advertising has been lifted in most countries, many still impose deontological restrictions. These rules often draw a distinction between permissible advertising and impermissible propaganda,[1371] maintaining professional integrity while allowing for limited promotional activity.

In particular, the European Lawyers' Code of Conduct explicitly prohibited *quota litis* agreements, stating that 'a lawyer shall not be entitled to make a pactum de quota litis'. It also permitted publicity, provided it is truthful and objective.[1372]

National regulations often go further. For instance, the Portuguese Bar Association Statute not only bans *quota litis* agreements but also prohibits unsolicited direct advertising[1373] – effectively ruling out the kind of client solicitation common in the US. France maintains similar restrictions, forbidding lawyers from soliciting clients in person or by telephone. In Spain, the rules are even more specific: lawyers are prohibited from inciting litigation or conflict, whether generically or specifically, and from offering professional services to victims of accidents, disasters, public calamities, or other events involving mass harm, unless explicitly requested by the victim.[1374]

It is important to note, however, that several Member States – including the Czech Republic, Estonia, Hungary, Latvia, Lithuania, Malta, Slovakia, and even Germany – currently permit *quota litis* agreements or contingency fees, albeit under specific limitations. A similar approach is followed in the UK, where contingency fees are

1367. *See* Jill E. Fisch, *Class Action Reform, Qui Tam, and the Role of the Plaintiff*, Penn Law, Legal Scholarship Repository, 1997, p. 171.
1368. *See* s. 3.4.1 above.
1369. *See* Sjoerd Claessens et al., *Evaluation of the Legal Framework for the Free Movement of Lawyers*, Final Report, Project number: BA03973, Study has been financed by the European Commission, DG Internal Market and Services (MARKT/2011/071/E), 28 November 2012, p. 103.
1370. *See* s. 3.6.5.4 above.
1371. *See* Pedro Petiz Viana, *Online Legal Platforms: The Beginning of the 4.0 Law Practice?*, UNIO – EU Law Journal, vol. 5, No. 2, July 2019, pp. 43-62, p. 45 https://doi.org/10.21814/unio.5.2.2291.
1372. *See* Articles 2.6-1 and 3.3-1.
1373. *See* Articles 94(4)e) and 106.
1374. *Law Firm Advertising Rules Around the World – Interlegal.*

allowed exclusively in opt-in actions, while conditional fee arrangements are permitted across all types of class actions.[1375]

All of the above proposals suggest that the limited development of competition law class actions in the EU cannot be effectively addressed without introducing contingency fee arrangements in those Member States where they are currently prohibited.

Charlotte Leskinen goes further, arguing that the European Commission should initially recommend the adoption of contingency fees. In a second phase (once collective redress mechanisms become more widespread), she advocates for the mandatory incorporation of such fee structures into national legislation. This, she contends, should be accompanied by binding rules for Member States on cost capping and exceptions to the 'loser pays' principle, drawing inspiration from existing EU legislation on intellectual property.[1376]

Similarly, Eda Şahin supports the introduction of both conditional and contingency fee arrangements. However, she also proposes a more transformative shift: the adoption of the US model, which places lawyers at the centre of the litigation initiative. According to Şahin, this model raises important questions about how to monitor lawyers' performance to ensure alignment with the interests of the represented group.[1377]

On this point, this book largely disagrees with the proposals advanced thus far. As previously noted,[1378] both the prohibition of *quota litis* agreements and the application of the loser pays principle are deeply rooted in European legal tradition. While there are exceptions – ranging from newer Member States to the UK and even one of the founding Member States, Germany – these remain limited and context-specific. A legislative initiative at the EU level that would mandate the abandonment of these legal constructs risks not only undermining long-standing legal cultures but also facing significant political resistance. Such a proposal should therefore be approached with caution and not be made lightly.

Although we acknowledge that removing certain procedural barriers could facilitate the use of class actions in competition law, we remain unconvinced by the assumption that such reforms are essential. In our view, the rationale underpinning the loser pays principle is more compelling than that behind the prohibition of *quota litis* agreements. The former is grounded in the idea of rewarding meritorious claims or incentivising settlement, while the latter rests on the presumption of a conflict of interest between a lawyer's ethical obligations and the pursuit of profit.

Importantly, despite the theoretical appeal of relaxing these rules, there is no empirical evidence establishing a causal link between their existence and the low number of competition law class actions in the EU. Correlation alone does not justify sweeping legislative changes, particularly when such changes would challenge long-standing legal traditions and risk unintended consequences.

1375. *See* s. 3.6.5.4 above.
1376. *See* Charlotte Leskinen, *Collective Actions: Rethinking Funding and National Cost Rules*, The Competition Law Review, vol. 8, No. 1, December 2011, p. 117.
1377. *See* Eda Şahin, *Collective Redress and EU Competition Law*, Routledge, 2019, p. 152.
1378. *See* ss 3.6.5.4 and 3.6.5.5 above.

Indeed, the comparative analysis of European paradigm case – summarised in the table and figure above[1379] – did not reveal that the legal traditions discussed were decisive factors in determining the number of existing lawsuits.

In fact, all States apply the loser pays principle (though in the UK, the Court has discretion in its application). Notably, until 2025, at least seventy-one lawsuits were filed in Portugal and the UK combined, compared to just one in France and none in Belgium. This disparity suggests that the presence of the loser pays principle alone does not account for the variation in the number of competition law class actions across Member States.

Moreover, the example cited by Charlotte Leskinen – namely, the limitation of the costs recoverable by the losing party – is not, strictly speaking, a derogation from the loser pays principle, but rather a cost cap. As she herself acknowledges, this is reflected in Article 14 of Directive 2004/48/EC,[1380] which provides that 'Member States shall ensure that reasonable and proportionate legal costs and other expenses incurred by the successful party shall, as a general rule, be borne by the unsuccessful party, unless equity does not allow this.'

However, the ECJ has clarified that this provision cannot justify national legislation that imposes fixed cost ceilings significantly below the average fees typically charged for legal services in that Member State.[1381] In other words, the Directive merely aims to ensure that reimbursable costs are reasonable, taking into account factors such as the nature of the dispute, the amount at stake, and the complexity of the legal work involved.[1382]

Consequently, a provision of this kind – far from having a substantial practical impact – may in fact serve as a further disincentive for lawyers to invest in such cases.

What was previously observed regarding the loser pays principle in the table and figure[1383] also applies to the prohibition of *quota litis* agreements. In the examined jurisdictions, only success fees are permitted, with the exception of the UK where *quota litis* agreements are allowed but only in opt-in class actions.

On this point, there appears to be a contradiction in Charlotte Leskinen's proposal. It is unclear why, in a context where collective actions are largely absent, she advocates only a non-binding recommendation from the European Commission, yet, at a later stage – when the urgency for intervention would presumably be lower – she proposes a legislative imposition. This sequencing seems inconsistent and raises questions about the underlying rationale.

However, assigning lawyers the primary responsibility for initiating and promoting class actions – as proposed by Eda Şahin[1384] and, to some extent, Charlotte Leskinen, who even suggests that lawyers should bear the opposing party's costs in the event of

1379. *See* s. 3.4.7 above.
1380. *See* s. 3.6.4 above.
1381. *See United Video Properties v. Telenet NV*, of 28 July 2016, Case C-57/15, p. 26.
1382. *See* Yves Van Couter et al., *IP Alert: Ground-Breaking CJEU Judgment on Reimbursement of Lawyers' Fees in IP Litigation*, 2 August 2016, available at IP Alert: Ground-breaking CJEU judgment on reimbursement of lawyers' fees in IP litigation - Ludology.
1383. *See* s. 3.4.7 above.
1384. *See* Eda Şahin, *Collective Redress and EU Competition Law*, Routledge, 2019, p. 166.

defeat[1385] – stands in tension with the ethical traditions of many Member States. These traditions diverge significantly from the North American model of the legal profession, which is more commercially oriented and litigation-driven. In several European jurisdictions, such a shift would challenge long-standing conceptions of legal ethics and professional responsibility.

What is more, the general authorisation of success fees serves as a strong incentive for lawyers to invest their own resources in litigation. It encourages them to reduce or even waive fixed fees, particularly in jurisdictions where there are no caps or limitations on the percentage of the overall compensation they may claim. This flexibility can significantly enhance access to justice by aligning the lawyer's financial interest with the success of the case.

The data presented in the table and figure above[1386] clearly indicate that in those Member States where representative organisations have access to funding, the number of competition law class actions has increased significantly. This is unsurprising, given that consumer protection associations (typically the entities authorised to bring such actions) are non-profit organisations that often lack both the financial and technical resources, particularly in the field of competition law, to initiate and sustain complex litigation. For this reason, we must disagree with Eda Şahin's argument[1387] that these organisations should remain the sole actors entitled to bring collective actions, based solely on the legal traditions of the Member States. Her position appears internally inconsistent: while she invokes European legal heritage to justify the continued role of these organisations, she simultaneously proposes a departure from that same tradition by advocating for the introduction of contingency fees (precisely to address the funding challenges these organisations face. This contradiction underscores the need for a more coherent and context-sensitive approach to reform).

This is not to say that such entities should be excluded from bringing collective actions; rather, they should not hold exclusive standing, as previously argued, particularly because they may not represent the most effective solution. This is precisely why the concept of 'qualified entities' adopted in Directive 2020/1828 is inadequate in the context of competition law, at least in the absence of a requirement to permit private funding. Indeed, not only does the Directive fail to mandate such financial support but it also includes a provision allowing individual consumers to be held liable for procedural costs resulting from intentional or negligent conduct. This clause, due to its vagueness, risks deterring consumer participation in opt-in actions.[1388]

Such a framework does not serve the specific demands of competition law enforcement (and arguably falls short even in the consumer law context). If it were truly effective, one could simply advocate for its extension to competition litigation without the need for further legislative intervention at the EU level.

1385. In *Collective Actions: Rethinking Funding and National Cost Rules, The Competition Law Review*, vol. 8, No. 1, December 2011, p. 109.

1386. *See* s. 3.4.7 above.

1387. *See* Eda Şahin, *Collective Redress and EU Competition Law*, Routledge, 2019, pp. 126, 136, 148 and 156.

1388. *See* s. 3.3.7 above.

In reality, litigation costs remain the primary barrier to initiating competition law class actions. If the preferred approach - arguably the most appropriate and politically feasible for EU-level legislation and national transposition - is to preserve foundational legal traditions such as the loser pays principle and the prohibition of *quota litis* agreements, then the solution must lie in promoting access to public or private funding mechanisms. Without such financial support, the procedural framework alone is unlikely to generate meaningful increases in collective redress activity in this area.

It was from this perspective that this book examined the viability of public funding,[1389] after-the-event (ATE) insurance,[1390] and private litigation funding.[1391] Our analysis concluded that the first two mechanisms are not only insufficient but also raise several concerns. As previously discussed,[1392] the costs associated with collective actions, particularly in the field of antitrust law, extend far beyond legal fees. They stem largely from the complexity of these cases and the multitude of actors involved. More specifically, they include the costs of initiating proceedings, issuing notices, navigating the certification phase (where applicable), covering lawyers' and economic experts' fees (often payable at least in part upfront), as well as managing compensation distribution in the event of success, and other court-related or party-incurred expenses.

While class actions, especially under the opt-out model, can generate economies of scale and efficiency in resource allocation, the overall costs remain substantial - arguably too high to be sustainably covered by public funding alone.

Furthermore, as previously discussed,[1393] the use of public funds to support civil litigation remains contentious (even when those funds originate from collected fines). While the creation of a special fund financed by undistributed compensation, as proposed by Eda Şahin, may appear more acceptable given that the original beneficiaries are private individuals, this approach raises important legal and ethical concerns. If compensation rightfully belongs to the claimants, diverting a portion of it to a third party - such as a public fund - would require their explicit consent through a formal funding agreement. More critically, this proposal fails to address the core issue: the current scarcity of collective actions and, consequently, the absence of compensation to redistribute. In this context, the proposed mechanism is not only premature but also ineffective in resolving the underlying problem of insufficient litigation activity in competition law.

The same concerns apply to legal ATE insurance. As previously discussed,[1394] these mechanisms are ill-suited to the high costs associated with this type of litigation, which extend well beyond court fees and often require significant upfront payments. Legal aid, in particular, presents additional challenges: in some Member States, it does not permit the assignment of legal persons in competition cases to lawyers with relevant expertise. ATE insurance, meanwhile, typically covers only the opposing party's costs

1389. *See* s. 3.6.5.3 above.
1390. *See* s. 3.6.5.6 above.
1391. *See* s. 3.6.5.1 above.
1392. *Ibid.*
1393. *See* s. 3.6.5.3 above.
1394. *See* ss 3.6.5.3 and 3.6.5.6 above.

in the event of a loss and is generally unattractive to insurers unless the premium is set at a high level – thereby discouraging claimants from using this option in the first place.

In addition to the exemption from court fees – as implemented in Portugal,[1395] which this book considers a positive measure – the most viable public funding mechanism, in this book's view,[1396] would be the creation of a national or EU-level fund financed through the Union's budget.[1397] However, if such a solution were to be adopted, it should be conceived as a temporary measure aimed at jumpstarting this type of litigation. Even then, it is not the approach this book advocates. The use of public funds should be avoided, particularly when private funding mechanisms have proven effective and profitable – not only in the US, where they originated, but also in European jurisdictions such as the UK and Portugal, albeit with varying degrees of regulatory oversight.

This book advocates for a model in which the costs associated with competition law class actions are privately financed in exchange for a percentage of the total compensation awarded. When combined with success fees for lawyers – also calculated as a percentage of the compensation – this approach offers a pragmatic and sustainable solution for fostering collective redress in the EU. It aligns financial incentives with case outcomes, reduces the burden on public resources, and has already demonstrated viability in other jurisdictions.

This study further argues that litigation funding should be subject to regulation[1398] – ideally through the same directive that required Member States to establish a specific collective action regime for competition law, as previously discussed.

This book's support for regulating private litigation funding – despite its existing presence in several Member States without formal oversight – is not driven[1399] by concerns over abusive litigation. As previously noted, such fears are largely unfounded in the EU context: (i) there is no litigation culture comparable to that of the US and (ii) funders are incentivised to support only meritorious claims, particularly follow-on actions, since they are remunerated only in the event of success and may be liable for the opposing party's costs in the event of defeat. This economic logic naturally steers funders towards viable cases, especially those benefiting from the evidentiary presumptions established under Article 9 of the EU Damages Directive.

This book believes that regulating public funding is justified (as previously argued)[1400] due to its incentivising effect on beneficiaries. Such regulation would provide legal certainty that funders are professional, possess the necessary economic capacity, and operate under ethical principles that ensure both the absence of conflicts of interest and the protection of confidential information.

1395. *See* Table 3.1 – Comparison of Antitrust Class Actions in Selected European Jurisdictions, s. 3.4.7 above.
1396. *See* s. 3.6.5.3 above.
1397. *See* Eda Şahin, *Collective Redress and EU Competition Law*, Routledge, 2019, p. 159.
1398. *See* Michael Napier et al., *Improved Access to Justice: Funding Options & Proportionate Costs, A Series of Recommendations to the Lord Chancellor to Improve Access to Justice through the Development of Improved Funding Structures*, Civil Justice Council, June 2007, p. 53.
1399. *See* s. 3.6.5.1.1 above.
1400. *See* s. 3.6.5.1.2 above.

The European Parliament's initiative to recommend the adoption of a directive on this matter is a step in the right direction.[1401] However, as previously argued[1402] and in contrast to the Parliament's recommendation, it is essential to eliminate Member States' discretion in allowing such mechanisms. These mechanisms are crucial to addressing the current shortage of litigation and, consequently, the lack of compensation for small victims (primarily SMEs and consumers) of competition law violations within the EU. Allowing Member States discretion in this area would risk creating unequal conditions in the enforcement of Articles 101 and 102 of the TFEU.

Among the criticisms this study raised[1403] regarding the European Parliament's Resolution on responsible private funding of litigation, one particularly noteworthy omission is the exclusion of defendants as potential beneficiaries of such funding. While this may be a less common scenario, if the resolution's objective is to ensure a level playing field between injured parties and offenders, then the possibility of defendants accessing private funding should also be considered.

Finally, this book supports the introduction of a cap on the percentage of remuneration for third-party funders and lawyers, provided it adheres to the principle of proportionality. This cap could be determined either by the National Courts, based on the complexity of the case, or established by law, as suggested by the European Parliament.[1404]

However, this book strongly opposes the imposition of joint and several liability on third-party funders or lawyers for litigation costs. Such liability undermines the necessary separation between these entities and the parties to the proceedings - separation that is vital to avoiding conflicts of interest and maintaining incentives for investment. It is worth noting that, as previously mentioned,[1405] the European Parliament proposes that third-party funders should have no control over the management of litigation costs, yet paradoxically recommends granting National Courts or administrative authorities the power to order them to bear those costs. Instead, the appropriate role of these authorities should be to determine the share of overall compensation allocated to funders and lawyers[1406] - particularly in opt-out collective actions, where the absence of identified beneficiaries at the outset makes it impossible for them to commit to reimbursing the funders.

In summary, this book advocates a model that combines the following:

- *Success fees* for lawyers, already permitted in most Member States.
- *TPLF*, regulated to ensure transparency, financial capacity, and ethical safeguards.

1401. *See* s. 3.3.8 above.
1402. *See* s. 3.6.5.1.2 above.
1403. *See* s. 3.3.8 above.
1404. *See* s. 3.3.7 above.
1405. *Ibid.*
1406. *See* s. 3.6.5.2 above.

- *Optional public funding,*[1407] ideally through a temporary EU or national fund financed through the EU's budget,[1408] to stimulate early adoption.

Also, *this book supports the European Parliament's initiative to regulate private funding* but stresses that Member States should not have discretion on this. Allowing such discretion would perpetuate disparities in the enforcement of Articles 101 and 102 TFEU. Regulation should include the following:

- Licensing and oversight of funders.
- Transparency of funding agreements.
- Proportional caps on funders' and lawyers' remunerations.
- Clear separation between funders and parties to avoid conflicts of interest.

In conclusion, *the key to unlocking competition law class actions in the EU lies not in dismantling foundational legal principles, but in enabling a robust, regulated framework for private funding* - complemented by *success fees* and, where necessary, transitional *public support.*

1407. *See* Table 3.1 - Comparison of Antitrust Class Actions in Selected European Jurisdictions, s. 3.4.7 above.
1408. *See* Eda Şahin, *Collective Redress and EU Competition Law*, Routledge, 2019, p. 159.

CHAPTER 6

Conclusion: Why and How a Competition Law Class Action Mechanism Should Be Established at EU Level

To revisit the central questions posed at the outset:

(i) Is it necessary to create a competition law class action mechanism at the EU level?
(ii) If so, in what form?

This book aims to offer an innovative solution to a clearly defined legal problem. One of the core objectives of the EU Damages Directive was to ensure the consistent and effective application of EU competition law – specifically Articles 101 and 102 TFEU – by strengthening the right to compensation for those harmed by anticompetitive conduct. This objective is rooted in the principle of effectiveness of EU law, which includes the right to effective judicial protection.

However, as this study has demonstrated, that objective has not been achieved. SMEs and consumers remain largely unprotected. The complexity of competition law disputes, the asymmetry of information between parties, and the high costs relative to the typically low individual harm make individual actions impractical. For these groups, only a class action mechanism can realistically ensure access to redress and judicial protection.

Given the scarcity of competition law class actions across the EU and the fragmentation of national legal frameworks, this book proposes the adoption of a dedicated EU-level mechanism for collective redress in competition law – an area notably excluded from Directive 2020/1828 supposed harmonisation. This mechanism should be complemented by the EU institutions' recent initiatives to regulate private litigation funding, which must be strengthened, particularly regarding funders' obligations and the removal of Member State discretion in this domain (where costs are an obstacle to the exercise of the right to redress by injured parties, especially SMEs and consumers, for reasons of economic rationality).

Our Proposal: A Distinctive and Balanced Framework

Our proposal, which diverges from existing models, consists of the following key elements:

(1) *A Directive,* as the legislative instrument, respecting the EU's legal tradition and allowing for national adaptation.
(2) *Scope*: Applicable to collective actions involving infringements of Articles 101 and 102 TFEU.
(3) *Model*: A mandatory opt-out regime, with the possibility for Member States to also allow opt-in actions. In such cases, National Courts must assess whether the number of injured parties is small and easily identifiable, and whether the individual harm is significant enough to justify opt-in.
(4) *Evidence access*: a mechanism for pre-filing access to evidence, essential for substantiating the core facts of the action (to be combined with the EU Damages Directive provisions).
(5) *Standing*: legal standing granted to any person (excluding public enforcers), whether or not a member of the injured class, provided they are authorised by law or by judicial approval - mirroring models in Portugal and the UK.
(6) *Funding*: regulation of private litigation funding, allowing funders to cover the costs of the action in exchange for a share of the compensation, alongside success fees for lawyers.

Why This Proposal Is Innovative

Unlike proposals that seek to replicate the US model, our approach is rooted in EU legal principles and institutional realities. It aims to resolve the persistent under-enforcement of competition law in a way that is both effective and politically viable. It respects core legal traditions - such as the prohibition of punitive damages, the loser pays principle (with the possibility of caps), and restrictions on *quota litis* agreements - while introducing targeted innovations to overcome structural barriers to access to justice.

Final Reflection

Harmonising collective redress in competition law must be guided by the general principles of the EU law, the effectiveness of EU competition law, and the legal traditions of the Member States. Without a coherent and enforceable EU-level mechanism, the right to redress for SMEs and consumers will remain illusory, and the private enforcement of competition law will continue to fall short of its intended goals.

APPENDIX I

EU Damages Directive Implementation Table

Member State	*Legislation Adopted*	*Date*
Germany	Neuntes Gesetz zur Änderung des Gesetzes gegen Wettbewerbsbeschränkungen	8 June 2017
Austria	Kartell- und Wettbewerbsrechts-Änderungsgesetz 2017	24 April 2017
Belgium	Loi portant insertion d'un Titre 3 'L'action en dommages et intérêts pour les infractions au droit de la concurrence' dans le Livre XVII du Code de droit économique	6 June 2017
Bulgaria	Закон за изменение и допълнение на Закона за защита на конкуренцията	3 January 2018
Cyprus	Αριθμός 113(Ι) του 2017	21 July 2017
Croatia	Zakon o postupcima naknade štete zbog povreda prava tržišnog naTJUEecanja	5 July 2017

Member State	*Legislation Adopted*	*Date*
Denmark	Lov om behandling af erstatningssager vedrørende overtrædelser af konkurrenceretten	13 December 2016
Slovakia	ZÁKON z 29. novembra 2016 o niektorých pravidlách uplatňovania nárokov na náhradu škody spôsobenej porušením práva hospodárskej sút'aže	29 November 2016
Slovenia	Zakon o spremembah in dopolnitvah Zakona o preprečevanju omejevanja konkurence	3 May 2017
Spain	Real Decreto-ley 9/2017, de 26 de mayo, por el que se transponen directivas of the European Union in the financial, commercial and health fields, and on the displacement of workers	27 May 2017
Estonia	Konkurentsiseaduse muutmise ja sellega seonduvalt teiste seaduste muutmise seadus	10 May 2017
Finland	Laki kilpailuoikeudellisist vahingonkorvauksista Laki kilpailulain muuttamisesta	14 December 2016
France	Decree No. 2017-305 of 9 March 2017 on actions for damages and interests arising from anticompetitive practices Ordonnance n° 2017-303 du 9 mars 2017 relative aux actions en dommages et intérêts du fait des pratiques anticoncurrentielles	10 March 2017

Member State	*Legislation Adopted*	*Date*
Greece	ΝΟΜΟΣ ΥΠ' ΑΡΙΘΜ. 4529 – Ενσωμάτωση στην ελληνική νομοθεσία της Οδηγίας 2014/104/ΕΕ	23 March 2018
Hungary	Törvény a tisztességtelen piaci magatartás és a versenykorlátozás tilalmáról szóló 1996. évi LVII. évi XLVII. törvény módosításáról	13 June 2017
Ireland	EU (Actions for Damages) Regulations 2017	17 February 2017
Italy	LEGISLATIVE DECREE 19 gennaio 2017, n. 3 Implementation of Directive 2014/104/EU	19 January 2017
Latvia	Grozījumi Konkurences likumā	5 October 2017
	Grozījumi Civilprocesa likumā	19 October 2017
Lithuania	Pakeisti Lietuvos Respublikos konkurencijos įstatymą Nr. VIII-1099	12 January 2017
Luxembourg	Loi relative à certaines règles régissant les actions en dommages et intérêts pour les violations du droit de la concurrence et modifiant la loi modifiée du 23 octobre 2011 relative à la concurrence	5 December 2016
Malta	Competition Law Infringements (Actions for Damages) Regulations 2017	26 April 2017
	Competition (Amendment) Act 2017	13 October 2017
The Netherlands	Wet houdende wijziging van Boek 6 van het Burgerlijk Wetboek en het Wetboek van Burgerlijke Rechtsvordering	25 January 2017

Member State	*Legislation Adopted*	*Date*
Poland	USTAWA or roszczeniach or naprawienie szkody wyrządzonej przez naruszenie prawa konkurencji	21 April 2017
Portugal	Law No. 23/2018, of 5 June - Right to compensation for infringement of competition law, transposes Directive 2014/104/EU, and makes the first amendment to Law No. 19/2012, of 8 May, which approves the new legal framework for competition, and the fourth amendment to Law No. 62/2013, of 26 August, the Law on the Organisation of the Judicial System.	5 June 2018
The Czech Republic	Zákon o náhradě škody v oblasti hospodářské soutěže	18 August 2017
Romania	ORDONANŢĂ DE URGENŢĂ nr. 39 privind acţiunile în despăgubire în cazurile de încălcare a dispoziţiilor legislaţiei în materie de concurenţă	31 May 2017
Sweden	Konkurrensskadelag Lag om ändring i konkurrenslagen Lag om ändring i lagen om grupprättegång Lag om ändring i lagen om patent- och marknadsdomstolar	3 November 2016

APPENDIX II

Survey[1409] of Recent[1410] Competition Law[1411] Private Enforcement Cases[1412] in Portugal[1413]

1409. Portugal does not maintain a public database of actions for damages resulting from violations of competition rules. Accordingly, the table presented includes only those cases – and the related information – that have been made public or were accessible to the author.

1410. Mostly following the transposition of the EU Damages Directive in 2018. A study identified 203 cases involving the private enforcement of competition law between 1988 and 2016. However, in the vast majority of these, private enforcement was a secondary issue – typically arising in the context of contractual liability, labour disputes or public procurement conflicts. *See* Miguel Sousa Ferro, *Jurisprudence of 'Private Enforcement'*, CIDEEFF Working Paper, 2016, available at *Jurisprudencia_de_Private_Enforcement.pdf (cideeff.pt)* and, more recently, Barry Rodger, Miguel Sousa Ferro and Francisco Marcos (eds) *Chapter 16: Portugal and Spain, in Research Handbook on Competition Law Private Enforcement in the EU*, Elgar Publishing, 2023, available at 1657735663951 (licdn.com).

1411. Between 2021 and 2025, Ius Omnibus filed six additional class actions for damages against Daimler/Mercedes-Benz, Stellantis/Fiat Chrysler Automobiles, Estée Lauder (Clinique), TikTok (two actions) and Flo Health, Inc. These actions were based exclusively on other branches of law, including unfair commercial practices, personality rights, advertising, data protection, and sector-specific regulation. DECO also brought several popular actions, at least between 1999 and 2015, based on violations unrelated to competition law. For further details, *see* Sofia Oliveira Pais, *Private Antitrust Enforcement: A New Era for Collective Redress?* Yearbook of Antitrust and Regulatory Studies, vol. 8, No. 12, CARS, 2015 https://doi.org/10.7172/1689-9024.yars.2015.8.12.1, p. 29, and *Observatoire des Actions de Groupe et autres Actions Collectives*, 2021, available at Acoes_DECO-2021.pdf (observatoireactionsdegroupe.com). Particularly noteworthy is the legal action brought against Portugal Telecom, which concluded with a settlement (STJ ruling of 10 July 2003, Case 03A1243).

1412. Damages actions only.

1413. It should be noted that Miguel Sousa Ferro has created a similar table but focusing on class actions filed in Portugal since 2020, *see Consumer Antitrust Private Enforcement in Europe: As Complete a Survey as Possible (Extended Version)*, 23 October 2022, available at https://ssrn.com/abstract=4223770, pp. 18 and 19.

Case	*Infringement*	*Date*[1414]	*Damages*[1415] *(Euros)*	*Individual/ Collective Action*[1416] *(No. of SMEs/ consumers)*	*Follow-On/ Stand-Alone/Mixed/ Disclosure of Documents*	*Private Funding*	*Highlights*
Recensere et al v. Tabaqueira TJCL 49/11.8TVLSB	102 TFEU + 11 and 12 PCL Discriminatory pricing	N/I[1417]	~ 16.5 million	Individual (23)	Stand-Alone	N/I	Final decision pending (Sentencing decision of the TRL on 10 August 2020)
Onitelecom v. Portugal Telecom TJCL 2271/11.8TVLSB	102 TFEU + and 11 PCL Artificial and unfair price-fixing, among other practices	2011	~ 1.5 million	Individual	Follow-On (PRC/2003/5 – however, on 4 October 2011, the TCL was declared extinguished by the statute of limitations)	N/I	The right to compensation was declared time-barred, and the reference for a preliminary ruling was dismissed, according to the judgment of the TRL on 31 October 2013

1414. Cases are displayed in ascending order, from the oldest to the most recent.
1415. Global figures, initially estimates.
1416. *Stricto sensu*, corresponding to the popular action (a single action on behalf of everyone). As this type of action is the focus of this study, these actions are marked in grey to make them easier to identify.
1417. No information.

NOS v. Portugal Telecom TJCL 1774/11.9TVLSB	102 TFEU + and 11 PCL Artificial and unfair price-fixing, among other practices	2011	~ 8.6 million	Individual	*Follow-On* (PRC/2003/5 – however, on 4 October 2011, the TCL was declared extinguished by the statute of limitations)	N/I	Claim dismissed at first instance on the grounds of lack of proof of compression of margins
Cogeco v. Sport TV TJCL 5754/15.7T8LSB	11th PCL Imposition of unfair transaction conditions	27 February 2015	~ 11.5 million	Individual	Follow-On (PRC/2010/2)	N/I	The right to compensation was declared statute-barred, apparently contrary to the ECJ's answer to the question referred for a preliminary ruling in the case, to the effect that EU law had infringed national legislation which provided for the limitation period
Cabovisão/ NOWO v. Sport TV TJCL S/I	102 TFEU + and 11 PCL Imposition of unfair transaction conditions	N/I	N/I	Individual	Follow-On (PRC/2010/2)	N/I	Settlement – waiver of claims and fair sharing of costs
OdC v. Sport TV TJCL 7074/15.8T8LSB. L1	102 TFEU + and 11 PCL Imposition of unfair transaction conditions	12 May 2015	N/I	Collective	Follow-On (PRC/2010/2)	N/I	Pre-trial phase (on 12 April 2018, the TRL ruled that this association had legal standing to bring the action – 7074/15.8T8LSB. L1-1))

Case	*Infringement*	*Date*[1414]	*Damages*[1415] *(Euros)*	*Individual/ Collective Action*[1416] *(No. of SMEs/ consumers)*	*Follow-On/ Stand-Alone/Mixed/ Disclosure of Documents*	*Private Funding*	*Highlights*
Parque Escolar v. UEM et al TCRS 73/19.2YQSTR	101 TFEU + 9 PCL Cartel practice of market sharing and price-fixing in public tenders	N/I	N/I	Individual	Follow-On (PRC/2014/2)	N/I	Decision pending
Trnsveiva and others v. AB Volvo[1418] TCRS 12/19.0YQSTR	101 TFEU + 9 PCL Price cartels and price increases	2019	~ 556 thousand	Individual	Follow-On (AT.39824)	N/I	Ruling of 12 September 2025
Transportes Guilherme Fernandes v. Renault Trucks TCRS 54/19.6YQSTR	101 TFEU + 9 PCL Price cartels and price increases	2019	180 thousand	Individual	Follow-On (AT.39824)	N/I	Ruling of 13 February 2025
Transfrugal v. Daf Trucks TCRS 71/19.6YQSTR	101 TFEU + 9 PCL Price cartels and price increases	22 August 2019	~ 15.5 thousand	Individual	Follow-On (AT.39824)	N/I	Ruling of 6 November 2022

1418. There are approximately hundred more individual *follow-on* actions against the so-called Trucks Cartel pending before the TCRS.

Ius Omnibus v. Mastercard TCRS 19/20.5YQSTR	101 TFEU + 9 PCL Cross-border restrictions and excessive intra-regional MIFs[1419]	2 December 2020	~400 million	Collective (8 million)	Mixed (AT.40049 + increase in material and temporal scope)	Yes (Nivalion)	Injured cited on 22 January 2021
Ius Omnibus v. Super Bock TCRS 20/20.9YQSTR	101 TFEU + 9 PCL Setting minimum prices and other transaction conditions	14 December 2020	~401 million	Collective (8 million)	Mixed (PRC/2016/4 + increase in time scope)	Yes (Telluride)	Proceedings suspended (TRL confirmation of 20 February 2023) as a result of the administrative offence proceedings – meanwhile confirmed by the Ruling of 12 September 2023 of the TRL (on 10 March 2023, the TRL annulled an Order of the TJCL ordering the preservation of evidence, for lack of reasoning and error in the applicable procedural means)
Ius Omnibus v. Meliá TCRS 6/21.6YQSTR	101 TFEU + 9 PCL Conclusion and/or implementation of vertical contracts that differentiated EEA	23 October 2023	N/A[1420]	Collective	Disclosure of documents	N/I	Ordered access to documents and confirmed the possibility of ordering access to documents created *ex novo*, with respect for

1419. Multilateral Interbank Commissions.
1420. Not applicable.

Case	*Infringement*	*Date*[1414]	*Damages*[1415] *(Euros)*	*Individual/ Collective Action*[1416] *(No. of SMEs/ consumers)*	*Follow-On/ Stand-Alone/Mixed/ Disclosure of Documents*	*Private Funding*	*Highlights*
	consumers on the basis of their country of residence						the principle of proportionality, based on ECJ's judgment in the case of *Paccar* and *DAF Trucks*
Ius Omnibus v. Comcast/ Universal Studios TCRS /21.4YQSTR, 8/21.2YQSTR, 9/21.0YQSTR, 10/21.4YQSTR, 11/21.2YQSTR, 12/21.0YQSTR, 13/21.9YQSTR and 14/21.7YQSTR	101 TFEU + 9 PCL Restriction of sales of Universal *merchandising* products by licensees	9 July 2021	N/A	Collective	Disclosure of documents	N/I	Initial phase
Ius Omnibus v. ANT TCRS 15/21.5YQSTR	101 TFEU + 9 PCL Pricing in the market for surveying services	12 July 2021	N/I	Collective	Follow-On (PRC/2020/2)	No	Settlement – ANT agreed to compensate the consumers represented in the lawsuit, in an amount equivalent to 5% of the gross amount paid for the services in question

Ius Omnibus v. Apple (iPhone) TJCL 17713/21.6T8LSB	Consumer law – passing on information and misleading advertising about the iPhone's resistance to liquids (Competition law invoked additionally – 102 TFEU + 11 PCL)	19 July 2021	~ 137 million	Collective (1 million)	Stand-Alone	No	Initial phase
Ius Omnibus v. EDP TCRS 18/21.0YQSTR	102 TFEU + 11 PCL Manipulation of the offer of tele-regulation services	6 September 2021	~ 95 million	Collective (2.5 million)	Follow-on (PRC/2016/5)	No	Defendant contested on 21 December 2021 (the TCRS had previously issued an order (i) rejecting the exceptions raised regarding the admissibility of the action and the active legitimacy of the plaintiff, (ii) referring the decision on the statute of limitations raised to after the production of evidence and (iii) suspending the proceedings until the final judgment of the Misdemeanour Procedure, which occurred on 1 June 2022 – 309/19.0YUSTR-F.L1)

Case	*Infringement*	*Date*[1414]	*Damages*[1415] *(Euros)*	*Individual/ Collective Action*[1416] *(No. of SMEs/ consumers)*	*Follow-On/ Stand-Alone/Mixed/ Disclosure of Documents*	*Private Funding*	*Highlights*
VASP and Iberomail v. CTT TCRS 19/21.8YQSTR	102 TFEU + 11 PCL Refusal to contract and grant wholesale access to its postal network, among other practices	18 January 2022	~ 189 million	Individual	Stand-alone (although based on PRC/2015/04 filed with commitments)	N/I	At the Preliminary Hearing stage
Ius Omnibus v. Apple (App Store) TCRS 3/22.4YQSTR	101 and 102 TFEU + 10 and 11 PCL Mandatory use of Apple's iOS operating system on your devices (iPhones, iPads and iPod Touch)	21 March 2022	Not estimated	Collective (2.9 million)	Stand-Alone (although these infringements have been invoked in damages actions pending in other jurisdictions against Apple, namely in the US, UK and the Netherlands, and similar infringements have motivated the opening of an investigation by the EC)	Yes	Initial phase

Ius Omnibus v. Google (Play Store) TCRS 4/22.2YQSTR	101 and 102 TFEU + 10 and 11 PCL Mandatory use of the Android operating system and Android applications and content	21 March 2022	Not estimated	Collective (3.6 million)	Stand-Alone (although these infringements have been invoked in actions for damages pending in other jurisdictions against Google, namely in the US, UK and the Netherlands, and these infringements have already been partially declared by an EC decision, confirmed by the EGC on 14.09.2022)	Yes	Initial phase
Fabrizio Esposito v. Google (Play Store) TCRS 61/22.1YQSTR	102 TFEU + 11 PCLMandatory use of the Android operating system and Android applications and content	June 2022	~ 100 million	Collective (3.6 million)	Stand-Alone (although these infringements have been invoked in actions for damages pending in other jurisdictions against	Yes	Initial phase

Case	*Infringement*	*Date*[1414]	*Damages*[1415] *(Euros)*	*Individual/ Collective Action*[1416] *(No. of SMEs/ consumers)*	*Follow-On/ Stand-Alone/Mixed/ Disclosure of Documents*	*Private Funding*	*Highlights*
					Google, namely in the US, UK and the Netherlands, and these infringements have already been partially declared by an EC decision, confirmed by the EGC on 14.9.2022)		
Ius Omnibus v. ABanca and Others TCRS 3/24.0YQSTR 4/24.8YQSTR 5/24.6YQSTR 2/24.1YQSTR 6/24.4YQSTR	101 TFEU + 9 PCL Exchange of sensitive information on prices and other conditions	18 January 2024	~ 5368 million	Collective (2.5 million)	Follow-On (PRC/2012/9)	N/I	Initial phase

Bibliography

Adams, Maurice, *Doing What Doesn't Come Naturally. On the Distinctiveness of Comparative Law*, in *Methodologies of Legal Research: Which Kind of Method for What Kind of Discipline?*, Mark Van Hoech (ed.), Oxford and Portland, Oregon, Hart Publishing, Bloomsbury, 2011.

Adkins Bernardine and Beighton, Samuel, *Private Antitrust Litigation: Jurisdictional Comparisons*, European Lawyer Reference, 2013.

Águila-Real, *Contra la armonización positiva; la Propuesta de la Comisión para reforzar el private enforcemente del Derecho de la Competencia*, Indret 3/2009.

Agulló, Diego, *Directive 2020/1828: A New Era for 'European Class Actions'?*, UNIO – EU Law Journal, 22 November 2021, available at https://officialblogofunio.com/2021/11/22/directive-2020-1828-a-new-era-for-european-class-actions/.

Agulló, Diego, *Directive 2020/1828 on Representative Actions for the Protection of the Collective Interests of Consumers: An Overview*, UNIO – EU Law Journal, vol. 8, No. 1, December 2022, pp. 127-142.

Albors-Llorens, Albertina and Cafaggi, Fabrizio (eds), *Consumer Law, Competition Law and the Europeanisation of Private Law, The Institutional Framework of European Private Law*, Oxford University Press, 2006.

Albuquerque, Paulo Pinto de, *Comentários do Código* de *Processo Penal à Luz da Constituição da República e da Convenção Europeia dos Direitos do Homem*, 4th Edition, Editora Universidade Católica, 2011.

Albuquerque, Paulo Pinto de, *Comentários do Regime Geral das Contraordenações à luz da Constituição da República e da Convenção Europeia dos Direitos do Homem*, Paulo Pinto de Albuquerque, Gabriel Mateus de Albuquerque (ed.), Universidade Católica Editora, 2022.

Alexander, Janet Cooper, *Contingent Fees* and Class Actions, DePaul Law Review, vol. 47, No. 2, Winter 1998: Symposium – Contingency Fee Financing of Litigation in America, Article 7.

Almeida, Carlos Ferreira de and Carvalho, Jorge Morais, *Introduction to Comparative Law*, Almedina, 3rd ed., 2017.

Alter, Karen J., *Establishing the Supremacy of European Law: The Making of an International Rule of Law in Europe*, Oxford University Press, 2003.

Alves, João, *Ministério Público na área cível: a nota discriminativa e justificativa de custos de parte*, Revista do Ministério Público No. 157, January and March 2019, pp. 171-173.

Alves, João, *Ação popular: a intervenção acessória do Ministério Público na jurisdição civil*, Revista do Ministério Público No. 160, October and December 2019, pp. 131-151.

Amaro, Rafael, Le *Contentieux Privé des Pratiques Anticoncurrentielles, Etude des Contentieux Autonome et Complémentaire devant les Jurisdictions Judiciaires*, Bruylant, 2013.

Amaro, Rafael (ed.), *Private Enforcemente of Competition Law in Europe: Directive 2014/104/EU and Beyond*, Bruylant, 2021.

Amorim, Luís Miguel Caldas Ribeiro Silva, *The Punitive Function of Civil Liability*, Coimbra, 2014, dissertation available at https://eg.uc.pt/bitstream/10316/34853/1/A%20Funcao%20Punitiva%20da%20Responsabilidade%20Civil.pdf.

Anastácio, Catarina, *O dever de colaboração no âmbito dos processos de contra-ordenação por infracção às regras de defesa da concorrência e o princípio nemo tenetur se ipsum accusare, Revista Concorrência e Regulação*, Ano I, N.º 1, January/March, 2010.

Anastácio, Gonçalo, *Portugal, The Private Competition Enforcement Review*, Law Business Research, 10th ed., 2017.

Andreangeli, Arianna, *Private Enforcement of Antitrust: Regulating Corporative Behaviour Through Collective Claims in the EU and US*, Edward Elgar, 2014.

Antunes, Henrique Sousa, *Once Upon a Time in America, Occasional Papers in Comparative Law*, No. 2, April 2005, published by the Portuguese-American Comparative Law Centre, Roger Williams University Ralph R. Papitto School of Law, p. 22.

Antunes, Henrique Sousa and Mulheron, Rachael, *Competition Law Cases under the Opt-out Regimes of Australia, Canada and Portugal*, A Research Paper for submission to the Department for Business, Enterprise and Regulatory Reform – BERR, 2003.

Antunes, Henrique Sousa, *Class Actions, Group Litigation & Other Forms of Collective Litigation (Portuguese Report)*, The Annals of the American Academy of Political and Social Science, vol. 622, 2009, pp. 161 et seq.

Antunes, Henrique Sousa, *In Intellectual Property Rights: Infringement and Calculation of Damages: A Comment on the Judgment of the Court of Justice of the European Union (Fifth Chamber) Stowarzyszenie 'Olawska Telewizja Kablowa' v Stowarzyszenie Filmowców Polskich, 25 January 2017 (Case C-367/15)104*, vol. I, No. 2, Católica Law Review, May 2017, pp. 95 to 109, available at 1983_article_4255_1_10_20191020.pdf (ucp.pt).

Antunes, Henrique Sousa, *Das Funções Reconstitutivas e Punitiva da Responsabilidade Civil: Propostas de Reforma do Código Civil Português, in Novos Desafios da Responsabilidade Civil: Atas das II Jornadas Luso-Brasileiras de Responsabilidade Civil,*

Mafalda Miranda Barbosa, Nelson Rosenvald and Francisco Muniz (eds), University of Coimbra, June 2019, pp. 121 and 144.

Antunes, Luís Miguel Pais, *Direito da Concorrência: Os Poderes de Investigação da Comunidade Europeia e a Protecção dos Direitos Fundamentais,* Almedina, 1995.

Anzini, Martina et al., *Making European Policies Work, Evolving Challenges and New Approaches in EU Law Enforcement*, October 2021, available at https://www.eipa.eu/wp-content/uploads/2025/03/Edward-Best_Making_European_Policies_Work_Evolving_Challenges.pdf, pp. 12 and 13.

Ashton, David and Henry, David, *Competition Damages Action in the EU: Law and Practice,* economics contribution from Maier-Rigaud, Frank and Schawalbe, Ulrich, Elgar, *Competition Law and Practice*, 2013.

Ashton, David, *Competition Damages Action in the EU: Law and Practice*, economics contribution from Frank Maier-Rigaud and Ulrich Schawalbe, Elgar, *Competition Law and Practice*, 2nd ed., 2018.

Athanassiou, Lia, *Collective Redress and Competition Policy, in Cross-Border Class Actions*, Arnaud Nuyts and Nikitas E. Hatzimihail (eds), Otto Schmidt and De Gruyter European Law Publishers, 2013.

Attrill, Wayne, *Ethical Issues in Litigation Funding*, 16 February 2009, available at https://portal.omnibridgeway.com/docs/default-source/site-documents/ethical-issues-paper-imf09---globalaw-conference.pdf.

Backhaus, Jürgen G., Cassone, Alberto and Ramello, Giovanni B. (eds), *The Law and Economics of Class Actions in Europe: Lessons from America*, Edward Elgar Publishing, 2012.

Bagnoli, Vicente, *Designing Competition Policy in Digital Markets for Developing Economies: How the EU Can Contribute with the Digital Markets Act and Digital Services Act,* Revista de Defesa da Concorrência, Brasília, vol. 9, No. 2, 2021, pp. 133-158, available at: https://revista.cade.gov.br/index.php/revistadedefesadaconcorrencia/article/view/957.

Baquero, Ingrid S. Ortiz, *La Aplicación Privada del Derecho de la Competencia*, La Ley, 2011.

Balasingham, Baskaran, *International Antitrust Litigation: Conflict of Laws and Coordination, Global Antitrust Review*, Hart Publishing, Oxford, 2012.

Bansal, Dee et al., *United States: Class Actions – Litigation, Policy and Latest Developments*, 2 December 2022, available at Class actions hub - Global Competition Review.

Basedow, Jürgen, *Private Enforcement of EC Competition Law,* Alphen Aan den Rijn, Kluwer Law International, 2007.

Basedow, Jürgen, Terhechte, Jörg Philipp and Tichý, Lubos, *Private Enforcement of Competition Law*, Nomos, 2011.

Basedow, Jürgen, Francq, Stéphanie and Idot, Laurence, *International Antitrust Litigation: Conflict of Laws and Coordination*, Oxford, Hart Publishing, 2012.

Batchelor, Bill, Macaulay, Bruce and Hunt, Sym, *UK Class Actions Update: Merricks Secures Uncontested CPO, But the Competition Appeal Tribunal Shows It Retains Significant Teeth to Narrow Claims*, 14 September 2021, available at UK Class Actions Update: Merricks Secures Uncontested CPO, But the Competition Appeal

Tribunal Shows It Retains Significant Teeth to Narrow Claims | Insights | Skadden, Arps, Slate, Meagher & Flom LLP.

Baumann, Marion et al., *The Enforcement of Abuse of Economic Dependence in the EU*, 28 January 2021, available at The Enforcement of Abuse of Economic Dependence in the EU | HUB | K&L Gates (klgates.com).

Batchelor, Bill et al., *European Union and Unite Kingdom: A New Dawn for Class Actions*, 24 June 2022, available at The European, Middle East and African Antitrust Review - Global Competition Review.

Benacchio, Gian Antonio and Carpagnano, Michele G., *L'azione di Risarcimento del Danno per Violazione delle Regole Comunitarie sulla Concorrenza*, Trento, Università degli Studi di Trento, 2007.

Benör, Iris, *EU Consumer Law and Human Rights*, Oxford University Press, 2013.

Bergh, Roger Van Den, *Private Enforcement of European Competition Law and the Persisting Collective Action Problem*, Maastricht Journal of European and Comparative Law, SAGE Publications, vol. 20, No. 1, 3 January 2013.

Bergström, Maria, Iacovides, Marios and Strand, Magnus, *Harmonising EU Competition Litigation: The New Directive and Beyond*, Swedish Studies in European Law, vol. 8, Oxford, Hart Publishing, 2016.

Bernard, Kent S., *On Judgments and Settlements in Antitrust Litigation: When Should Damages Be Trebled?*, St. John's Law Review, vol. 56, No. 1, Fall 1981, available at https://scholarship.law.sTJUEohns.edu/cgi/viewcontent.cgi?article=2259&context=lawreview.

Bishop, Simon and Walker, Mike, *Economics of EC Competition Law*, Sweet & Maxwell, 3rd ed., 2010.

Blanco, Luis Ortiz, Sanz, Angel Givaja and Lamadrid De Pablo, Alfonso, *Fine Arts in Brussels: Punishment and Settlement of Cartel Cases under EC Competition Law, Antitrust: between EC Law and National Law*, Bruylant, 2008.

Blanke, Gondon and Nazzini, Renato (eds), *International Competition Litigation: A Multi-jurisdictional Handbook*, Kluwer Law International, 2012.

Bockel, W.B. van., *The Ne Bis in Idem Principle in EU Law: A Conceptual and Jurisprudential Analysis*, Meijers-reeks, 16 June 2009, available at https://scholarlypublications.universiteitleiden.nl/access/item%3A2875411/view.

Bolwerk, Aloísio and Júnior, José Eustáquio de Melo, *Considerações sobre a Tutela do Processo Coletivo no Brasil e em Portugal*, Revista Jurídica Luso-Brasileira, Year 7, No. 6, 2021, pp. 75-101.

Borges, Marta Alexandra Frias, *Algumas Reflexões em Matéria de Litigância de Má-Fé*, Master's dissertation, University of Coimbra, 2014.

Bosco, David, *Le financement par les tiers de l'action collective: l'exemple* de *l'Union européenne*, Bulletin de Droit Économique, 2015, 1/2, available at http://www.droit-economique.org/wp-content/uploads/2015/11/DB-Le-financement-par-les-tiers-final-29-oct-15.pdf.

Botta, Marco, *The Economic Succession Doctrine in Private Enforcement of EU Competition Law: 'Nothing Extraordinary' after Skanska Industrial?*, Market and Competition Law Review, vol. 3, No. 2, pp. 171-186, available at https://revistas.ucp.pt/index.php/mclawreview/article/view/1828.

Botteman, Yves and Hughes, Paul, *Access to File: Striking the Balance Between Leniency and Private Enforcement Tools, The European Antitrust Review 2013*, Global Competition Review, 2013.

Bridges, Tom, *Australia, The Private Competition Enforcement Review*, Law Business Research, 10th ed., 2017.

Buccirossi, Paolo, Marvão, Catarina and Spagnolo, Giancarlo, *Leniency and Damages*, Working Paper No. 32, Stockholm Institute of Transition Economics, February 2015.

Búrca, Gráinne de and Weiler, J.H.H., *The European Court of Justice*, Oxford University Press, 2001.

Campos, João Mota de and Campos, João Luiz Mota de, *Manual* de *Direito Comunitário*, Coimbra Editora, 5th ed., 2007.

Campos, Marta, *De novo o direito à não autoincriminação em processos de contraordenação por práticas restritivas da concorrência contra pessoas coletivas*, Revista de Concorrência & Regulação, Lisbon, No. 36, 2018.

Cauffman, Caroline, *The Interaction of Leniency Programmes and Actions for Damages*, The Competition Law Review, vol. 7, No. 2, July 2011.

Cauffman Caroline and Philipsen, Niels, *Who Does What in Competition Law: Harmonising the Rules on Damages for Infringements of the EU Competition Rules?*, Maastricht European Private Law Institute Working Paper No. 2014/19, 7 November 2014.

Carmeliet, Tine, *How Lenient is the European Leniency System? An Overview of Current (Dis)Incentives to Blow the Whistle*, Jg. 48, No. 3, 2011-2012.

Carstensen, Peter C., *The Goals of Competition Law: Ends v. Means, in Albert A. Foer, A Consumer Voice in the Antitrust Arena, Liber Amicorum*, Nicolas Charbit and Sonia Ahmad (eds), Concurrences, 2020.

Carvalho, Margarida Sousa Lobo de, *Collective Indemnity Proceedings*, Master's Dissertation, Lisbon, Universidade Católica Portuguesa, 2020.

Casanova, Nuno Salazar and Rosa, Madalena Afra, *The Class Actions Law Review: Portugal*, 21 April 2022, available at The Class Actions Law Review - The Law Reviews.

Chappatte, Philippe and Walter, Paul, *United kingdom, in The Cartels and Leniency Review*, Chistine A. Verney (ed.), Law Business Research, 2nd ed., 2014.

Cheren, Daniella Soares and Carvalho, Juliana Brina Correa Lima de, *O Método Jurídico (Interpretação), O Direito e a Ciência: Tempo e Métodos*, Alf Ross (ed.), Movimento Editorial da Faculdade de Direito da UFMG, 2006.

Chevalier, Rémi, *Recommendations for Responsible Private Funding Of Litigation: European Parliament Resolution 2022/2130(INL)*, 6 March 2023, available at Recommendations For Responsible Private Funding Of Litigation: European Parliament Resolution 2022/2130(INL) - Trials & Appeals & Compensation - European Union (mondaq.com).

Choi, Dosoung and Philippatos, George C., *The Review of Economics and Statistics*, vol. 65, No. 3, August 1983, pp. 501-506.

Claessens, Sjoerd et al., *Evaluation of the Legal Framework for the Free Movement of Lawyers*, Final Report, Project number: BA03973, Study has been financed by the

European Commission, DG Internal Market and Services (MARKT/2011/071/E), 28 November 2012.

Cleynenbreugel, Pieter Van, *Private Damages Actions in EU Competition Law and Restorative Justice: Towards a More Streamlined Institutional Framework?*, Market and Competition Law Review, vol. 3, No. 2, pp. 15-49, available at https://doi.org/10.7559/mclawreview.2019.1826.

Cisotta, Roberto, *Some Considerations on the Last Developments on Antitrust Damages Actions and Collective Redress in the European Union*, The Competition Law Review, vol. 10, 2014.

Connor, Charley, *Portuguese Court Rejects ECJ's Cogeco Preliminary Ruling*, 13 November 2020, available at Portuguese court rejects ECJ's Cogeco preliminary ruling – Global Competition Review.

Correia, Vasco Marques, *O Logro das Sociedades ditas Multidisciplinares*, available at https://www.oa.pt/upl/%7Bc7112026-0691-483e-8bc8-880eefd42049%7D.pdf.

Costa, Adalberto, *O Novo Regime Jurídico da Concorrência Anotado e Comentado*, Vida Económica, 2014.

Costa, Guilherme Oliveira e, *The First Preliminary Ruling on Directive 2014/104/EU: Case 637/17 Cogeco*, 3 July 2019, available at The first preliminary ruling on Directive 2014/104/EU: Case 637/17 Cogeco - European Law Blog.

Costa, Tiago Branco da, *O sistema português* da *ação coletiva*, Dereito, Revista Xurídica da Universidade de Santiago de Compostela, vol. 28, No. 1, 2019, pp. 85-107.

Costeira, Maria José, *The Transposition of the Private Enforcement Directive: A Critical Perspective*, UNIO – EU Law Journal, vol. 3, No. 2, July 2017, pp. 175-184.

Couter, Yves Van et al., *IP Alert: Ground-breaking CJEU Judgment on Reimbursement of Lawyers' Fees in IP Litigation*, 2 August 2016, available at IP Alert: Ground-breaking CJEU judgment on reimbursement of lawyers' fees in IP litigation - Ludology.

Crowther, Peter Crowther and Holzhäuser, Michael, *ECJ Rules on Third Party Access to Leniency Documents: Pfleiderer AG v Bundeskartellamt*, 20 June 2011, http://awa2012.concurrences.com/business/article/ecj-rules-on-third-party-access-to.

Crump, Richard, *The Biggest UK Antitrust Class Action Cases to Watch*, 9 March 2020, https://www.law360.com/articles/1250361.

Cumming, George, Spitz, Brad and Janal, Ruth, *Civil Procedure Used for Enforcement of EC Competition Law by the English, French and German Civil Courts*, Kluwer Law International, 2007.

Cunha, Carolina et al., *Lei da Concorrência: Comentário Conimbricense*, Almedina, 2013.

Daly, K., *Public v. Private Enforcement: Why Competition Litigation will not Save the Public Enforcement Deficit, The Private Competition Enforcement Review*, Law Business Research, 7th ed., 2015.

Davies, Martin, Middleton, Oliver and Watret, Tom, *The Increasing Prevalence of Class Actions in the UK*, Business Law Review, vol. 42, No. 4, 2021, pp. 168-174.

Deffains, Bruno and Demougin, Dominique, *Class Actions, Compliance, and Moral Cost, in Contract Governance: Dimensions in Law and Interdisciplinary Research*,

Stefan Grundmann, Florian Möslein and Karl Riesenhuber (eds), Oxford University Press, 1 July 2015.

Dietzel, Kim et al., *Collective or Class Actions and Claims Aggregation in the United Kingdom, in EGCR's Private Litigation Guide*, Nicholas and Heaton and Benhamin Holt (eds), 3rd ed., 22 November 2021, available at Private Litigation Guide - Global Competition Review.

Dobson, Sarah-Jane and Hepsworth, Camille, *Collective Redress & Class Actions 2021: UK*, 9 November 2021, available at https://chambers.com/downloads/gpg/814/collective_redress__and__class_actions_2021.pdf.

Du, Tian-Yu, *Research on Conflicts of Interest Arising from Third-Party Funding In International Investment Arbitration*, Advances in Social Science, Education and Humanities Research, vol. 281, 4th International Conference on Social Science and Contemporary Humanity Development (SSCHD 2018).

Edelson, Ken, Boylan, Liam and Vinis, Petros, *In Antitrust and Private Enforcement: A Recent Judgment by EU's Top Court Requires Defendants to Produce New Documents That Can Be Used Against Them*, 21 November 2022, available at Antitrust and Private Enforcement: A Recent Judgment by EU's Top Court Requires Defendants to Produce New Documents That Can Be Used Against Them | Wilson Sonsini (wsgr.com).

Eizenga, Michael A. and Davis, Emrys, *A History of Class Actions: Modern Lessons from Deep Roots*, Canadian Class Action Review, vol. 7 No. 1, October 2011.

Fairgrieve, Duncan and Howells, Geraint, *Collective Redress Procedures: European Debates*, The International and Comparative Law Quarterly, vol. 58, No. 2, April 2009, 379-409.

Fairgrieve, Duncan and Salim, Rhonson, *Collective Redress in Europe: Moving Forward or Treading Water?*, Cambridge University Press for the British Institute of International and Comparative Law, 2022.

Falla, Élodie, *The Role of the Court in Collective Redress Litigation: Comparative Report*, Collection de l'Unité de droit économique de l'ULB, Edition Larcier, 2014.

Faria, Rita Lynce de, *A Inversão do ónus da Prova no Direito Civil Português*, Editora Lex, 2001.

Fausten, Thomas and Hammesfahr, Robert, *Punitive Damages in Europe: Concern, Threat or Non-issue*, Richard Heard (ed.), Swiss Re, 2012, available at punitive_damage_in_europe.pdf (biztositasiszemle.hu).

Ferro, Miguel Sousa, *Collective Redress: Will Portugal Show the Way?*, Journal of European Competition Law & Practice, vol. 6, No. 5, 2015, available at Collective Redress: Will Portugal Show the Way? by Miguel Sousa Ferro:: SSRN.

Ferro, Miguel Sousa, *Jurisprudência de 'Private Enforcement' (Private Enforcement Case-Law), Portuguese Competition Law Jurisprudence Chapter 7: Private Enforcement Case-Law*, 2016, available at https://papers.ssrn.com/sol3/papers.cfm?abstract_id=3077488.

Ferro, Miguel Sousa, *Antitrust Private Enforcement and the Binding Effect of Public Enforcement Decisions*, Market and Competition Law Review, vol. 3, No. 2, pp. 51-80, available at Antitrust Private Enforcement and the Binding Effect of Public Enforcement Decisions | Market and Competition Law Review (ucp.pt).

Ferro, Miguel Sousa and Costa, Guilherme Oliveira e, *Otis: Another Great Judgment on Private Enforcement from the CJEU ... But It Could be Better, Competition Policy International,* 22 January 2020, https://www.competitionpolicyinternational.com/otis-another-great-judgment-on-private-enforcement-from-the-cjeu-but-it-could-be-better/.

Ferro, Miguel Sousa, *The Reality of Access in Antitrust Private Enforcement: Overview of 3 Years' Experience in Portugal,* Revista de Concorrência e Regulação, Year XIII, Nos 46-47, Almedina, 2021, pp. 37-71, available at CR 46-47_Miguel Sousa Ferro.pdf (concorrencia.pt).

Ferro, Miguel Sousa and Salpico, Nuno, *Consumer Compensation as a Priority for Regulators,* Revista da Faculdade de Direito da Universidade de Lisboa, vol. LXII, No. 2, 2021 pp. 407-445, available at Miguel-Sousa-Ferro-Nuno-Salpico.pdf (ulisboa.pt).

Ferro, Miguel Sousa, *Class Actions in Portugal: The Little Regime That Could, in Mass Claims,* No. 2, December 2021, Class Actions in Portugal - Mass Claims - Uitgeverij Den Hollander.

Ferro, Miguel Sousa, *Ações populares cíveis em Portugal,* Revista de Direito Comercial, 23 February 2022, pp. 411-448.

Ferro, Miguel Sousa, *Consumer Antitrust Private Enforcement in Europe: As Complete a Survey as Possible (Extended Version),* 23 October 2022, available at https://ssrn.com/abstract=4223770.

Fikfak, Veronika, *Changing State Behaviour: Damages before the European Court of Human Rights,* The European Journal of International Law, vol. 29, No. 4, Oxford University Press, 2019, p. 1095.

Fisch, Jill E., *Class Action Reform, Qui Tam, and the Role of the Plaintiff,* Penn Law, Legal Scholarship Repository, 1997.

Fischel, Daniel R., *Multidisciplinary Practice,* The Business Lawyer, vol. 55, No. 3, May 2000, pp. 951-974.

Fitzpatrick, Brian T. and Thomas, Randall S., *The Cambridge Handbook of Class Actions: An International Survey,* Cambridge University Press, 2021.

Foer, Albert A. and Cuneo, Jonathan W. (eds), *The International Handbook on Private Enforcement of Competition Law,* Edward Elgar Publishing, 2012.

Freitas, José Lebre de, *Regime of the Popular Action of Art. 19 of Law 23/2018,* Revista de Direito Comercial, 23 March 2022, pp. 557-594.

Freund, Benedikt, *Heralds of Change: In the Aftermath of Skanska (C-724/17) and Sumal (C-882/19),* International Review of Intellectual Property and Competition Law, vol. 53, Springer, 15 February 2022, pp. 246-263, available at https://link.springer.com/content/pdf/10.1007/s40319-022-01150-5.pdf.

Gac, Maciej, *In Group Litigation as an Instrument of Competition Law Enforcement: Analysis Based on European, French and Polish experience,* Centre for Antitrust and Regulatory Studies, University of Warsaw, Faculty of Management, Eighty third Publication of the Publishing Programme, Series: Textbooks and Monographs (25), Prof. Dr. Tadeusz Skoczny (Series ed.), 2017, available at CARS 25 - Group litigation-Gac.indd (uw.edu.pl).

Gal, Michal S. and Dahan, Rivi, *Legal Obstacles to Private Enforcement of Competition Law*, Market and Competition Law Review, vol. 3, No. 2, pp. 133-152, available at https://doi.org/10.7559/mclawreview.2019.1835.

Gaudet, Robert, JR, *Turning a Blind Eye: The Commission's Rejection of Opt-out Class Actions Overlooks Swedish, Norwegian, Danish and Dutch Experience*, European Competition Law Review, vol. 30, No. 3, 2009.

Geider, Andreas, *The End of the EU Cartel Leniency Programme*, available at https://www.euractiv.com/section/competition/opinion/the-end-of-the-eu-cartel-leniency-programme/, 23 June 2011.

Geradin, Damien, *Collective Redress for Antitrust Damages in the European Union: Is this Reality Now?*, George Mason Law Review, Nos 15-16, 2015.

Gerven, Walter van, *Of Rights, Remedies and Procedures*, Common Market Law Review, vol. 37, No. 3, 2000.

Glendon, Mary Ann, Gordon, Michael Wallace and Osakwe, Christopher, *Comparative Legal Traditions: Text, Materials and Cases, American Casebook Series*, West Publishing CO., 1985.

Gomes, José Luís Caramelo, *Lições de Direito da Concorrência*, Almedina, 2016.

Gomes, Júlio, *Uma função punitiva para a responsabilidade civil e uma função reparatória para a responsabilidade penal?*, Revista de Direito e Economia, University of Coimbra, 1989.

Gorjão-Henriques, Miguel, *Direito da União, História, Direito, Cidadania, Mercado Interno e Concorrência*, Almedina, 7th ed., 2014.

Gotanda, John Y., *Charting Developments Concerning Punitive Damages: Is the Tide Changing?*, Villanova University Charles Widger School of Law Digital Repository, 2006, available at https://digitalcommons.law.villanova.edu/cgi/viewcontent.cgi?params=/context/wps/article/1065/&path_info=.

Guedes, Agostinho Cardoso, *Actions for Damages under Portuguese Law for Infringements of the Competition Law, Competition Law Challenges in the Next Decade*, Sofia Oliveira Pais (ed.), P.I.E. Peter Lang, 2016.

Guerrin, Maurice and Kyriazis, Georgios, *Cartels: Proof and Procedural Issues*, Fordham International Law Journal, vol. 16, 2nd ed., 2nd Article, 1992.

Guillermin, Guy, *Un Traité en Trompe L'ŒIL, Le Traité de Lisbonne: Reconfiguration ou Déconstitutionnalisation de l'Union Européenne?*, Bruylant, 2009.

Gulińska, Anna, *Collecting Evidence Through Access to Competition Authorities' Files: Interplay or Potential Conflicts Between Private and Public Enforcement Proceedings?*, Yearbook of Antitrust and Regulatory Studies, vol. 8, No. 12, CARS, 2015.

Gürkaynak, Gönenç, Uçar, Ali Kağan and Buharal, Zeynep, *Frédéric Jenny, Standing up for Convergence and Relevance in Antitrust: Liber Amicorum*, Nicolas Charbit and Sonia Ahmad (eds), vol. I, Concurrences Review, 2019, pp. 293-310.

Hayek, Friedrich A., *Individualism and Economic Order*, The University Of Chicago Press, 1948.

Hausfeld, Michael D. and Scher, Irving, *Can U.S. Class Action Law Serve as Guidelines for the UK Indirect Purchaser Mastercard Case?*, Hausfeld Competition Bulletin, 18 August 2020, available at Hausfeld | Can U.S. class action law serve as guidelines for the UK indirect purchaser Mastercard case?.

Heaton, Nicholas and Holt, Benhamin (eds), *EGCR's Private Litigation Guide,* 3rd ed., 2021, asset download – Global Competition Review.

Heijer, Maarten den, Abeelen, Teun van Os van den and Maslyka, Antanina, *On the Use and Misuse of Recitals in European Union Law,* Amsterdam Law School Research Paper No. 2019-31, 3 September 2029.

Henderson, Kenny, Gluyas, Lee and Scrine, Jonathan, *Funder Liable to Pay Substantial Adverse Costs in Group Litigation,* 20 July 2020, available at Funder liable to pay substantial adverse costs in group litigation (cms-lawnow.com).

Henriques, Duarte Gorjão, *'Third Party Funding' or the Financing of Litigation by Third Parties in Portugal,* Revista da Ordem dos Advogados, vol. 75, No. 3, 2015, pp. 573-624.

Hennah, James and Barrat, Haidee, *United Kingdom: Class Actions – Litigation, Policy and Latest Developments,* 2 December 2022, available at Class actions hub - Global Competition Review.

Herrmann, Volker, Enzberg, Donata Freiin and Bär, Kerstin, *Die EU-Richtlinie über Verbandsklagen tritt in Kraft* (The EU Directive on Representative Consumer Actions Enters into Force), 29 January 2021, available at tw-2021---die-eu-richtlinie-ber-verbandsklagen-tritt-in-kraft.pdf (taylorwessing.com).

Hodges, Christopher, *Competition Enforcement, Regulation and Civil Justice: What Is the Case?,* Common Market Law Review, vol. 43, No. 5, 2006, pp. 1381-1407.

Hodges, Christopher, *The Reform of Class and Representative Actions in European Legal Systems: A New Framework for Collective Redress in Europe,* Oxford, Hart, 2008.

Hodges, Christopher, *In Current Discussions on Consumer Redress: Collective Redress and ADR,* ERA Forum, Springerlink, June 2012.

Hodges, Christopher, Peysner, John and Nurse, Angus, *Litigation Funding: Status and Issues,* Oxford Legal Studies Research Paper No. 55/2012, September 2012.

Hodges, Christopher, *Collective Redress: The Need for New Technologies,* Journal of Consumer Policy, vol. 42, Nos 59-90, 2019, pp. 59-90.

Hoecke, Mark Van, *Methodology of Comparative Legal Research,* https://www.bjutijdschriften.nl/tijdschrift/lawandmethod/2015/12/RENM-D-14-00001.

Höppner, Thomas and Westerhoff, Philipp, *EU General Court Confirms Landmark Google Android Decision with Strong Signal for Tougher Antitrust Enforcement in Digital Ecosystems,* 14 September 2022, available at EU General Court confirms landmark Google Android decision with strong signal for tougher antitrust enforcement in digital ecosystems - Lexology.

Hornkohl, Lena, *Of Adequate Cost Rules, Judicial Damages Estimation, and Fundamental Principles of Antitrust Damages Actions: Tráficos Manuel Ferrer, C-312/21,* 17 February 2023, available at Of Adequate Cost Rules, Judicial Damages Estimation, and Fundamental Principles of Antitrust Damages Actions - Tráficos Manuel Ferrer, C-312/21 - Kluwer Competition Law Blog.

Hou, Liyang, *Excessive Prices Within EU* Competition *Law,* European Competition Journal, vol. 7, pp. 47-70, *in Dominance and Monopolization,* vol. II, Rosa Greaves (ed.), 2012.

Humphreys, Llio et al., *Mapping Recitals to Normative Provisions in EU Legislation to Assist Legal Interpretation*, Legal Knowledge and Information Systems: JURIX 2015: The Twenty-Eighth Annual Conference, 9 January 2015.

Humphries, Mark, *The Ethics of Litigation* Funding, 17 September 2014, available at The_Ethics_of_Litigation_Funding_17.09.14.pdf (humphrieskerstetter.com).

Hurst, Samia A. and Mauron, Alex, *A Question of Method. The Ethics of Managing Conflicts of Interest*, EMBO Rep. February 2008, vol. 9, No. 2, pp. 119-123.

Hüschelrath, Kai, *Is It Worth All the Trouble?: The Costs and Benefits of Antitrust Enforcement*, Discussion Paper No. 08-107, Centre for European Economic Research (ZEW) of Germany, available at DP 08-107 (zew.de).

Hüschelrath, Kai and Peyer, Sebastian, *Public and Private Enforcement of Competition Law: A Differentiated Approach*, ZEW – Centre for European Economic Research Discussion Paper No. 29, June 2013, available at https://papers.ssrn.com/sol3/papers.cfm?abstract_id=2278839.

Imgarten, Nils, *Disclosure of Documents in Parallel Public and Private Enforcement of Competition Law: The ECJ's Judgment in C-57/21 – RegioJet*, 1 February 2023, available at Disclosure of Documents in Parallel Public and Private Enforcement of Competition Law - The ECJ's Judgment in C-57/21 - RegioJet - Kluwer Competition Law Blog.

Issacharoff, Samuel and Miller, Geoffrey P., *Will Aggregate Litigation Come to Europe?*, Vanderbilt Law Review, vol. 62, 2019, p. 177, available at https://scholarship.law.vanderbilt.edu/cgi/viewcontent.cgi?article=1448&context=vlr.

Jerez, Horacio Vedia, *Competition Law Enforcement and Compliance Across the World: A Comparative Review*, Wolters Kluwer, 2015.

Johnston, Peter, *Consumer Representative Actions: Floodgates Opening Soon?*, 27 July 2022, available at Consumer Representative Actions - Floodgates ... | Mason Hayes Curran (mhc.ie).

Jones, Alison and Sufrin, Brenda, *EC Competition Law*, Oxford University Press, 3rd ed., 2008.

Jones, Clifford, *Private Enforcement of Antitrust Law in the EU, UK and USA*, Oxford University Press, 1st ed., 1999.

Jones, Emilie and Weißbach, Johfanna, *EU Plans to Regulate Third-Party Litigation Funders Meet Mixed Response*, 12 January 2023, available at EU plans to regulate third-party litigation funders meet mixed response | ICLG.com Briefings.

Juška, Žygimantas, *Obstacles in European Competition Law Enforcement: A Potential Solution from Collective Redress*, European Journal of Legal Studies, vol. 7, No. 1, 2014, pp. 125-153.

Juška, Žygimantas, *The Effectiveness of Antitrust Collective Litigation in the European Union: A Study of the Principle of Full Compensation*, International Review of Intellectual Property and Competition Law, vol. 49, 2018, pp. 63-93.

Juška, Žygimantas, *The Role of Collective Redress Actions to Achieve Full Compensation for Violations of European Union Competition Law*, PhD thesis defended at Leiden University on 23 June 2019, available at view (universiteitleiden.nl).

Kakouris, Constantinos, *Do the Member States Possess Judicial Procedural 'Autonomy'*, Common Market Law Review, vol. 34, No. 6, 1997.

Kerse, Christopher Stephen, *EEC Antitrust Procedure*, European Law Centre Ltd., 2nd ed., 1988.

Kersting, Christian, *Practical Difficulties with Privileging the Successful Leniency Applicant in Relation to the Injured Parties, Proposal for a Private Enforcement Directive, COM(2013) 404 final*, Heinrich Heine University, 28 September 2013.

Kirst, Philipp, *The Impact of the Damages Directive on the Enforcement of EU Competition Law: A Law and Economics Analysis*, Edward Elgar, 2021.

Kliebard, Kenneth M. et al., *Class/Collective Actions in the United States: Overview*, 1 September 2020, available at Class/collective actions in the United States: overview | Practical Law (thomsonreuters.com).

Klimas, Tadas and Vaitiukait, Jflrate, *The Law of Recitals in European Community Legislation*, ILSA Journal of International & Comparative Law, vol. 15, No. 1, 2008.

Knigge, Albert and Cornelissen, Rick, *The Judgment of the CJEU in Otis and Others (C-435/18): Indirect Losses May Need to Be Compensated*, Lexology, 16 January 2020, https://www.lexology.com/library/detail.aspx?g=bb549a7b-d0da-4bb6-9a91-37a5ca375637.

Kokkoris, Ioannis and Olivares-Caminal, Rodrigo, *Antitrust Law Amidst Financial Crises*, Cambridge University Press, 2010.

Komnimos, Assimakis P., *Private Antitrust Damages Actions in the EU: Second Generation Questions, Revista de Regulação e Concorrência*, Year III, No. 9, Almedina, January/March 2012.

König, Thomas and Luetjueert, Brooke, *Troubles with Transposition? Explaining Trends in Member-State Notification and the Delayed Transposition of EU Directives*, Cambridge University Press, 10 November 2008, available at ConantBackgroundReading4 (eui.eu).

Krüger, Carsten, *Revival of the 'Claims Assignment Class Action' in German Private Antitrust Enforcement (and Beyond)*, 8 May 2021, available at Revival of the 'claims assignment class action' in German private antitrust enforcement (and beyond) - CDC (carteldamageclaims.com).

Lamego, José, *Elements of Legal Methodology*, Almedina, 2016.

Landini, Sara, *Private Enforcement and Market Regulation*, Market and Competition Law Review, vol. 2, No. 2, pp. 47-70, available at Private Enforcement and Market Regulation | Market and Competition Law Review (ucp.pt).

Larenz, Karl, *Metodologia da Ciência do Direito*, Calouste Gulbenkian Foundation, 2nd ed., 1997.

Lavoire, Chantal, *Court of Justice Ruling in Skanska: EU Competition Law Concept of 'Undertakings' and Principle of Economic Continuity to the Rescue in Civil Damages Claims*, Kluwer Competition Law Blog, 22 March 2019, http://competitionlawblog.kluwercompetitionlaw.com/2019/03/22/court-of-justice-ruling-in-skanska-eu-competition-law-concept-of-undertakings-and-principle-of-economic-continuity-to-the-rescue-in-civil-damages-claims/?doing_wp_cron=1591108238.9130420684814453125000.

Ledesma, Carmen Alonso, Sáenz, Joseba A. Echebarría and Gilsanz, Javier Gutiérrez, *Private Enforcement of Competition Law*, Lex Nova, 2011.

Legg, Michael, *The Rise and Regulation of Litigation Funding in Australian Class Actions*, Erasmus Law Review, vol. 14, No. 4, 2021.

Leskinen, Charlotte, *Recent Developments on Collective Antitrust Damages Actions in the EU*, Global Competition Litigation Review, vol. 4, No. 2, 2010, pp. 79-88.

Leskinen, Charlotte, *Collective Antitrust Damages Actions in the EU: The Opt-in v. Opt-Out Model*, Working Paper IE Law School, 2010, available at http://ssrn.com/abstract=1612731.

Leskinen, Charlotte, *Collective Actions: Rethinking Funding and National Cost Rules*, The Competition Law Review, vol. 8, No. 1, December 2011, pp. 87-121.

Leslie, Christopher R, *Editorial: Antitrust Leniency Programmes*, The Competition Law Review, vol. 7, No. 2, July 2011.

Levine, Jason, *The Role of Litigation Finance in Antitrust Lawsuits*, 30 March 2022, available at The role of litigation finance in antitrust lawsuits (omnibridgeway.com).

Lewis, Sebastian, *Precedent and the Rule of Law*, Oxford Journal of Legal Studies, vol. 41, No. 4, Winter 2021, pp. 873-898.

Lima, José Reinaldo de and Courtis, Christian (eds), *Regla y Compás, O Metodología para un Trabajo Jurídico Senato, in Observar la ley: Ensayos sobre Metodología* de *La Investigación Jurídica*, Editorial Trotta, 2006.

Lopez, Fernando Peña, *Issues and Problems Regarding U.S. Competition Law Private Enforcement: Damages and Nullity Actions, The* USV Annals of Economics and Public Administration, vol. 13, No. 1(17), 2013.

Lourenço, Paula Meira, *Public Hearing on a Horizontal Instrument for Collective Redress in Europe*, Brussels, 12 July 2011.

Lourenço, Nuno Calaim, *The European Commission's Directive on Antitrust Damages Actions*, Revista de Concorrência e Regulação, Ano V, N.º 18, Almedina, 2014, pp. 65-87.

Lourenço, Paula Meira, *A Indemnização Punitiva e os Critérios para a sua Determinação*, Colloquium organised by the Supreme Court of Justice, under the theme Civil Liability - Novas Prespectivas, held on 13 and 14 March 2008, available at https://www.academia.edu/37199605/MEIRA_LOURENCO_P_A_indemniza%C3%A7%C3%A3o_punitiva_e_os_crit%C3%A9rios_para_a_sua_determina%C3%A7%C3%A3o_03_2008_.

Marcos, Francisco, *In Prescripción y daño en las reclamaciones de daños por conductas anticompetitivas: luces y sembras de la sentencia del Tribunal de Justicia UE de 22/6/22 (C-267/20 DAF TRUCKS NV and AB VOLVO/RM) (Statute of Limitations and Harm in Antitrust Damages Claims: Light and Shadows on the CJEU Judgment of 22/6/22 (C-267/20 DAF Trucks NV & AB Volvo))*, 9 September 2022, available at https://ssrn.com/abstract=4244690.

Marcos, Francisco, Rodger, Barry and Ferro, Miguel Sousa, *Promotion and Harmonisation of Antitrust Damage Claims by Directive EU/2014/104*, Working Paper IE Law School AJ8-242-I, 13 June 2018.

Marder, Neal Ross et al., *UK Supreme Court Hands Down New Guidance for Collective Claim Certification*, Thomson Reuters Wesrlaw, 25 January 2021, *available at* pi_marder.pdf (akingump.com).

Marques, Maria Manuel Leitão, *A Course in Competition Law*, Coimbra Editora, 2002.

Marques, Nuno Castro, *Os fundamentos políticos da concorrência: alinhando a defesa da concorrência com a constituição económica e o modelo económico-social* português, ULP Law Review Special Is, 2022, pp. 42-58, available at http://dx.doi.org/10.46294/ulplr-rdulp.siv1a4.

Martínez, Ignacio García-Perrote, *AG Rantos: Temporal Scope of the Damages Directive, Substantive and Procedural Provisions and Limitation Periods*, Kluwer Competition Law Blog, 19 February 2022, available at AG Rantos: Temporal scope of the Damages Directive, substantive and procedural provisions and limitation periods - Kluwer Competition Law Blog.

Martins, Patrícia Fragoso, *Rethinking Access by Private Parties to the Court of Justice of the European Union: Judicial Review of Union Acts Before and after the Lisbon Treaty*, Universidade Católica Editora, 2016.

Massa, Claudia, *The Disclosure of Leniency Statements and Other Evidence under Directive 2014/104/EU: An Undue Prominence of Public Enforcement?*, Market and Competition Law Review, vol. 2, No. 1, pp. 149-169, available at The Disclosure of Leniency Statements and Other Evidence under Directive 2014/104/EU: An Undue Prominence of Public Enforcement? | Market and Competition Law Review (ucp.pt).

McClure, Daniel and Dekovich, Matthew, *Class and Group Actions Laws and Regulations: USA*, 9 November 2022, available at Class and Group Actions Laws and Regulations Report 2023 USA (iclg.com).

Mcconville, Mike and Chui, Wing Hong, *Research Methods for Law*, Edinburgh University Press, 2007.

McGovern, Francis E., *Punitive Damages and Class Actions*, Louisiana Law Review, vol. 70, No. 2, Symposium on Punitive Damages, Winter 2010.

Meeûs, Charlotte de, *The EU Court of Justice Clarifies the Temporal Scope of the Damages Directive (Volvo/DAF Trucks)*, e-Competitions, 22 June 2022, Article No. 107667.

Mehren, Arthur Taylor von, *Law in The United States: A General and Comparative View*, Kluwer, 1989.

Melíssias, Maria João, *The Art of Consistency Between Public and Private Antitrust Enforcement: Practical Challenges in Implementing the Damage Directive in Portugal*, Revista Concorrência e Regulação, Year VII, No. 26, April/June, 2016.

Mendes, Castro and Sousa, Miguel Teixeira de, *Manual de Processo Civil*, vol. I, AAFDL, 2022.

Mendes, Paulo de Sousa, *As garantias* de *defesa no processo sanancional especial por práticas restritivas da concorrência confrontadas com a jurisprudência do Tribunal Europeu dos Direitos do Homem, Revista Concorrência e Regulação*, Ano I, N.º 1, January/March, 2010.

Miller, Arthur R., *The American Class Action: From Birth to Maturity Theoretical Inquiries in Law*, vol. 19, No. 1, 13 February 2018.

Moniz, Carlos Botelho, *Competition Law Annotated*, Almedina, 2016.

Monteiro, António Pedro Pinto and Júdice, José Miguel, *Class Actions & Arbitration in the European Union: Portugal*, Studies in Honour of Miguel Galvão Teles, vol. II, Almedina, 2012, pp. 189-205.

Morais, Luís D. S., *Os Conceitos de Objecto e Efeito Restritivos da Concorrência e a Prescrição de Infracções de Concorrência*, Almedina, 2009.
Morais, Luís Silva, *Integrating Public and Private Enforcement of Competition Law in Europe: Legal and Jurisdictional Issues,* available at https://papers.ssrn.com/sol3/papers.cfm?abstract_id=2657570.
Morony, Elizabeth, Jasper, Ben and Carroll, Oliver, *England & Wales, Private Antitrust Litigation 2020*, Francesca Richmond (ed.), July 2019.
Morpurgo, Marco de, *A Comparative legal and Economic Approach to Third-Party Litigation Funding,* 11 January 2011, available at A COMPARATIVE LEGAL AND ECONOMIC APPROACH TO THIRD-PARTY LITIGATION FUNDING (cejamericas.org).
Motta, Massimo, *Competition Policy: Theory and Practice*, Cambridge University Press, 2004.
Moussis, Vassili and Yamada, Atsushi, *Abuse of Economic Dependence, Global Dictionary of Competition Law*, Concurrences, Article No. 86372.
Mulheron, Rachael, *Reform of Collective Redress in England and Wales: A Perspective of Need*, Civil Justice Council, 2008, available at https://www.judiciary.uk/wp-content/uploads/JCO/Documents/CJC/Publications/Other+papers/reform-of-collective-redress.pdf.
Mulheron, Rachael, *The United Kingdom's New Opt-out Class Action: The Unique Perspective of a 'Third Generation' Statute*, Oxford Journal of Legal Studies, vol. 37, No. 4, Oxford University Press, 2017, pp. 814-843.
Mulheron, Rachael, *Class Actions and Government*, Cambridge University Press, 2020.
Nagy, Csongor István, *Has the Time Come to Federalise Private Competition Law? The Autonomous Concept of Undertaking in the CJEU's Ruling in Case C-724/17 Vantaa v. Skanska*, Maastricht Journal of European and Comparative Law, vol. 26, No. 5, 2019, pp. 720-728.
Nagy, Csongor István, *Collective Actions in Europe: A Comparative, Economic and Transsystemic Analysis,* Springer Open, 2019, available at https://link.springer.com/content/pdf/10.1007/978-3-030-24222-0.pdf.
Napier, Michael et al., *Improved Access to Justice: Funding Options & Proportionate Costs, A Series of Recommendations to the Lord Chancellor to Improve Access to Justice Through the Development of Improved Funding Structures*, Civil Justice Council, June 2007.
Nascimbene, Juan and Anderson, Olivia, *EU Plans To Regulate Third-Party Funding in Litigation and International Arbitration*, 3 April 2023, available at EU Plans To Regulate Third-Party Funding in Litigation and International Arbitration - Lexology.
Neale, Alan Derrett, *The Antitrust Laws of the United States of America: A Study of Competition Enforced by Law*, University Press, 1960.
Neto, Susana, *Quota Litis: da Evidência da sua Proibição*, Revista da Ordem dos Advogados, Lisbon, A.61, No. 2, April 2001, pp. 1121-1140, available at https://portal.oa.pt/publicacoes/revista-da-ordem-dos-advogados/ano-2001/ano-61-vol-ii-abr-2001/temas/susana-neto-quota-litis-da-evidencia-da-sua-proibicao/.
Neves, Castanheira A., *Legal Methodology: Fundamental Problems, Bulletin of the Faculty of Law*, Coimbra Editora, 2013.

Nielsen, Laura Beth, Cane, Peter, Kritzer, Herbert M., *The Need for Multi-Method Approaches, The Oxford Handbook of Empirical Legal Research*, Oxford University Press, 2010.

Nnona, George C., *Multidisciplinary Practice in the International Context: Realigning the Perspective on the European Union's Regulatory Regime*, Cornell International Law Journal, vol. 37, No. 1, 2004, Article 4.

Nowag, Julian and Tarkkila, Liisa, *In How Much Effectiveness for the EU Damages Directive?: Contractual Clauses and Antitrust Damages Actions*, Common Market Law Review, vol. 57, No. 2, 2020, available at https://doi.org/10.54648/cola2020 033.

O'Regan, Matthew, *United Kingdom: Consumer Rights Act 2015 Introduces New Procedures for Competition Litigation, Including Collective Follow-on Damages Actions*, Kluwer Competition Law Blog, 5 October 2015, *http://competitionlawblog.kluwercompetitionlaw.com/2015/10/05/united-kingdom-consumer-rights-act-2015-introduces-new-procedures-for-competition-litigation-including-collective-follow-on-damages-actions/.*

Otero, Paulo, A *acção popular: configuração e valor no actual Direito português*, Revista da Ordem dos Advogados, vol. III, 1999, pp. 871-893.

Pais, Sofia, *Algumas Reflexões sobre o Princípio da Interpretação Conforme no Contexto da 'Transposição Judicial' das Diretivas, Revista da Faculdade e Direito da Universidade do Porto*, Year VII, 2010.

Pais, Sofia Oliveira, *Between Innovation and Competition: In Defence of a European Model*, Universidade Católica Editora, 2011.

Pais, Sofia Oliveira, *Between Clemency and Responsibility: A Success Story?, Judgement of the Court of Justice (Grand Chamber) of 14.6.2011, Case C-360/09, Cadernos de Direito Privado*, ISSN 1645-7242, No. 37, 2012.

Pais, Sofia Oliveira, *Direito da União Europeia: Legislação e* Jurisprudência *Fundamentais*, Quid Juris - Sociedade Editora, 2nd ed., 2013.

Pais, Sofia Oliveira, *A União faz a força? Breves reflexões sobre os mecanismos coletivos de reparação no contexto da aplicação privada do direito da concorrência da união, Liber Amicorum em Homenagem ao Prof. Doutor João Mota de Campos*, Coimbra Editora, 2013.

Pais, Sofia Oliveira and Piszcz, Anna, *Package on Actions for Damages Based on Breaches of EU Competition Rules: Can One Size Fit All?*, Yearbook of Antitrust and Regulatory Studies, vol. 7, No. 10, CARS, 2014.

Pais, Sofia Oliveira, *Estudos de Direito da União Europeia*, Almedina, 3rd ed., 2014.

Pais, Sofia Oliveira, *Private Antitrust Enforcement: A New Era for Collective Redress?* Yearbook of Antitrust and Regulatory Studies, vol. 8, No. 12, CARS, 2015, available at 3Private Antitrust Enforcement.pdf.

Pais, Sofia Oliveira, *National Report: Portugal, XXVII FIDE Congress*, Budapest, Hungary, 18-21 May 2016, Private Enforcement and Collective Redress in European Competition Law - Congress Proceedings, Kluwer Law International, 2016, available at Microsoft Word - FIDE 2016 Topic 2.docx (apde.org.pt).

Pais, Sofia Oliveira, *Judgment of the Court of Justice of 5 February 1963: Case 26/62 Van Gend en Loos v. Dutch Tax Administration, Fundamental Principles of European Union Law, A Jurisprudential Approach*, Almedina, 3rd ed., 2017.

Pais, Sofia Oliveira, *Judgment of the Court of Justice of 13 November 1990: Case C-106/89 Marleasing SA v. La Comercial Internacional de Alimentación SA, Fundamental Principles of European Union Law, A Jurisprudential Approach*, Almedina, 3rd ed., 2017.

Pais, Sofia, *Judgment of the Court of Justice of 30 September 2003: Case C-224/01 Gerhard Köbler v. Republik Österreich, Fundamental Principles of European Union Law, A Jurisprudential Approach*, Almedina, 3rd ed., 2017.

Pais, Sofia, *A First Look at the Portuguese Act 23/2018 Transposing the Private Enforcement Directive in EU Competition Litigation: Transposition and First Experiences of the New Regime*, Magnus Strand, Vladimir Bastidas Venegas and Marios C. Iacovides (eds), Oxford Hart Publishing, 2019, pp. 63-76, available at untitled (ucp.pt).

Pak, Chul and Weick, Daniel P., *United States, The Private Competition Enforcement Review*, Law Business Research, 10th ed., 2017.

Pakamanis, Mantas, *The Role of Class Actions in Ensuring Effective Enforcement of Competition Law Infringements in the European Union*, International Comparative Jurisprudence, vol. 2, No. 2, December 2016, pp. 122-130.

Palma, Augusta Ferreira, *Das Pequenas e Médias Empresas: Algumas Questões (Maxime, no Direito da Concorrência)*, Almedina, 2011.

Palmer, Ellie (eds), *Access to Justice: Beyond the Policies and Politics of Austerity*, Bloomsbury Publishing, 26 April 2018.

Parcu, Pier Luigi, Monti, Giorgio and Botta, Marco (eds), *Private Enforcement of EU Competition Law: The Impact of the Damages Directive*, Elgar, 2018, p. 92.

Pärn-Lee, Evelin, *Effect of National Decisions on Actions for Competition Damages in the CEE Countries*, Yearbook of Antitrust and Regulatory Studies, vol. 10, No. 15, 2017, pp. 177-196, available at Effect of National Decisions on Actions for Competition Damages in the CEE Countries by Evelin Pärn-Lee:: SSRN.

Pejovic, Caslav, *Civil Law and Common Law: Two Different Paths Leading to the Same Goal*, July 2001, available at https://www.researchgate.net/publication/265244573_Civil_Law_and_Common_Law_Two_Different_Paths_Leading_to_the_Same_Goal.

Perales, Carmen, *European Parliament Litigation Funding Resolution Criticised by Experts*, ION Analytics, 13 December 2022, available at European Parliament litigation funding resolution criticised by experts | ION Analytics Community.

Pereira, Miguel Mendes, *Competition Law:* Annotated, Coimbra Editora, 2009.

Peres, Catarina Vieira, *The Cogeco Case: The First Preliminary Ruling on the Private Enforcement Directive*, Market and Competition Law Review, vol. 3, No. 2, pp. 81-106, available at The Cogeco Case: The First Preliminary Ruling on the Private Enforcement Directive | Market and Competition Law Review (ucp.pt).

Pérez, Gerardo Sáer Pérez, *Estudio e Investigación del Derecho*, Universidad de Carabono, 1974.

Peters, Frank, Krekels, Michelle and Berger, Louis, *New European Directive Gives Teeth to Consumer Rights (and There Are Many ...!)*, 20 January 2021, available at New European Directive gives teeth to consumer rights (and there are many ...!) - Bureau Brandeis.

Petrasiscu, Alex and Unseld, Christopher, *Collective Redress in Germany for Cartel Damages Claims*, Lexology, 24 August 2022, available at Collective redress in Germany for cartel damages claims - Lexology.

Peyer, Sebastian, *Injunctive Relief and Private Antitrust Enforcement*, CCP Working Paper 11-7, 2011.

Peyer, Sebastian, *Has the CAT's MasterCard Decision Killed off Opt-out Class Actions by Indirect Purchasers?*, Centre for Competition Policy, 10 August 2017, available at Has the CAT's MasterCard decision killed off opt-out class actions by indirect purchasers? | Centre for Competition Policy.

Pietrini, Silvia, *L'action en droit des pratiques anticoncurrentielles: Perspectives nationale, européenne et internationale*, Concurrences, Bruylant, 2012.

Pike, Richard and Cousins, Katherine, *Too Big, Too Small, Not Yet 'Just Right': UK Collective Actions Regime Still to Find Its Goldilocks*, Global Competition Litigation Review, No. 1, 2018, pp. 42-45.

Pinto De Albuquerque, Paulo and Aaken, Anne van, *12 Punitive Damages in Strasbourg, in The European Convention on Human Rights and General International Law*, Anne van Aaken and Iulia Motoc (eds), Oxford University Press, 2018, pp. 230-248.

Piszcz, Anna, *Piecemeal Harmonisation Through the Damages Directive? Remarks on What Received Too Little Attention in Relation to Private Enforcement of EU Competition Law*, Yearbook of Antitrust and Regulatory Studies, vol. 8, No. 12, CARS, 2015.

Piszcz, Anna, *Implementation of the EU Damages Directive in Central and Eastern European Countries*, Centre for Antitrust and Regulatory Studies, University of Warsaw Faculty of Management Press, 2017, available at CARS 24 Implementation of the EU.indd (uw.edu.pl).

Plasschaert, Emmanuel, *Les PME et les indépendants ont désormais accès à l'action en réparation collective*, 7 June 2018, available at https://www.lecho.be/opinions/carte-blanche/les-pme-et-les-independants-ont-desormais-acces-a-l-action-en-reparation-collective/10018844.html.

Porto, Manuel Carlos Lopes and Anastácio, Gonçalo, *Tratado de Lisboa: Anotado e Comentado*, Almedina, 2012.

Prosperetti, Luigi, *Antitrust Damages in Europe: an Economic Perspective, VII Conference European Lawyers Union*, Bruylant, 2007.

Ramos, *European Constitution and Constitution of the Portuguese Republic, Europe and the Challenges of the 21st Century: International Conference*, Almedina, 2008.

Ramos, Maria Elisabete, *Situation of Private Enforcement of Competition in Portugal*, Revista de Concorrência e Regulação, Year VII, No. 27/28, July/December, 2016.

Ramos, Maria Elisabete, *Private Enforcement and Opt-out System Risks, Rewards and Legal Safeguards*, Yearbook of Antitrust and Regulatory Studies, vol. 11, No. 18, 2018, pp. 85-114, available at available at https://doi.org/10.7172/1689-9024.yars.2018.11.18.4.

Rangel, Paulo Castro, *Advocacy and Prejudice*, Revista da Ordem dos Advogados (ROA) Year 2002 Year 62, vol. II, April 2002.

Rasmussen, H., *The European Court of Justice*, GadJura, 1998.

Reale, Miguel, Teoria *Tridimensional do Direito, Teoria da Justiça, Fontes e Modelos do Direito*, Imprensa Nacional-Casa da Moeda, Estudos Gerais, Série Universitária, 2003.

Reich, Norbert, *General Principles of EU Civil Law*, Cambridge Intersentia Publishing, 2014.

Reis, José António Sá, *in 'Make Antitrust Great Again'?: Perspectives for US Competition Law in the Post-truth Era*, Revista Eletrónica de Direito, No. 2, June 2017.

Render, Adrian and Peyer, Sebastian, *Are Cases Too Good to Litigate? Cost Recovery in Antitrust Collective Actions in the UK*, European Competition Law Review, vol. 41, No. 1, 2020, pp. 3-12, available at Are cases too good to litigate? Cost recovery in antitrust collective actions in the UK - UEA Digital Repository.

Renner, Christina and Manong, Cécile, *Collective Actions in the EU: The Past, the Present, the Future*, Thomson Reuters Practical Law, 1 March 2020.

Review, Michigan Law, *Class Actions for Punitive Damages*, Michigan Law Review, vol. 81, 1983, p. 1787, available at 'Class Actions for Punitive Damages' by Michigan Law Review (umich.edu).

Richards, J. Douglas, Eisenkraft, Michael B. and Shafrith, Abigail E., *Class Actions, Private Enforcement of Antitrust Law in the United States: A Handbook*, Albert A. Foer and Randy M. Stutz (eds), Edward Elgar, 2012.

Richards, Tom, *Cats, Bags, Rings and Rooms: The Problem of Confidentiality*, Competition Bulletin, 11 October 2013, available at Cats, bags, rings and rooms: the problem of confidentiality | Competition Bulletin.

Richter, Ann-Christin, *In ECJ Rules on Temporal Applicability of the Cartel Damages Directive and Clarifies the Statute of Limitation in Cartel Damage Cases*, Competition Bulletin, 24 August 2022, available at Hausfeld | ECJ rules on temporal applicability of the cartel Damages Directive and clarifies the statute of limitation in cartel damage cases.

Riley, Alan and Peysner, John, *Damages in EC Antitrust Actions: Who Pays the Piper?*, European Law Review, ISSN 0307-5400, vol. 31, No. 5, 2006, pp. 748-761.

Rodger, Barry (ed.), *Competition Law, Comparative Private Enforcement and Collective Redress Across the EU*, Kluwer Law International, 2014.

Rodger, Barry, Ferro, Miguel Sousa and Marcos, Francisco (eds), *The EU Antitrust Damages Directive: Transposition in the Member States*, Oxford University Press, 2018.

Rodger, Barry, Ferro, Miguel Sousa and Marcos, Francisco, *A Panacea for Competition Law Damages Actions in the EU? A Comparative View of the Implementation of the EU Antitrust Damages Directive in Sixteen Member States*, Maastricht Journal of European and Comparative Law, vol. 26, No. 4, 2019, pp. 480-504.

Rodger, Barry, Ferro, Miguel Sousa and Marcos, Francisco (eds), *Research Handbook on Competition Law Private Enforcement in the EU*, Edward Elgar, 2023.

Rodrigues, Vasco, *Economic Analysis of Law*, Almedina, 2nd ed., 2016.

Rossi, Leonor and Ferro, Miguel Sousa, *Private Enforcement of Competition Law, in Portugal (I): An Overview of Case-law*, Revista de Concorrência e Regulação, Year III, No. 10, Almedina April/June 2012.

Rossi, Leonor and Ferro, Miguel Sousa, *Private Enforcement of Competition Law in Portugal (II): Actio Popularis – Facts, Fictions and Dreams*, Revista de Concorrência e Regulação, Year IV, No. 13, Almedina, January/March 2013.

Rossi-Maccanico, Pierpaolo, *A Reasoned Approach to Prohibiting the Bis in Idem Between the Double and the Triple Identities*, Associations for European Criminal Law and the Protection of Financial Interests of the EU, No. 4, 2021, pp. 266-273, available at https://eucrim.eu/media/issue/pdf/eucrim_issue_2021-04.pdf#page =72.

Rotondo, Elisabetta, *Is the EU's Use of Regulations Becoming a Trend?*, Thomson Reuters Practical Law Public Sector Blog, 24 July 2013 available at Is the EU's use of regulations becoming a trend? | Public Sector Blog (practicallaw.com).

Saavedra, Alberto, *The Relationship Between the Leniency Programme and Private Actions for Damages at the EU Level*, Revista de Concorrência e Regulação, 1 December 2010.

Saavedra, Alberto, *Access by National Courts and Private Plaintiffs to Leniency Documents Held by the Commission*, Revista de Concorrência e Regulação, No. 10, Year III, April/June 2012.

Sadeleer, Nicolas de, *Les actes hors nomenclature et le soft law européen*, *in* Les *Sources du Droit Revisitées*, Université Saint-Louis Bruxelles, vol. 1, Anthemis, 2012.

Şahin, Eda, *Collective Redress and EU Competition Law*, Routledge, 2019.

Salpico, Nuno A. Pires, *The Effectiveness of Private Enforcement of Competition Law: Deterrent, Collective Actions and Third-party Ligation Funding*, Revista de Concorrência & Regulação, Lisbon, No. 45, 2021, pp. 103-141.

Sauter, Wolf, *Coherence in EU Competition Law*, OUP Oxford, 2016.

Schwab, Andreas, *Finding the Right Balance: the Deliberations of the European Parliament on the Draft Legislation Regarding Damage Claims*, Journal of European Competition Law & Practice, vol. 5, No. 2, 2014.

Scott, Peter et al., *England & Wales, The Private Competition Enforcement Review*, Law Business Research, 10th ed., 2017.

Shah, Omar, *Class Actions: A Global Guide from Practical Law*, Thomson Reuters, 2015.

Silva, Miguel Moura e, *Inovação, Transferência de Tecnologia e Concorrência: Estudo Comparado do Direito da Concorrência dos Estados Unidos* e *da União* Europeia, Almedina, 2003.

Silva, Miguel Moura e, *Direito da Concorrência: Uma introdução Jurisprudencial*, Almedina, 2008.

Silva, Sara Monteiro Pinto Ferreira da, *Danos Punitivos: Problemas em relação à sua admissibilidade no ordenamento jurídico português*, UCP, 2012, dissertation available at https://repositorio.ucp.pt/entities/publication/6ce1156d-85b2-4e5c-9c01-bc469ad265db.

Silveiro, Fernando Xarepe, *Commentary on European Union Case Law, Judgment of the Court of Justice of the European Union of 6 June 2013, in Case C-536/11, Donau*

Chemie, Revista de Concorrência e Regulação, Year IV, Nos 14 and 15, April/ September, 2013.

Silver, Charles, *We're Scared to Death: Class Certification and Blackmail*, New York University Law Review, vol. 78, No. 4, October 2003, We're Scared to Death: Class Certification and Blackmail (nyulawreview.org).

Siragusa, Mario and Rizza, Cesare, *Cartels and Collusive Behaviour: Restrictive Agreements and Practices between Competitors*, Claeys & Casteels, 2012.

Siredey-Garnier, Fabienne, *Sanctions pénales*, Dictionnaire de droit de la concurrence, Concurrences, Article No. 88941.

Siska, Juraj and Seegers, Martin, *CJEU Clarifies the Temporal Application of the New EU Damages Directive's Five-Year Limitation in Cartel Cases*, Cartel Damage Claims, 24 June 2022, available at CJEU clarifies the temporal application of the new EU Damages Directive's five-year limitation in cartel cases - CDC (carteldamageclaims.com).

Skara, Gentjuean, *Europeanisation of Private Enforcement of Competition Law: The Case of Albania*, Springer, 2022.

Soares, António Goucha, *A Aplicação Descentralizada das Normas Comunitárias da Concorrência: o sistema de competências paralelas estabelecida pelo Regulamento n.º 1/2003, Concorrência: Estudos*, under his coordination and that of Marques, Maria Manuel Leitão, Almedina, 2006.

Solas, Gian Marco, *Third Party Funding: Law, Economic and Policy*, Cambridge University Press, 2019.

Sousa, Miguel Teixeira de, *A Legitimidade Popular na Tutela dos Interesses Difusos*, LEX, 2003.

Stadler, Astrid, *Are Class Actions Finally (Re)conquering Europe?: Some Remarks on Directive 2020/1828*, Juridica International, 30 March 2021.

Stanikunas, Rimantas and Burinskas, Arunas, *The Interaction of Public and Private Enforcement of Competition Law in Lithuania*, Yearbook of Antitrust and Regulatory Studies, vol. 8, No. 12, CARS, 2015.

Stefano, Gianni de, *Access of Damage Claimants to Evidence Arising out of EU Cartel Investigations: A Fast-evolving Scenario*, Global Competition Litigation Review, vol. 3, 2012.

Stellakis, Elysia-Elena, *5 Things We Learnt about Class Actions, Practical Law Dispute Resolution*, 8 March 2023, available at 5 things we learnt about class actions | Dispute Resolution blog (practicallaw.com).

Stephan, Andreas, *Does the EU's Drive for Private Enforcement of Competition Law Have a Coherent Purpose?*, 2018, pp. 11 and 16, available at Accepted_manuscript.pdf (uea.acórdãk).

Stöhr, Alexander, *In The Implementation of Collective Redress: A Comparative Approach*, German Law Journal, vol. 21, 2020, pp. 1606-1624.

Strand, Magnus, *Competition Damages Betwixt and Between Past and Future: Cogeco*, Common Market Law Review, vol. 57, 2020, pp. 569-590.

Tettenborn, Andrew, *Punitive Damages: A View from England*, San Diego Law Review, vol. 41, 2004.

Trstenjak, Verica and Weingerl, Petra, *Collective Actions in the European Union: American or European Model?*, Beijing Law Review, vol. 5, 2014, pp. 155-162.

Turtle, Edward, *New EU Class Actions Mechanisms to be Implemented by Christmas*, 11 October 2022, available at New EU Class Actions Mechanisms to be Implemented by Christmas - Lexology.

Ullrich, Hanns, *Private Enforcement of the EU Rules on Competition: Nullity Neglected*, Max Planck Institute for Innovation & Competition Research Paper No. 21-09, pp. 606-635, available at https://link.springer.com/content/pdf/10.1007/s40319-021-01054-w.pdf.

Unger, Roberto Mangabeira and Rawlings, Richard (eds), *Legal Analysis as Institutional Imagination, Law, Society, and Economy: Centenary Essays for the London School of Economics and Political Science (1895-1995)*, Clarendon Press, 1997.

Uzelac, Alan and Voet, Stefaan (eds), *Class Actions in Europe: Holy Grail or a Wrong Trail?*, Springer, 2021.

Vanleenhove, Cedric, *Punitive Damages and European Law: Quo Vademus?, in The Power of Punitive Damages: Is Europe Missing Out?*, Lotte Meurkens and Emily Nordin (eds), Cambridge-Antwerp-Portland, Intersentia, 2012, pp. 337-353.

Venda, Sílvia Bessa, *As regras antitrust e o direito a uma reparação efetiva: O acesso às declarações de clemência*, Colecção Estudos Instituto do Conhecimento AB, No. 6, Almedina, 2017, 299-343, available at Estudos do Instituto do Conhecimento AB No. 6 (abreuadvogados.com).

Venda, Sílvia Bessa, *The Disclosure of Documents Collected by Competition Authorities Before and After the EU Damages Directive, 60 Years of EU Competition Law: Stocktaking and Future Prospects*, Roberto Mastroianni and Amedeo Arena (eds), Editoriale Scientifica, Naples, 2017, pp. 99-112.

Venda, Sílvia Bessa, *Otis II: Light at the End of the Tunnel for Damages Indirectly Caused by Competition Law Infringements*, ULP Law Review/Revista de Direito da ULP, vol. 13 No. 1, 2020, available at Otis II: light at the end of the tunnel for damages indirectly caused by competition law infringements | ULP Law Review - Revista de Direito da ULP (ulusofona.pt).

Verhulst, Michiel, *CJEU Finds National Limitation Periods in Conflict with the EU Law Principle of Effectiveness*, 2 July 2020, available at CJEU finds national limitation periods in conflict with the EU law principle of effectiveness - CDC (carteldamage-claims.com).

Viana, Pedro Petiz, *Online Legal Platforms: The Beginning of the 4.0 Law Practice?*, UNIO – EU Law Journal, vol. 5, No. 2, July 2019, pp 43-62.

Vicente, Dário Moura, *Comparative Law*, vol. I, Almedina, 3rd ed., 2014.

Walle, Simon Vande, *Private Antitrust Litigation in the European Union and Japan*, Maklu, 2013.

Waller, Spencer Weber, *The Incoherence of Punishment in Antitrust*, Chicago-Kent Law Review, vol. 78, No. 1, Symposium: Private Law, Punishment, and Disgorgement, April 2003, Article 8.

Wamel, David Van, *Otis II: A Lost Opportunity to Clear the Mist*, Lexxion Competition Blogs, 25 March 2020, https://www.lexxion.eu/en/coreblogpost/otis-ii-a-lost-opportunity-to-clear-the-mist/.

Warringto, Giles and Riisager, Tim, *United Kingdom, Cartels 2020*, Nigel Parr and Euan Burrowns (eds), Global Legal Group, 8th ed., 17 February 2020, https://www.globallegalinsights.com/practice-areas/cartels-laws-and-regulations/united-kingdom.

Webley, Lisa, CANE, Peter and M. Kritzer, Herber (eds), *The Oxford Handbook of Empirical Legal Research*, Oxford University Press, 2010, pp. 927-950.

Whish, Richard and Bailey, David, *Competition Law*, Oxford University Press, 2012.

Williams, Sarina, Shardlow-Wrest, Jason and Chung, Alice, *A Little Less Conversation: CAT Restricts Defendants' Communications with Actual or Potential Class Members*, 21 February 2023, available at Class actions hub - Global Competition Review.

Wilman, Folkert, *The End of the Absence? The Growing Body of EU Legislation on Private Enforcement and the Main Remedies It Provides for*, Common Market Law Review, vol. 53, No. 4, 2016, pp. 887-935, available at https://kluwerlawonline.com/journalarticle/Common+Market+Law+Review/53.4/COLA2016088.

Wils, Wouter PJ, *Should Private Antitrust Enforcement Be Encouraged in Europe?*, World Competition: Law and Economics Review, vol. 26, No. 3, 2003.

Wils, Wouter PJ, *Efficiency and Justice in European Antitrust Enforcement*, Hard Publishing, 2008.

winters, Gary A., *Trial Issues In Consolidated Direct And Indirect Purchaser Cases: Lessons From the Sram Litigation*, ABA Antitrust Trial Practice Newsletter, Spring 2011, available at trialissues.pdf (mayerbrown.com).

Wisking, Stephen, Dietzel, Kim and Herron, Molly, *EU Overview, The Private Competition Enforcement Review*, Law Business Research, 10th ed., 2017.

Wrbka, Stefan, Uytsel, Steven Van and Siems, Mathias (eds), *Collective Actions: Enhancing Access to Justice and Reconciling Multilayer Interests?*, Cambridge University Press, 2012.

Woods, Donncadh, *Private Enforcement of Antitrust Rules: Modernisation of the EU Rules and the Road Ahead*, Loyola Consumer Law Review, vol. 16, 2004, pp. 431-460.

Xavier, Rita Lobo, Folhadela, Inês and Castro, Gonçalo Andrade e, *Elements of Civil Procedural Law: General Theory – Principles – Assumptions*, Universidade Católica Portuguesa Editora – Porto, 2nd ed., 2018.

Zacharodimos, George, *Excessive Pricing*, 21 October 2022, available at Guide to Life Sciences - Global Competition Review.

Zwehl, Felix von and Stübinger, Malte, *The Third Party Litigation Funding Law Review: Germany*, Simon Latham and Augusta Ventures (eds), 6th ed., The Law Reviews, 8 December 2022.

Table of Cases*

CJEU

ECJ

* The most relevant one that has been cited throughout this work, apart from the one in Appendix II – Survey of Recent Competition Law Private Enforcement Cases in Portugal above.

UK

FR

ES

DE

Table of Decisions*

EC

PCA

OFT

* Quoted throughout this book, in addition to those included in Appendix II - Survey of Recent Competition Law Private Enforcement Cases in Portugal.

Table of Documents

EC

PE

Others

Table of Legislation*

EU

* The most relevant one that has been cited throughout this book, apart from the one presented in Appendix I - EU Damages Directive Implementation Table above.

Index

INTERNATIONAL COMPETITION LAW SERIES

1. Ignacio De Leon, *Latin American Competition Law and Policy: A Policy in Search of Identity*, 2001 (ISBN 90-411-1542-0).
2. Wim Dejonghe & Wouter Van de Voorde (eds), *M & A in Belgium*, 2001 (ISBN 90-411-1594-3).
3. Yang-Ching Chao, Gee San, Changfa Lo & Jiming Ho (eds), *International and Comparative Competition Law and Policies*, 2001 (ISBN 90-411-1643-5).
4. Martin Mendelsohn & Stephen Rose, *Guide to the EC Block Exemption for Vertical Agreements*, 2002 (ISBN 90-411-9813-X).
5. Clifford A. Jones & Mitsuo Matsushita (eds), *Competition Policy in the Global Trading System: Perspectives from the EU, Japan and the USA*, 2002 (ISBN 90-411-1758-X).
6. Christian Koenig, Andreas Bartosch, Jens-Daniel Braun & Marion Romes (eds), *EC Competition and Telecommunications Law*, Second Edition, 2009 (ISBN 978-90-411-2564-4).
7. Jürgen Basedow (ed.), *Limits and Control of Competition with a View to International Harmonization*, 2002 (ISBN 90-411-1967-1).
8. Maureen Brunt, Economic Essays on Australian and New Zealand Competition Law, 2003 (ISBN 90-411-1991-4).
9. Ky P. Ewing, Jr., *Competition Rules for the 21st Century: Principles from America's Experience*, Second Edition, 2006 (ISBN 90-411-2477-2).
10. Joseph Wilson, *Globalization and the Limits of National Merger Control Laws*, 2003 (ISBN 90-411-1996-5).
11. Peter Verloop & Valérie Landes (eds), *Merger Control in Europe: EU, Member States and Accession States*, Fourth Edition, 2003 (ISBN 90-411-2056-4).
12. Themistoklis K. Giannakopoulos, *Safeguarding Companies' Rights in Competition and Anti-dumping/Anti-subsidies Proceedings*, Second Edition, 2011 (ISBN 978-90-411-3404-2).
13. Marjorie Holmes & Lesley Davey (eds), *A Practical Guide to National Competition Rules across Europe*, Second Edition, 2007 (ISBN 978-90- 411-2607-8).
14. Sigrid Stroux, *US and EU Oligopoly Control*, 2004 (ISBN 90-411-2296-6).
15. Tzong-Leh Hwang and Chiyuan Chen (eds), *The Future Development of Competition Framework*, 2004 (ISBN 90-411-2305-9).

16. Phedon Nicolaides, Mihalis Kekelekis and Maria Kleis, *State Aid Policy in the European Community: Principles and Practice,* Second Edition, 2008 (ISBN 978-90-411-2754-9).
17. Doris Hildebrand, *Economic Analyses of Vertical Agreements: A Self- Assessment*, 2005 (ISBN 90-411-2328-8).
18. Frauke Henning-Bodewig, *Unfair Competition Law: European Union and Member States*, 2005 (ISBN 90-411-2329-6).
19. Duarte Brito & Margarida Catalão-Lopes, *Mergers and Acquisitions: The Industrial Organization Perspective,* 2006 (ISBN 90-411-2451-9).
20. Nikos Th. Nikolinakos, *EU Competition Law and Regulation in the Converging Telecommunications, Media and IT Sectors*, 2006 (ISBN 90-411- 2469-1).
21. Mihalis Kekelekis, *The EC Merger Control Regulation: Rights of Defence. A Critical Analysis of DG COMP Practice and Community Courts' Jurisprudence,* 2006 (ISBN 90-411-2553-1).
22. Mark R. Joelson, *An International Antitrust Primer: A Guide to the Operation of United States, European Union and Other Key Competition Laws in the Global Economy*, Third Edition, 2006 (ISBN 90-411-2468-3).
23. Themistoklis K. Giannakopoulos, *A Concise Guide to the EU Anti-dumping/ Anti-subsidies Procedures*, 2006 (ISBN 90-411-2464-0).
24. George Cumming, Brad Spitz & Ruth Janal, *Civil Procedure Used for Enforcement of EC Competition Law by the English, French and German Civil Courts,* 2007 (ISBN 978-90-411-2471-5).
25. Jürgen Basedow (ed.), *Private Enforcement of EC Competition Law,* 2007 (ISBN 978-90-411-2613-9).
26. Jung Wook Cho, *Innovation and Competition in the Digital Network Economy: A Legal and Economic Assessment on Multi-tying Practices and Network Effects*, 2007 (ISBN 978-90-411-2574-3).
27. Akira Inoue, *Japanese Antitrust Law Manual: Law, Cases and Interpretation of the Japanese Antimonopoly Act*, 2007 (ISBN 978-90-411-2627-6).
28. René Barents, *Directory of EC Case Law on Competition,* 2007 (ISBN 978-90-411-2656-6).
29. Paul F. Nemitz (ed.), *The Effective Application of EU State Aid Procedures: The Role of National Law and Practice*, 2007 (ISBN 978-90-411-2657-3).
30. Jurian Langer, *Tying and Bundling as a Leveraging Concern under EC Competition Law*, 2007 (ISBN 978-90-411-2575-0).
31. Abel M. Mateus & Teresa Moreira (eds), *Competition Law and Economics – Advances in Competition Policy and Antitrust Enforcement*, 2007 (ISBN 978-90-411-2632-0).
32. Alberto Santa Maria, *Competition and State Aid: An Analysis of the EC Practice*, 2007 (ISBN 978-90-411-2617-7).
33. Barry J. Rodger (ed.), *Article 234 and Competition Law: An Analysis,* 2007 (ISBN 978-90-411-2605-4).

34. Alla Pozdnakova, *Liner Shipping and EU Competition Law*, 2008 (ISBN 978-90-411-2717-4).
35. Milena Stoyanova, *Competition Problems in Liberalized Telecommunications: Regulatory Solutions to Promote Effective Competition*, 2008 (ISBN 978-90-411-2736-5).
36. *EC State Aid Law/Le Droit des Aides d'Etat dans la CE. Liber Amicorum Francisco Santaolalla Gadea*, 2008 (ISBN 978-90-411-2774-7).
37. Cees Dekker, *Directory of EU Case Law on State Aids*, Fifth Edition, 2024 (ISBN 978-94-035-3708-5).
38. Ignacio De Leon, *An Institutional Assessment of Antitrust Policy: The Latin American Experience*, 2009 (ISBN 978-90-411-2478-4).
39. Doris Hildebrand, *The Role of Economic Analysis in EU Competition Law: The European School*, Fourth Edition, 2016 (ISBN 978-90-411-6245-8).
40. Eugène Buttigieg, *Competition Law: Safeguarding the Consumer Interest. A Comparative Analysis of US Antitrust Law and EC Competition Law*, 2009 (ISBN 978-90-411-3119-5).
41. Ioannis Lianos & Ioannis Kokkoris (eds), *The Reform of EC Competition Law: New Challenges*, 2010 (ISBN 978-90-411-2692-4).
42. George Cumming & Mirjam Freudenthal, *Civil Procedure in EU Competition Cases before the English and Dutch Courts*, 2010 (ISBN 978-90-411-3192-8).
43. A.E. Rodriguez & Ashok Menon, *The Limits of Competition Policy: The Shortcomings of Antitrust in Developing and Reforming Economies*, 2010 (ISBN 978-90-411-3177-5).
44. Mika Oinonen, *Does EU Merger Control Discriminate against Small Market Companies? Diagnosing the Argument with Conclusions*, 2010 (ISBN 978-90-411-3261-1).
45. Eirik Østerud, *Identifying Exclusionary Abuses by Dominant Undertakings under EU Competition Law: The Spectrum of Tests*, 2010 (ISBN 978-90-411-3271-0).
46. Marco Botta, *Merger Control Regimes in Emerging Economies: A Case Study on Brazil and Argentina*, 2011 (ISBN 978-90-411-3402-8).
47. Jürgen Basedow & Wolfgang Wurmnest (eds), *Structure and Effects in EU Competition Law: Studies on Exclusionary Conduct and State Aid*, 2011 (ISBN 978-90-411-3174-4).
48. George Cumming (ed.), *Merger Decisions and the Rules of Procedure of the European Community Courts*, 2012 (ISBN 978-90-411-3671-8).
49. Eduardo Molan Gaban & Juliana Oliveira Domingues (eds), *Antitrust Law in Brazil: Fighting Cartels*, 2012 (ISBN 978-90-411-3670-1).
50. Giandonato Caggiano, Gabriella Muscolo & Marina Tavassi (eds), *Competition Law and Intellectual Property: A European Perspective*, 2012 (ISBN 978-90-411-3447-9).
51. Ben Van Rompuy, *Economic Efficiency: The Sole Concern of Modern Antitrust Policy? Non-efficiency Considerations under Article 101 TFEU*, 2012 (ISBN 978-90-411-3870-5).

52. Liyang Hou, *Competition Law and Regulation of the EU Electronic Communications Sector: A Comparative Legal Approach*, 2012 (ISBN 978-90-411-4047-0).
53. Barry Rodger, *Landmark Cases in Competition Law: Around the World in Fourteen Stories*, 2012 (ISBN 978-90-411-3843-9).
54. Andreas Scordamaglia-Tousis, *EU Cartel Enforcement: Reconciling Effective Public Enforcement with Fundamental Rights*, 2013 (ISBN 978-90-411-4758-5).
55. Bernardo Cortese (ed.), *EU Competition Law: Between Public and Private Enforcement*, 2014 (ISBN 978-90-411-4677-9).
56. Barry Rodger (ed.), *Competition Law: Comparative Private Enforcement and Collective Redress across the EU*, 2014 (ISBN 978-90-411-4559-8).
57. Nada Ina Pauer, *The Single Economic Entity Doctrine and Corporate Group Responsibility in European Antitrust Law*, 2014 (ISBN 978-90-411-5262-6).
58. Urška Petrovčič, *Competition Law and Standard Essential Patents: A Transatlantic Perspective*, 2014 (ISBN 978-90-411-4960-2).
59. David Telyas, *The Interface between Competition Law, Patents and Technical Standards*, 2014 (ISBN 978-90-411-5418-7).
60. Katerina Maniadaki, *EU Competition Law, Regulation and the Internet: The Case of Net Neutrality*, 2014 (ISBN 978-90-411-4140-8).
61. Horacio Vedia Jerez, *Competition Law Enforcement and Compliance across the World: A Comparative Review*, 2015 (ISBN 978-90-411-5815-4).
62. Kadir Baş, *The Substantive Appraisal of Joint Ventures under the EU Merger Control Regime*, 2015 (ISBN 978-90-411-5816-1).
63. Alberto Santa Maria, *Competition and State Aid: An Analysis of the EU Practice*, Third Edition, 2025 (ISBN 978-94-035-2768-0).
64. Lúcio Tomé Feteira, *The Interplay between European and National Competition Law after Regulation 1/2003: "United (Should) We Stand?"*, 2016 (ISBN 978-90-411-5663-1).
65. Giovanni Pitruzzella & Gabriella Muscolo (eds), *Competition and Patent Law in the Pharmaceutical Sector: An International Perspective*, 2016 (ISBN 978-90-411-5927-4).
66. Małgorzata Cyndecka, *The Market Economy Investor Test in EU State Aid Law: Applicability and Application*, 2016 (ISBN 978-90-411-6102-4).
67. Damiano Canapa, *Trademarks and Brands in Merger Control: An Analysis of the European and Swiss Legal Orders*, 2016 (ISBN 978-90-411-6717-0).
68. Inge Graef, *EU Competition Law, Data Protection and Online Platforms: Data as Essential Facility*, 2016 (ISBN 978-90-411-8324-8).
69. Anders Jessen, *Exclusionary Abuse after the* Post Danmark I *Case: The Role of the Effects-Based Approach under Article 102 TFEU*, 2017 (ISBN 978-90-411-8996-7).
70. Baskaran Balasingham, *The EU Leniency Policy: Reconciling Effectiveness and Fairness*, 2017 (ISBN 978-90-411-8479-5).
71. Eugene Stuart & Iana Roginska-Green, *Sixty Years of EU State Aid Law and Policy: Analysis and Assessment*, 2018 (ISBN 978-90-411-8869-4).

72. Anna Renata Pisarkiewicz, *Margin Squeeze in the Electronic Communications Sector: Critical Analysis of the Decisional Practice and Case Law*, 2018 (ISBN 978-90-411-6246-5).
73. Ploykaew Porananond, *Competition Law in the ASEAN Countries: Regional Law and National Systems*, 2018 (ISBN 978-90-411-9102-1).
74. Corinne Ruechardt, *EU State Aid Control of Infrastructure Funding*, 2018 (ISBN 978-90-411-9099-4).
75. Amalia Athanasiadou, *Patent Settlements in the Pharmaceutical Industry under US Antitrust and EU Competition Law*, 2018 (ISBN 978-94-035-0113-0).
76. Miroslava Marinova, *Fidelity Rebates in Competition Law: Application of the 'As Efficient Competitor' Test*, 2018 (ISBN 978-94-035-0570-1).
77. Gabriella Muscolo & Marina Tavassi, *The Interplay Between Competition Law and Intellectual Property: An International Perspective*, 2019 (ISBN 978-90-411-8687-4).
78. Fevzi Toksoy, Bahadir Balki & Hanna Stakheyeva, *Merger Control in the EU and Turkey: A Comparative Guide*, Second Edition, 2022 (ISBN 978-94-035-4303-1).
79. Paulo Burnier da Silveira & William Evan Kovacic (eds), *Global Competition Enforcement: New Players, New Challenges*, 2019 (ISBN 978-94-035-0283-0).
80. Giovanna Massarotto, *Antitrust Settlements: How a Simple Agreement Can Drive the Economy*, 2019 (ISBN 978-94-035-1133-7).
81. Marc Veenbrink, *Criminal Law Principles and the Enforcement of EU and National Competition Law: A Silent Takeover?*, 2020 (ISBN 978-94-035-1434-5).
82. Ferdinand Wollenschläger, Wolfgang Wurmnest & Thomas M.J. Möllers (eds), *Private Enforcement of European Competition and State Aid Law: Current Challenges and the Way Forward*, 2020 (ISBN 978-94-035-0281-6).
83. Jorge Marcos Ramos, *Firm Dominance in EU Competition Law: The Competitive Process and the Origins of Market Power*, 2020 (ISBN 978-94-035-2030-8).
84. Ingrid Margrethe Halvorsen Barlund, *Leniency in EU Competition Law*, 2020 (ISBN 978-94-035-1722-3).
85. Jan Blockx, Mens Rea *in EU Antitrust Law: When Intentions Matter*, 2020 (ISBN 978-94-035-2353-8).
86. Maria Wasastjerna, *Competition, Data and Privacy in the Digital Economy: Towards a Privacy Dimension in Competition Policy?*, 2020 (ISBN 978-94-035-2220-3).
87. Maria Fernanda Caporale Madi, *Regulating Vertical Agreements: A Comparative Law and Economics Review of the EU and Brazil*, 2020 (ISBN 978-94-035-2650-8).
88. Martin Gassler, *Information Exchange Between Competitors in EU Competition Law*, 2021 (ISBN 978-94-035-3183-0).

89. Andrea Biondi, Gabriella Muscolo & Renato Nazzini (eds), *After the Damages Directive: Policy and Practice in the EU Member States and the United Kingdom*, 2022 (ISBN 978-94-035-1302-7).
90. Angelika S. Murer, *Blocking Patents in European Competition Law: The Implications of the Concept of Abuse*, 2022 (ISBN 978-94-035-3814-3).
91. Barry Rodger and Or Brook, Maciej Bernatt, Francisco Marcos & Annalies Outhuijse, *Judicial Review of Competition Law Enforcement in the EU Member States and the UK*, 2024 (ISBN 978-94-035-0238-0).
92. Nils Stock, *Big Tech Acquisitions and Merger Control: Challenges Posed by Digital Platforms and Ecosystems*, 2025 (ISBN 978-94-035-2759-8).
93. Sílvia Bessa Venda, *Private Enforcement of EU Competition Law and Class Actions: Has the Force Awakened?*, 2026 (ISBN 978-94-035-2139-8).

www.ingramcontent.com/pod-product-compliance
Ingram Content Group UK Ltd.
Pitfield, Milton Keynes, MK11 3LW, UK
UKHW020845290926
15470UKWH00004B/1567

9 789403 521398